# PIONEERING STUDIES IN SOCIONOMICS

Socionomics — The Science of History
and Social Prediction, Volume 2

*by*

*Robert R. Prechter*

Socionomics Institute Press

ISBN: 978-1-946597-03-8
Library of Congress Catalog Card Number: 2014959905

Publisher: Socionomics Institute Press
Gainesville, Georgia USA
Address for comments: institute@socionomics.net

The Socionomic Institute
www.socionomics.net

*This book is dedicated to Robert Prechter, Sr., Barbara Prechter, Douglas Rumble, Margaret O. Bynum, Marilyn Hopkins, Jim Futral, David Larkin, Gretchen Mieszkowski, Irving Janis, Marty Kugell, Creighton Hooker, Phil Roth, Bob Nurock, Dick Diamond, Bob Meier, Liebe Geft, Sue Abbott, Hernan Cortes and John Casti.*

# Acknowledgments

I would like to acknowledge invaluable assistance from Dave Allman, Leigh Tipton, Angie Barringer, Rachel Webb and Sally Webb. The jacket design is by Darrell King and Roberta Machcinski. Thanks especially to the brave souls who are this book's guest contributors.

*Editor's Note*: *The Wave Principle of Human Social Behavior* (1999) incorporated most of the socionomics-related ideas that had appeared in *The Elliott Wave Theorist* from inception through early 1999. This book fills in a few missing pieces from those earlier times and includes key essays published from 1999 through 2003. This new edition adds two items from 2004 and two more recent essays and brings Section VI to an updated conclusion. Our 2016 and 2017 books on socionomics pick up where this book leaves off. The original essays herein have been lightly edited for grammar, clarity and precision.

# CONTENTS

*Appendix*: **Toward Quantifying Sociometers Other than
the Stock Market**

# *Foreword: A Socionomic Manifesto*

Men have tried for millennia to forecast human events. In the long history of social forecasting, the chronic propensity for immense error has resulted from linear thinking, the extrapolation of current trends into the future. This nearly ubiquitous approach is a result of the assumption that laws governing billiard ball behavior apply to human behavior. Simply stated, most people, including economists, are social mechanists. They believe that markets and societies share the property of an object in motion, which will continue along a calculable path until some new outside influence—a force or an obstruction—alters its trajectory. It remains a source of amazement to me how often I am asked what events will cause (or, in modified form, what "catalyst" will "precipitate") a change in the direction of the market, politics or the economy, a query which has as its basis the unquestioned assumption that the record of human history is a record of events causing events. Usually the question is not asked in the context of truly outside influences, such as earthquakes, volcanoes and floods but with regard to one presumed social influence over another presumed social effect. Yet social forces cannot be "outside influences" because they reside within the human social experience, in which all elements are interrelated. The general assumption of outside causality nevertheless persists and has as its result the continuing bizarre state of affairs in which most people involved in areas of life where the future is important waste hours debating the various potential "causes" of the trends they hope to predict. They usually conclude that forecasting with any reliability is impossible, yet they persist in the exercise anyway! Successful anticipation of future events *is* possible. It is possible, however, only with the knowledge that human social behavior usually changes as a result not of external forces but of internal ones.

Generally speaking, the human mind has two aspects, which impel two types of actions. Rational, conscious mental processes can induce actions that create airplanes, computers and skyscrapers. Unconscious mental processes do not produce goods and services but rather generate emotional signals that trigger impulsive actions. These emotional

signals developed through eons of evolution, which is why they impel
all kinds of actions with respect to concerns that are common to lower
animals, such as territorialism, fighting, fleeing and sex. (The production
of art probably involves both mental aspects, which is why it provides
the richest experiences.) One of the unconscious mind's occupations is
attempting to increase the chances of survival through mimicking, which
is reflected in the herding impulse, a fact that provides a biological and
psychological basis for socionomics.

Conventional economists have been mired in the assumption that
trends in finance result from the exercise of the first type of thinking:
the rational and the conscious. It is a false premise, which has just
begun to be undermined. In twenty years, academic economists have
gone from believing that markets are rational, efficient calculators of
intrinsic value—and therefore random—to believing that psychology
occasionally might have something to do with extremes in short term
financial valuation. Someday, a large segment of the profession will
surely come to understand that a mix of randomness and psychology
is not the answer to overall financial market behavior. At the forefront
of the new understanding is the Chairman of Psychiatry at Metro West
Medical Center (Boston), Dr. John Schott, who is also an instructor at
Harvard and Tufts medical schools and a successful money manager.
Even on the subject of practical investing for the individual, he states
unequivocally, "Emotions are central; they are the entire ball game."[†]
Emotions are central to enough investors that decisions by the rare few
making individually informed and rational decisions cancel each other
out, so what remains on the stock market graph is a record of the trends
of shared emotion, the mood of the herd.

It is not in the social nature of mankind to accept and be content with
stasis. If there is one constant regarding social mood and social action, it
is their continuous flux. Yet the fact that social mood is ever-changing is
not, as many would assume, an impediment to forecasting; it is the key to
it. Investigation by R.N. Elliott in the 1930s and 1940s yielded the crucial
knowledge that social behavior changes not randomly but according to
a particular fractal pattern. Social mood *does* have constancy, but it is a
dynamic one. While social mood, experiences and conditions vary from
time to time and place to place, the patterns of behavior that lead to reversals in trend do not. In order to anticipate changes in society reliably,
one must understand the consistent pattern of society's mood dynamics.

---

[†] Schott, John W. and Arbeiter, Jean S. (1998). *Mind Over Money*. Boston:
Little Brown & Co., p.3.

Social mood trends result from forces endogenous to the process of collective mental interaction. These forces are not rational but impulsive, probably deriving from herding behavior governed by the basal ganglia and the limbic system, which are pre-rational portions of the brain. This dynamic creates social *attitudes*, which are manifest instantaneously in investment trends, political sentiment, the character of popular cultural symbols and other such immediately expressible outlets for the prevailing social mood. These attitudes fluctuate according to the Wave Principle, which is a robust fractal governed by Fibonacci mathematics.

Because the naturally patterned interaction of individual limbic systems governs the dynamics of social mood, it ultimately compels the consciously undertaken social actions that are generally considered historically significant. *Non-social* yet significant events, such as natural disasters, clearly do not affect the patterned social-mood dynamic and are irrelevant to it. On the other hand, *social* actions temporally follow *and* are in sympathy with the patterned social-mood dynamic. The conclusion best fitting these data is that the social-mood dynamic regulates the character of human social action and is therefore its primary stylistic motivator.

Social actions come in two types. The first is *collective action*, which is group-based action, such as a labor strike. It takes purposeful cooperation and a majority decision by a group or a group's leader(s) to effect collective action. The second type is *aggregate action*, a summation of individual actions, such as trends in cigarette smoking. Both types follow Elliott waves because they have the same basis. In each case, people's decisions to act are based not primarily upon independent reason but upon substantial influence from others. Interaction and communication with others leads to a shared attitude, or "social mood," which prompts collectively shared opinions, which prompts and shapes social actions.

All macroeconomic, political and cultural developments are shaped and guided by the Wave Principle of human social behavior. It is the engine of everything from popular fads and fashions to the events of collective action that make history. Because the social mood dynamic unfolds according to a principle governed by *phi* (the Fibonacci, or "golden," ratio), which is the basis for many processes of growth and decay, expansion and contraction, and progress and regress in nature, we can see that humanity's social experience reflects an essential aspect of the processes of life and the universe in general.

Once you understand the fundamentality of social mood change, you approach the socionomic insight. The socionomic insight is that conventional assumptions about the direction of social causality are not only incorrect but opposite to what actually occurs. Social events do not compel social mood, as is widely supposed; rather, the patterns of social mood impel social events. For example, the state of the economy does not underlie social mood; social mood underlies the state of the economy. Politics do not affect social mood; social mood affects politics. Demographics do not determine stock market trends; the social mood that determines stock market trends determines demographics. Rising stock trends do not improve people's mood; people's improving mood makes stock prices rise. Styles of popular art and entertainment do not affect social mood; social mood determines the popularity of various styles of popular art and entertainment. War and peace do not impact stock trends; the mood that governs stock trends determines propensities for war and peace. And so on.

Before carefully considering the issue, I had assumed that mood formed a feedback loop with events, which in turn reinforced the mood. I have since seen that this idea is erroneous. Our studies on the Enron scandal and the terrorist attacks (see Chapters 31 and 32) demonstrate this point empirically: Events *do not* affect aggregate mood. Theoretically speaking, moreover, it is abundantly clear that events *cannot* affect social mood. If events formed a positive feedback loop with mood, then social trends would never end. Each new extreme in mood in a particular direction would cause more reinforcing actions, and those actions would reinforce that same mood, and so on forever. This is an untenable idea.

The only feedback that occurs is one involving the propagation of Elliott waves through human minds. In order to participate in social Elliott waves, minds must *interact* with others and become synchronized with them. All types of communication media, from facial expressions to voice timbre, from face-to-face discussion to satellite television news, serve to effect this interaction.

This interaction produces Elliott waves, and Elliott waves determine the trends of social mood, and those trends stimulate actions, which are reported as events. The actions and events are end results *with no consequences of their own in terms of the waves*. This must be so, because Elliott waves exist and because events produce no consistent results in terms of stock market movement. Events do affect minds to the extent that they often cause emotional reactions and/or shape specific actions that owners of those minds take, but they do not alter or affect the path of social mood.

The socionomic dynamic unfolds regardless of whether humans create a gauge of it or not. But when a gauge (such as the Dow Jones

Industrial Average) is created and widely observed, people may incorporate the gauge itself into the process of mental interaction. It is a conscious reference point for the individual participants and an unconscious reference point for the socionomic dynamic. Consciously rendered changes in the components of the gauge (such as occasionally replacing one or two of the stocks in the Dow), then, seem to be irrelevant to the more important fact that the unconscious dynamic uses the gauge as a reference regardless of its components.

People do not notice the operation of the socionomic dynamic because they're not looking. Indeed, given the opportunity, they typically reject the idea outright because such dynamics are contrary to the natural, mechanistic assumptions that people make about how societies (and more narrowly, markets) progress and regress. Ironically, that these processes be unknown or rejected by virtually all people is a prerequisite for their operation. Only people who are blind to the principles that govern the social dynamic can behave so as to produce it, because only then can they be passionate, active participants in it.

An individual who can disengage himself from the social trends that sweep along his fellows so that he can observe their operation has an incalculable advantage over all those who do not. He has a basis upon which to anticipate the future, not every time and not perfectly, but well enough to have immense value. Anticipating the social future has always appeared to be a gift unavailable to humanity. That has been true until now not because the task is impossible but because it requires detailed knowledge of the patterns of social behavior and an ability to think and act in a fashion contrary to that impelled by unenlightened human nature as directed by the primitive brain stem and limbic system. Armed with the knowledge of patterned social behavior, a wise individual can train his reasoning cerebral cortex to recognize at least some of his emotionally driven thought processes and thus observe many activities of groups and societies calmly, as of from Olympus. He cannot avoid human society and thus cannot avoid the social dynamic. But he can make conscious, rational decisions to aid his prosperity, and at times even his survival, while others, who participate fully in the dynamic unconsciously, use rationalization to justify emotional decisions, never once seeing the forest for the trees and, sadly, without even knowing there's a forest to be seen.

Merely to accept the fact of social flux is to be prepared for the future in a way that no linear thinker can be. Even at this primitive level of understanding, a forecaster will have a much better chance of avoiding the mistakes of the crowd in chasing one investment fad after another, in expecting a certain futures because that is the trend of the past, in taking on debt at the peak of an economic expansion, in selling productive assets at the bottom of a depression, in getting caught up in the latest political trend or in rushing off to war. Paradoxically, when linear thinkers live as if today's conditions are the way the world will always be, their error causes a buildup of excesses, thus resulting in the very cyclicality that they deny or of which they are unaware.

Successful social forecasting is possible only on the basis of probabilities. Often, when knowledge is sufficient, one can say with some certainty what those probabilities are. In the long run, acting in accordance with the most probable future conditions will result in a more successful life. Unfortunately, people tend to demand certainty in forecasting, and if they cannot get it, they do not change their behavior. This has been, and will continue to be, a recipe for personal disaster. In 1929, it was those who were entirely unprepared for the crash and Great Depression, who were mortgaged to the hilt betting on further expansion and had become convinced that a "new era" had dawned, who ended up in bread lines or jumping out of windows. In 1980, it was those who were entirely unprepared for an era of prosperity, who were invested to the hilt in gold and silver and Swiss francs and had become convinced that recovery was impossible, who ended up losing much of their fortunes and missing out on two decades of productive success. Today is perhaps one of the best times ever to be socionomically aware, but the vast majority of people are again unprepared for yet another major sea change.

At the very least, *psychological* preparation for changes in the social and economic climate is a worthwhile goal. Financial and physical preparation for downturns, even if the downturns do not occur, should be considered a reasonable cost of insurance. On the other hand, when events *do* occur along the lines of the greatest probability, whether in the case of emerging uptrends or downtrends, your preparedness will be invaluable to you, your family and perhaps even your progeny.

This book is about using socionomics to evaluate social conditions and make social predictions. Predictions involve two levels of complexity: the *general character* of coming events and the specific events themselves. The primary aspects of the social dynamic are its formological imperative, which governs the former, and its chaotic process, which governs the latter.

A formological system is one within which the essential cause of events is an imperative of form rather than of preceding events or conditions or of outside influences. (For a discussion of this term, see *The Wave Principle of Human Social Behavior and the New Science of Socionomics*, pp. 17, 399-400.) Social mood trends are, and must be, independent of social-event causality because their primary register—aggregate stock prices—is patterned per the Wave Principle. Social mood trends, and therefore trends in the *character* of social action, are thus determined formologically, not by antecedent events.

Socionomics recognizes that *specific* social events, which are among the results of social mood trends, have specific antecedents and derive from the chaotic aspect of social activity. As an example of the difference, trends of social goodwill vs. bellicosity are formologically determined, but the specific manifestations of those impulses—which peace treaties will be proposed or signed and which leaders will take adversaries into war, and so on—result from the workings of chaos with antecedents in prior events.

Formological developments are far more deterministic and predictable than chaotic ones. Nevertheless, such developments provide the context within which specific events occur and so aid in the attempt to anticipate various specifics as well. Predicting trends and changes in the character of social behavior is an ability available only to those who fully incorporate the socionomic insight. Those who hold this insight are also therefore better equipped to predict trends and changes in specific social circumstances as well.

Before diving into these essays, you should at least be familiar with the basics of the Wave Principle, as presented in Chapter 1 of *The Wave Principle of Human Social Behavior*. The rest of that volume provides the proper grounding fully to appreciate the studies collected here. On the other hand, there is some adventure in following along "blind" as we developed and applied our ideas in the early days.

This book primarily chronicles the sociological studies and forecasts that Pete Kendall and I conducted between 1985 and 2002, covering not only various formological aspects of the real-time social present and future but also some of their specific manifestations. I have also included a few guest editorials. As the human experience, particularly in the aggregate, is a stew of joy, pain, wisdom and folly, many of these studies make for lively reading. We hope you enjoy reading these pages as much as we did writing them.

—Robert R. Prechter, December 2002

# Part I:

## POPULAR CULTURE

Prechter
*The Elliott Wave Theorist*
as published on the dates shown

## Chapter 1

# Early Socionomic Commentary

*August 3, 1979*

[This commentary accompanied the display of a multi-year symmetrical wave pattern with certain mathematical properties. The full report is reprinted in *Market Analysis for the New Millennium* (2002).]

**What's Going On?**

[The] wave structure I have shown here unfolded its pattern quite clearly regardless of wars, energy crises, speeches, assassinations, Watergates, Peanutgates, jawboning or the weather. To a phenomenal extent, the DJIA appeared to know exactly where it was, exactly where it had been, and exactly where it was going. But *why* is an average of thirty [major industrial] stocks so reliable in exhibiting over and over again these phenomena of construction? For a hundred years, investors have noticed that events external to the market often seem to have no effect on the market's progress. With the knowledge that the market continuously unfolds in waves that are related to each other through *form* and *ratio*, we can see why there is little connection. *The market has a life of its own.* Now what ultimately *causes* that particular pattern of the market's life is open to debate. It can be surmised, though, that it is *mass human psychology* that is registering its changes in the barometer known as the DJIA. This idea helps to explain the cause of future events: changes in the mass emotional outlook. That's what comes first. The market is a mirror of the forces, whatever they may be, which are affecting humanity both *in* and *out* of the market arena. The market doesn't "see into the future" as the discounting idea suggests; it reflects the causes of the future. Increasingly optimistic people expand business; increasingly depressed people contract their businesses. The *results* show up later as a "discounted" future. It's not the politicians who gallantly "save" a bear market by returning to policies of economic sanity, it's the mass emotional environment, as reflected by the market, which forces them at some critical point to do it. Events do not shape the forces of the market; it is the forces behind the market that shape events.

*October 17, 1983*
## But Why?

Most investors are uncomfortable with technical logic. They demand current-event "reasons" why a market should move in one direction or the other. Such reasons always come out later. If you wait for them, you'll act too late every time.

*June 3, 1985*
## Has Market Behavior Changed?

Technical analyst George Lindsay, in his very last market letter, recently wrote, "Most professional market men whose comments I've read in the newspapers and those I know and have talked with personally call this a 'crazy,' 'outlandish' or even 'weird' market. I can see nothing about it that differs materially from other strong advances...." I agree with him.

I often hear comments that the market is acting completely differently today from the way it did in years gone by. Some argue that new products, such as futures and options, have changed the market. Others argue that computers have made it behave strangely. A few just say that the market acts more irrationally every day, that it "doesn't make sense anymore," as if it did in real time in the past.

With respect to markets, people never change. The specific tools of the trade are irrelevant to the dynamics of the process. It is unlikely that anyone on Wall Street could recognize a difference in price behavior between a chart of today's stock market and one of a comparable period 40 years ago or 140 years ago.

The main reason the market "doesn't make sense" to people is that their premise about causality is false. Most investors believe that they are dealing with a law of cause and effect with the market's action on the "effect" side of the equation. The market, if it does operate in a cause and effect world, is a reading of what is on the "cause" side; it is a manifestation of naturally fluctuating mass mood change. Price patterns reveal this basic law of human nature, and human nature hasn't changed.

A chicken appears crazy only if you expect it to behave like a fox. Similarly, the market appears crazy only if you expect it to behave according to the laws of physics rather than those of human nature.

*Chapter 2*

# Popular Culture
# and the Stock Market

Most people believe that stock market movement is caused by fundamental economic and political conditions and events. Experienced stock market watchers have recognized that such events "cast their shadow before," on the stock exchange. However, the assumption even among veteran market students is that the stock market foreshadows events because "smart money" is correctly guessing future events. This report is an attempt to lend some justification[†] to an alternate explanation. The reasoning is as follows:

1) Popular art, fashion and mores are a reflection of the dominant public mood.

2) Because the stock market changes direction in step with these expressions of mood, it is another coincident register of the dominant public mood and changes in it.

3) Because a substantial change in mood in a positive or negative direction foreshadows the character of what are generally considered to be historically important events, mood changes must be considered as possibly, if not probably, being the basic cause of ensuing events.

Both a study of the stock market and a study of trends in popular attitudes support the conclusion that the movement of aggregate stock prices is a direct recording of mood and mood change within the investment community, and by extension, within the society at large. It is clear that extremes in popular cultural trends coincide with extremes in stock

---

[†] *This report is designed as a rough introduction to an idea, not a final statement. My intention is to indicate a field of study that others may wish to pursue. All facts presented herein were checked, most with first-hand sources but some with second-hand sources (particularly in the pre-1950s data), which may have produced errors. I would appreciate notice of any errors, which will be corrected in any future printing(s).*

prices, since they peak and trough coincidentally in their reflection of the popular mood. The stock market is the best place to study mood change because it is the only field of mass behavior where specific, detailed and voluminous numerical data exists. It was only with such data that R.N. Elliott was able to discover the Wave Principle, which reveals that mass mood changes are natural, rhythmic and precise. The stock market is literally a drawing of how the scales of mass mood are tipping. A decline indicates an increasing "negative" mood on balance, and an advance indicates an increasing "positive" mood on balance.

Major historic events which are often considered important to the future (i.e., economic activity, lawmaking, war) are not causes of change; they are the result of mass mood changes that have already occurred. The reason that such events are lagging indicators of mood change is that it takes a good deal of time and an extensive swing in mood throughout the populace for the shared mood change to result in such events. For instance, to motivate a society or a body which represents the society to undertake a collective action such as creating a sweeping new law, electing a new regime or starting a war, the new mood must have taken root throughout much of the society and reached extreme proportions.

In some cases, extremes in mood permit actions that impose a structural (usually political) rigidity on the society. The effects of this institutionalization may continue to be felt for a long period because it takes time to mobilize machinery and play out the consequences of the actions initially taken at the extreme point of mass mood. As an example, the collective mood in Germany in 1933 was so negative that its expression resulted in the granting of power to Adolf Hitler. Although the underlying public mood was changing toward the less negative from that date forward, the consequences of that popular action took twelve years to play out because the representatives of the negative popular mood at the low gained such great political power. The collective mood in the United States also reached a negative extreme in 1933, the year the depression hit its depths. As one manifestation, enrollment in and disruptive activity by the Communist Party in the United States peaked in the 1930s. In contrast to the German experience, however, those forces never achieved political control, so the improving mood was allowed to express itself in the years that followed.

Any activity that by its nature quickly reflects a change in how people in general feel is a coincident indicator of mood change and thus an advance indicator of important social events. A person communicates his mood when he puts on a record, chooses a movie, decides what sporting event to see or chooses a book to read. Many people, as is obvious from the swings in elections, base their votes on their then-current mood rather than on rational thought. The availability in a free society of numerous books, records, styles, entertainment events and candidates to choose from is a requisite for the attainment of reliable, detailed data. The relative popularity of the styles available then reflects the dominant mood. It should be stressed that the record of these overall societal changes says nothing necessarily about how an individual or a specific group might feel or act, but it is an indication of the "net" mood of the society at large (and apparently at times of humanity at large). For the overall change in mood to express itself, all that is required is for *some* particularly susceptible people to undergo a *substantial* change in mood and/or for *most* people to undergo *some* change in mood. The latter explanation is more convincing to this writer, after ten years of watching individuals' behavior as the stock market ebbs and flows. In this case, those individuals whose state of mind placed them closest to taking action in the direction of the changing trend can be stirred to action as a result of just a slight change in mood, which pushes them past the threshold. The further the swing in public mood carries, the larger will be the number of people stirred to action.

If mass mood change is indeed the cause, and its manifestation a visible indicator, of coming social events, then evidence of mood change is the single most important area of discovery for those who wish to peek into the future of social events. In the world of popular culture, "trendsetters" and the avant-garde must be carefully observed since their ideas are often an expression of the leading edge of public mood.

Trends in music, movies, fashion, literature, television, popular philosophy, sports, dance, automobile styling, mores, sexual identity,[1] family life, campus activities, politics and poetry all reflect the prevailing mood, sometimes in subtle ways. Noticeable changes in slower-moving mediums such as the movie industry more readily reveal changes in larger degrees of trend, such as the Cycle. More sensitive mediums such as television change quickly enough to reflect changes in the Primary trends of popular mood. Intermediate and Minor trends are likely paralleled by current song hits, which can rush up and down the sales charts as people change moods. Of course, *all* of these media of expression are influenced by mood changes of all degrees (i.e. extents and time spans). The net impression communicated is a result of the *mix and dominance* of the forces in all these areas at any given moment.

# Direction of Mood Trend

**Cultural Manifestation**

| AREA OF CULTURE | RISING TRANSITION | PEAK POSITIVE MOOD | FALLING TRANSITION | PEAK NEGATIVE MOOD |
|---|---|---|---|---|
| CAMPUS TRENDS | Work hard, have fun | Positive-minded save-the-world social concern | Rebellious, angry social concern | From riots to sudden quiet |
| CREATIVITY | Positive mood creativity | Positive mood creative trend fully realized | Negative mood creativity; lack of creativity | Negative mood creative trend fully realized; destruction |
| DANCE | Partners together, tempo speeds up, partners separate | Partners apart, fast tempo | Partners come back together; tempos slow down | Partners together |
| FAMILY LIFE | Babies popular, family orientation, marriage | Trend reaches extreme | Children a negative value, divorce, "single" life preferred | Trend reaches extreme |
| FASHION (color) | Colors emerge | Bright colors dominate | Drabness emerges | Drab colors dominate |
| FASHION (covering) | Men's ties narrow | Bodies exposed, short skirts, bikinis for women, tight pants for men | Men's ties widen | Bodies covered; floor-length dresses, baggy pants |
| FASHION (style) | "Correctness" stressed | Flamboyant individuality for men and women | Anti-fashion fashions | Conservative dress returns |
| FITNESS/HEALTH | Healthy lifestyle, physical fitness practiced, encouraged | Body admired. Body-building peaks. Smoking, "junk" foods taboo | Fitness fanaticism wanes rapidly. Social concern replaces concern with self | "Working out" is out of fashion. |
| GOOD vs. EVIL | Bad guys vs. good guys (movies, pro wrestling). Heroes celebrated | Everybody's a good guy | There are no bad guys and no good guys. Heroes trashed | Everybody's a bad guy |
| JUDGMENTS | Answers are black and white | There is good in all | Who's to judge? | There is evil in all |
| MOVIES/TV/LITERATURE | "G" rated themes, adventure | Celebrate life; upbeat, entertaining themes | Social concern, symbolism, heaviness, anti-heroes | Horror, dead-end themes |
| NOSTALGIA | Nostalgia for black-and-white values | Focus on now | Nostalgia for mythical simpler times (back to the earth) | Focus on now |
| POETRY | Structured | Lyrical | Anarchic | Ugly |

| AREA OF CULTURE | RISING TRANSITION | PEAK POSITIVE MOOD | FALLING TRANSITION | PEAK NEGATIVE MOOD |
|---|---|---|---|---|
| POLITICIANS (perceptions of) | Politicians revered (Camelot, "Teflon") | Strengths magnified, weaknesses overlooked | Weaknesses magnified, strengths overlooked | Politicians hated or deified |
| POLITICS | Relative stability | Desire to maintain status quo | Old styles fail | Radical parties and solutions |
| POP ART | Structured, traditional | Colorful, wild, "alive" | Anarchic --anything goes | Deliberately ugly, heavy, sedate |
| POP MUSIC (Arrangement) | Simplicity peaks, complexity returns | | Complexity peaks, simplicity returns | |
| POP MUSIC (Image) | Dirty, happy | Clean, happy | Clean, angry | Dirty, angry |
| POP MUSIC (Lyrics) | Any non-negative theme OK | Joyous celebration and love songs | Anxious, socially conscious themes emerge | Songs of despair, hate, violence; also happy denial |
| POP MUSIC (Melody) | Melody emerges as a key ingredient | Lifting, complex, inventive melodies and harmony | Melody is eclipsed by various elements: rhythm, arrangement | Little melody or chord structure |
| POP MUSIC (Mood) | Upbeat, major keys | Upbeat, major and minor keys | Minor keys, downbeat, arty | Distorted sounds, atonality, dissonance |
| POP PHILOSOPHY | Achievement is possible and desirable | Love will save the world | Achievement is a waste of time | Hate and destruction will give the world what it deserves |
| RELIGION | Conservative religion but increasingly subdominant | Religious tolerance and inclusiveness | Religion is openly questioned and passionately reintroduced | Powerful fundamentalist religions and cults |
| SEXUAL CULTURE² | Stereotypical masculinity and femininity | Broader range of relationships accepted, celebrated | Conflict over norms; expressions shock or degrade | Repression |
| | Focus on Love | | Focus on Sex | |
| SPORTS | Clean "good guy" sports | | Rough "bad guy" sports | |
| STOCK MARKET (popular valuation of productive enterprise) | Rising | Topping | Falling or correcting | Bottoming |
| WAR | Old wars fought and concluded | Little conflict | More conflict; new wars begin | New wars begin or intensify |

Forecasting the mood changes themselves can best be accomplished through a knowledge of the Wave Principle[3] and a study of the record of the relative strength of "positive mood" and "negative mood"[4] manifestations at all degrees of trend. Although the stock market would probably remain the single best indicator because of its reliably precise measurement of mood and mood change, other social phenomena *could* be detailed, numericized and studied, and used to forecast social events and even changes in the mood trends themselves when extremes are achieved. If reliable data on social activities other than stock valuation were available, we could undoubtedly graph and interpret them with a similar degree of reliability. The main difficulty in assessing indicators of mood other than stock prices is the woeful lack of precise numerical data produced by social scientists. A precise, measurable detailing of sporting event attendance figures, the number of notes and note changes in popular melodies, the lyrical content of popular songs, story content in popular books, hemline lengths, tie widths, heel heights, the prominence of various fashion and pop art colors, the angularity vs. roundness of automobile styling, the construction of various architectural styles and a host of other reflections of the popular mood, all weighted according to volume of sales, would allow us to read graphs of the public mood in the same way we read graphs of aggregate stock prices now. By comparing the evidence to stock price movement, their implications could be assessed and the general hypothesis presented here could be tested. It is highly likely that plots of the net existence and dominance of these various popular cultural elements on a daily basis would parallel those of aggregate stock prices and reflect the Wave Principle. It would take a multi-year research project to gather such data, so for now some general observations will have to suffice.

**Fashion**

Stock broker Ralph Rotnem observed, rather casually, that the long-term trends of stock prices and of the hemlines on women's skirts appear to be in concert. Skirt heights rose to mini-skirt brevity in the 1920s and in the 1960s, peaking with stock prices both times. Floor-length fashions appeared in the 1930s and 1970s (the Maxi), bottoming with stock prices. This is not likely a frivolous observation. In my judgment, it is not unreasonable to hypothesize that a rise in both hemlines and stock prices reflects a general increase in friskiness and daring among the population, and a decline in both, a decrease. Because skirt lengths have limits (the floor and the upper thigh, respectively), the reaching of a limit would imply that a maximum of positive or negative mood had been achieved.

Similar changes appear in fashion *colors*. Bright colors are associated with market tops and dull, dark colors with bottoms. It is not coincidence, then, that, generally speaking, the smaller the skirt or swimsuit, the brighter the color(s). Floor-length fashions, in turn, are more often associated with dull, dark colors such as brown, black and gray. These fashion elements reflect the same general mood. Tie width, heel height, pants leg style, and flamboyance or conservatism in men's fashions (remember London's Carnaby Street, which peaked in influence when the Value Line topped in 1968?) also fit the trends in the stock market.

The idea that outside events could cause a rising trend in skirt heights would appear ridiculous on the surface of it. Skirts' hemlines didn't suddenly jump to above the knee because Lyndon Johnson created ebullience by announcing the formation of the Great Society. Skirt heights had been rising for years and merely continued along the established trend, as did the trends toward brightly colored clothes and bikinis. The announcement of the Great Society programs was merely an expression of how far the ebullient mood had carried in the previous 20 years, so far that the public representatives wanted it institutionalized. In the same way, isn't it ridiculous to assume that outside events would cause a rise in the stock market? It appears more sensible to recognize that the mood reflected by rising stock prices is the impetus for later grand-scale events.

**Popular Art**

The late 1960s produced Peter Max, who specialized in adorning objects for public consumption with bright primary colors. The brightness of color peaked with Day-Glo poster art, which sported shimmering alive colors when showered with ultraviolet light. The irony of Day-Glo art was that it was intended to be viewed in pitch darkness, a curious mixture of experience (the brightest possible colors in the darkest possible surroundings). Fittingly, it occurred during the transition phase from peak positive mood to bear market that took place from 1966 to 1969. 1970s' pop art, produced during the long bear market from 1969-1982, generally consisted of massive hunks of dark or heavy sculpture, much of which was detested for its ugliness and later removed. In both cases, a common question was, "Is it really art?" The avant-garde is always questioned (properly so), but our concern is not whether it is art, but whether it expresses a light, bright, positive mood or a heavy, dark, negative one. The former is found in bull markets and in extremes at market tops; the latter is found in bear markets and in extremes at market bottoms. (Perhaps an upcoming peak will be accompanied by brightly colored laser art.)

## Movies

While musicals, adventures, and comedies weave into the pattern, one particularly clear example of correlation with the stock market is provided by horror movies. Horror movies descended upon the American scene in 1930-1933, the years the Dow Jones Industrials collapsed. Five classic horror films were all produced in less than three short years. *Frankenstein* and *Dracula* premiered in 1931, in the middle of the great bear market. *Dr. Jekyll and Mr. Hyde* played in 1932, the bear market bottom year and the only year that a horror film actor was ever granted an Oscar. *The Mummy* and *King Kong* hit the screen in 1933, on the double bottom. These are *the* classic horror films of all time, along with the new breed in the 1970s, and they all sold big. The message appeared to be that people had an inhuman, horrible side to them. Just to prove the vision correct, Hitler was placed in power in 1933 (an expression of the darkest public mood in decades) and fulfilled it. For thirteen years, lasting only slightly past the stock market bottom of 1942, films continued to feature Frankenstein monsters, vampires, werewolves and undead mummies. Ironically, Hollywood tried to introduce a new monster in 1935 during a bull market, but *Werewolf of London* was a flop. When film makers tried again in 1941, in the depths of a bear market, *The Wolf Man* was a smash hit.

Shortly after the bull market in stocks resumed in 1942, films abandoned dark, foreboding horror in the most sure-fire way: by laughing at it. When Abbott and Costello met Frankenstein, horror had no power. That decade treated moviegoers to patriotic war films and love themes. The 1950s gave us sci-fi adventures in a celebration of man's abilities; all the while, the bull market in stocks raged on. The early 1960s introduced exciting James Bond adventures and happy musicals. The milder horror styles of the bull market years and the limited extent of their popularity stand in stark contrast to those of the bear market years.

Then a change hit. Just about the time the stock market was peaking, film makers became introspective, doubting and cynical. How far the change in cinematic mood had carried didn't become fully clear until 1969-1970, when *Night of the Living Dead* and *The Texas Chainsaw Massacre* debuted. Just look at the chart of the Dow and you'll see the crash in mood that inspired those movies. The trend was set for the 1970s, as slice-and-dice horror hit the screen. There also appeared a rash of re-makes of the old Dracula and Frankenstein stories, but as a dominant theme, Frankenstein couldn't cut it; we weren't afraid of him any more. Hollywood had to horrify us to satisfy us, and it did. The bloody slasher-on-the-loose movies were shocking versions of the '30s' monster shows, while the equally gory zombie films had a modern twist. In the 1930s, Dracula was a fitting allegory for the perceived fear of the day, that the aristocrat was sucking the blood of the common people.

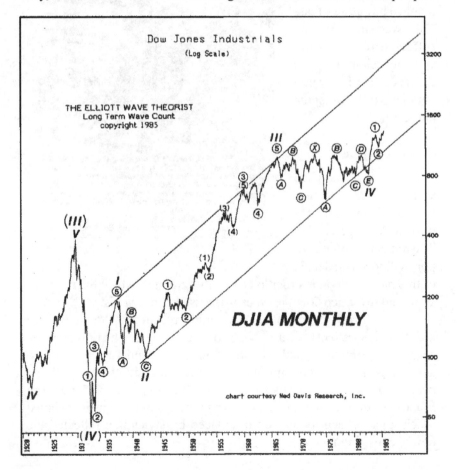

In the 1970s, horror was perpetrated by a *group* eating people alive, not an individual monster. An army of dead-but-moving flesh-eating zombies devouring every living person in sight was a fitting allegory for the new horror of the day, voracious government and the welfare state, and the pressures that most people felt as a result. The nature of late '70s' warfare ultimately reflected the mass-devouring visions, with the destruction of internal populations in Cambodia and China.

## Popular Music

Pop music has been virtually in lock step with the Dow Jones Industrial Average as well. The remainder of this report will focus on details

of this phenomenon in order to clarify the extent to which the relationship (and, by extension, the others discussed above) exists.

As a 78-rpm record collector put it in a recent *Wall Street Journal* article, music reflects "every fiber of life" in the U.S. The timing of the careers of dominant youth-oriented (since the young are quickest to adopt new fashions) pop musicians has been perfectly in line with the peaks and troughs in the stock market. At turns in prices (and therefore mood), the dominant popular singers and groups of the time have faded quickly into obscurity and were replaced by styles that reflected the newly emerging mood.

The 1920s' bull market gave us hyper-fast dance music and jazz. The 1930s' bear years brought folk music laments ("Buddy, Can You Spare a Dime?"), and mellow ballroom dance music. The 1932-1937 bull market brought lively "swing" music. 1937 ushered in the Andrews Sisters, who enjoyed their greatest success during the corrective years of 1937-1942 ("girl groups" may be a corrective wave phenomenon; more on that later). The 1940s featured uptempo big band music, which dominated until the market peaked in 1945-46. The ensuing late-1940s' stock market correction featured "cool jazz" and mellow love ballad crooners, both male and female, whose styles reflected the dampened public mood.

The post-war bull market's initial advancing wave, wave (1) from 1949 through 1953, brought a flood of new grassroots-style music to the charts. During that period, 49 Country or Western music titles suddenly sold over a million copies each, and "race" music sold strongly enough to require its own sales charts in the industry's trade magazines. Interest in the more powerful black music by whites grew so strong during the early years of the bull market that Cleveland disc jockey Alan Freed arranged a "Rock and Roll Party" show in March 1953. Ironically, the show was canceled due to the chaos resulting from 30,000 people (two-thirds of whom were white) demanding to sit in a 10,000-seat arena. It was not re-staged until the exact month in the fall that kicked off wave (3) of ③, an upside acceleration, in the stock market's wave structure.

From that point on, the emerging excitement of an improving public mood could no longer be contained. The grassroots styles of music began to merge, and high energy rock 'n' roll exploded on the scene. Within a few years, the trendsetters were jitterbugging like crazy to work off their collective emotional high. By the late '50s, some of the doo-wop song tempos were so fast that the singers and musicians could barely keep up with the pace. 1959 was the year that wave ③ peaked and the year that all the joyous, celebrative rock 'n' rollers' careers came to a sudden stop. They either died (Buddy Holly, Eddie Cochran, Ritchie Valens, and J.P. Richardson), were drafted (Elvis Presley), quit the scene (Little Richard, Chuck Berry) or faded quickly from popularity (Bo Diddley, Jerry Lee Lewis and a hundred Northeast doo-wop groups).

Popular music went into what rock 'n' roll historians consider somewhat of a stagnancy (producing many great songs, but little in-novation) between 1959 and 1962, which just happens to be the period of the wave ④ stock market correction.[5] The correction in stock prices

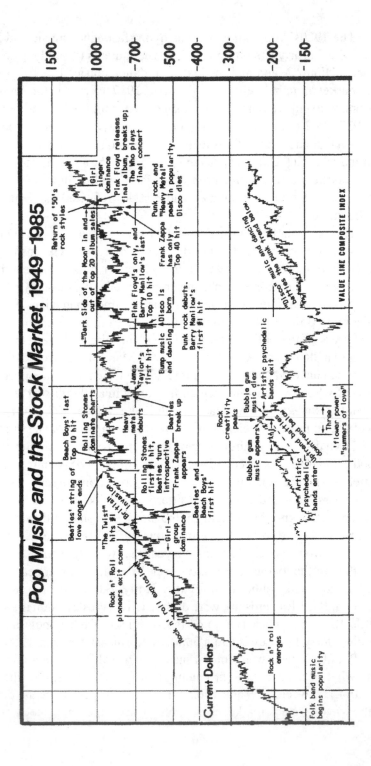

*Pop Music and the Stock Market, 1949–1985*

copyright © 1985

THE ELLIOTT WAVE THEORIST
Gainesville, GA

Dow Jones Industrial Average

Constant Dollars

Angry
rock
is born

Happy rock n'
roll peaks

Rolling Stones, The Who, Pink Floyd, Barry Manilow, Heavy Metal, Punk Rock

Celebrative rock
"double tops"

INCREASINGLY NEGATIVE MOOD (16.5 years)

Lyndon Johnson legislates
the "have it all" society.

Nixon legislates cutbacks
(wage and price controls,
55 mph limit).

Jimmy Carter legislates
the sacrificial society
and decries "crisis of
confidence."

Angry rock
"double bottoms";
happy rock n' roll

Bill Haley, Little Richard, Everly Brothers, Motown
Chuck Berry, Buddy Holly, Beach Boys,
Do-Wop, Elvis, Beatles,

INCREASINGLY POSITIVE MOOD (16.5 years)

Grassroots styles (country
music, rhythm and blues)

Rock n' roll
is born

and the "correction" in popular musical innovation coincided precisely. This phase was marked by three phenomena in the realm of pop music and dance: phony made-by-the-record-company "stars," who were marketed on the basis of a handsome face or TV popularity and who copycatted rather than innovated, the emergence of "girl groups" on the charts and a basic change in social dance with the advent of the Twist (more on that later). Twist king Chubby Checker (a record-company-created star whose name was borrowed from Fats Domino and whose hit was stolen from Hank Ballard) and other copycats topped the charts from 1960 through 1962, then abruptly lost their dominance.[6] During these years, Chubby Checker's popularity was so strong that his hit, "The Twist," reached the #1 position on Billboard's list *twice*, once in August 1960 and again in November 1961, a feat not achieved by any record before or since. If you study the Dow Jones Industrials, you'll see that each of these months was the exact month of the peak of a "B" wave within the Primary wave ④ correction. As readers of *Elliott Wave Principle* know, "B" waves reflect excitability, and the Twist let people express it. Checker's last Top 10 hit peaked on the charts in September 1962, one month prior to the orthodox bottom of the 3-year stock market correction.

The energetic, positive emotions that Primary wave ③ exhibited up to 1959 turned out to be only a warm-up for the euphoric joy expressed by the Beatles and the melodic, harmonic music of the "British Invasion" and American bands that dominated the charts during Primary wave ⑤ from 1962 to 1966. The Beach Boys' first hit made the charts in September 1962. The Beatles' first hit was released almost simultaneously in October 1962, the month of the orthodox bottom in stocks. It wasn't until the Beatles' next release in January 1963 that they zoomed to #1 status in Britain and began moving toward their dominance of the pop-music world. That same month, Chubby Checker's final Top Ten hit began dropping from the charts. (Try as he did over the ensuing years, his message was "out," and the public would no longer buy it.) Three months later, the Beach Boys scored their first Top Ten hit and soared in popularity in the States. During the acceleration phase, wave (3) (not shown on the chart) of ⑤, the "fun music" phenomenon exploded as had rock 'n' roll's itself in wave (3) of ③. In January 1964, Britain's happy music flooded into the U.S. In February, the Beatles accounted for 60% of U.S. record sales and in March, *Meet the Beatles* became the biggest selling album in history.

During the entirety of Primary wave ⑤, the public wanted upbeat, joyous high-energy songs about love and fun, and for three years, they got them, from the Beatles (12 of their 16 hits of 1964 had the word "love" in the lyrics), the Beach Boys (whose hit songs included "Dance, Dance, Dance" and "Fun, Fun, Fun"), various "British Invasion" bands, Motown artists, Frat Party bands and others. That mood ended promptly with the bull market.

The first #1 hit by the Rolling Stones appeared in June 1965, the exact month of the correction low that preceded the final run to new highs in stocks. After trying for more than a year, the Stones finally began gaining the upper hand as avant-garde expressors of the popular mood. Their message was one initially of dissatisfaction and impatience, about the most strongly negative attitudes the public was willing to experience. The same month marked a dramatic style change for the Beatles, separating their three-year "innocent love song" period from their introspective period, introduced by "Help" and "Yesterday" in August and October 1965 respectively.[7] Precisely these same months ushered in three years of hard-edged "soul" music by blacks[8] and turned even Bob Dylan's electrified taunts into hit material. These events foreshadowed the bull market top just months later in January 1966. In 1966, the Rolling Stones suddenly outdid the Beatles in the number of Top Ten hits, with themes of drugs, mental breakdown, crying and death, with their final hit of the year coming in October. Look at the crash in stock prices from January to October 1966 and see how precisely it reflected the new mass mood. By mid-1966, says Philip Norman in *Shout*, "The latter-day Mersey groups had all gone home to settle down as pork butchers and damp-course engineers." The same thing happened to other happy-music bands who did not change musical direction, such as the Beach Boys, Herman's Hermits, Gary Lewis & the Playboys, etc., whose strings of Top Ten hits ended abruptly in 1966.[9] The public was now looking for something else and found it in the Stones, Bob Dylan (who had sung prophetically, "The Times, They Are A-Changin'"), soul music, the more worldly British and San Francisco bands and others. Coincidentally, the name for rhythmic popular music changed, from "rock and roll" to just plain "rock," a name that correctly suggested the hardness of the new musical style.

The Beatles, who remained innovators, did not yet retire, but changed precisely in line with the times. In August 1966, two months before that year's crash bottom in stocks, they announced their retirement from live performing and released an album cover featuring dismembered toy dolls and bloody joints of meat. The public's mood had changed so dramatically that the Beatles as a group suffered a worldwide hate campaign (the stated reasons are irrelevant) even as they adapted to the new mood. Not coincidentally, as a bull market returned in late 1966, the "butcher" album cover (now a collector's item) was quickly recalled and replaced with a bland photo. In June 1967, the Beatles "committed suicide," announcing their reincarnation as a new band (Sargent Pepper's Lonely Hearts Club Band) with a complex identity reflecting both the peace/love sentiments of the emerging psychedelic "flower power" era and the more worldly style that had been expressed on their previous two albums. This mood mixture precisely reflected the bull market/bear market battle that was raging on Wall Street, with the secondary indexes heading for new highs against the Dow Industrials, which had made their orthodox top in January 1966 and were already declining, particularly in real-dollar terms. In a reflection of the rich sea change in mood that was taking place in those years, rock music became consciously artistic and flowered in terms of innovation, creativity, subtlety and complexity, as exemplified by the compositions and arrangements of Jimi Hendrix, Chicago, Santana, Quicksilver, Jefferson Airplane, Big Brother, Cream, The Who, Spirit, The Grateful Dead, Blood Sweat & Tears and a host of other bands.

Then in the fall of 1968, as the secondary stock bull market was preparing to enter its top, "heavy metal" music entered the scene, as hits by Iron Butterfly, Deep Purple and Steppenwolf all entered the charts concurrently. The sudden popularity of this new style at the bottom of the correction preceding the final peak foreshadowed the stock market top in December 1968 just as the Rolling Stones' two #1 hits in the second half of 1965 had foreshadowed the peak of January 1966.

The peace-love sentiments of the psychedelic era coincided with the last hurrah in the stock market, which peaked in a speculative frenzy with new all-time highs in the Value Line index (representing the dominance of secondary stocks). The good intentions found generally in bull market music peaked at the same time, with a string of studio-manufactured "Bubble Gum" hits, a sickly-sweet extreme in trend. Despite their agility in navigating the newest change in mood, the Beatles were apparently still a "bull market" band.[10] In January 1969, just as stock prices turned down and the bear market began to take firm hold, George Harrison walked out of the tension-filled *Let It Be* sessions, foreshadowing the final breakup of the band. Their final recordings, which had already been in the making, were released later that year.

Innovation, musical creativity and complexity in rock peaked at the same time, as the flood of ground-breaking bands came to an abrupt halt. Releases of the new music continued into the new year, and the momentum carried just long enough to produce the Woodstock festival that summer, the general disarray of which came off like the celebration of a bear market rally. As a New York ABC radio personality flatly said later in a front page *Wall Street Journal* article, "Rock peaked in 1969."

The Beatles themselves fought throughout the following year, with the final split coming in April 1970, as the stock market crashed toward its multi-year low. *Let It Be*,[11] a movie that chronicled the group's frictions (in dramatic contrast to their good-natured 1964 and 1965 movies), premiered on May 20, 1970, days from the crash bottom in stocks and the shootings of students at Kent State University. During the same period, the pop-music groups and stars that had shaped the topping phase abruptly fell from popularity, quit, broke up, or died in droves (Jimi Hendrix, Cass Elliot, Janis Joplin, Jim Morrison, Duane Allman).

A distinct change in rhythm occurred in the 1970s; it was as if someone had thrown a bucket of sludge into the pop music machine. Many songs were presented in a half-speed tempo (i.e., a backbeat every four beats instead of every two, "The Night They Drove Old Dixie Down," "I Shot the Sheriff," "Lonely People," for example). Some former hits were re-recorded at dramatically slower tempos ("Breaking Up Is Hard to Do," "Handy Man," "Higher and Higher," for example). Ballads were sung an octave lower than the previous average or pounded out at an agonizingly plodding pace as if the musicians were exhausted (James Taylor and Barry Manilow, for example). The timing of these artists' appearances followed immediately upon the exit of the "topping phase" bands. James Taylor (who, ironically, was discovered by the Beatles and recorded by Apple) had his first hit, "Fire and Rain," on the heels of the 1970 crash bottom in stocks, just a few months after the Beatles' breakup. (As with so many of the "negative mood" artists, his last hit was in 1981, near the end of the negative-mood period.) Barry Manilow's first dirge-like hit soared to #1 on the exact week of the major stock market bottom in December 1974, ending a crash in mood that expressed itself partly in a general blinding hatred of Richard Nixon, who had been forced from office in a sea of scandal. (Manilow's last Top Ten hit fell from the charts in late March, 1980 as the last of the stock market "massacres" bottomed; he remained in the lower areas of the charts into 1983.) Dance music also suddenly became slower in 1974, the year of the crash bottom. That year, a phenomenon known as "bump" music performed the function of bringing dance couples back together again. It was with only a tentative fanny-bump, but it paved the way for the later emergence of "disco" dance, which required fully cooperating partners, a typical occurrence near the end of corrective waves.

While the ballad buyers and dancers felt depressed, the kids felt angry. The bear market dating from 1966 that accelerated in 1969 supported bands whose accent was on the negative. The Rolling Stones thrived on themes of war, sex and the devil. Heavy metal bands, which had originally been satisfied to present merely a noisy, foreboding sound, adopted a calculated theatrical approach to their recordings and performances and sported names such as Black Sabbath, Blue Oyster Cult, Queen, AC/DC, The Scorpions and Kiss, suggesting darkness, sexual ambiguity and general nastiness. In a related development, early psychedelic "garage bands" gave way to groups that specialized in long, hypnotic compositions with negative-mood themes. The most accomplished and successful of these was Pink Floyd, which formed shortly after the onset of the wave IV bear market and which eventually became the strongest selling group in "downer theme" history, singing songs about self-destruction, axe murderers, money grubbing, war and alienation, all to a comfortably numbing or gratingly distorted soundtrack. Their classic album *Dark Side of the Moon* floated continually into the Top 20 album sales charts during the years from 1973 to 1982 (the final bear market year in real terms), when the group's popularity began to wane.

The most extreme musical development of the mid-1970s was the emergence of punk rock. The lyrics of these bands' compositions, as pointed out by Tom Landess, associate editor of *The Southern Partisan*, resemble T.S. Eliot's classic poem "The Waste Land," which was written during the 'teens, when the *last* Cycle wave IV correction was in force (a time when the worldwide negative mood allowed the communists to take power in Russia). The attendant music was as anti-"musical" (i.e., non-melodic, relying on one or two chords and two or three melody notes, screaming vocals, no vocal harmony, dissonance and noise), as were Bartok's compositions from the 1930s. It wasn't just that the performers of punk rock would suffer a heart attack if called upon to change chords or sing more than two notes on the musical scale, it was that they made it a *point* to be non-musical minimalists and to create ugliness, as artists. The early punk rockers from England and Canada conveyed an even more threatening image than did the heavy metal bands because they abandoned all the trappings of theatre and presented their message as reality, preaching violence and anarchy while brandishing swastikas. Their names—Johnny Rotten, Sid Vicious, Nazi Dog, The Damned, The Viletones, etc.—and their song titles and lyrics—"Anarchy in the U.K.," "Auschwitz Jerk," "The Blitzkrieg Bop," "You say you've solved all our problems? You're the problem! You're the problem!" and "There's no future! no future! no future!"—were reactionary lashings out at the stultifying welfare statism of England and their doom to life on the dole, similar to the Nazis' backlash answer to a situation of unrest in 1920s and 1930s Germany. Actually, of course, it didn't matter what conditions were attacked. The most negative mood since the 1930s (as implied by stock market action) required release, period. These bands took bad-natured sentiment to the same extreme that the pop groups of the mid-1960s had taken good-natured sentiment.[12] The public at that time felt joy, benevolence, fearlessness and love, and they demanded it on the airwaves. The public in the late 1970s felt misery, anger, fear and hate, and they got exactly what they wanted to hear. (Luckily, the hate that punk rockers' reflected was not institutionalized, but then, this was only a Cycle wave low, not a Supercycle wave low as in 1932.) The speed of the songs was usually breakneck, as the negative mood fell into its depths, just as the breakneck speed of doo-wop music from the late 1950s marked the peak of the energetic mood of wave ③. Ironically, even the punk rock audience had its way of re-introducing a "partners touching" style of dance in a unique frenzied frontal ramming-together of each other's bodies called "slam dancing." (One way or another, bear market bottoms bring couples back together!) These bands' domination of the airwaves lasted until the early 1980s, when Cycle wave IV, the great bear market that began in 1966, ended.[13]

In summary, an "I feel good and I love you" sentiment in music paralleled a bull market in stocks, while an amorphous, euphoric "Oh, wow, I feel great and I love *everybody*" sentiment (such as in the late '60s) was a major sell signal for mood and therefore for stocks. Conversely, an "I'm depressed and I hate you" sentiment in music reflected a bear market, while an amorphous tortured "Argh! I'm in agony and I hate *everybody*" sentiment (such as in the late '70s) was a major buy signal.[14]

## Leading Up to Today

Just as the beginning of Cycle wave IV was a sloppy process with two peaks (January 1966 and December 1968), its end was as well, with two bottoms (December 1974 and August 1982[15]). The music scene between the two *tops* resembled a complex battle between good and evil, which, in a sense, it was. The music scene between the two bottoms was schizophrenic as well, with disco music doing its best to affirm the happy positive and punk rock and heavy metal asserting the dominance of the angry negative. In the early 1980s, the negative mood manifestations reached extremes that signaled a major bottom, while truly positive forces (excluding disco itself, which, like the Twist, was only a transition-phase phenomenon), one by one, began claiming major victories in turning the tide.

The first big victory for the positive-mood forces in general was the public adoption of "bootstrap" psychology. It was as if people had tired of the negative and were determined to pull themselves, each as an individual, out of that mood. The first hint was the jogging fad, which turned into a full-blown craze for physical self-improvement. The 1980 method for spreading the craze was through video. Guess what was popular in that very analogous year (more on that later), 1920: workout *audio*. The new-fangled technology of *that* period gave us phonograph records to do exercises by. There was a new energy building in the early 1980s, and humans had to express it by running, lifting and jumping up and down. This was a coincident indicator of an *emerging* bull market for stocks. (Few embraced exercise in 1970.) This same "I'm sick of hearing the negative!" psychology was reflected in the blockbusting popularity of the film, *Rocky*, which expressed the new mood that "you can succeed (or at least avoid the natural state of failure) if you try like hell and push yourself to the limit." Four years later, a "bootstrap" president was elected.

The next big hint of change was the emergence of the nostalgia craze. All of a sudden, the social scene changed, and 1950s styles in just about everything were adopted. The country witnessed the return of family values, Disney movies, Ray-Ban sunglasses, campus rest, Boy Scout popularity, baseball popularity, etiquette, macho men, westerns, marriage and babies. Even nerds became "cool," and science began replacing sociology as the study of preference. '50s' pop music per-formers began touring again for "oldie" concerts and showing up, dead or alive, on TV programs (Jerry Lee Lewis, Elvis, Chuck Berry, Carl

Perkins, etc.). New bands which flatly copied the styles of the 1950s became popular (Stray Cats), and performers who powerfully resembled stylists of the 1950s (always with an '80s' twist) became stars (Michael Jackson echoed Elvis Presley's breathy vocals and girl-melting physical movement; Prince echoed Little Richard's combination of wildness and overt sexual lyrics). 1983 in particular witnessed a flood of articles on fashion, art and culture that reflected "conservative" times reminiscent of the 1950s or early 1920s, when bull markets were young.

At the same time, Christian rock music (Amy Grant, etc.) burst upon the scene and rose quickly in popularity. Sound tracks by "tech-no-pop" bands reflected the herky-jerky computer age while greatly mellowing the jagged edges of the still-remaining punk influence. Even the heavy metal band Kiss removed its horror-theatre makeup in the early 1980s. Melody hadn't yet returned to a dominant role in pop music, but the hate element was dissipating.

There was also a discernible shift in the sentiment of popular song lyrics in the early '80s. With "All we are is dust in the wind..." still echoing from Kansas' hit of February 1978, the month of an intermediate stock market bottom,[16] John Lennon[17] in late 1980 remained on the cutting edge of the newest mood by releasing an immensely popular album of sweet love songs to his family. October 1982 actually brought a social-commentary style hit that was upbeat, optimistic, and celebrated the computer and transportation revolution, concluding, "What a beautiful world this will be; What a glorious time to be free," with a favorable mention of the "Stars and Stripes" thrown in for good measure. The love song returned as an acceptable, if not dominant, theme for pop hits as the bull market of 1982-1983 took off. Even Lou Reed, an early leader in '70s' "downer theme" music, emerged from obscurity singing, "I Love You, Suzanne"! In 1983, Pink Floyd, after ten years of popularity, released its last album and broke up as a band. The Who, an aggressively toned and relatively anarchic rock group whose music remained a strong seller from the exact start of the negative-mood trend (having achieved notice originally with an auto-destructive stage act that included smashing guitars, amps and drums and releasing smoke bombs), played its last concert and disbanded. [They both reunited briefly for tours and live albums in subsequent years. —Ed.] Both of these groups, as well as numerous punk bands, exhausted themselves under the pressure of the new trend, as happened to the "fun" bands in 1966 and the Beatles in 1970.

After Primary wave ① peaked in 1983, the '50s' craze in music began to wane. The 1950s' styles, while still very much in evidence, yielded dominance to those of the early 1960s, specifically the years 1960-1962, which were transition years prior to the next big bull market advance in stocks. In the dance and music fields, the main trends that took over in 1984 were break dancing, girl groups and cutesy copycat rockers.

After ten years of "partners touching" disco dancing,[18] the new style, once again having taken hold despite the warnings of doctors and the dismay of parents, was "break dancing," the new "Twist." In 1960, the Twist was a major event, a basic change in dance style from a partners-touching style of dance to a partners-separate style. It was as if each dancer had so much energy that to stay together was just too dangerous. The Twist was denounced by doctors as potentially damaging to the sacroiliac, but the dancers loved it anyway. In the recent transition, it was "break dancing" that pushed partners apart from the partners-touching disco dancing convention and turned each into a whirling dervish impervious to his doctor's warnings. Again, everybody "on the scene" loved it, to the extent that several break dancing movies became box office hits. The dancing seen on prime time TV programs today is almost all partners-separate again, as opposed to the myriad partners-touching disco programs of the late 1970s. The girl-group phenomenon hardly needs elaboration. Female pop singers have returned in droves, successfully invading the traditionally male idiom once again. Some of the biggest sensations of the pop-music world recently have been women, including the Go-Go's, the Pointer Sisters, Madonna, Cyndi Lauper, Tina Turner, Pat Benatar and others. They own the airwaves, as they did in the early 1960s. As a final parallel with the early '60s, lightweight copycat rockers Wham! (like Bobby Vee and others in 1960-1962) sold records and cavorted on video wearing "Choose Life" T-shirts. Can it be just coincidence that after all these years, the Everly Brothers staged a packed-house "reunion" concert and Chubby Checker is touring again?

**Where Are We Now?**

What may be important for signaling another mood change is that the dominance of women in pop music appears to have reached an extreme this year. Cyndi Lauper graced the March 4 cover of *Newsweek*,

Sweaters set

daring

NEW
Bold
son's sw
tradition
signs sh
patterns
out geo
squiggles
bounty o
tinues th
and brill
ing yelle

**Life in fast lane:**
**USA ignores 55 mph**

More motorists are ignoring the 55-mph speed limit

U.S. Department of Transportation surveys show an average of 42 percent of us drove faster than 55 last year. On rural interstates, 3 of 4 sped.

"People are driving faster."

There's no doubt about it," said DOT spokesman Bob Beasley.

"Interstates are designed for '70 miles an hour. People get on 'em and go like hell," said Bob Sherman, aide to Vermont Gov. Madeleine Kunin.

**SEC Approves**

## Increased Limits

## On Option Positions

WASHINGTON—The Securities and I change Commission gave four exchang approval to increase their limits on optio positions, enabling investors to hold mo options contracts.

The new position limits will
—8,000 contracts on stocks with a s month trading volume of 40 million sha or a 30 million-share volume and a put float of 120 million shares outstanding
—5,500 contracts on stocks with a s month volume of 20 million shares or a million-share volume and 40 million sha outstanding.

—3,000 contracts on less active sto

**Deregulating**
**Stock Credit**

For more than 50 years Federal regulators have told stockbrokers how much credit they can extend to their customers to purchase stock, a practice known as buying on margin. Under the rules in effect since the Depression, investors had to post at least 40 percent, using the stock as collateral for the balance.

The Federal Reserve Board suggested last week that changes in the market had rendered those rules obsolete. The board wants to turn over responsibility for regulating credit to the stock exchanges, and Treasury Secretary Donald T. Regan suggested they should consider abolishing requirements completely.

Congress restricted the purchase of stock on margin in 1934 partly in an effort to control dramatic fluctua-

## Katrina and crew really
## 'Walking on Sunshine'

"I think the timing was just right," she says. "People are ready for a good band singing down-to-earth pop songs, and people are in the mood for summer."

"It's going to be in the same vein," Miss Leskanich says. "Maybe a bit more rocked up, but we're going to keep the innocent, honest, band-next-door approach.

"I like to think we come off sounding friendly — like we're nice people. Even if that might get us labeled a pop band — which some people think is a derogatory status — success is success."     June 8, 1985

**WANT SOMETHING FULL OF PEP**
**THAT COMES IN A FIVE-PACK AND**
**MAKES YOU SMILE? TRY NEW EDITION**

**C**hief, I think I've found someone for the new bubble-gum campaign. I know you wanted the Jacksons, but let's face it, they're going to be pricey. So how about New Edition? It's a five-kid group from Boston's Roxbury ghetto, and their music is known as—get this—bubble-gum soul. Perfecto, no?

The kids sign, sing, and poppo! zoom to No. 1 on the black-singles chart. Sure, the lyrics are kind of drippy—*You look so sweet/You're a special treat*—but they might be just the thing for the TV spots, eh, chief? But here's the capper: These kids

are *nice*. They come from working-class families, don't do drugs ("We were raised differently," says Ralph) and even travel with a tutor. In fact, our only problem might be that they're *too* popular right now. Some 5,000 fans showed up for an October autograph-

**'Silly Love Songs'**
**Sweep the Country**

If you turn your radio dial carelessly these days, you may well come across a station that promises you "Love Songs—Nothing but Love Songs." Like fast food and other forms of mush, the "love song" format that has emerged recently is a uniquely American invention. Although it is aimed at the age 25-49 market, the explosion of love-song programming suggests some interesting trends in popular music. At the very moment when West European rock music is becoming more and more political, American pop has become dominated by love songs that are increasingly banal

**In the Silicon Valley,**
**L'Enfant Terrible Is**

## Also L'Enfant Riche

SCOTTS VALLEY, Calif.—The spotlight shivers on a fuming wall of dry ice. A drum roll sounds, the crowded ballroom falls silent. Even the guests ripping slabs of meat from the whole roast pig on the buffet turn to watch.

Eventually, the night's host glides into center stage, his considerable girth draped in a purple and gold tent—er, toga—and a wreath of grape leaves on his head. "All hail Bacchus," someone bellows. He hoists his saxophone in salute and begins to play.

The saxophonist and host is Philippe Kahn, the founder and owner of Borland International and the self-appointed court jester of Silicon Valley. Even here, where extravagant indulgence and eccentricity are commonplace, the expansive software publisher has become a legend within two years of his arrival from his native France.

His toga party is costing him $45,000, with a gluttonous mob of 600 on hand, including an ersatz satyr wearing little more than a shepskin loincloth and a pair of horns. A trapeze artist performs, and merrymakers pelt one another with balloons filled with shaving cream.

A local newspaper subsequently calls the affair "a drunken orgy." Mr. Kahn replies, with a melodramatic sigh, "I can't quarrel with the drunken part. I only wish I remembered the orgy."

"I have all the money I need," he says. "Now, I dedicate myself to fun."

## When Inflation Rate Is 116,000%, Prices Change by the Hour

Bolivians aren't yet lugging their money about in wheelbarrows, as the Germans did during the legendary hyperinflation of the Weimar Republic in the 1920s, when prices increased 10 billionfold. But Bolivia seems headed in that direction.

"This isn't even good as toilet paper," says pharmacist Ruth Aranda, holding up a 100-peso bill. Indeed, she points out, admission to a public toilet costs 300 pesos.

Three years ago, she says, she bought a new luxury Toyota auto for what she now sells three boxes of aspirin for. "We're headed for the garbage can."

tions in the market. The sale of stock on credit with only a fraction of the price paid in advance was widely blamed for having inflated prices during the unregulated days of the 1920's. A slight decline in value could wipe out a customer's investment, with his collateral for the balance (the stock) declining as well. A crash, as occurred in 1929, could break thousands of investors and leave the creditors to collect only a few cents on the dollar.

In a study of margin requirements released last week, the board argued that the market had largely outgrown the dangers of these leveraged purchases.

"My concern is that the exchanges might compete on margins," said Nicholas Giordano, president of the Philadelphia Stock Exchange. "Traders would like to have no margin at all, and it puts us in a difficult position. The stock exchanges are competing with the options and financial futures markets, so they could be pressured to go to the lowest common denominator so they can compete."

## Pop rockers Wham!

Wham! Just like that, they've got the No. 1 record in the USA.

How did an obscure British dance band manage to push past such heavyweights as Prince and Stevie Wonder?

It's simple, says the band's lead singer. "We're cute," explains George Michael, who, along with guitarist Andrew Ridgeley, turned Wake Me Up Before You Go-Go into one of the most lightweight, but infectious, pop hits of the year.

"You have to have a strong rhythm track to make a hit pop record. Wake Me Up has a lightweight, sing-along melody but it also has an intense rhythm track. ...

Michael, who produces, arranges and writes the music, feels Wham! has a formula for success. "Our songs may seem familiar because we've used as our foundation some of the great commercial artists, especially the Motown sound. The melodies we have are very simple and easy to hum."

## TWILIGHT ZONE

USA TODAY · THURSDAY, APRIL 4, 1985

HOLLYWOOD — This fall, the mystery anthology format is back big.

Out of favor since the glory days of *Alfred Hitchcock Presents* and *The Twilight Zone* and off the tube entirely since ABC's *Darkroom* in 1982, the style will enjoy a rebirth with CBS' *Twilight Zone* and Steven Spielberg's *Amazing Stories* on NBC.

Compared to the old series, "some things have changed and some haven't," he says.

Of the first shows, all the segments are new stories except two remakes:

■ "Night of the Week." A 1960 Rod Serling teleplay featuring Art Carney as a drunken department store Santa Claus who "enters a strange kind of North Pole ...part of the magic that can only be found in the *Twilight Zone*."

■ "Dead Man's Shoes." In 1962, Warren Stevens played a bum who steals shoes from a dead gangster, puts them on and becomes the gangster. In the new version, the bum will have his gender changed to a brunette.

## Boot lovers go gaga over go-go — again

By Elizabeth Sporkin
USA TODAY

NEW YORK — With miniskirts and lace stockings reviving 1960s style, can go-go boots be far behind?

on Broadway in March. De-Mora snapped up eight pairs for the opening number; dancers will wear them with miniskirts and midriff tops.

"They should never have gone away," says deMora of

## fall fashion scene
## designs and color

Thursday, August 1, 1985

YORK, N.Y. — ...raphics make this sea-...eaters stand out from the ...al crowd of the past. De-ow a new daring with that range brom blocked-metrics, to new wave ...tapestry mosaics and a ...fancy florals. Color con-...e emphasis on boldness ance. Electric blue, jolt-...w, fiery red and stark

black and white add to the vivid appeal of this year's sweater set.

One clear winner, *Seventeen's* fashion editors predict, will be an updated Aztec graphic in the attention-getting color combination of black, white and grey zapped with bright yellow. Worn with a white and yellow striped cotton shirt and strip-light yellow mini skirt, the look is sure to end up in the fashion spotlight.

## Guys get familiar with fashion

1922...1962...1985?

Much to the surprise of the store — which expected the avant-garde look to have limited appeal — the $125 sweater by designer Andrew Fezza immediately sold out.

Other USA stores — such as Marshall Field's in Chicago and Macy's in New York — also report that the most fashion-forward men's looks are selling faster than traditional ones. Men, it seems, are beginning to cotton to clothes like never before.

"Anything dabbled in by women is now dabbled in by men. Men are much more experimental with fabrics, silhouettes and color," says Howard Sussman, Macy's men's fashion coordinator. "There's never been a time like this in men's fashion."

ing 1960s style, can go-go boots be far behind?

"There's definitely an upswing" in interest in white boots, says Lois Kopf of Courreges, the Paris design house that first introduced the mid-calf-high go-go boot in 1964.

This year, Courreges has brought back restyled versions in white and silver, with cutouts at the tops — to some of its 15 USA boutiques. "They're selling like crazy in Beverly Hills and there has been growing interest in New York," Kopf reports.

One customer was Bob deMora, costume designer for *Leader of the Pack!*, a musical set in the 1960s that will open

"They should never have gone away," says deMora of the boots.

Shoe manufacturer Two City Kids also will bring out updated go-go boots with a punch-out design that allows stockings to show through.

"Fashion is cyclical and things do repeat themselves," says avant-garde shoe designer Kenneth Cole, who late this spring will bring out a new version of the go-go boot: short white boots that are tight around the ankle. Some have high heels; some are flat.

"I think miniskirts call for something that comes up the foot," he says. "It just feels right again."

*Women's Wear Daily* has ushered in the new spring season with "The Short Age." The fashion mag places the "in" hems about four inches above the knee.

**FAB FAD:** Fishnet stockings and updated go-go boots by Courreges, are finally back in vogue. In colors: White and silver.

"Anything dabbled in by women is now dabbled in by men. Men are much more experimental with fabrics, silhouettes and color," says Howard Sussman, Macy's men's fashion coordinator. "There's never been a time like this in men's fashion."

# Two-piece swimsuits resurface on beaches

By Elizabeth Sporkin
USA TODAY

NEW YORK — 1985's most stylish swimmers will shun the long-popular maillot for a splash from the past: the two-piece.

Not a teeny bikini, mind you, but a suit that covers a little more hip, thigh and stomach.

"There's a whole generation who have never seen these suits before," says Doug Arbetman, spokesman for Cole of California, which offers a style that can be rolled up or down for more or less coverage. "They really have a fun fashion look."

After three years of one-piece predominance. "This is a natural evolution," says designer Norma Kamali.

By MICHAEL POLLOCK
Press Staff Writer

OCEAN CITY — They were a product of the late 1950s and 1960s, a time of prosperity and two-car garages. The stock market appeared to be a bull market that would ride forever and small investors wanted to ride the bull in their own tiny herds.

Investment clubs were chic and novel, as popular as outdoor barbecues and "The Donna Reed Show."

There may not be as many investment clubs around today as there were in the 1960s, but there are still a reported 25,000 such clubs active in the United States.

Investment clubs are gatherings of people with a common interest: investing in the stock market.

The National Association of Investment Clubs, based in Royal Oak, Mich., reports that the average member invests $13 a month. The entire association, representing 115,000 investors in 5,900 clubs, invests $4.4 million a month.

"It's not a get-rich-quick program," warned Thomas O'Hara, association chairman and co-founder. "It's an accumulation program."

O'Hara credited the bull market which began in August 1982 with renewing much of the interest in investment clubs. The NAIC, which had nearly 14,000 members in 1969, was down to fewer than 4,000 in 1980.

# Family life is 'in'
# 1950's return

## Parents renew an emphasis on etiquette

FRIDAY, FEBRUARY 8, 1985 · USA TODAY

# Scouting is 75 yrs. today and growing

For some children, learning to say "please" and "thank you" is as difficult as learning to eat with a knife and fork — and about as much fun. When parents nag them to do or say things "correctly," they are hard pressed to understand what all the fuss is about.

Today, parents are making more of a fuss over manners — the art of doing things correctly — than they did during the free-for-all 1960s.

Respect for age, wisdom and the establishment are back, and an emphasis on good manners is part of this return to more traditional values.

## Funicello at 41: Back to basics with Disney

Some things never change. The sun rises in the East. April showers bring May flowers. And Annette Funicello exudes as much exuberance about life at 41 as she did in her Mouseketeer years—

"When I heard the name Disney, I jumped at the chance," says Funicello. Her last Disney film was *Monkey's Uncle* nearly 20 years ago.

"I have the kids that watched the Mickey Mouse Club that are now my age, the kids that watched the

## Casual sex on campus declines

PALM SPRINGS, Calif.

From a peak of 4.9 million in 1972, BSA's youth membership fell by more than a third to a low of just 3.3 million in 1979. The number of adult volunteers also dropped dramatically. "It was the tenor of the times," Chief Scout Executive Ben H. Love said. "There was rebellion against anything that had traditional values. Some of the things we believe in — patriotism, duty to God — were being challenged."

In the past five years, the organization has managed to reverse its slide. Preliminary 1984 figures show youth membership at nearly 3.7 million, a 2.5 percent increase over 1983. Scouting is benefiting, Love said, from what he sees as a national return to "basic values and basic beliefs." (Scouts, after all, still take an oath to be "physically strong, mentally awake and morally straight.")

# Explode

## with the rebirth of Westerns

# RAMBO

**Macho strides back**

May 19, 1985

**12 states move to cut taxes**

By Richard Benedetto
USA TODAY

The cuts are proposed or probable in 12 states this year, in a bid to trim budget surpluses. Income tax USA and up to $4.15 billion.

In 21 taxpayers' and interest taxpayers' pockets too far ... with 14 years coming today. America's have ..... but far ... state have transformed the dollar

**Dollar, Wall St. hit highs**

**Dear Ann: Hugs beat sex**

72%

JANUARY 13, 1985, USA TODAY

5-19-85

Ron Kirchoff, a real estate agent here, started his club five years ago "just to be sociable, to have fun. We're not trying to make a killing."

The club, which began in June 1983 with five members, "just looks for anything that looks half-decent," Kirchoff said.

"We're down, to be honest with you."

College students today are less likely to engage in casual sex than they were a decade ago and they feel more guilty about their sexual behavior, suggests a new study to be released here Saturday.

In 1974 and 1984, researchers surveyed 100 students at Northern Iowa University in Cedar Falls on their sexual attitudes and practices. The study will be presented at the annual meeting of the Society for the Scientific Study of Sex

"The changes in sexual behavior just go along with the conservative shift in our society's values over the past 10 years," says Marilyn Story, a family studies professor at Northern Iowa.

"Sexual guilt, for example, correlates with being religious and a more conservative political orientation. That's what we're seeing on campuses and in society at large."

## Jane Pauley: 'new father' is a myth

the kids that watching the beach pictures that are now young adults, and the little kids who are now watching the Skippy (peanut butter) commercials."

DICK'S HAMBURGERS, is a startup outfit (with experienced management) that plans to open drive-in fast-food restaurants that resemble those that were popular in the 1950s. JUNE 4, 1985.

"Our reports show everybody likes it," says an ecstatic Jerry Esbin, Tri-Star vice president. "What this film reality is doing is saying we're coming out of the closet as far as Vietnam is concerned."

"Phil Donahue is an endangered species," says Arthur Cooper, editor of *Gentlemen's Quarterly* magazine. "For a while, men were defining themselves in terms of their reactions to the feminist movement. Now, they've said, 'Enough

"I see it as a healthy antidote to *Strawberry Fields Forever* and all the peace-love junk of the '60s," says Art Murphy, an industry analyst for *Variety* and University of Southern California film professor.

already.' They don't want to see themselves as Jimmy Cagney, but they're not silent sobbers either. *Masculine* is what's happening."

I may be wrong, but there seems to be a mood in America at the moment which is reflected in the kind of television that America produces. And something of the spirit of that is reflected in this miniseries."

And what mood is that? "A sort of patriotism," he said. "A feeling that there is hope, that one can press forward and achieve. Above anything else, Christopher Columbus was a great achiever. And there's great respect, I think, in America for the achiever, for the man who brooks no obstacle and is determined to achieve his end. And I think that's something that American audiences will relate to."

# Fashions a-go-go for '60s look

AUGUST 18, 1985

By Betsa Marsh
USA TODAY

Skirts are short, pants are pegged and shoes are pointed.

The time is now, but the look is unmistakably 1960s.

Twenty years and one generation after fishnet stockings, miniskirts and turtleneck dickeys blasted onto the fashion scene, they're back — thanks to the sons and daughters of the men and women who wore them the first time around.

Teens and college students are scouring the secondhand shops for '60s garb and completing the look with dramatic eye makeup, teased hair and flashy sunglasses.

"Most of the kids are 16 to 18," says Jon Bok of Cowboys and Poodles' boutique in Los Angeles, where the '60s fashion fad seems to be hottest.

For several months, he says, $20 paisley shirts and $20 miniskirts — unused clothing from manufacturers' and retailers' overstocked warehouses — have been selling out.

"The kids are into '60s music, like the Monkees and the Shangri-Las," Bok says, "and that sort of led them into the clothes."

Until last summer, sales were roughly 80 percent from '50s clothes and 20 percent from '60s styles, Bok says. The '60s sales "skyrocketed" when school was out. Now, '60s clothes are 80 percent of the sales.

Especially popular are Beatles boots, polka dots, op-art designs, go-go boots and oversized jewelry in Day-Glo colors.

In New York, the '60s fad has been "definitely there, but not a major influence," says R__ Goodman of Trash and __deville.

U nless you have been sequestered in a cave for the past few months, you must know that stir-rup pants are the latest trousers for young fashionables to sport on the streets. Slim and narrow, they bring the legs into focus, with an emphasis on fit. Stirrups first sauntered

onto the fashion scene for skiing in the early '20s, boasting jodhpur-type legs. Gradually the leg got slimmer and sleeker, thanks to innovations in fabrics, especially of the stretch variety.

During the '60s, noted Italian fashion designer Emilio Pucci brought out sleek-looking stirrup pants, according to Sol Kent, Rich's fashion director, who to this day doesn't have much use for them. "At that time, everyone looked like hookers in these pants," he said, "wearing them with high-heeled mules. El-len Melinkoff quoted several women who wore stretch stirrups during the '60s. One said, "I remember hating ski pants or stretch pants even though I wore them.

However, women clung to these pants and by 1961, they made their first general appearance in the stores for street wear. Called stretch pants —

1923----1962?

1985?

By Barb Kinney, USA TODAY

**PAST IS PRESENT:** A dickey, pegged pants for him; a minidress, fishnet stockings for her. Classic Clothing, Washington, D.C.

# Break dancing fever hits Germany

West Germany (AP) — Break dancing, the street sensation of the South Bronx, has boogied across the Atlantic to Germany.

West German youngsters are doing the supple falls, gyrations and gymnastics of break dancing for tips in shopping malls, and some department stores are luring customers with break dance exhibitions. Cinemas, television and magazines also are featuring the acrobatic steps.

Dancers dazzle onlookers with their spins and struts in Frankfurt's main shopping district, and earn about $78 a day in small change.

A local disco called the No Name holds weekly break dance competitions. The winner gets a prize of $196.

"It's like a fever right now," said Peter Boehm, 32, who works at the City Music store in downtown Frankfurt.

Break dancing is the latest fad in a country where successive generations of teen-agers since World War II have been quick to adopt American styles in music, dance and clothes.

The West German Dance Teachers' Association estimates that 360,-000 young Germans are caught up in the craze.

# London goes prim in the age of punk

LONDON—Punk is passé. Prim is in.

That's the message London's young, trendy women are sending out these days.

Outrageous outfits are giving way to grown-up gowns. Suddenly young women have taken to looking like their moms: Elbow-length gloves, black cocktail dresses, high heels, severe hairdos, lots of costume jewelry, bright lipstick, heavy mascara.

Nowhere is the new look more evident than at Hyper Hyper, the market-stall designer hall opened a year ago as a showcase for young English designers.

Some 70 of these stalls are found in Hyper Hyper, which is much larger and more sophisticated than the Kensington Market, another designer market across the street. Kensington, which got its start in the 1960s, faded in the 1970s and is currently undergoing a revival.

## Spring fling: Short skirts

When it comes to skirts for spring, the thigh's the limit.

After a winter of sidewalk-sweeping hemlines, "It's time to see a little bit of leg," says designer Perry Ellis. His spring 1985 collection features above-the-knee skirts after four years of predominantly long styles. "Suddenly, the short skirts and soft shapes look refreshingly feminine."

Other USA designers short-ening skirts (and showing leg-revealing shorts): Calvin Klein, Ralph Lauren, Willi Smith and Norma Kamali, who unveil their collections Oct. 29-Nov. 9 in New York.

Will they sell? "I think they're real cute as long as they're not too short, and as long as they look good on you," says Edwina Richard, 21, a model from Tucson, Ariz.

■ Europe also goes short 3D

---

## Short skirts, shorts reign at Paris show

PARIS (AP) — Short skirts got the nod at Karl Lagerfeld's summer ready-to-wear show Saturday, and designer Claude Montana unveiled hot pants and micro-skirts from beneath long duster coats.

There were even white cuffed shorts in Lagerfeld's bridal wear.

Lagerfeld also showed some long pleated skirts, but his clear preference was for leg-revealing minis and micros.

which featured the lead article, "Rock and Roll: Woman Power." In January, *USA Today* quoted Patti LaBelle (who had her first "girl group" hit herself in 1962) as saying "We (women) are taking over." On May 27, Madonna made the cover of *Time*. As Paul Montgomery's studies of magazine covers would indicate, this year must mark the peak of girl-group popularity.

Now let's move up to the present. *Playboy* and *Penthouse* magazines, trying to cash in on the girl-singer craze, hoped to sell out their August issues with nude pictures of Madonna. An interesting thing happened. Sales were brisk, but not as good as hoped. Remember those headlines about the one-day crash in Utility stocks on July 29th? "Worst Day For Utilities in 23 Years," they read, referring to May 28, 1962, one month before the price low in the wave ④ correction in stocks and five months before the orthodox bottom. And as if to seal the fate of the "available female" as a pop image, Madonna got married last Friday night (August 16). Meanwhile, the upbeat love-song trend that began in 1980 and has been flashing in and out of style is again picking up steam. Even the Beach Boys have been touring again.[19] From late 1982 to the present, there has been an undercurrent of happy pop music that, according to this model, should be about to explode on the scene as the dominant style, featuring melody, harmony and relative creativity. The message from the state of today's popular music is that the uncertain, corrective phase is nearing its end and that a full-fledged speculative bull market in mood is preparing to emerge.

A "fundamental" (i.e., outside of the market itself, but seemingly related) event that is akin to a bad earnings report after the stock has declined is the sudden new insistence that popular music albums utilize a rating system. If lyrics have gotten so disgusting that people are finally reacting, the peak in negative lyrics has passed. This fundamental event is not unlike Congress's move during the 1973-1974 bear market to institutionalize the nation's depressed pace by mandating a 55-mph speed limit nationwide. Laws like this merely signal that an extreme has been reached and therefore that the trend is about to change. They certainly can't, short of iron military enforcement (which *is* an option), stop a trend that is aching to express itself.

This month, another fascinating event occurred, the release of a movie entitled, *Return of the Living Dead*, billed as a *spoof* of the zombie horror movies. In other words, it's Abbott & Costello meet the Zombies. The power of horror is dying right now, strongly suggesting

Rarely have so many women performing rock had so many hit records on the charts. Never have so many women with such strong images so dominated the music videos shown on MTV, the rock-and-roll cable network (page 54). Madonna's new album, "Like a Virgin" (Sire), recently No. 1 for three weeks, is already "triple platinum." In 14 weeks it's sold some 3.5 million copies—a staggering amount, particularly since her first tour doesn't start until April. Turner, the Pointer Sisters, Pat Benatar and Chaka Khan all have current albums that have topped the million mark. And after 63 weeks, Cyndi Lauper's album, "She's So Unusual" (Portrait), is still charted in the Top 30, with nearly 4 million copies sold. Lauper's recordings have earned five Grammy nominations and her album has produced four Top Five singles—a new record for female singers.

The first big break for women in rock came in the early '60s, with girl groups like the Shirelles, the Ronettes and the Crystals. The songs the girls sang, like "Be My Baby" and "(Today I Met) The Boy I'm Gonna Marry," may have given marriage a false glow of paradise. But their bee-hive hairdos and stiletto heels gave the game away. The boy they wanted to marry was probably a biker.

Some insiders point to Madonna's steamy image and argue that little has really changed for women in rock and roll since the days of "girl groups" like the Ronettes.

"I get so much bad press for being overtly sexual," sighs Madonna. "When someone like Prince, Elvis or Jagger does the same thing, they are being honest, sensual human beings. But when I do it: 'Oh, please. Madonna, you're setting the women's movement back a million years'." Lauper agrees: "How can you criticize a woman for having a sexuality when men for years and years have been singing about nothing else? She's just doing her thing. My thing happens to be different. Women have a sexuality that shouldn't be suppressed."

Rodgers, her current producer, concocted a relentless rhythm track for "Like a Virgin" that suggests a bright, major-key version of Michael Jackson's "Billie Jean." The lyrics—all about how true love makes a girl feel "shiny and new, just like a virgin"—fit like a glove. So does Madonna's vocal. Her singing evokes the pie-eyed kid in "Bobby's Girl," the pert Marcie Blane hit of 1962. But when Madonna summons a nervous, fey hiccup on the chorus, she sounds more like the giddy vixen of the video version. It's a perfect pop epiphany—pure erotic fluff.

---

Even Madonna's staunchest fans would not claim that their idol is a radical ground-breaker. Indeed, the most beguiling aspect of Madonna is the way in which she is a throwback to interesting "girl" vocalists of years past.

LaBelle started singing in a more innocent era. In the early '60s, she led Patti LaBelle and the Bluebells in her native Philadelphia. The combo, which included former Supreme Cindy Birdsong, scored its first hit in 1962 with *I Sold My Heart to the Junkman.*

In the '70s, Patti and Bluebells Nona Hendryx and Sarah Dash transformed themselves into Labelle. A blazing fusion of sexy space-funk, raw rock power and provocative social commentary, Labelle was ahead of its time — and paid the price for it.

"It was something too different; something nobody was willing to accept," says LaBelle. "There was no category for three outrageous women at the time.... We were saying things that women were afraid to say — sexual, political, whatever we felt."

When the group split up in 1977, LaBelle's solo career was launched. She's pleased with the changes that have come for women over the years: "We're takin' over the charts," she jokes. And she's still carrying the hot stuff — right onto Broadway.

courtesy Newsweek,  USA Today

that *Halloween, Part 17* and *Friday the 13th, Part 32* will never be made.[20] The newest trend in movie themes is that science and brains are not nerdy but cool. Films such as *Weird Science*, *My Science Project*, *Real Genius* and computer-oriented adventure stories are coinciding with kids' new desire to run computers and manipulate technology, in stark contrast to the values of the late 1960s and 1970s. These are all hints that better times lie ahead.

As with music and movies, it is still too early to characterize the fashion trends as typical of a major top. Fashion designers keep try-ing to re-introduce mini-skirts, but as yet, the public hasn't rushed to buy them. On the longer-term trend, women have been slowly raising hemlines, but as one article puts it, "Will they [shorter skirts] sell? 'I think they're real cute as long as they're *not too short*,' says a model from Tucson." No, it's not the *late* '20s or '60s yet! Two-piece bathing suits are making a comeback, but skimpy bikinis are still worn only by a minority at the beaches. "Daring colors" are being introduced by some fashion designers, while reactionaries are trying to re-introduce the Maxi-skirt as the stock market corrects. The bright colors and shorter hemlines should win this battle, but while it is still a battle, and until the newly introduced styles make the covers of *Time* and *Newsweek* and are seen everywhere at the shopping malls, the bull market should have more to go.

The years 1921 through 1929 experienced a *fifth* Cycle-degree wave in stocks, the same wave label and degree of the current bull market, which dates from August 1982 in the Dow Industrials. The parallels today with the mid-1920s (a period similar to the early 1960s) are becoming more and more obvious. There have been a number of parallel economic phenomena occurring in recent years, including the end of inflation in 1980, which corresponds to the inflationary peak of 1920, the end of the constant-dollar Dow's bear market in 1982, which corresponds to the same event in 1921, the current runaway inflation in South America, which corresponds to the same phenomenon in 1923 Germany, and the proposal to eliminate legal margin requirements for stock purchases, a widely recognized prerequisite for the speculative heights achieved in the bull market of the 1920s. More to the point, however, is that the *social* scene of today is beginning to resemble that of the mid-1920s, with advertisements for "Great Gatsby" parties and articles about computer business multi-millionaires whose new-found goal is to party all night long. As yet, however, evidence that the party-crazed mini-skirted *late* '20s have arrived is not to be found. By the time Cycle wave V is over, the trendsetters should have reached that point, living life in a new version of the late '20s and mid-to-late '60s.

There are many indications that Cycle wave V is a nostalgia wave that is doing its best to re-create the glories of the past. (I don't know whether the 1920s exhibited a similar tendency.) In stocks, it should end with the old-line Dow Industrials providing the final run. In politics, the longing to return to "old-time values" elected a president. In fashion, nostalgia has its hand on the helm, and the speeded-up replay of the fashions of Cycle wave III should continue right into a re-creation of the mini-skirted, foppish, frenzied peak of the late 1960s. "There's definitely a '60s' inspiration in today's hair fashions," says a representative of Vidal Sassoon on TV, "not a copying, but a creative inspiration...." The pop-music world is rushing through a re-creation of the trends in the 1940s (Linda Ronstadt's prom-queen music revival), 1950s and 1960s. In fact, re-formations of groups from the 1960s and small-scale tours and TV appearances are beginning already.

What is the implication of nostalgia as a driving cultural force? One of the observations revealed by a study of the Wave Principle is that third waves are accompanied by increasingly favorable "fundamental" news events, while fifth waves' fundamentals are less impressive by comparison. In a similar way, '50s' & '60s' music, produced during a third wave, was a strong step forward because it was *innovative*, while '80s' music is less impressive because it's *derivative*. (The great symphonic music was undoubtedly produced during the latter stages of a third wave of Supercycle and/or Grand Supercycle degree.) For those who lived through the 1950s and 1960s, the modern echo has been hollow, in the same way that the bull market in stocks has lacked the solid breadth (percentage of stocks advancing) of the bull market of 1942-1966. In other words, all indications are that the advance in mood which began in 1982 *is* a fifth (Cycle wave V), and that ultimately, this wave, in all its manifestations, is doomed to usher in another collapse in stocks and in mood. In the meantime, enjoy it, profit from it, and don't sell it short too soon.

## NOTES

[1] Men are more "masculine" during bull markets, and women more "feminine." "Feminism" gains power during corrections, as it did in the 1850s during Supercycle wave (II), around World War I during Cycle wave IV of (III), and again in the 1970s, during Cycle wave IV of (V).

[2] Due to new research in 2018, these cells have been refined from the original article.

[3] History suggests that creativity in all fields (entrepreneurial, philosophic, literary, scientific, musical, etc.) peaks with third waves.

[4] Evidence of these directional forces lends support to the idea of Yin and Yang in Eastern philosophy. It will take the approach of a Western frame of mind, however, to gather and interpret the specific data to substantiate the concept.

[5] Artists such as Ricky Nelson, Bobby Vee  and the Everly Brothers took over. Their sweet melodies and harmonies kept them popular through the 1959-1962 correction. Their consecutive string of hits ended in 1962 in both cases.

[6] "Girl groups" continued to produce hits into 1964 until the Beatles took over, and on a lesser scale right into the orthodox top in January 1966; after that time, the only women who could make it in rock music were the ones who could act rougher than men, such as Grace Slick and Janis Joplin.

[7] In "Help!", John Lennon sang, "Help me if you can, I'm feeling down; Help me get my feet back on the ground; Won't you please, please help me?" In "Yesterday", Paul McCartney sang, "Yesterday all my troubles seemed so far away; Now it looks as though they're here to stay...."

[8] Soul music singers went out of style in 1969, so their reign covered the period of the double top in stocks.

[9] These bands' appearance at lower levels on the charts continued until late 1968-early 1969, ending abruptly with the second top in the bull market. Brian Wilson, leader of the Beach Boys, went into seclusion and suffered psychological problems.

[10] Paul McCartney, particularly, kept in tune with the last gasp of the bull market that had carried to new highs in the secondary stock indexes. John Lennon, on the other hand, switched immediately and powerfully into the new mood. His post-1965 song contributions became darker and darker until his input on the White Album in 1968 prompted these (admiring) liner notes:

> The harshness of the imagery is, if anything, even harsher;
> 'The eagle picks my eye/The worm he locks my bone.' Black

birds, black clouds, broken wings, lizards, destruction. And, most grotesque of all, there is a terrifying track just called 'Revolution 9,' which comprises sound effects, overheard gossip, backwards-tapes, janglings from the subconscious memories of a floundering civilisation. Cruel, paranoiac, burning, agonised, hopeless, it is given shape by an anonymous bingo voice which just goes on repeating 'Number nine, number nine, number nine'—until you want to scream.

As a trend setter, Lennon, whose popular career began in 1962 with (effectively) the simple emphatic announcement, "the bull market is on!" was saying simply and increasingly emphatically, "the bear market is on," a statement that began with "Help!" in August 1965.

[11] The Beatles' last album, of the same title, was labeled not with a green apple symbol but with a red one. This simple statement not only indicated that they knew, unlike many groups who self-destructed, exactly "where they were" but that they understood on some level the importance of their band's demise.

[12] A number of socially conscious people have attacked negative-sentiment movies, rock music, literature and art as *causing* a pervasive negative psychology, an inversion of the relationship. One wonders if they give the same styles of artistic expression the credit for causing *good* feelings in the 1950s and early 1960s. The only reason the underlying sentiments are manifested is that Western culture enjoys freedom of expression. To remove that would remove the manifestation but not the reality behind it, which would merely be vented via other avenues. A case could be made that musical, artistic, literary and sports expression of negative sentiments is a healthy release, as opposed to some possible alternatives. Negative-mood music and sports, for instance, do not exist to make the listener or watcher feel bad. If that were so, it wouldn't sell. On the contrary, it makes people feel good because it mirrors their feelings. Hearing a happy song when you feel angry is an annoyance. It can actually make you feel worse. An angry song says, "Go ahead and feel your anger," which probably helps dissipate it. Imagine how you would feel in a rigid society which only allowed elevator music. Would you really walk around all day with a bland smile on your face, or would you eventually want to lash out, screaming?

[13] One of the last gasp punk (renamed "new wave" in the U.S., whose music buyers didn't feel as angry as their British cousins) groups managed to put out this record two years ago, apparently misspelling its own name:

> **Fibonnaccis**, *Fibonnaccis* (Enigma): The country's most obscure cult band releases a three-song, 12-inch 45 rpm record.

[14] The sexual progression in pop music from 1954 to 1974 which appears to be beginning again as of the early 1980s, is, Men: "I'm a man!"; Women: "I'm cute and available—come and get me!" (speeding up the dance); Men: "I love you!" Men: "Enough happiness; I need thrills!" Men and Women: "Let's get D-I-V-O-R-C-E-D." Men and Women: "Let's kiss, make up, and have a slow dance."

[15] A climax of sorts also seems to have occurred in early 1980, coinciding with the last of three yearly stock market "massacres," the lowest recorded value for the Dow Jones Industrials since early in the rise off the 1974 low, and the lowest value for stocks in terms of gold since 1932.

[16] Intermediate highs and lows also correlate with hit songs. Paul McCartney's "Silly Love Songs" (which implored, "Some people want to fill the world with silly love songs—what's wrong with that?") was the biggest hit of 1976, the year of an important intermediate-term top in the Dow.

[17] Lennon's early '70s' music fit into the hard-edged sound with *grating protest songs* and long recordings of his wife's distinctive caterwauling. After a five-year hibernation in the late '70s, he again burst on the scene in 1980 with "(Just Like) Starting Over," effectively announcing, earlier than the crowd, the start of another bull market. He was murdered a month later by someone who was still caught in the grip of the slowly dying bear, which didn't breathe its last until a year and a half later.

[18] Linda Ronstadt engineered a brief revival among older people of crooning ballads and partners-touching ballroom dancing in 1984, around the Primary wave ② low.

[19] Remember James Watt's embarrassment when he canceled the Beach Boys concert in Washington, D.C. in 1983 to keep out "undesirable elements"? Everyone laughed because the Beach Boys don't attract undesirable elements—they're a bull market band.

[20] An even more horrible slew of movies and songs will undoubtedly be released at the bottom of the next Supercycle (and perhaps Grand Supercycle) crash, due in the 1990s. [2000s.—Ed.] There are many straws in the wind of very bad things to come. The appearance of AIDS, for instance, is the most serious plague-like threat since the Dark Ages.

## Chapter 3

# A Few Examples of Applied
# Social Observation

*February 7, 1983*

What's the social scene like these days? Roaring '20s' parties, '30s' style gangland "hits," tramp camps for the unemployed, falling prices, conservative values, increasing religion, a move to "clean up 42nd Street" and fashion from the '20s and '50s. All are part of the typical social background in the early stages of a long bull market.

# Get out circle skirts, pedal pushers; '50s come sashaying back into style

And what is the venerable Hemline Theory saying? The split skirt, a perfect symbol for the split market of the late '70s, is "out." Conservative dress is "in," and minis are still nowhere to be seen. Remember, rising hemlines, not high hemlines, coincide with healthy bull markets. If the mini-skirt returns, it may signal the approaching peak of a bull market (the last mini came out in 1967 in England and hit the U.S. in 1968). In other words, the social and mass psychological extremes occur together. So be happy if the move back to minis takes awhile.

*August 18, 1983*

The position of the market under the Wave Principle is a direct reflection of how people feel about the future. Wave positions analogous to those that have occurred in the past are often accompanied by similar attitudes among the public and therefore similar phenomena in the art and fashion worlds, which are highly responsive to the shifting winds of public sentiment. The current wave position has some things in common with the early 1920s, since that was also the beginning stage of a fifth wave of Cycle degree, with the mid-1930s, since wave

V should be similar in time, extent and construction to wave I, and with the 1940s and 1950s since that was the early stage of the most recent wave of Cycle degree. The social scene should reflect those similarities, and I think it does (see collage below). By the top, however, the nostalgic conservatism of the current social scene should give way to a wild abandon characteristic of the late 1920s and late 1960s.

**Rockabilly:**

**It's all the rage**

**Old and new**

Delta's 6,000 flight attendants will be wearing new jet-age uniforms — with a touch of propeller-age styling — starting March 1. After a decade during which attendants of major airlines were attired in what mostly looked like sportswear, Delta has decided to return to more structured uniforms. In that respect, the new fashions are similar to those worn by Delta's first attendants in 1940 (above). Although the new uniforms will be all-season clothes, they are the same color as the winter version of the '40 style, navy blue. Both men and

*Chloé suit, Calvin Klein dress: Tailored '20s chic, '50s flair*

**1950s rock '83 teen fashions**

Clothes for today's young Gidgets are rolling out of the 1950s to rock around the 1980s — at least around spring '83.

Teenyboppers can choose from all the former groovy favorites: Bobby sox, pedal pushers, cropped tops,

shorts, bowling skirts, bandstand skirts, sorority sweater sets and more.

Some trends stores have even set up special departments to house these 1950s fashion reincarnations. And don't be surprised to see Marilyn Monroe shops featuring adaptations of the sexy lady's clothes — Bloomingdale's in New York has one.

NEWSWEEK/JUNE 27, 1983

If some influential high-fashion designers—led by Karl Lagerfeld of Chanel and Chloé—have revived the longline, tailored silhouettes of the '20s, complete with luxurious accessories like gloves and brimmed hats, some designers are also bringing back the look of the '50s: returning to herringbone patterns, circle skirts, nipped-in waists, wide belts and strapless cocktail dresses.

At the heart of this revival, of both the '20s and the '50s, is an inventive, freewheeling geometry inspired by the original modern movement.

# Ronstadt swings into an older era

Linda Ronstadt is kicking off her rock 'n' roll shoes come summer's end.

Ronstadt, rock's leading female vocalist for the past decade, will release an album of Sinatra-style pop standards next month and will follow it up with September performances on both coasts in which she will be backed by a full orchestra.

"It's a period that's really fascinated me ever since I was a kid," says Ronstadt of the 1930s, '40s and '50s tunes she features on the new album.

CROONER: Linda Ronstadt is releasing Sinatra-style album.

**Goin' All the Way**

A giggle-jiggle film, owned of those who pipped out on "Porky's." As the title suggests, the plot concerns the efforts of a high school senior to get his girlfriend into bed. The '80s are sounding more like the '50s every day. Omni.

The Elliott Wave Theory, says Prechter, holds that mass psychology creates waves of optimism and pessimism in the economy, which determine — rather than result from — prevailing economic indicators. Gold prices, stock market averages and hemlines all are measures of that confidence.

"When people are feeling more optimistic, friskier and more energetic, men wear louder ties and women let their hemlines rise," Prechter pointed out.

"Gold is very reflective of how human beings feel about the future; it's virtually a barometer. I don't know the mechanism for it, why people change, but they do."

## Old is new!

**Update '80s styles back to '50s chic**

By PATRICIA WEISS
Times/Gannett News Service

Maybe it's just a fad, this obsession with Marilyn Monroe, pedal pushers, poodle skirts and fabulous '50s chic.

Long-lived or not, the latest fashion craze is a revival, not something new. That means economical dressing — turning castaways from your closet or the thrift shop into high-fashion finds.

Perhaps you don't still fit into your red tulle and taffeta prom dress from 1955. But surely you have a cardigan sweater to wear buttoned up the back. The problem is not finding the basic necessities, but knowing how to put them together.

To this end, Susan McGraw is traveling around the nation to promote the "deja vu" concept of dressing.

# Neil Young's latest rock rolls back the clock to '50s

EAST TROY, Wis. — Like a magician possessed, Neil Young continues to pull rabbits out of his amazing career. The latest surprising phase for the veteran rocker is mid-'50s rock 'n' roll, as represented by Bobby Freeman's *Betty Lou's Got a New Pair of Shoes* and *Do You Want to Dance?* and such early Elvis Presley hits as *It's All Right, Mama.*

* * *

The SEC proposes to temporarily limit exchanges to trading only two new stock-index option instruments. The limit is designed to prevent the new instruments from multiplying more quickly than they can be handled by brokers.

## From Elvis to the Stray Cats

Pop music periodically recycles itself, drawing on the styles of earlier periods for musical as well as sartorial inspiration. Until recently, the latest stratum to be excavated in detail was the 1950's, which provided the original models for pop phenomena as disparate as the current rockabilly revival and the ascension to television-rerun valhalla of the Fonz and "Happy Days." But the 1960's are next on the agenda. In fact, though it may seem a bit premature, a 1960's revival is already upon us.

**Teens cut drug use**

# In Pop, a 1960's Revival Has Already Begun

*August 6, 1984*

The social scene still reflects the assumed position of the market within the overall wave structure. If the January high were a 1929 or 1968 type of top with a monstrous bear market having just begun, then social behavior would probably be similar to that of the wild and happy late 1920s or late 1960s. Those were great times, and judging from personal experiences (at least as far as '60s go!), we're not there yet. Today's fun and fashion is still typical of conservative times (see collage, next page).

*September 30, 1985*

Lately a number of dire warnings have been issued regarding some institutions' buying index futures and selling stock when they believe that futures premiums are too low. Some have gone as far as to say that this simple arbitrage game "threatens the integrity and stability of America's stock markets." Every imaginable new structural event in the history of stock trading has produced such pronouncements. They usually appear during downtrends when people are losing money. In the 'teens, the big money boys were supposedly "rigging" the markets. In 1929, the "shorts" had "engineered" the crash. In the later 1930's, the Dow Theory's popularity was blamed for the occurrence of several "confirmed" tops and bottoms in the market. In the late 1970s, options were supposed to be the tail that "wagged the dog." Now it's futures contracts! The danger in believing these theories is that market losers will place the blame for their losses on someone else and thus fail to learn anything about trading. (I hate making mistakes, but I don't blame someone else for them.) Such an "out" is almost irresistable, like a conspiracy theory. Here are some observations:

1) The wave structures on the hourly chart look no different from those of the past, so no effect of this nefarious practice on price patterns is evident. The times when these structural selloffs and rallies are supposed to be occurring just happen to fit right into places such as the "third wave" position of the smaller waves, a natural place to expect volatility.

2) I was told at a meeting of the San Francisco Society of Technical Analysts that computer studies of volatility showed no support for the widely held belief that the market is more volatile today than at all other times in the past.

## Tradition registers high Oldies but goodies revived on newlyweds' wish lists as ad execs remember when

By Elizabeth Sporkin
USA TODAY

Never mind the age or background of the couple. When it comes to setting up house, "tradition has come back," says *Bride's* magazine editor Barbara Tober. "Everybody wants still on wish lists, have been eclipsed by formal serving pieces, tableware and linens.

The pot-luck suppers of the 1960s and '70s have given way to more formal dinners at home, Tober says, and brides want to host them in style. So woks and fondue pots, while more elegance."

### Hats Are Back

Easter may be the celebration of everlasting life, but one thing associated with it, the Easter bonnet, almost expired permanently. Almost, that is. But fitting to the season, it is a style that is being resurrected.

That's especially true in California. "Even little women there wear brims out to their shoulders. They look sometimes like toadstool," he chuckles. Californians also go to lunch sporting huge cabbage roses and ostrich plumes, like in the good old hat days of the 1950s.

*According to fashion, the market ain't crashin'!*

After years of selling Comet cleanser on TV, Josephine the Plumber finally piped down in 1973. If you thought she'd not be heard from again, you were sadly mistaken.

Bert and Harry, the beer-selling Piel brothers, were a popular success — and a marketing flop — in the mid-60s. They were retired — but not forever.

Speedy Alka-Seltzer left the advertising scene in 1963. Was he all fizzled out? Hardly. Ad-

Ray Ban Wayfarers — popularized by Buddy Holly in the '50s, favored by the late blues singer Muddy Waters, and donned by jaunty Tom Cruise in the summer smash *Risky Business* — are once again the rage.

The dark glasses, designed by Bausch & Lomb in the '50s, have seen waves of popularity. (John) Belushi and (Dan) Aykroyd wore them in their Blues Brothers skits," says Lee Hill of Bausch & Lomb.

ADVERTISING
& MARKETING
BY ROBERT
GARFIELD

vertising is not like real life. The qualifications for resurrection are modest.

A parallel case: the famous Hathaway man. After serving as the persona of C.F. Hathaway & Co. dress shirts since 1951, the man with the eye patch vanished in the mid-1970s. After two aborted revivals, he seems to be back.

### Ray Bans: We've got it made in '50s shades

By Richard David Story
USA TODAY

18,000 Wayfarers were sold in 1981; so far in 1983, more than 250,000. Next spring, watch for the Wayfarer Woody, timed to co-incide with "rediscovery" of the 1950s wood-paneled station wagon.

## Fine points of etiquette aren't passe

Once again, boys and girls are learning the right way to walk, talk, eat and dress

By Ellen Brown
USA TODAY

OCONOMOWOC, Wis. — This classroom is a luncheon table. And served with the soup is a lesson on the proper way to eat it: From the center of the bowl, lift the spoon up and away from you, then bring it to the lips. Never, ever, lean toward the bowl.

Jenny Hepp, 14, from Plymouth, Wis., and 15-year-old Julie Pekar of Cudahy, Wis., listen while Janet Sherkow, an instructor for Menars Studios at the Olympia Spa here, details tried-and-true table manners at the four-day, $600 Teen Finishing course — a 4-month-old program born from a rising interest across the USA in teaching manners to the young.

"For a few decades people dropped what they thought wasn't important at the time," says Sherkow. "You can always eat a hamburger at McDonald's, but you'll feel more confident if you know which is the fish fork, and the proper way to gracefully eat a Napoleon."

■ Last month, 14 young gentlemen in the making and six budding young ladies, ages 8 to 14, attended the first Emily Post Summer Camp at the posh Breakers Hotel in Palm Beach, Fla. They learned telephone and thank-you-note manners, "dressing for the occasion," and ballroom dancing.

## Fraternities back — and in trouble

By Rick Friedman
**AMHERST MAN:** Keith Dawson 'devastated.'

By Barbara Palmer
and Richard Price
USA TODAY

Social fraternities and sororities, which faded from campus life in the early 1970s, are enjoying a big comeback — and stirring controversy again, too.

The latest battleground: Amherst, Mass., where G. Armour Craig, acting president of Amherst College, was booed Monday during a chapel assembly as he tried to explain why the board of trustees has voted to abolish the school's coeducational frats.

3) The idea that arbitrage tactics will "snowball" the market into a bottomless pit or unstoppable rally is ridiculous. It's the same case we hear every time the market makes a major bottom. Remember? It goes like this: "The margin accounts' equity is so low that it will force more liquidation, which will force the market lower, which will force more liquidation," etc. There's always an article to that effect on the week of a bottom.

4) At some point, the arbitrage game becomes only marginally profitable. When a large enough number of institutions catches on to the profits available, they will act to keep a very tight reign on futures premiums. The arbitrage will then be just another service, like shoe-shining, and will be paid accordingly.

5) Arbitrage is actually a *good* thing. It provides, without intention, a service for less accomplished traders, particularly the public. If futures premiums were not arbitraged, their values relative to the cash markets would fluctuate even more wildly than they do now, making it even harder for the "average investor" to profit. (Check out the wide spreads in the Value Line contracts in 1981!) The professional traders, who can smell panic and greed, would do even better. A professional day-trader might be all in favor of outlawing the practice of futures premium arbitrage.

I recently received a letter from a subscriber who quit investing in the market, saying, "the odds of figuring out the direction of the market have changed drastically since these institutional programs have begun to dominate the market. The *Business Week* issue of September 16 finally convinced me I have no chance." "Changed drastically"? From what? I think *that's* the poor guy who was done a disservice, by those who blame their investment difficulties on manipulation and conspiracies. Such thinking is also a product of negative mood. Once the market turns up again, you probably won't hear any more about it.

*November 4, 1985*

I would like to take the space to clear up a misconception among many who wrote in August and September worrying about the appearance of various expressions of negative mood. The point made in my Special Report was not that cultural fads precede changes in psychology, but that they are a direct reflection of it, as is the position and trend of the market. Expressions of popular mood are not a leading indicator of stock trends but a *coincident* one. In other words, the widespread popularity of miniskirts doesn't forecast a top, it *is* the top. Therefore, this summer's appearance of dark fashion colors (notably offset by pink tennis shoes among the trendsetters, just to show they're not that serious about sporting black), long skirts, negative-theme books on the *New York Times* book review, etc., *is not bearish*. It is merely a cultural reflection of the mood correction that also showed up on Wall Street with falling prices and record put buying. The only forecasting value in these phenomena currently is that observations of popular cultural trends clearly indicate that the public mood, and therefore the market, is not at a major top of historic proportion. Thus, although a decline is possible on that evidence, a 1929-style collapse is highly improbable. It's the only implication about the future one can draw, but it is knowledge of some value.

*August 10, 1987*

The most important popular cultural event is occurring not in the U.S. but in Russia. The USSR is typically about 30 years behind the West in popular culture (wasn't it about 30 years ago that they officially accepted jazz?). Now glasnost may have bitten off more than it can chew. Allowing private taxis and tailors is one thing. But now that the Soviets have let rock 'n' roll get a foot in the door, there will be no easy turning back from the desire for greater knowledge of the tempting joys of the freedom-loving West. This terrifically written article by Edna Gundersen of *USA Today*, reproduced on the next page, says it all. It sounds like a scene from 1957 in the U.S....

*February 1989*

**The Role of Fundamentals**

Many people insist upon "reasons" *ahead of time* for why the market will go up or down, by which they mean reasons other than those derived from market analysis. The Wave Principle makes it clear that conditions and events that are presumed to cause market trends in fact lag those trends. Aggregate stock prices represent people's opinion of the value of society's productive enterprise. That opinion is determined primarily by social mood, which also ultimately determines the quality and quantity of economic output. Thus, the direction and level of the stock market, which adjusts *immediately* to mood change, usually provides an early warning of changes in the economy, which result from actions taken as a result of mood change. Price patterns, which reflect social psychological changes, are precisely what forecast a change in outside events. Therefore, use of the Wave Principle makes unnecessary any discussion of so-called "fundamental" causes. Insisting upon a full understanding of such causes for change among current events can in fact be counterproductive, since such evidence is always available well after a change in trend has occurred. Ironically, since most investors misunderstand the relationship between the market and events, it is

# Joel rocks 'em back in the U.S.S.R.

MOSCOW — The man at the piano spoke in broken Russian: "Hi, my name is Billy Joel. I'm nervous."

He had reason to be. Sunday night's 2½-hour concert at the Olympic Sports Complex began sluggishly. About 20,000 Soviets sat politely in silence as the first USA rock star to tour the U.S.S.R. energetically belted out one hit after another.

But an hour into the show, Joel pointedly invited the audience to join him at the stage, and the night was transformed. Thousands streamed from the stands to stomp and cheer and whistle and — flouting house rules — dance with abandon.

The performance grew more dramatic and surprising with each slickly performed tune. During *Angry Young Man*, a Soviet boy in Adidas high-top sneakers raised a USA flag. Others quickly joined him. Joel prompted roars of approval when he dedicated *Honesty* to the late Vladimir Vysotsky — the Soviet Bob Dylan — a balladeer revered for his brazen social commentary.

(Saturday, Joel visited Vysotsky's gravesite, along with 4,000 Muscovites. "It touched me deeply that a man that suc-cessful could find the time to see my son's grave," said Maximava Vysotsky after Sunday's concert.)

But most of the show's notes were joyous. The barbershop harmonies of *For the Longest Time* set the crowd clapping and the hard-rocking treatment of *A Matter of Trust* brought even stern-faced parents to their feet.

Joel was a tornado of vitality. He introduced songs with earnest jokes and bittersweet speeches, explaining the inspiration behind the distinctly back-home *Allentown* and *Goodnight Saigon*.

Sweat streaming down his neck, he twirled and strutted, at one point leaping into the throng to grasp the hands of startled onlookers.

Gradually, the shell-shocked Soviets answered the call to rock 'n' roll. Girls shimmied; boys stood on their feet and shouted.

And when the band let loose with a full-throttled *Still Rock and Roll to Me*, starch-collared crowd-control soldiers clapped and danced, throwing caution to the sudden wind of change. Even the military guards who had first attempted to blockade the stampede surrendered to Joel's spell with toe-tapping and rare smiles.

Though Joel earlier complained of a sore throat brought on by an unplanned jam session in Tbilisi, he sang with dizzying passion and bravado. His grinning musicians rocked with unstoppable glee. Crowd-wowing saxophonist Mark Rivera and drummer Liberty DeVitto were especially luminous.

Joel's wife, Christie Brinkley, also was flushed with pride. Wearing a ruffled denim miniskirt and white sneakers, she snaked through crowded aisles unescorted, a video camera on her shoulder.

The one sobering snag in this intoxicating conquest came when Joel said goodnight and the audience, unschooled in the art of commanding encores, obediently shuffled to the exits. Joel returned anyway, and perplexed fans scurried back for roof-raising renditions of *Back in the U.S.S.R.* and *Big Shot.*

By Edna Gundersen
USA TODAY

precisely the changes in events which persuade many people to join a trend after it has substantially progressed. That is also the reason they are caught fully invested at the top and in cash at the bottom. Thus, an armchair argument about why current conditions do or do not support the case for change is a waste of time. The true fundamentals are the wave patterns.

*August 28, 1992*

## Exclusionism in Bear Markets

Major bear markets are accompanied by a reduction in the size of people's unit of allegiance, the group that they consider to be like themselves. At the peak, there is a perceived brotherhood of men and nations. Even mythical aliens are included in the brotherhood of the universe. During the reduction process in the size of the social unit of allegiance, the "in group" becomes smaller and smaller, moving from the universe to the world to the nation to the ethnic, religious, regional or sexual group to the city or feudal estate to the family to the individual. The trend halts at a point dependent upon the extent of the economic and psychological contraction. When the extent is substantial, the unit of allegiance is very small. In the Dark Ages, for instance, the feudal estate was the largest unit of allegiance in Europe. In times of starvation (such as in parts of Africa today), even the family unit can disintegrate, as individuals fend for themselves.

In other words, at a peak, it's all "we"; everyone is a potential friend. At a bottom it's all "they"; everyone is a potential enemy. When times are good, tolerance is greater and boundaries weaker. When times are bad, intolerance for differences grows, and people build walls and fences to shut out those perceived to be different. Ultimately, persecution and war result.

New social trends are born out of the old. There is a backlash to every state of affairs. Every trend is pushed to an extreme, and people, at a point determined by the Wave Principle, become sick of it and demand change. Take one example. Today's term for the entrenched political and social mores, particularly involving pressure group patronization, is "political correctness." One upcoming major socio-political trend will be a backlash against p.c.

*March 18, 1994*

## Social Implications of Negative-Mood Trends

Trends of negative social psychology are characterized primarily by *polarization* between and among various perceived groups, whether political, racial, ideological, religious, geographical or financial ("class"). The result is a net trend toward anger, fear, intolerance, disagreement and exclusion, as opposed to bull market years, whose net trend is toward benevolence, confidence, tolerance, agreement and inclusion. The shift toward negative mood typically brings conflict in many forms, and evidence of it is visible in all types of social organizations. Political manifestations include protectionism in trade matters, separatist movements, emotional political oustings (whether by vote, resignation, impeachment or coup), a polarized and vocal electorate, the dissolution of old alliances and parties and the emergence of radical ones. All of these manifestations will surface in the next Supercycle-degree bear market. *The Elliott Wave Theorist* said in 1982 that given the outlook for a Cycle degree bull market, which portended an increasingly gentle social sentiment, there would be "no major war for at least ten years." A bear market of Grand Supercycle degree will include at least one major war, if not several wars or protracted warring. For whatever reason, disease sometimes plays a prominent role in major corrective periods, with some Cycle and Supercycle degree corrections containing epidemics and larger ones pandemics. The most dangerous time socially and politically will be during and for a few years after wave C, whenever it occurs.

Keep in mind that such expectations are relative. Conflict is always with us, as are joy and harmony. Throughout even the major corrective periods of history, most people have lived normal and fulfilling lives while an unfortunate few get caught up in the various social maelstroms that such periods produce. One point of foreknowledge is to be prepared mentally so that you can recognize the centers of conflict as they are brewing, and act to avoid them if necessary. Another is to become positioned to prosper from the impending change. Dramatic markets present rare profit making opportunities for those who are capable of seizing the opportunities.

*August 26, 1994*

**Rationalization**

The engine of markets is psychological change. Its turns are marked by psychological extremes, which are justified by rationalization. Rationalization is the visa that allows emotionally based thoughts to pass through the cerebral cortex unaccosted. Smart people are very good at it, and employ it freely, particularly if they have little market experience.

*Chapter 4*

# Reflections of Social Mood in Religion

Religious events and trends reflect a social emotional high. Headlines have noted that Pope John Paul II's "mass appeal" extends beyond denomination. Throngs filled Aqueduct Race Track in New York City and Giant Stadium in New Jersey and sat mesmerized with joy, undaunted by hours of rain. One typical fan was quoted as saying she could not describe how "exuberant and exhilarated" she felt. With rifts between the Pope and Catholic advocates of women in the priesthood, birth control, pre-and extra-marital sex, divorce, gay rights and abortion, *Time* magazine asks "Why are these Catholics so happy?" Only the elevated social mood explains it, showing once again that for societies, events do not determine mood. In the past, jubilant receptions of the Pope in New York City have been quickly followed by big declines on Wall Street. The first Pope to visit the New World was Pope Paul VI, who spoke to four million people. That was in October 1965, four months before the Cycle Wave III high of February 1966. In October 1979, an outpouring of emotion greeted Pope John Paul on his first American visit, and the stock market immediately began one of its famous October "massacres." John Paul's next visit took place in September 1987, the month before that year's infamous crash. Followers were ecstatic then as well, but the current state of euphoria, to judge from the news reports, is even greater.

October 22, 1995

# HOLY LAUGHTER

Some other denominations, also caught up in the spirit of the times, are, say newspapers, "giggling before God." Worshippers lie down on church floors to receive the holy spirit, thereby engaging in uncontrollable "holy laughter." The phenomenon originated in Toronto right before the January 31, 1994 stock market high and has spread to congregations throughout North America. *Christianity Today* reports that in addition to laughing, worshippers bark like dogs, roar like lions, peck like chickens and get so staggeringly "drunk in the spirit" that some churches have to appoint designated drivers.

This activity is the polar opposite of what took place in 1348, which *The Elliott Wave Theorist* has previously identified as the likely end of a Millennium-degree bear market. In that year, the bubonic plague reached its zenith and the Flagellant Movement swept parts of Europe. As in 1995, the Flagellants would lie down on church floors to receive what many believed to be divinely inspired impulses, but they were not laughing. *The Black Death* by Robert Gottfried (1983, The Free Press), recounts that from 1348 to 1350, the celebrants were "literally whipping themselves into a frenzy," tearing their own flesh to appease what they presumed must be an angry God. At times, they drove spikes so deeply into their bodies that they could only be pulled out with a wrench.

These manifestations of mass mood in the field of religion, 6½ centuries apart, are exquisitely reflective of the position of the long term Elliott wave structure and the collective emotional conditions it has implied. Today, religious groups, like other social groups, are reveling in the emotional good feeling of a topping social mood trend of Grand Supercycle degree. At the next Grand Supercycle bottom, ideally due decades hence, religious groups—along with many others—will once again act out a tortured social mood.

## 2002 Addition:

There is also some evidence that religion becomes more important to people as bear markets progress and less important as bull markets progress. At the stock market low of wave (II) in 1857, 22 years after the peak of wave (I) in 1835, newspapers reported that people in New York City were lined up for blocks to join churches for the first time. In contrast, it was on April 8, 1966, just two months after a multi-decade stock market top, that *Time* magazine filled its cover with the bold question, "Is God Dead?" In extended periods of social depression, such as the Dark Ages, religion is generally a central aspect of people's lives. In long periods of social ebullience, religion plays a secondary role. Thus, social mood trends appear to affect not only the style of religious practices, but also the very importance of religion itself. We can see both aspects of this influence in the dramatic rise of fundamentalism in the form of terrorist activities by radical Muslims and efforts by Baptists to get stories in Genesis taught as science, both having emerged since the stock market peaked in 2000. *The Wave Principle of Human Social Behavior* (Chapter 14) anticipated the character of these events.

*Chapter 5*

# A Socionomic Study of Restaurants

## Munching on Evidence of a Grand Supercycle Peak

When people feel good, they like to get out, be seen, eat well and drink socially. This makes restaurants a focal point for the expression of a bull market mood. In our town, chain restaurants now seem to spring up a row at a time, which led us to dig up the following highlights in the history of the restaurant industry.

Data show that the urge to eat out has been synonymous with the urge to buy stock for the duration of the Grand Supercycle bull market. The first true restaurant was the Grande Taverne de Londres, which was established in Paris around 1782, approximately the year that we believe Supercycle wave (I) began. Delmonico's, the first American restaurant, was established during the final leg of Supercycle wave (I). Between its establishment and the stock top of 1835, the Delmonico brothers and two other proprietors became the first to "operate multiple restaurants which functioned as a complex organism—the use of the same name, almost duplicate menus, and similar genetic consistencies to create clones," according to the book, *From Boarding House to Bistro*. Through the middle of the 19th century, restaurants became more common, but the choppy stock market conditions were reflected in a high failure rate. Of the 497 different addresses in New York City from 1850 to 1860, only 11, or 2%, were open under the same proprietor in both years. True chains appeared after the Civil War, as Supercycle wave (III) began its steady advance. In 1875, in the middle of wave (III), the Harvey House, which ultimately grew to a highly standardized family of 50 restaurants, revolutionized the industry. "Like the Delmonicos, Fred Harvey was at the right spot at the right time," records *America Eats Out*, a history of the restaurant business. "[His] effect was immediate, populist, and spread through the entire country, [setting] the course of culinary history." In the bull market of the 1920s, cafeterias, speakeasies and White Castle hamburger joints spread rapidly across the country. Howard Johnson, Marriott Corp. and countless other "white box" hamburger stands tapped into the mass appeal that White Castle had uncovered. The next "revolution" was called "fast food," which *From Boarding House to Bistro* dates to 1949, the exact year of the start of Supercycle wave (V) in inflation-adjusted stock prices, when the McDonald brothers established a walk-up hamburger stand. In many ways, "McDonald's story was a re-enactment of the [White Castle system] in the 1920s." In 1954, as the "third of the third wave" entered its acceleration phase, Ray Kroc bought the franchise rights, capturing what may be America's No.1 brand name by introducing speed, efficiency and mass marketing to the industry. McDonald's capped off a decade of rapid growth with the first major offering of a restaurant stock in 1965, a few months before the wave III peak.

Through the first 200 years of the Grand Supercycle bull market, the relatively fragmented and faddish nature of the industry kept most eateries from being listed on the stock exchange. McDonald's still makes up almost 80% of the S&P restaurant index because it remains one of just four well-established restaurant-chain stocks. Appropriately, however, in this final decade of the advance, the public has assumed much of the risk that is inherent in catering literally to tastes. In the 1990s, the number of restaurant stock offerings has mushroomed into the 100s, financing an unprecedented boom in restaurant-industry growth. Almost 45% of the money spent on food now is spent in restaurants. In some multi-purpose establishments, dining has been upgraded to a full-sensory experience known as "eatertainment." At the Rainforest Café, patrons are treated to an "environmentally conscious 'family adventure' featuring live tropical birds, simulated nature sounds, waterfalls, aromatic scents and a gift shop retail area." Planet Hollywood packages its fare around the aura of celebrities from movies, sports and music. Both are publicly traded.

The stock market is an advance-warning device, so it is of interest that the stocks of these two companies have fallen substantially. In fact, it's hard to find a restaurant stock that is still participating in the bull market. Even McDonald's is struggling to regain "it's golden touch." Over the last two years, McDonald's shares have been flat versus a 70% gain in the S&P. Suddenly, "the company that once seemed a half-step ahead of pop culture" cannot even "construct an appealing new lunch sandwich." Our view is that McDonald's and the restaurant business are powerful reflections of a positive social mood. The quantity, diversity and increasing complexity of restaurants reflect the same aspects of the bull market. The inability of their stock prices to match the bull market hints of a coming retrenchment in the industry. That, in turn, portends an end to the long term economic uptrend that has supported their success.

Kendall
*The Elliott Wave Financial Forecast*
March 31, 2000


## Chapter 6

# *Broadstreet*


The following chart of annual gross revenues for Broadway theaters paints a revealing portrait of the correlation between a rising social mood and the demand for popular stage shows. Over the last half century, Broadway's box office performance has ebbed and flowed with the Cycle-degree trends in the stock market. Just like stocks, ticket sales had a long rise to a double top in 1966 and 1968 (attendance topped in 1966 and revenues in 1968), a major bottom in 1974 and another long advance through the end of the 1990s. Broadway's recent take suggests that a trend change is at hand. Projections for the year ending May 31 call for little more than a slight increase of $1 million. This slowing would fit our Elliott wave case for stock market downturn of at least Cycle degree.

Lending support to this quantitative assessment is the more qualitative analysis that appeared in the August 1997 issue of *The Elliott Wave Theorist*. A study of New York City's theater district at past peaks revealed a clear tendency to finish long advances with a flourish of activity and showmanship. "Entertainment industry histories covering the Supercycle peaks of 1835 and 1929 show that flashy but shallow drama is a recurrent theme in fifth waves of Cycle degree." The same word, "spectacles," continually surfaces in descriptions of Broadway's earlier fifth wave peaks and its latest era. "You have two kinds of shows on Broadway—revivals and the same kind of musicals over and over again, all spectacles," laments Stephen Sondheim, who was recently tabbed "the Broadway musical's last great artist." "Broadway today is more than ever about spectacle than real drama or real emotions, more about giving audiences an 'experience.'" Like the figures for Broadway ticket sales, this more subjective confirmation of a fifth wave also carries a clear sign its impending demise. "*Cats*, the longest running production in Broadway history will close June 25," says *The New York Times*. "*Cats* fundamentally reshaped the Broadway landscape by ushering in the era of the megamusicals: big flashy spectacles that required little theatrical sophistication or knowledge of the English language to appreciate." *Cats* came to Broadway on October 7, 1982, a few weeks after the stock market's upturn in August 1982. When the curtain falls June 25, *Cats'* many critics will undoubtedly applaud, but probably not for long. "In 1930," *Times Square*, a history of the NYC district notes, "the frivolity of the 1920s gave way to a serious, if not grim tone." By 1932 only six shows were playing on Broadway. That compares to an all-time high in 1928 of 294! The show will go on, but not without drastic changes in tone and reductions in number.

*Part II:*

# *SOCIAL CAUSALITY*

Prechter
Adapted from a speech delivered to the Market Technicians Association
May 1986

## Chapter 7

# The Fractal Design of Social Progress

While for years some theoreticians have argued that stock price movements are random because all investors make fully informed and rational decisions, those who study the market and its participants know that few investment and trading decisions are based on reason, logic and knowledge gained from comprehensive research. Some decision making is informed and rational, but most apparently reasonable explanations for investors' decisions are merely *rationalizations* of emotionally based decisions.

The primary mover of aggregate stock market prices is mass emotional change. The Wave Principle reveals that aggregate stock price movement, and therefore mass emotional change, is patterned. It is patterned, moreover, independently from concurrent news. Thus, social mood and changes in it must simply be a reflection of the workings of human nature in society. The determinants of the specifics of market action are the naturally occurring direction, speed and extent of social mood changes.

Social mood change does not necessarily affect every individual involved, but in the aggregate, the people participating in markets are acting as a crowd. An early observer of crowd psychology once made the observation that a very rational and sensible human being, when part of a crowd, becomes a "blockhead." To be more precise, he ceases to think independently and reasonably. Wall Street is certainly a crowd. Every day, investors read the same newspapers, listen to the same TV shows and watch the same market indices go up and down. Millions of people involved in the market watch and hear all the same things. It is almost as if the participants are on a town square, and an orator trying to whip up revolution is standing on a balcony, making the crowd's emotions wax and wane with each change in content, tone and volume. In the case of markets, however, the orator and crowd are usually one and the same. Much of Wall Street's information (such as price level,

direction, speed of price change and volume) is self generated, and
just like a crowd, Wall Street feeds off its own frenzies. (This process
involves the feedback of result back into the system as a new cause,
making it a candidate for study under chaos theory.) Because crowds
have a nature all their own and a behavioral style that reflects it, mass
emotional change has a fair degree of predictability.

R.N. Elliott's discovery of the Wave Principle fifty years ago was
a major breakthrough in sociology. His observations reveal that social
psychological dynamics create the same pattern of "waves" in aggregate
stock price movement from the smallest to the largest degree of trend
(see Figure 1). In fact, there is a new science, the science of fractals,
indicating that much of nature is made up of the kind of patterns and
relationships that Elliott recognized and described.

The modern pioneer in the concept is Benoit Mandelbrot, a former
professor at Harvard, Yale and the Einstein College of Medicine, who
wrote a book called *The Fractal Geometry of Nature*. It documents his
discovery that many natural forms that scientists had assumed were
disorderly are not. In looking at clouds, seacoasts and mountain ranges,

© Robert R. Prechter, Jr.          *Figure 1*

for instance, the typical conclusion was that they were governed by no specific geometry. Mandelbrot said that that wasn't true; they display a relational form that scientists hadn't considered.

Here are some excerpts from a *New York Times* article of five months ago [December 1985] about Mandelbrot's ideas on the way nature develops.

> He has invented a new way of describing, calculating and thinking about shapes that are irregular and fragmented, jagged and broken up. A new geometry has emerged, and it turns out to be nature's own.... The interesting feature of a lightning bolt's path, for example, is not the straight line direction, but rather the distribution of its zigs and zags.... A new kind of symmetry has emerged, not of left to right or front to back, but of small scale patterns to patterns on larger and larger scales, the self similarity of a broccoli floret whose tiny bifurcations echo the branching of the stalk as a whole.... Oddly, the mathematical description of them seemed to apply just as well to very different problems, from fluctuating cotton prices since the 19th century to the rising and falling of the Nile River through two millenniums.... In unexpectedly orderly fashion, they have self similarity on different scales.

This description echoes Elliott's observation that stock market movements trace out five waves in the direction of the one larger trend and three waves (or a variation thereof) against that trend at all degrees, or sizes, of trend, producing self similarity on different scales. Daily, hourly and shorter term charts all show the same patterns as do longer term charts. The article continues,

> When you zoom in, looking closer and closer, the irregularities don't smooth out. Rather, they tend to look exactly as irregular as before. Some of Mandelbrot's fractal patterns looked indistinguishable from records of stock market prices. Economists needed to understand the heretical idea that prices don't change in a smooth, continuous flow. [Why an idea that reflects reality may be labeled "heretical" is a question only for academia, not for those who deal intimately with markets.—Ed.] "They can change abruptly in instantaneous jumps. And dam builders, reservoir builders, and risk insurers of all kinds needed to understand that traditional notions of probability were leading them to underestimate the likelihood of the rarest, most catastrophic events.

Similarly, Elliott recognized that big bear markets are no different in basic shape from short-term reactions. They are just of a larger scale and thus occur less often. They do not, however, occur less often *relative to the scale of advances that precede them*. A headline-making market "crash," for instance, is merely a large version of what happens all the time on smaller scales. Likewise, bull markets and minor degree rallies have the same basic shape.

The article continues, "The same question applies to economics. Daily fluctuations are treated one way, while the great changes that bring prosperity or depression are thought to belong to a different order of things. In each case, Mandelbrot said, my attitude is: Let's see what's different from the point of view of geometry. What comes out all seems to fall on a continuum; the mechanisms don't seem to be different." This was precisely one of R.N. Elliott's revolutionary messages.

Just to show one kind of structure produced by Mandelbrot's ideas, Figure 2 presents a line that moves either up or sideways according to a formula employing a fractal dimension. Unfortunately, this particular computer-generated illustration does not include declines, which would have made it look even more like a chart of financial market prices.

Figure 3, though it looks substantially different, brings us nearer to another of R.N. Elliott's revolutionary observations. It shows a computer generated snowflake. In this example, unlike Figure 2, the whole is a replica of its parts, from the largest size component to the next and the next. If your observations were to continue at smaller degrees, you would forever find the same shape. Figure 4 shows a computer generated tree. Notice that when you observe the smaller degrees, it continues to be the same picture, just like the snowflake. These pictures actually more closely reflect what R.N. Elliott said happens in the stock market. The smaller advancing and declining patterns depicted in the illustrative diagram of Figure 1 not only display discontinuity (i.e., size and frequency of internal trend reversals) to the same extent as the larger ones, but they also form component *replicas* of the larger patterns. The entire structure is based on one simple pattern. [*The Wave Principle, like many of nature's fractals (trees for example), is what The Wave Principle of Human Social Behavior identifies as a "robust fractal," which is neither as infinitely indefinite as clouds and seacoasts nor as precisely repetitive as Figures 2 through 4 but rather a definite basic structure with infinite subordinate variability.—Ed.*]

*Figure 2*

Snowflake

*Figure 3*

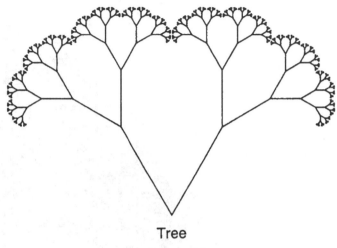

**Tree**

*Figure 4*

Although Elliott came to his conclusions fifty years before this new science blossomed, he went a great step further than current observers of natural processes. He explained not only that the progress of the market was fractal in nature but discovered and described the component patterns. He catalogued five specific simple pattern units that combine to compose the stock market's behavior. These five patterns occur over and over, and a combination of them on a small degree will create one of those same shapes on the next larger degree, and so on.

The further time extends, the larger the degrees of trend get, implying a geometric expansion in the size of the advances and retrenchments that form mankind's progress, the entire structure propelled by the ebb and flow of mass mood. Figure 5 conveys this idea visually with a spiraling line connecting the top of each first wave of increasingly higher degree. While forms such as triangles, squares and circles (and concepts such as "cycles" in markets or human experience) imply stasis or precise repetition, a spiral implies net growth or decay, expansion or contraction. The largest degree depicted in the illustration, of course, would be the first wave up of the *next* larger degree, and so on.

The process, moreover, is not governed by mathematics that are applicable only in this case. As Elliott explained in his final unifying conclusion, the Fibonacci ratio (.618..., 1.618...) governs the number of waves which form in the movement of aggregate stock prices, in an expansion upon the underlying 5:3 relationship. The same ratio governs growth and decay processes found in nature and expanding and

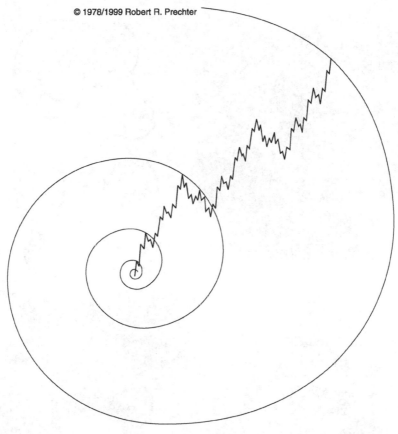

*Figure 5*

contracting phenomena found throughout the universe (see examples, Figure 6). Stock prices are the popular evaluation of productive enterprise, in other words, how people value their ability to produce. Thus, the form of the progress and regress of the valuation of mankind's productive enterprise through history follows an expansion/contraction pattern that is typical of processes in nature that display patterned growth.

Whether specific component forms and governing ratios also exist for river meanders or seacoasts remains to be discovered, but I would contend that it is a possibility. For now, we must be content to contemplate the simple yet profound idea that on the whole, mankind's progress through history, propelled by the natural ebb and flow of social mood, follows a grand fractal design governed by the Fibonacci ratio, the same ratio that governs patterns of growth and expansion found throughout the universe.

Figure 6

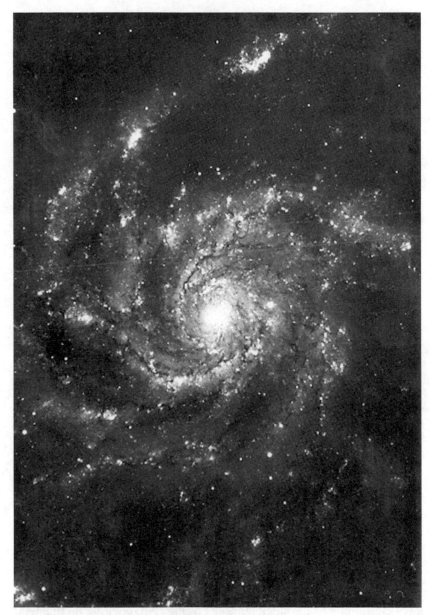

*Figure 6 (cont'd)*

Illustrations from *Fascinating Fibonaccis* by Trudi H. Garland (1987, Dale Seymour Publications), *1929 Again?* by Terry R. Rudd (1988, Bell Curve Research) and *The Fractal Geometry of Nature* by Benoit Mandelbrot (1988, W.H. Freeman).

*Chapter 8*

# Socionomics in a Nutshell

Understanding socionomics requires comprehending the contrast between two postulations:

(1) <u>The standard presumption</u>: Social mood is buffeted by economic, political and cultural trends and events. News of such events affects the social mood, which in turn affects people's penchant for investing.

(2) <u>The socionomic hypothesis</u>: Social mood is a natural product of human interaction and is patterned according to the Wave Principle. Its trends and extent determine the character of social action, including the economic, political and cultural.

The contrast between these two positions comes down to this: The standard presumption is that in the social setting, *events govern mood*; the socionomic hypothesis is that *mood governs events*. In both cases, the stock market is seen as an efficient mechanism. In the first instance, it presumably revalues stocks continually and rationally in reaction to events; in the second, it revalues stocks continually and impulsively as the independent social mood changes. We will now investigate five presumed "outside forces" to see which of these views their relationship to the stock market supports.

## The Economy

The standard presumption is that the state of the economy is a key determinant of the stock market's trends. All day long on financial television and year after year in financial print media, investors debate the state of the economy for clues to the future course of the stock market. If this presumed causal relationship actually existed, then there would be some evidence that the economy leads the stock market. On

*Figure 1*

the contrary, for decades, the Commerce Department of the federal government has identified the stock market as a leading indicator of the economy, which is indeed the case.

If the standard presumption were true, then changes in the economy would coincide with or *precede* trend changes in aggregate stock prices. However, a study of Figure 1 will show that changes in the economy coincide with or *follow* trend changes in aggregate stock prices. Except for the timing of the recession of 1946 (which supports neither case), all economic *contractions* came upon or after a *downturn* in aggregate stock prices, and all economic *recoveries* came upon or after an *upturn* in aggregate stock prices.[1] In *not one case* did a contraction or recovery precede a like change in aggregate stock prices, which would repeatedly be the case if investors in fact *reacted* to economic trends and events. This chronology persists back into the nineteenth century as far as the data goes.

The socionomic hypothesis explains the data. Changes in the stock market immediately reflect the changes in endogenous social mood. As social mood becomes increasingly positive, productive activity increases; as social mood becomes increasingly negative, productive activity decreases. These results show up in lagging economic statistics as expansions and recessions. The standard presumption has no explanation for the relative timing of these two phenomena.

## Politics

The standard presumption is that political trends are a key determinant of the stock market's trends. As an election approaches, commentators debate the effect that its outcome will have on stock prices. Investors argue over which candidate would likely influence the market to go up or down. "If so-and-so gets elected, it will be good/bad for the market," we often hear. If this causal relationship were valid, then there would be evidence that a change in power from one party's leader to another affects the stock market. There would also be evidence that certain political parties or policies reliably produced bull or bear markets. To the contrary, there is no study that shows any such connection.

A socionomist, on the other hand, can show the opposite causality at work. Examine Figure 2 and observe that strong and persistent trends in the stock market determine whether an incumbent president will be re-elected in a landslide or defeated in one. In all cases where an incumbent remained in office in a landslide, the stock market's trend was up. In all cases where an incumbent was rejected by a landslide, the stock market's trend was down.[2] In *not one case* did an incumbent win re-election despite a deeply falling stock market or lose in a landslide despite a strongly rising stock market.[3]

The socionomic conclusion is this: When social mood waxes positive, as reflected by persistently rising stock prices, voters desire to retain the leader who symbolizes their upbeat feelings and who they presume helped cause the conditions attending them. When the social mood becomes more negative, as reflected by persistently falling stock prices, voters decide to throw out the incumbent who symbolizes their downbeat feelings and who they presume helped cause the conditions attending them. *The political policies of the incumbent and his challenger are irrelevant to this dynamic*. The key is a desire for change *per se*, not any particular type of change. The standard presumption has no explanation for reconciling the relationship between these phenomena.

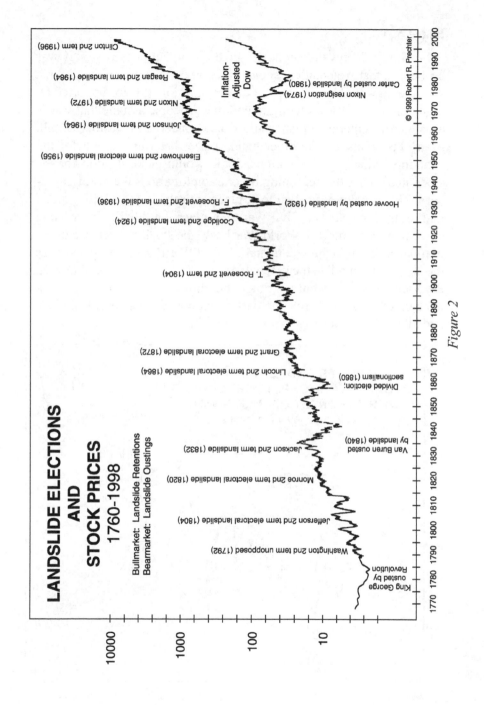

*Figure 2*

## Peace & War

"Surely," says the supporter of the conventional view, "if war broke out, that would affect social mood and the stock market." Such a comment would be, and is, an utter assumption. It is unsupported by argument or history. As to argument, many people assume that war is a dangerous enterprise that would cause concerned investors to sell. Many historians, on the other hand, argue that war is good for the economy, which by conventional logic would make it good for the stock market. As this reasoning is contradictory, so is the historical record. The Revolutionary War took place entirely during a falling stock market in England. The Civil War took place entirely during a rising stock market in the U.S. World War I saw the stock market rise in the first half and fall in the second half. World War II saw the opposite, as the stock market fell in the first half and rose in the second half. During the Vietnam War, it went up, down, up, down and up, finishing about unchanged. In sum, there is no data to support the conventional view, and all the data taken together contradict it.

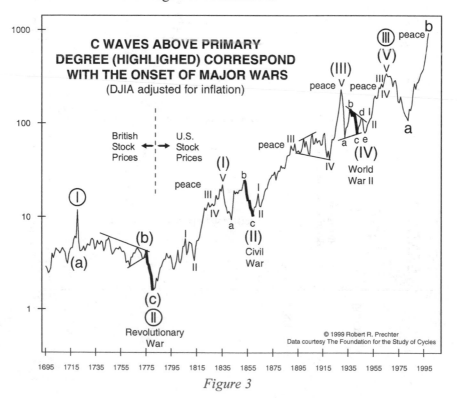

*Figure 3*

Socionomics, in contrast, points out a *consistent* correlation with a *consistent* rationale. Because social mood governs the character of social activity, a persistently *rising* stock market, reflecting feelings of increasing goodwill and social harmony, should consistently lead to peace, and a persistently *falling* stock market, reflecting feelings of increasing ill will and social conflict, should consistently lead to war. Figure 3 bears out this expectation. Long rises in the stock market unerringly result in climates of peace. Similarly, we find that major wars virtually always erupt during or immediately following "C" waves of Elliott wave corrections above Cycle degree. The Revolutionary War took place during wave (c) of the Grand Supercycle bear market from 1720 to 1784. The Civil War broke out shortly after the end of wave c of the Supercycle bear market from 1835 to 1959. World War II started during wave c of the Supercycle bear market (in inflation-adjusted terms) from 1929 to 1949. In every case, a rising social mood eventually brought an end to the war.[4]

### Demographics

Currently fashionable is the idea that demographics determine stock market trends. It was discovered, when sliding birth data around on top of a chart of the stock market, that there is a four-decade correlation when birth data are moved forward 46-49 years. The explanation for this correlation, roughly stated, is that people spend and invest more when in their 40s, so the stock market will go up and down with the percentage of people in their 40s. It seems so sensible to the conventional mindset that people across the country have embraced this thesis.

The first problem with this case is that when data may be moved around at will, apparent correlations appear often. I can find three different multi-decade periods of correlation between immigration data and the stock market when I am allowed to slide the two series around until they fit. The second problem with this case is that the available data prior to the mid-1950s diverges so significantly from this postulation that it disproves any causality. At least four studies[5, 6, 7, 8] have debunked the assertion.

What is the socionomic position on demographic causality? Think about it for a minute. We have already seen that social mood determines the trends of the economy, politics, and the conditions for peace and war. Might social mood also determine demographics?

*Figure 4*

Figure 4 shows that demographic data line up almost perfectly with the stock market, particularly when it is expressed in terms of the advance-decline line, which reflects how many stocks are going up or down. The a-d line is a broad measure, and therefore is more useful to compare and contrast with the full population's participation in national demographics (as opposed to data on the economy, which can be propelled by a narrow list of industry leaders). The data shown in bars is annual birth data, lagged by one year to reflect (within three months) the number of annual *conceptions*. The major stock market lows of 1932 and 1974 coincide exactly with the major nadirs in procreational activity. The peaks in procreational activity correspond to peaks in the a-d line.

There is not enough data to be certain of a causal relationship, but it is nearly twice as long a correlation as the one that convinces so many people of the "demographics determine stock prices" case. More important, and in contrast to the aforementioned case, this correlation holds *throughout all the available data*, which dates from 1908 for conceptions and 1926 for the a-d line. No data contradict it. The socionomic hypothesis can account for this correlation. As people in general feel more energetic, confident and happy, they have more children. Conversely, as people in general feel more sluggish, fearful and unhappy, they have fewer children. Thus, social mood determines aggregate procreational activity. Once again, the hypothesis is simple and elegant and explains the data.

**Nuclear Explosions**

"O.K., Bob," a skeptic might say, "Maybe I can accept the idea that social mood determines the economy, politics, peace and war, and maybe even the birth rate. But you can't claim, as you appear to be doing, that no outside forces affect the stock market. I mean, what if, out of the blue, somebody detonated a nuclear bomb in a major city? You can't

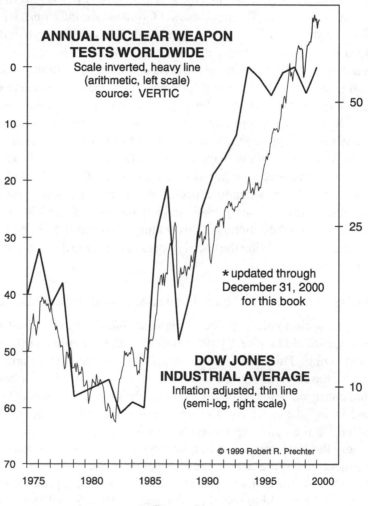

*Figure 5*

say that wouldn't affect people's mood or the stock market!" Clearly, this person has yet to incorporate fully the socionomic point of view. What does he mean, "out of the blue"? This is the same fictional "out of the blue" that we have already debunked in economics, politics, peace, war and demographics. Every social act has an antecedent in mood, so nuclear explosions are unlikely to be an exception. Not only do I claim, based on the fact that social mood is patterned, that the detonation of a nuclear bomb would have no effect on social mood, but also once again, the causality is the other way around: *Social mood determines the penchant for exploding nuclear devices*.

Figure 5 demonstrates that the socionomic hypothesis governs even here. As you can see, the stock market (adjusted for inflation), which is a direct reflection of social mood, correlates almost perfectly with the rate at which governments detonate nuclear bombs. The reason is this: As social mood becomes more positive, people become more confident, trusting and content. They feel little need to prepare a defensive or offensive force. As social mood becomes more negative, people become more fearful, distrusting and angry. They are impelled to prepare to defend themselves or attack an enemy. As in politics and economics, if you would like a view to the future in this area, just watch our most responsive and precise reflector of social mood, the stock market. Its trends will tell you when to expect more or fewer nuclear explosions, and whether they are more likely to be deployed defensively or offensively.[9] The blackest moods of this century occurred in 1932 and 1942, the latter time providing the social impetus to develop the nuclear bomb in the first place.

### The Degree of Mood Change Determines the Degree of the Results

The socionomic hypothesis suggests that the extremity of social behavior should be directly proportional to the extremity of the social mood swing. This is indeed the case. The longer, further and more broadly the stock market rises, reflecting a waxing positive mood, the more consistently the economy expands, the more citizens vote to "stay the course," the more children people produce and the more broadly peaceful is the resulting social climate. The longer, further and more broadly the stock market falls, reflecting a greater swing toward negative mood, the more deeply the economy contracts, the more citizens vote to "throw the bums out," the fewer children people produce and the greater is the resulting social tension and conflict. Small stock market corrections beget recessions, mild defeats at the polls and minor wars. For example, the Primary degree correction of 1959-1962 led to a mild recession in 1960 and the Cuban Missile Crisis of 1962, a near minor war. (Had 1962 been an election year, the incumbent would have lost.) The Primary-degree correction of 1987-1990 led to the moderate Gulf War in 1990 and a brief recession in 1991. In 1992, the incumbent lost the election by a small margin. The larger Cycle degree correction of 1966-1974, in contrast, led to two major recessions (in 1970 and 1974), the ousting of a president by resignation and the comparatively severe Vietnam War. Larger stock market corrections, such as those highlighted in Figure 3, beget depressions, political upheaval and all-out war. Corrections of Millennium degree, such as the Dark Ages, destroy economies, political systems and entire nations, and warring becomes chronic. Conversely, small uptrends produce moderate benefits, while uptrends of the highest degree produce the greatest social achievements of mankind such as the Renaissance, the Industrial Revolution and the Information Age.

## Summary

As social mood becomes more positive, people buy more stocks, behave more productively, vote for more incumbents, have more children, blow off fewer bombs and act peacefully toward their neighbors. Conversely, as social mood becomes more negative, people sell more stocks, behave less productively, vote for more challengers, have fewer children, blow off more bombs and act belligerently toward their neighbors. All this correlation is consistent with the idea that all these activities have a common engine, which is social mood. Of course, social mood dynamics produce countless other manifestations, such as trends in art, music, entertainment, mores and fashion, to name but a few.

Because social mood change, as revealed by stock market's form, is patterned according to the Wave Principle, we can propose a larger socionomic hypothesis, that the Wave Principle ultimately shapes the dynamics underlying the character of all human social activity. The Wave Principle, in brief, is the engine of history.

## NOTES

[1] We may also say that every downturn in aggregate stock prices of at least Primary degree produced an economic contraction, as long as we define "downturn in aggregate stock prices" as the onset of an Elliott wave correction (see letter labels in Figure 1). Thereafter, the resulting recession may occur in wave A, C or both.

[2] To this summary we may add Richard Nixon, who, after being re-elected on a landslide as the DJIA rose to an all-time high, was forced to resign during the 1973-1974 bear market.

[3] Narrowly contested elections sometimes hinge on near-term market trends and/or the lagging performance of the economy, as in the cases of Truman and Bush.

[4] This is where historians get the bizarre notion that war is good for the economy. Actually, each war is triggered by an extreme low in mood, typically in the climate of economic depression. The social mood then reverses naturally and brings about both increased productivity and, eventually, peace.

[5] *Bank Credit Analyst.* (1997, January and 1999, March). Toronto.

[6] Holt, Derek. (1997, June 20). Royal Bank of Canada, as quoted on Bloomberg.

[7] Poterba, James M. (1998, October). "Population age structure and asset returns: An empirical investigation." Cambridge: Massachusetts Institute of Technology.

[8] Prechter, Robert R., Jr. (1999, September 17). Debate with Harry S. Dent, presented by Bill Good Marketing, Chateau Elan, Braselton, GA.

[9] In the last two decades, there has been no Elliott wave correction large enough to induce anything beyond nuclear weapons *testing*. The next "C" wave of larger than Cycle degree will undoubtedly impel the use of nuclear weapons for offensive purposes.

Prechter
*The Elliott Wave Theorist*
September 1999

## Chapter 9

# A Socionomic View of Demographic Trends
### or
## Stocks & Sex

Most people think that the economy is a key determinant of stock market behavior. Pages 260 through 264 of *The Wave Principle of Human Social Behavior and the New Science of Socionomics*[1] demonstrate that actually, social mood trends, as reflected by the trends of the stock market, determine the direction of economic activity. Most people think that politics affect the stock market. Pages 272 through 282 in the book show that the social mood, as reflected by the stock market, controls the selection of leaders and therefore the direction and outcome of politics. Most people think that peace and war mightily affect the valuation of stocks. Pages 265 through 270 show that aggregate mood trends, as reflected by stock prices, determine social climates that are conducive to peace or war. The fundamental observation of the new science of socionomics is that social mood, which is patterned according to the Wave Principle, is the generator of social action, be it economic, political or cultural. The key insight of socionomics is that the *direction of causality* between social mood and social action is precisely the opposite of that which is almost universally presumed; the former dictates the character of the latter, not vice versa.

Most people who attempt to relate demographics to the stock market operate under the standard presumption that, if there is any relationship at all, demographic changes (like changes in politics, economics, cultural events, and so on) would be causal to the trends of the stock market. In reviewing related studies, one finds full agreement on that starting point and utter disagreement thereafter. Of course, in any instance when there is a paucity of data and a researcher has the option of sliding two series around until he finds a fit, it is quite easy to find confluence somewhere.[2] With respect to demographics and the stock market, one study, based on a cycle theory, postulates a 20-year lag in the stock market's reaction to the number of births.[3] Another, based on the hypothesis that people in their forties spend and invest more than those in other age groups, shows a 44-to-49-year lag between birth rates and stock price trends from 1956 to the present.[4,5] Another researcher disputes this claim, pointing out that the number of 44-to-49-year olds "kept rising right through the 1929[-1932] crash, [which] calls the reliability of 'the spending wave' as a stock market indicator into question." To improve the correlation, he constructs a five-year moving average of the rate of change of a "saver/spender ratio" (in this case, the number of 40-to-49-year-olds divided by the number of 25-to-34-year-olds) that correlates with broad stock trends in the U.S. and Japan since 1948 and 1965 respectively, but not well beforehand.[6] At least three studies, including one from academia, argue that there is too little data, too little cross-cultural correspondence and far too much divergence in pre-1956 data to suggest any relationship at all between the stock market and lagged birth trends.[7,8,9] It is clear from the disagreement among the proponent studies and the statistical analysis in the opponent studies that there is in fact, as the latter conclude, little or no basis for proposing that there is a causal relationship between demographic trends and later stock market trends. However, that is as far as these studies go, because social researchers cannot imagine a basis for investigating any other correlation.

What all of these studies have in common, despite their wide differences, is the presumption that if there is any causality at all, it is demographics that would be causal to the stock market's trends. This stance reflects the standard misconception of causality, i.e., the idea that social mood, and therefore the stock market, is a slave to "outside" influences. The socionomist understands that this view with respect to demographics, as with every other major social phenomenon, is precisely backwards; the *premise* is false. Naturally, this false presumption has led, as it has with studies relating stocks to economic or political causation, to utter chaos in the aggregated conclusions, as the wide disagreements catalogued above reveal.

How may we state the correct premise for the purposes of testing its validity? We must start from the socionomic perspective on social causality. We know that social mood, as reflected by the stock market, determines the expansions and contractions in the economy. We know that extremes in social mood, as reflected by extremes in the stock market, determine whether a landslide election will favor the incumbent or

*Figure 1*

the challenger. We know that the direction and extent of social mood change, as reflected by the stock market, determine the extent of peace or whether there is a social mindset conducive to the outbreak of war. Is it possible to imagine that social mood also determines demographics? Most people would never pose such a question; I hope to suggest an answer.

Figure 1 shows stock market prices plotted against total births from 1909 to the present. The data is shown with *no lag*. The first thing to notice is that there is a fairly noticeable correlation between the two sets of data.

Why would births and the stock market trend together, if they do at all? Sometimes answers can be found in subtleties. Notice that the deepest low in births this century came in 1933, the year after the deepest low in the stock market this century. Notice that the second most important low in births occurred again in 1975, one year after the second most important stock market low of this century. Why would there be a one-year lag? Well, can you think of any activity that always precedes a

birth by about a year? If so, could this activity be correlated directly with
people's moods and therefore the trend and level of the stock market?
Chapter 14 of *The Wave Principle of Human Social Behavior* characterizes a rising social mood trend as correlating, among other things, with
"friskiness, daring and confidence," a falling trend with "somberness,
defensiveness and fear." We now have a tenuous basis for a socionomic
hypothesis regarding demographic trends. When aggregate feelings of
friskiness, daring and confidence wax, people engage in more sexual
activity with the aim of having children. When these feelings wane, so
does the desire for generating offspring. It takes about nine months between the procreative impulse and a child's birth, which is why, at least
at market bottoms, annual data on births lag annual data on the stock
market by one year. Figure 2 shows the same data, lagged by one year
to reflect conceptions. The result is not an extrapolation or theory, nor
is it the result of elaborate exercises in data fitting, as we find so often
with hypotheses that demographics drive the economy. We *know* that a
procreative decision or impulse is required nine months prior to a birth,

*Figure 2*

so there is no theoretical presumption in repositioning and renaming this data.[10] Now the two major lows line up exactly.

Let's investigate the relationship at market tops. As you can see from the slash marks imposed upon Figure 2, the rate of procreation has declined prior to major tops in the Dow Jones Industrial Average. This is precisely the same behavior exhibited by indicators of market breath and rates of change for stock averages, which always peak and begin declining before the major blue-chip averages top out. To visualize the similarity, let's graph the relationship between procreative activity and the success of the broad stock market, not just the blue chips.

A stock market indicator known as the advance-decline line records the cumulative trading activity of *all* stocks on the New York Stock Exchange that have advanced and declined each day. It reflects trends of stock prices throughout the country, even down to smaller local companies. In other words, it reflects, more deeply and broadly than the DJIA, the breadth of overall corporate success and thus the overall mood, which is the engine of buying and selling among all stocks. Presumably, the a-d line would therefore better reflect the

*Figure 3*

mood of a broad segment of the population that might be tempted to a procreative decision, not just the mood of people who influence the trend of advancing blue chip stocks. Figure 3 shows the same procreation data plotted against the advance-decline line. As you can see, this correlation is far tighter. In light of this relationship, one might be excused for concluding that during the twentieth century, the stock market's advance-decline line (despite its imperfections in this role) has been a fairly accurate ongoing real-time reflection of the number of U.S. couples that are engaging in procreation.

This contemporaneous relationship holds for all of the available data in both series, which is far more time than the lagged data: 73 years as opposed to only 43 years. Thus, there is a stronger correlation between these two sets of data than there is in any argument involving a multi-decade lag. Therefore, if you think that the popular "spenders" correlation is valid simply by how it looks when graphed from 1956 to the present, then you must accord this relationship nearly twice the validity on longevity alone. What's more, its expression is restricted only by a lack of breadth data prior to 1926 and of birth data prior to 1909, *not* a glaring divergence from the hypothesis as is encountered with the lagged data prior to the 1950s. Thus, unlike the demographics-as-first-cause argument, all available data supports the socionomic conclusion, and none contradicts it.

It is at least possible to suggest, based on this limited evidence, that human social mood, the engine that drives the stock market, also regulates aggregate impulses to procreate. This engine is fired by the interactive limbic systems of people, which are impulsively driven. *If there is any connection between demographics and the stock market, then, it is that social mood, as reflected by stock market trends and levels, determines demographics, not the other way around.* Like all socionomic observations, this one reveals the proper direction of causality, which is the opposite of the one that forms the false premise and foundation of most economic and sociological study.

## Demographics and the Socionomic Hypothesis

Socionomics differs from conventional economics and sociology in one crucial aspect: It recognizes that social causality is precisely the opposite of the standard presumption. Most researchers begin with the presumption that the economy, politics, peace and war, demographics, and all kinds of other cultural events and situations influence people's thinking, and therefore the social mood, and therefore the trend of the stock market. Socionomics recognizes that the social mood is endogenous and patterned, the result of cooperating impulsive human limbic systems. The result is a patterned series of waves of human social mood, which in turn determine the character of social and cultural events, including economics, politics, demographics, peace, war, fashion and culture. When the socionomic premise is adopted, the proper correlation among various cultural and societal trends becomes readily apparent. For the first time, the various products of human interaction make sense together. This result is in dramatic contrast to the chaotic sea of uncertainty and cross-inapplicability that pervades the fields of economics and sociology today.

The demographic data presented here, while they are too limited for a firm conclusion, are nevertheless undeniably compatible with the socionomic hypothesis. Humans inherited a primitive pre-rational portion of their brains that engages in impulsive mentation[11] and controls activities crucial to animal survival such as herding, the selection of leaders, fighting and *mating*. Because of the demonstrated commonality among all these activities in our graphs of economic, political and cultural activity, it appears that this portion of the brain actually generates a single mood-regulating impulse, which is the basis for unity in the trends and aggregate character of these activities. Since the stock market is the most accurate sociometer we have, one need hardly be surprised that these data show a tight correlation between its trends and the procreative impulse. If further studies show that the demographic correlation described in Figure 3 holds over the centuries and throughout cultures, they will strengthen our socionomic hypothesis that social mood trends are the genesis of demographic trends.

While the procreative impulse appears to result from feelings of "daring, friskiness and confidence," one must not presume that the latter term rests upon rationality regarding the wisdom of having children. The key word is *feelings*, which originate in the limbic system. It might seem attractive to argue that people have fewer children because when the economy contracts, they restrain themselves due to poverty and the cost of child rearing. If this thought entered your mind, you were exercising (probably in seconds; am I right?) the conventional style of rationalization. We should not be surprised that sociologists rationalize the practicality factor *in the opposite way* when they declare that people in poor countries must be having many children in the quest to produce more family workers or have someone around to take care of them in their old age. On one hand, they opine that poverty induces people to restrict child-bearing, and on the other, they say that it induces people to expand it. Needless to say, contradiction has never halted conventional theorizing about social causality. Traditional thinking makes people naturally offer such event-causal arguments. They are, however, anti-socionomic and assuredly wrong.

Is it reasonable that people *respond* to a contracting economy by having fewer children? First, as you can see in Figure 2, rises and falls in the conception rate coincide with rises and falls in the advance-decline line, which is a register of social mood. This correlation means that trends in conceptions significantly *precede* expansions and contractions in the economy, which lag the a-d line, usually by years. Most noticeably, the lows in procreation coincide with *stock market lows, not economic lows*, which follow shortly thereafter. For example, procreative activity bottomed in 1932 with the stock market, *not* in 1933 with the economy. This chronology contradicts the conventional explanation. Second, as it happens, we have some data on the subject of procreative causality. In ancient Rome, Augustus Caesar tried to make couples poorer if they *refused* to produce the desired number of children. Here is the result:

> In 18 B.C., Augustus passed a series of laws that are often referred to as his "social" or "moral" reforms, in which he regulated, or tried to regulate, marriage and procreation. These laws made adultery a criminal offence for the first time…. He also passed laws encouraging couples to have children, mainly through *large tax penalties* on those who did not. These laws…*didn't work*… the divorce rate did not notably go down, *the birth rate did not notably go up*….[12]

In other words, practicality for the couples involved has little to do with decisions for or against procreation. Such responses support my case that impulsion has everything to do with it.

In the social aggregate, increasing procreation results from increasing *feelings* of confidence more so than with actual family economics. In the aggregate, procreative decisions, like stock-buying decisions and leader selection, are more commonly impulsive/emotional than meditative/rational. In the case of procreation, they are the result of couples in a state of excitement agreeing either, "Let's have a baby!" or "Let's risk sex that could lead to conception!" Any associated discussion by prospective parents is undertaken mostly to rationalize an impulsive desire that they cannot actually explain.

There also exists an offset correlation between aggregate procreation and aggregate prosperity *per se* because prosperity results from the shared feelings of increasing confidence that also spur the procreative impulse. This socionomic perspective reveals why the trends of the economy *lag* trends in both the stock market and procreation. As is the case with all socionomic observations, one must realize that the economy is not an isolated outside force that independently influences procreative decisions. Like interest rates, politics and war, the economy is the result of human interaction; it is an intimately intertwined element of the human social experience, not an isolated outside cause.

**Trend Divergence and Practical Application**

As you can see in Figure 2, conceptions fell persistently against rising stock market averages in 1920-1929 and again in 1956-1966, i.e., in the ten years prior to the top of waves V of (III) and III of (V) respectively, the two biggest tops of this century. After each of those periods, aggregate stock prices rapidly joined the trend of procreation on the downside. We might be tempted to suggest cavalierly that, like waning market breadth and velocity, waning procreative activity is a sentiment-based "sell signal" for the stock market because only the extremity of bullishness at an approaching major market top could make people more interested in stocks than in sex. It's a good line for speeches, anyway. However, I believe, based on our graphs relating stock trends to political trends as well as Figure 3, that it is more accurate to postulate *an intimate and contemporaneous relationship between the limbic system's impulses both to procreate and to herd.*[13] In relating sociometers, it is important to compare apples to apples; national procreation rates track the broad public's mood, which is better reflected by the a-d line than by the much narrower Dow. These two trends rarely diverge. Regardless of our hypothesis, *the same type of trend divergence that occurred prior to previous major market tops is again in evidence from 1989 to 1999,* portending a social mood reversal of like magnitude.

**NOTES**

[1] Prechter, Robert R., Jr. (1999). *The wave principle of human social behavior and the new science of socionomics*. Gainesville, GA: New Classics Library.

[2] With 180 years of data, I can slide graphs of the U.S. immigration rate and aggregate inflation-adjusted stock prices to show a tight 100-year period of correlation with a 20-year lead, a 35-year period of correlation with a 2-year lead, a 90-year period of correlation with a 20-year lag, and a 67-year period of correlation with an 80-year lag. One can construct a plausible "theory" to go with at least three of them, as I did in a speech in September 1999, which went more or less as follows:

> If you have two sets of data and slide them around, you can find countless correlations. I'm going to show you three.
>
> First let's look at concurrent trends, not shifted, in the first half of the 1800s. Had you been living back in the 1860s, you would have noticed that decade after decade the pace of immigration to the United States matched the ups and downs in the stock market. Somewhere around 1870 you write a book and offer this theory: When immigrants come off the boat, they're broke, so they have to go to work immediately, and all this new labor juices the economy.
>
> The only problem is that shortly afterward, the correlation completely breaks down. There is no connection between the lines anymore. Had you bet on it, you would have gone bankrupt many times over.
>
> Let's slide the immigration graph approximately 20 years into the future. Now the lines coincide perfectly with the boom of the 1920s and the crash and depression of the 1930s. Do you have a theory to explain it? Sure. You propose that 20 years after impoverished families land on the shores of the United States they are well enough off to start investing in the stock market.
>
> Unfortunately, as the country got into the biggest economic boom of the 20th century, from the early 1940s to the early 1970s, the correlation was the exact opposite. Immigration was falling the entire time. And in the worst economy since the Great Depression, during the 1970s, the immigration line was rising. Fooled again.
>
> Now I'm going to show you my favorite one. When you slide the immigration chart 80 years ahead, you get the longest positive correlation in the data, lasting 80 years, almost a full century. You might say, "Bob, that's crazy. What does immigration have to do with trends 80 years in the future?" Well, here's a good theory for it: Immigrants come off the boat; they haven't got a nickel; they have kids, who

work in the family bakery or whatever. When the second generation starts its own families, they have enough money to send their kids to private school. When their kids—the third generation—get into their 40s, they're wealthy enough to invest in the stock market. And that's why there's an 80-year lag between immigration and the stock market!

I can also slide these graphs to show that the stock market predicts immigration. You easily can make that theoretical case, too: As the stock market booms, it attracts immigrants. You can make up exogenous causes all day long. They offer a great basis for rationalization.

My point is that if you take the liberty of shifting data sets around and are willing to pull validity out of only part of the data, they will fit many ways. This practice, however, is not likely to lead to a valid claim.

My correlation doesn't have enough data, either. But I can say that conceptions and the stock market line up in concurrent time, without shifting anything, and all available data fit. No other demographic case can't say that.

[3] Berry, Brian. (1991). *Long wave rhythms in economic development and political behavior*. Baltimore: Johns Hopkins University Press.

[4] Dent, Harry S. (1993). *The great boom ahead*. New York: Hyperion.

[5] Dent, Harry S. (1998). *The roaring 2000s*. New York: Simon & Schuster.

[6] Carder, John. (1997, September). *Encyclopedia of historical charts*. Boulder, CO: Topline Graphics.

[7] *Bank Credit Analyst*. (1997, January and 1999, March). Toronto.

[8] Holt, Derek. (1997, June 20). Royal Bank of Canada, as quoted on Bloomberg.

[9] Poterba, James M. (1998, October). "Population age structure and asset returns: An empirical investigation." Cambridge: Massachusetts Institute of Technology.

[10] Obviously this extrapolation does not account for multiple births (twins, triplets, etc.), which would slightly reduce the conception numbers, or abortions, which would increase them. Abortions are not *necessarily* a factor, as sexual activity risking unwanted conception might increase *because* abortions are legally available, so the sum of aborted fetuses might equal the sum of conceptions that would not otherwise have taken place. Anyone who wants to take the time to refine the birth data to more precisely reflect procreative decisions is welcome to do so.

[11] MacLean, Paul. (1990). *The triune brain in evolution*. New York: Plenum Press.

[12] Vandiver, Elizabeth. (n.d.) "The *Aeneid* of Virgil." Course Number 303, Lecture 3, The Teaching Company audio tape.

[13]Indeed, procreation may be seen as herding in the sense that it increases the size of the herd. Further, because procreation undergoes long social trends, engaging in it or refraining from it may be an expression of herding for many people, who may be spurred to action or non-action by the spectacle of increasing or decreasing childbirths among their relatives, neighbors and friends.

Prechter
*The Elliott Wave Theorist*
February 27, 1998

*Chapter 10*

# Rationalizing Optimism with Demographics

In January, a *Barron's* headline boldly claimed: "Demography is Destiny." We were regaled yet again with the argument that stocks will continue higher for at least another decade as 9.7 million Americans turn 45 between now and 2008. Paul Montgomery (*Universal Economics*, Legg Mason Wood Walker, Newport News, VA) responded in a letter to the editor, noting that the $146 billion this segment is expected to bring to the market is nothing compared to the $450 billion the market took away in just one day last fall. Instead of calculating what boomers can do for the stock market, Montgomery concluded, boomers should consider "what the market can do to them." Proponents volleyed back with another *Barron's* feature ("Triple Play") on February 16. A long-time advocate of the demographics theory discovered another $25 *trillion* in inevitable stock market flows. The author's new study, "The Big Shift—Barely Begun," asserts that the stock market will triple again over the next 15 years simply by assuming that it will rise at a historical growth rate of 8% a year. We point out that if GDP were simultaneously to maintain its comparatively meager historical growth rate of 2.5% a year, it would bring stock market valuation to 500% of GDP. The figure as of September was 125%, 50% higher than the old record set in August 1929. Are we to be concerned with such things? "With an air of satisfaction," the article notes, "The nice thing about demographics is that you're not wrong unless there's a plague." So to some, the proposed relationship of demographics to the stock market is not a theory but a law of nature: the bull market as manifest destiny. We have discussed the flaws in this case before, in *The Elliott Wave Theorist*. Recent statistics show that baby boomers are not saving much, but they are saving differently. What used to go into the bank or a second home now goes right into the stock market. We think this change in behavior illustrates Montgomery's point: Investment is based on emotional, not mechanical, decision-making. We think that the demographics theory will ultimately prove to have been a rationalization of an emotional state.

## Chapter 11

# A Socionomic Study of Patents

After becoming adept at using the socionomic hypothesis to make social predictions, one can anticipate substantially what a new set of data—never before investigated from a socionomic perspective—will show.

Questions: (1) When do you think society would tend to come up with more technological innovations—when social mood is in a positive trend or a negative trend? (2) If you were going to use the frequency of patent grants to answer this question, would you expect those applications to be a leading or lagging sociometer? To check your answers, let's look at the data for patents granted in the United States over the past century.

Most economists would probably postulate that more patents would drive an upswing in the economy and vice versa. But our data show that the stock market, and shortly thereafter the economy, turn before patent grants do. In other words, social mood trends, as recorded by the Dow Jones Industrial Average, anticipate trend changes in patent grants, which constitute a lagging sociometer.

We knew that patent applications would be a lagging data series, because it generally takes two to five years from the formation of an idea until the prototypes are made, the drawings completed, the legal aspects investigated, the applications written and submitted and a patent finally granted. The ideas themselves arise more easily during a time of a rising and heightened social mood. A few years later, we see the result.

## Chapter 12

# *Social Behavior During Blackouts*

When a major loss of electricity affects a large urban area, economists may offer to predict the probable reaction in the stock market to such an expensive event, and sociologists may offer to predict people's behavioral reaction, using past events as a guide. These social scientists reflexively view the event as a cause and duly estimate the results.

The socionomic lens provides an utterly different perspective. Even though the cost to an economy might be substantial, the stock market won't react; it is priced according to endogenously regulated social mood. Even though the event is a surprise, it will not dispose people either to riot and loot or to cooperate and help each other; social mood does. Even though such events have happened before, the character of prior human behavior at such times is not a reliable basis for predicting how they will act the next time it happens; people's demeanor with respect to the event can differ radically, because it is regulated by social mood, not the event per se.

The largest electricity-service failure in the history of North America occurred on August 14, 2003. This event actually has its roots in socionomics, because over a century ago Congress formed the Interstate Commerce Commission, the first federal regulatory agency and the beginning of persistent governmental interference in U.S. production and services. The electrical production industry has suffered the same stultification as the railroad industry and for the same reason. It is not as far gone, but it is moving in that direction.

Yet the social-mood roots of the recent blackout run so far back in history that, in terms of its relationship to current human behavior, we may ignore it and treat the blackout itself as an isolated disaster, like a hurricane or tornado. The point of primary socionomic interest with regard to this event is not so much what caused the blackout but how people used it to express their mood.

## The Blackout Experience of 2003

One of the interesting aspects of the latest event is the good feelings expressed by many of those caught in the middle of it:

—"In city after city, people offered help to those they did not know."[1]

—"In New York, some risked life and limb to direct traffic when stoplights were paralyzed. Stores passed out free milk rather than allow it to spoil in the heat. Hotels passed out bedding to folks sleeping on the street."[1]

—"Residents banded together, sharing candles, radios, and stories."[2]

—"No-one's panicking. Everyone's cool. We're all helping each other. I love this."[3]

—"Detroit mayor Kwame Kirkpatrick said he believed the city was 'the calmest of all the cities that have been hit by this crisis.'"[1]

## The Blackout Experience of 1977

Contrast these beatific social images to those in evidence during the 1977 blackout:

—"The mood in the sweltering city quickly turned ugly. Looters destroyed sections of Brooklyn, Harlem and the South Bronx, with 2,000 stores picked clean."[4]

—"Police arrested 3,700 people. A headline in the July 16 New York Times read, 'Ravaged Slums Facing a Future of Uncertainty.'"[4]

—"'Uptown was trouble, uptown was looting.' said a pianist and artistic director of New York's Festival of Song. 'It saddened me. The blackout shouldn't have been an occasion for violence.'"[4]

—"[N]eighborhoods throughout New York exploded into violence. Stores were ransacked, looted and destroyed. Buildings were set ablaze. And the police, for the most part, stood helpless. In these stark contradictions, an unusual yet definitive moment left its mark on New York history-the night the lights went out."[5]

—"News broadcasts reported outbreaks of violence, looting, and fires. Areas of Harlem, Brooklyn, and the South Bronx experienced the most damage, where thousands of people took to the streets and smashed store windows looking for TVs, furniture, or clothing. In one report, 50 cars were stolen from a car dealership in the Bronx. The police made 3,776 arrests, although from all accounts, many thousands escaped before being caught. 1,037 fires burned throughout the City, six times the average rate, while the fire department also responded to 1,700 false alarms."[5]

—"The summer of 1977 permanently [not so] altered New York's self-image, and, perhaps as important, its self-confidence. Not only did crime and economic strain transform the City, but the blackout fused the significance of the two in a perception that New York, the largest city in the United States, was on the road to ruin. It had become the standard-bearer for the urban crisis. In future years, when New York would make dramatic strides to address the problems that surfaced in the seventies and forge a new image of national and world leadership, the memories of these times would linger as a reminder of how hard it could be to fall from skyscraper heights."[5]

## The Difference between the 1977 and 2003 Blackouts

The contrast between crowd behavior in the recent experience and that of 1977 is dramatic. It is so striking that it made headlines in many media, including *USA Today* and Bloomberg news. Here are some representative comments from the articles:

—"The nation's worst blackout generated not the 'night of terror' that followed a lesser blackout in New York in 1977, but a moment in which strangers became allies."[1]

—"Anna Ramirez, 70, looked out from her apartment on Manhattan's upper West Side when New York lost power shortly after 4 p.m. Thursday and feared a repetition of the violence that ravaged her neighborhood and others in the city during a 25-hour blackout on July 13, 1977. 'I was so scared,' Ramirez said, 'Looking out my window, it was like living in a war zone. Everything was on fire. But last night, people were so much calmer. They shared flashlights and helped me up the stairs.'"[6]

—"'In 1977, the city was on the edge of bankruptcy and people were at one another's throats,' Koch said. 'We had huge racial anger, which evaporated long ago. Now this city is just about the most civil place you could go to. And even though the city has fiscal problems, the city doesn't have the feel that it's out of control the way it was back then.'"[6]

—"'Last time I saw them carrying out furniture and appliances. This time my neighbors gave me flowers, candles and flashlights.'"[6]

—"'Instead of anger and fear, they saw grateful customers and smiling faces of customers whom they knew,' Tony Kumer said, 'People were really happy,' he said, 'they really appreciated us being open.'"[6]

—"The director of the Blackout History Project at George Mason University in Fairfax, Va., notes that the same grievances still exist in many neighborhoods. 'It's really telling that we haven't seen looting and rioting. It's deeply significant,' he says."[5]

Yes, it's significant. But why?

### Conventional Views

Conventional sociologists have offered many explanations for why most people were in a good mood and on their best behavior during the recent blackout. Let's review some of those that made it to press:

—"In retrospect, the social and economic conditions of 1977 provide many clues to the conflicting blackout experiences. The fiscal crisis and the ensuing cutbacks had been precipitated by a crippling economic recession which intensified growing public expressions of mistrust and consternation, leading some communities to lash out in the darkened night. [Why would a recession make you "lash out"?] Growing crime rates, [Why were they growing?] coinciding with a City government unable to grapple [Why was government impotent?] with escalating social and economic problems, also provided the backdrop for the explosion of violence. Contrasting with the good memories most New Yorkers had of a peaceful blackout only twelve years prior [in 1965], the garish images of the 1977 blackout confirmed just how much the City had changed in a decade. [Correct! But why?] The 'urban crisis' had become a permanent [sic] national emergency, claiming New York as its latest victim."[5]

—"It seems, say researchers who study America's psyche, that the country learned something profound from terrorists on Sept. 11, 2001."[1] [What terrorist attack taught America to be civil in 1965?]

—"'Someone noted that the terrorists hoped after 9/11 they had changed America forever, and they were right,' says a professor of psychiatry at Pennsylvania State University. 'They did.'"[1] ["Forever"? Like the way "the summer of 1977 permanently altered New York's self image"?]

—"After 9/11 there was a 'growing feeling that people needed to hang together to take care of each other,' said [a researcher of] post-traumatic stress disorder at Florida State University. 'Passengers immediately began to talk about 9/11. We got into that spirit, and appreciated how lucky we were' not to be in the middle of another terrorist horror. [He] describes their relief as 'post-traumatic euphoria' and says their relief 'enabled them to activate that part of themselves that wants to help others.'"[1] [What determines whether we have "post-traumatic stress" or "post-traumatic euphoria"?]

—"Another peaceful Rust Belt blackout that occurred in 1965 may help explain why. It occurred during the Cold War, another time when Americans felt themselves under threat. 'Americans in general are in a state of mind that's much closer to the Cold War,' he says. 'There's a sense of community that wasn't there in the '70s, and a greater respect for authority. And I wouldn't underestimate the fear factor'"[1] [If you throw in the Cold War, there is hardly a period in the past 70 years when Americans did not "feel themselves under threat."]

—"Former New York Mayor Edward Koch, who took office in 1978, said the disparities were striking and attributable to the changes in the city's economic, ethnic and political circumstances."[6] [What brought about these changes?]

—"Kelley said the Police Department, with 37,000 officers, is 15,000 over its 1977 staffing levels and uses more sophisticated technology, communications and personnel management techniques."[6] [I'm not sure about the latter three items, but it hardly seems that more cops diffused tension at Kent State in 1970.]

—"In those days [1977], New York's crime rate was soaring—a trend that would last until 1993, when former Major Rudolph Guiliani and then Police Commissioner William Bratton launched 'Zero Tolerance' policing, says [a professor at] Boston's Northeastern University."[1] [Does the crime rate correlate with the riot rate?]

—"Deputy Mayor Dennis Walcott, who for 12 years was president of New York Urban League, said the city had undergone a change over the past decade in which 'the consensus in minority communities has moved toward zero tolerance for anti-social behavior.'"[6] [So we just decided not to tolerate rioting. As Sir Robin said in *Monty Python and the Holy Grail*, "That's easy!"]

—"A study of the '77 blackout by researchers at three New York institutions, including Columbia University, linked looting to an incendiary mix of poverty, unemployment, mistrust of the justice system and other grievances."[1] [Do the poverty-stricken unemployed of Appalachia stage riots when the lights go out? If it was the "mix" of social circumstances, how did it get there? Why didn't New York's poor and unemployed riot this time?]

—"Because many of the problems behind the urban crisis remain unsolved despite the prosperity of recent years, the memories of the 1977 blackout have taken on the quality of morality play or myth, with widely diverging views of what the myth means."[5] [This is socio-babble.]

## The Blackout Experience of 1965

One key to understanding the difference in behavior between the two events is available in reports of crowd behavior during the preceding major NYC blackout of November 1965. It is described this way:

—"'Everybody was very cooperative and nobody panicked,' he recalled. 'It wasn't as scary as it was maddening.'"[4]

—"It was remarkable for what didn't happen: looting and violence. Police reported that the crime rate actually went down."[4]

—"Despite the confusion and disarray, New Yorkers spent the night in peace. There were no riots or widespread looting. Instead, New Yorkers helped each other. Some directed traffic. Others assisted the New York fire department as they rescued stranded subway passengers. In many cases, New Yorkers just shared extra candles and flashlights with neighbors, reveling in the opportunity to get to know the people who lived across the hall."[7]

—"This wasn't the case a dozen years later when New York's poorer boroughs turned ugly and violent, littered with broken glass and burned-out buildings."[4]

### The Socionomic Perspective

The question is, why did the public behave well in 1965, poorly in 1977 and well again in 2003? If you are a long-time reader of our socionomic studies, you may already have figured out the answer: The

*Figure 1*

years 1965 and 2003 are positioned near peaks of long-term positive social-mood trends, and the year 1977 is positioned near the bottom of a negative social-mood trend, as evidenced in the following graph of the constant-dollar Dow. Shared good feelings near the two tops manifested in constructive behavior, and shared bad feelings near the bottom manifested in destructive behavior. The event was the same each time, so its nature is irrelevant to the behavior.

The expressions of social goodwill during the 2003 blackout are in perfect accordance with today's readings on all the indicators of social mood that we maintain. Extreme optimism toward the stock market and net popular support for the President are but two of the other manifestations of the currently elevated social mood. Readings in 1965 were similarly elevated, and those in 1977 were depressed.

Americans did not "learn something profound from 9/11" or exhibit restraint because of a "fear factor" or "zero tolerance." Social mood regulates social behavior during blackouts and other disruptions of infrastructure. Further proof of this fact will come when, near the ultimate bottom of the next major bear market, an infrastructure disruption occurs and riots follow.

People yearn to express both their good feelings and bad. A service disruption simply provides an occasion to do so.

**Socionomic Value**

Not only can a socionomist use the position of the waves to determine the likely character of social events, but he can also use the character of social events to help confirm or contradict the presumed position of the waves. Judging from the sentiments revealed in the reaction to each of these blackouts, one could have deduced that the stock market was closer to a major top or to a major bottom based on the behavior people exhibited.

## REFERENCES

[1] Peterson, K.S. and Sternberg, S. (2003, August 18). "Blackout illuminates change for the  better." *USA Today*, 7D.

[2] Parker, Laura. (2003, August 15). "Small surge cascades into epic outage." *USA Today* (online).

[3] Abocar, Amran. (2003, August 15). "After blackout, Toronto wonders where leaders are." Reuters.

[4] Chapman, D. (2003, August 15). "Reactions different in earlier outrages." *The Atlanta Journal-Constitution*, A13.

[5] (2000, June 27). "Events/1977 (New York Blackout)." Blackout History Project, blackout@history.gmu.edu.

[6] Goldman, H. (2003, August 16). "New York's calm contrasts with violence of 1977 power failure." Bloomberg News.

[7] (2000, June 27). "Events/1965 (Great Northeast Blackout)." Blackout History Project, blackout@history.gmu.edu.

Prechter
*The Elliott Wave Theorist*
July 2002

## Chapter 13

# A Socionomic View of
# Central-Bank Causality

Both supporters and critics of the Federal Reserve System agree that the first cause of paper money inflation and credit expansion in the U.S. since 1913 is the Fed. How does a socionomist respond to this assertion?

Conventional statements about social causality always treat the purported cause as an isolated force, as if it appeared from nowhere, with no antecedent causes of its own. Likewise, the Fed is taken as akin to the Law of Gravity, and all consequences flow therefrom.

Certainly the Fed is the primary *engine* of inflation via money creation and the fostering of easy credit through the banking system. But an engine and a first cause are different things. The motor of an automobile is the engine of locomotion but it is not the cause of it. Somebody built the motor *in order that locomotion could occur*. Likewise, people built the Fed in order that credit could be made easy.

The socionomic insight provides a principle of social causation that requires an inversion of conventional statements of causality. To reverse the presumed direction of causality expressed in the first paragraph of this report, we may conclude that the proper reformulation is as follows: The Fed is not the root cause of money and credit inflation; the desire for money and credit inflation is the root cause of the Fed.

If this re-statement is true, then a socionomist should be able to find evidence of it in the record of the formal structure of social mood fluctuation, which is best manifest in the fluctuations of aggregate stock prices. As we shall see, a review of that record suggests that the Fed did not appear out of nowhere at a random time but in fact was a product of social mood forces desiring an engine of credit inflation. We come to this conclusion because in three out of four instances, central-bank formation occurred at almost exactly the same place in wave structure, i.e., in the progression of social psychology.

### Credit Engines as Products of Fourth and Fifth-Wave Psychology

Figure 1 shows the stock-price record from its beginning in 1695 in England. I would be remiss as a socionomist if I neglected to mention that the very appearance of reported stock prices was itself a symptom of fourth and fifth-wave social psychology, just as the appearance of financial network television was in the early 1980s. In other words, minds were turning to finance, and these outcomes were simply manifestations of that orientation.[1]

*Figure 1*

In Figure 1, the points of three central-bank formations are marked with arrows. The ensuing period that encompassed fourth and fifth waves are traced with a bold line. By the way, the labels on the graph are *not* retrofitted to this discussion. For over twenty years, publications of Elliott Wave International have labeled the wave structure consistently as shown.

Observe that there is a remarkable correlation between the wave position and central bank creation. These central banks all came into being during *fourth* waves of large degree:

— The first modern central bank was the Bank of England, constituted in 1694. **It appeared during wave ④ of III, just prior to wave IV of (V).**

— The second American experiment with central banking was the second Bank of the United States, chartered in 1816. **It appeared during wave ④ of III, just prior to wave IV of (I).**

— The latest incarnation of central banking in the U.S. is the Federal Reserve System, which was signed into law in 1913. **It appeared during wave IV of (III).**

In each of these three cases, government constituted the central bank in time to provide credit for the excesses of a Cycle-degree fourth wave and the ensuing Cycle-degree fifth wave. The Bank of England financed the ongoing Nine Years' War (also known as King Williams' War and the War of the Grand Alliance) with France during wave IV and then the South Sea Bubble, wave V. The second Bank of the United States created the credit to finance the War of 1812's debt legacy and then wave V, the Era of Good Feeling. The Federal Reserve System created credit to finance World War I during wave IV and then the Roaring Twenties, wave V. Probably because the next major correction was itself a fourth wave, wave (IV), the Fed remained in operation to finance the New Deal of wave (IV) in constant-dollar terms and the major expansion of wave (V), which culminated in wave V of (V), the Great Asset Mania of the 1980s and 1990s. So the Fed has accompanied not only a fourth and fifth wave of Cycle degree but also a fourth and fifth wave of Supercycle degree.

The second Bank of the United States was an object of political controversy. The presidential campaign of 1832 between Jackson and Clay was fought largely over the issue of re-chartering the second bank. Clay, who supported the bank, lost the election. The bank operated just long enough to finance waves IV and V of (I). In 1836, the first down year after the top, its 20-year charter was allowed to expire.

There is little question that the Federal Reserve System was a product of a certain necessary social psychology as well, because it came into being only after decades of political opposition to the idea of a central bank. In the 77 years following the expiration of the second Bank, promoters of central banking in the United States lost all of their political battles. In 1913, during a major fourth wave, resistance melted away, and proponents got their central bank.

## An Exception

There is one exception in our period of record. The *first* Bank of the United States, which Alexander Hamilton guided to formation in 1791, did not appear in the same wave position as the other three examples. It was formed in the midst of an economic depression substantially to finance Revolutionary War debts that had already been incurred. Thus, while we may postulate that the social psychology of fourth and fifth waves is conducive to facilitating the formation of a credit-expansion engine, such engines may come into being and operate at other times as well. It is probably pertinent that after the debts were paid, Congress closed the bank in 1811. Until we get evidence to the contrary, we might suggest that central banks formed in fourth waves will continue to operate through the ensuing fifth wave. Those formed at other times, such as the first Bank of the United States, will be discontinued fairly quickly because they have no fourth and fifth-wave social imperative to keep them going.

## First Cause

The chronology we have explored supports the socionomic premise that psychology is the first cause of the credit excesses of fifth waves. I conclude, then, that governments have formed central banks to facilitate credit in response to the psychological demands of major fourth and fifth waves. Fourth waves induce society to build the credit engine, and then fifth waves are propelled by it.

Because the Wave Principle is the first cause of the tenor of social events, we should properly conclude that had the specific event not occurred, had the Federal government not authorized a central bank, then during the terminal waves V of (III) and **(V)**, other banks and financial institutions would have exploited credit anyway, through their own ingenious methods and with much of the public happily participating throughout the process. Major fourth and fifth waves, we may safely postulate, encourage and thrive on easy credit no matter what the mechanism.

## A Moral Question

If this thesis is true, then is there any reason to object to central banking monopolies? Yes, because a free market in money and banking would allow prudent banks to operate independently from the incautious majority. They would advertise their safety services, and prudent people would have the opportunity to protect themselves with sound banks. Then only those choosing to take risk would get hurt. Under central banking, the innocent suffer the most.

## Future Prospects

Regarding this topic, what might we postulate with respect to the fact that at Grand Supercycle degree, the stock market is in wave Ⓘ, with wave Ⓥ due thereafter? Clearly, if a credit engine generally appears during major fourth waves to finance their attendant social profligacies and conflicts and then to accommodate the desire for speculation typical of fifth waves, and if fourth and fifth waves of immense degree are due, then we might anticipate the emergence of an unprecedented credit engine for waves Ⓘ and Ⓥ over the next two or three centuries. Some economists, such as Charles Kindleberger in the appendix to his book, *Manias, Panics, and Crashes*, advocate a "lender of last resort" to stave off deflation, in other words, a global super-Fed. This is like advocating crack smoking to save a cocaine addict, but sense has no force against the formological imperative. The existence of such a lender provides an excuse allowing people to abandon prudence under the assumption of safety, thus fueling the society-wide extension of credit to ever-weaker debtors. Such a proposal would forestall the next deflation only by generating an even greater credit expansion than has been accomplished by any previous monetary experiment. The ensuing crash and deflation would then be the largest ever.

Given the imperative of Grand Supercycle waves Ⓘ and Ⓥ, I suggest that authorities will embrace the "lender of last resort" proposal, or something like it, some time in the next hundred years as wave Ⓘ progresses. Wave Ⓥ will be the most spectacular credit inflation in the history of man and lead to the greatest credit bust in the history of man. After that experience, the wave position suggests that fiat-money central banking will go out of style for a millennium or so.

## NOTES

¹ As Marshall McLuhan said, "The medium is the message." That financial news networks came into being is far more important than their content. When (if) they go off the air in response to public disinterest, it will be in the vicinity of a major bottom in stock prices.

*Part III:*

# *SPORTS*

Prechter
*The Elliott Wave Theorist*
July 31, 1992

## Chapter 14

# An Elliott Wave in Olympics Participation

If you were to graph the number of nations competing in the Olympics since their renaissance in 1896, what picture would you see? Since it would track human behavior, you might expect to see an Elliott wave.[1]

Figure 1, on arithmetic scale, is reproduced from the newspaper, and Figure 2 shows the same data on semi-log scale. The new high in worldwide participation is one socionomic effect of a waxing positive social mood, which always engenders harmonious cooperation.

Notice that wave 4 pulled back approximately to the fourth subwave of wave 3, following the guidelines of impulse wave development. That was the year that the Olympics were held in Moscow and Russian troops were in Afghanistan. Why did the Olympic committee choose to hold the event in Moscow at such an emotional time? The "why" is elusive, but the decision fulfilled Elliott wave guidelines for how people *do* act. In 1916, 1940 and 1944, the Olympics were canceled due to war.

*Figure 1*

The wave structure suggests that among the next three Olympics scheduled, at least one will be canceled and/or will have fewer than 120 nations (the top of the previous fourth wave) competing, despite the larger number of nations now in the world resulting from the breakup of the Soviet Union.

*Figure 2*

## NOTES

[1] Wave 2 in these data ends lower than the start of wave 1, which does not occur in ongoing Elliott waves. The extension in the advance labeled wave 3 is typical of third waves, however, which justifies the labeling as shown. I consider the starting point of a brand new wave such as this to be zero. The same thing happened in gold in 1971. Wave II bottomed at $34.50, which is .50 below the fixed price of $35 that had held for decades. That lower low did not violate the Wave Principle because prior to wave I's burst upward, *there had been no market*. That is in essence what we have in these data, too.

## Chapter 15

# A Historic Extreme
# in Baseball Emotions

**November 1, 1991**

Sports can provide a background for extreme emotions socially expressed. Long time readers will remember that in the August 1985 Special Report, "Popular Culture and the Stock Market," football was listed as flourishing in bear markets, baseball in bull markets. In the early 1980s, at the end of the 16-year bear market pattern and the low for stocks in constant dollars, baseball bottomed in its slump at a low point that saw players on strike. Since then, baseball has been on a powerful "comeback" trend that has continued right through to this year. In fact, baseball players' salaries constitute one of the few speculative markets that have hit new all time highs this late in the 1987-to-present topping phase. The attention toward baseball this year has been nothing short of tremendous. What makes the story even more interesting is the party atmosphere and intense fan activity of the crowds attending the league playoffs and the World Series. Listen to baseball analyst Don Sutton, being interviewed before Game 3 of the NL playoffs:

> *Reporter*: "You normally see these kinds of crowds at college football games in the Southeast. It's hard to believe this is baseball and to see *this sort of enthusiasm*."

> *Sutton*: "Atlanta has become a very unusual baseball city. You normally see this *outflow of emotion* in a city like Chicago, negatively in cities like New York and Philadelphia. If you go to ball games in San Francisco or Los Angeles...you don't see this kind of *emotional outpouring*. And most of the time when people are really revved up and into it, it is from a negative standpoint, and not from a positive standpoint. In 28 years of being around baseball, *it has been the most remarkable phenomenon I've seen in baseball*."

"I have never seen anything more dramatic than what's happening in Atlanta today."

"It was great, super. We feel good. We feel happy. It's amazing."

— Quotes from fans, *The Atlanta Journal-Constitution*
October 1991

The "tomahawk chop," the "Indian war chant" and "homer hankies" were continually displayed in unison by *tens of thousands of people at a time*. 40 year olds acted like 20 year olds. Drums beat for weeks, game or no game. People showed up hours early at the ballpark to soak up the supercharged atmosphere of the crowd. These upbeat social rituals directly involved hundreds of thousands of people. Millions were involved indirectly via television. Victory celebrations in Atlanta and Minneapolis (despite sleet) attracted 760,000 people. The victory parade in Atlanta, with floats and 16 bands, attracted *the largest crowd ever to flood downtown for any event.* As one observer said on TV prior to a game, "*It's the Woodstock of sports.*"

## October 30, 1992

*A Top in Baseball?*

The first World Series game was held in 1903. This year was the Fibonacci *89th* World Series. The *emotion* surrounding the 88th and 89th World Series games was huge. The 1991 series was widely described as "the best World Series ever." It brought together two "worst-to-first" teams, a battle of underdogs (who are always popular). Fans were chanting and "tomahawk chopping" like college fraternity lunatics. The games attracted a high 24.0 share of TV viewers. The teams were greeted by throngs totaling nearly a million people at post-series hometown parades. The 1992 series was similarly emotional, particularly in Canada, as the Toronto Blue Jays took on the symbolism of national pride. Indeed, the Atlanta Braves were the only team ever to have been magically groomed for such a setting by a decade of billing as "America's Team." It was the first nationalistic World Series ever.

Among a list of overpriced items of the 1980s, most have fallen in value. Baseball players' salaries, as well as baseball cards and other memorabilia, are an exception. There is reason to believe these prices have just made a "spike top" along with fans' emotions. Here is a list of subtle hints that a major disaffection with baseball is in the offing.

1) The 1992 World Series had the *second lowest U.S. viewership ever*. (Experts say that the fact that one team was from out of the country was a minor factor.)

2) This year following the World Series, the Atlanta Braves were feted by *97% fewer* people than last year (24,000 vs. 750,000, according to newspapers).

3) CBS will have lost *half a billion dollars* broadcasting the World Series by the time its contract ends in *1993*.

4) On October 17, a 1937 jersey owned by the famed Lou Gehrig *failed to sell* at a Christie's auction. A Mickey Mantle card sold below expectations.

5) Veteran announcers and writers are griping on the air and in print about baseball's "selling out" to commercialism, evidenced by the World Series' nighttime TV scheduling, inflated salaries and players team-hopping for extra money. As one writer put it, "a unique event in our national life has been reduced to just another prime time special," too late for kids to watch, too late for dads to take them to the game and forty minutes longer due to commercials. "A leisurely and timeless event...is now about ratings and money." The national pastime is suddenly not *perceived* the same as it was. *This is a major change in the fans' emotional orientation toward baseball*, from the euphoric to the cynical.

6) While making money is certainly a virtue, baseball may be earning big dollars partly because today's adults enjoyed it as kids. If today's kids grow up without baseball, the money will disappear. In other words, baseball may be short sightedly living high off its capital base and not replacing it.

7) You may recall that our "Popular Culture" Special Report of 1985 concluded that baseball is a *bull market sport* (good guys are the good guys) and football a bear market sport (bad guys are the good guys). When the first World Series was played in October 1903, the Dow was making a low at 43. It was never lower during another World Series, enjoying an 89-year net uptrend. If stocks are topping in a major way as the Wave Principle argues, so is the uptrend in baseball's popularity. Here is corroborating evidence of a top. Atlanta acquired the Braves when it felt rich in 1966, the exact year of the top of Supercycle wave III (and the all time inflation-adjusted peak) in stocks. After all this time, the city has

now decided that it can afford a new $207 million state-of-the-art stadium, to begin construction in 1993. This decision qualifies as further evidence that the top of Supercycle wave V is upon us.

8) In the past few years, Hollywood has idolized baseball in *Field of Dreams, The Babe* and *A League of Their Own*. The widespread popularity of such sentiment toward a subject often coincides with a peak in interest among the population.

Could baseball be in for a 55-year period of decline in public favor? Signs of a turn are there. If you're an investor, take profits on baseball cards. If you're a player, sign a long term contract. If you're an owner, sell your club. Kids will soon be trading in their bats for helmets (or hockey pucks, soccer balls, or equipment for a more violent sport yet to come). If you're a real fan, you'll still find yourself griping about baseball some time in the 1990s.

## January 29, 1993

*The Elliott Wave Theorist* presented a full page of detailed discussion in the October 30 issue arguing that after 89 years, the trend of increasing popularity of baseball had given eight major signs of topping. (Immediately thereafter in the post-season, team owners signed 34 players to contracts guaranteeing $258 million. Barry Bonds will make over $45,000 a *game*, more than former top heroes made in a *year*; talk about locking in "Bond" yield....) That write-up apparently came at the top of a spike, just before a dramatic reversal. Here's a hot-off-the-press assessment of what's happened since.

Baseball-card stocks were hit by news that market leader Topps Co. will report its first quarterly loss in more than a decade.

Topps – which experienced strong insider selling last year – sank 31% to $8.50 from $12.25, on seven times its usual volume.

The announcement sent shares of several other companies in the sports-memorabilia business south yesterday. Among them was Marvel Entertainment group, the comic-book giant that purchased card manufacturer Fleer Corp. last September. Shares of Marvel, which according to analysts get roughly half its revenue from Fleer, slid $3.25, or 11.5%, to $24.875.

"The speculative bubble has burst in the new cards," said....
—*The Wall Street Journal*, January 27, 1993

Pete Kendall has just obtained the data on baseball attendance during this century. As you can see by the chart, the figures appear to have traced out an exceptional Elliott wave, ending with the 1991 season. Notice that the 1981 strike brought attendance back to the preceding fourth wave, just as it was scheduled to do. When the data is plotted on semilog scale (not shown), the entire rise from the World War I low in 1916 forms a wedge, which has bearish implications. At minimum, then, *baseball faces its largest percentage drop in attendance since it became the national sport.* At junctures such as this, it is even appropriate to consider that it may fall far enough out of favor in coming years to cease *being* the premier national sport.

Prechter
*The Elliott Wave Theorist* Special Report
September 29, 1994

*Chapter 16*

# Sports, Markets and Forecasting

*"Baseball faces its largest percentage drop in attendance since it became the national sport."*
— *The Elliott Wave Theorist*, January 29, 1993

The forecast cited above was based entirely on technical [socionomic] analysis, including (1) the Elliott wave pattern in baseball attendance figures, (2) Fibonacci time sequences, (3) the cultural connection between baseball popularity and bull markets in stocks, and (4) an extreme psychology, which included record attendance and revenue, record baseball card prices among collectors and "investors," record player salaries, highly emotional World Series in 1991 and 1992, and a period of production of numerous baseball movies. In other words, when baseball was at its all-time healthiest "fundamentally," that was the time to turn bearish.

The 1993 season was the biggest ever in terms of attendance, and that rise on the chart finished the "fifth of the fifth" wave from 1918. Bear market emotions were running high early in the 1994 season, as an amazing total of seven "bench-clearing brawls" had occurred in this gentleman's game before even two months had passed (ending near the May bottom in mood and the stock market). The 1994 season nevertheless promised a new home run record, a "first" in consecutive pitching awards, and a modern record for a batting average, keeping interest at fever pitch. The final sign of an exhaustive "blowoff" in national baseball psychology came with the production of Ken Burns' 18 1/2-hour PBS documentary, *Baseball*, which was completed literally days before the 1994 strike was called and therefore right at the peak of the long term trend. One observation by Burns is a loud echo of what *The Elliott Wave Theorist* has been saying, both in a specific and general sense: "We can measure our health as a country," says Burns, "by the health of the game itself." Burns' documentary divides baseball history into nine "innings," one for each decade. Is the game over?

As you can see by the chart, baseball's 1994 attendance figure has already resulted in the largest numerical drop in annual attendance in the history of baseball, thanks to a nationwide players' strike. This is a fitting start to what is expected to be the largest *percentage* drop in history. The 1995 season is reported to be in question, and if there is no season or a truncated season next year, the forecast will be fulfilled. However, corrective waves are often complex, so from now on, no particular year is crucial. The overall trend for many years should continue toward lower popularity, lower attendance (though a brief slight new high is possible within the corrective pattern) and more frustrating obstacles to success in resuming the old uptrend. As EWT postulated a year and a half ago, "At junctures such as this, it is even appropriate to consider

**Baseball Stadium Attendance Figures**
(in millions)

Source: Major League Baseball
© 1994 Elliott Wave International

---

## Is baseball on **Fallen Classic:**
## road to ruin?  **no Series in '94**

### Baseball season over with no end in sight to historical work stoppage

Baseball's season is over, sending the national pastime down a black hole

Wednesday, on the 34rd day of the second-longest work stoppage in major league history, acting baseball commissioner and owner of the Milwaukee Brewers Bud Selig canceled the remainder of the 1994 season.

And baseball fans have hit bottom.     SEPTEMBER 15, 1994

R.I.P. ... Baseball died in 1994. Oh, it'll be reinvented, but it'll never be the same and the game we all grew up with and loved is gone.

## **'95 in doubt**

## The Shortest Season
owners, union refuse to budge

Styles of Confrontation Made
A Bad Situation Worse;

## **a sad day for baseball**

---

that [baseball] may fall far enough out of favor in coming years to cease *being* the premier national sport." That thought, unthinkable at the time and outrageous today, still pertains. Certainly this warning from October 1992 has proved valid: "If you're a real fan, you'll still find yourself griping about baseball some time in the 1990s." The enormity of the trend change can be observed by the fact that only one other World Series was ever canceled, and that was in 1904.

For Fibonacci fans, it is worth noting that the remainder of the baseball season was canceled on the **34th** day of the players' strike. For stock market observers, it is worth noting that the players' union was *formed* in 1966, the year of the Grand Supercycle top in U.S. stocks, measured in constant dollars. Union activity, being exclusionary and confrontational, is a bear market phenomenon. The bear market in stocks and mood that should last a decade will undoubtedly wreak havoc on Major League Baseball, and will almost certainly result in an end to Major League Baseball's anti-trust law exemption and its absolute dominance of the profession. As *The Elliott Wave Theorist* said in October 1992, fans will begin turning to rougher sports, such as football, hockey, soccer "or a more violent sport yet to come." Since then, "gladiator" sports have become big on TV and no-rules boxing is back and selling tickets.

While EWT's forecast was one season early, the Fibonacci analysis employed actually therefore pertains to an even greater degree. The first World Series game was held in 1903, and there was none played in 1904, so EWT concluded that 1992 was the Fibonacci 89th World Series.

However, 1993 was the 89th *consecutive* World Series, apparently completing the Supercycle uptrend after an uninterrupted Fibonacci duration of 89 years. 1903's games were simply a false start. It was the 89th consecutive *season*, 1991, that produced the most emotionally charged playoffs ever (see description in November 1991 EWT), ending with what was widely called "the best World Series ever." 1991 and 1993, then, created a sort of a "double top," balancing, *each after 89 years*, the double beginning of 1903 and 1905.

The forecast cited at the start of this section was more important than most people realize, given its seemingly trivial subject. The first reason is that every successful forecast of this type serves further to demonstrate the breadth of application of the Wave Principle and technical analysis [socionomics]. Second, success in predicting social events *outside* markets serves to support the case in "Popular Culture and the Stock Market" (1985) that market trends and social trends are simply manifestations of deeper sociological trends. Third, it validates the specific conclusion in that essay that baseball, a "clean, good-guy sport," thrives in bull markets and suffers in bear markets when "rough, bad-guy sports" capture the fervor of the fans. Basketball is a bull market sport as well, and after coming from near bankruptcy at the end of Cycle wave IV and a roaring fifteen years of increasing success during wave V, it, too, now faces a players' strike. (In contrast, football should be on the verge of a surge in success.) Fourth is the practical value of such forecasts for people involved in a related industry. EWT was specific in its advice on October 30, 1992: "If you're an investor, take profits on baseball cards. If you're a player, sign a long term contract. If you're an owner, sell your club." Prices for collectible baseball cards peaked very near that time, and by April 1993, articles announced that "the market is crumbling." The stock of The Topps Company, Inc., maker of baseball cards, was at 16 at the time, and has now fallen 68% from its January 1992 record high of 20 1/4 (following the record-emotional 1991 season) to 6 1/2 today. The 1993 season, which set all-time attendance records, was the ideal time for any club owner to sell and the ideal time for a player to lock in a high salary, which many players did. Finally, correct forecasting of social trends increases the probability that our *market* forecasts will be accurate. As noted in the November 1992 EWT, "When the first World Series was played in October 1903, the Dow was making a low at 43. It was never lower during another World Series." The long term peak in baseball's fortunes is mirroring a peak in the long term value of stocks.

## Chapter 17

# *Basketball and the Bull Market*

**Introduction**

R.N. Elliott's discovery of the Wave Principle was derived from empirical evidence, in stock prices. Elliott soon realized, however, that the only possible explanation for the market's "rhythmical bias" was a mass psychological condition that went beyond Wall Street. In *The Wave Principle* (his first treatise on the subject in 1938), Elliott asserted that he had found a natural law that shapes "all social-economic processes." Until his death in 1947, Elliott focused almost exclusively on the stock market because it furnished an "abundance of reliable data," and it was the field where the predictive value of his work could be most practically applied. Elliott's greatest contribution in this regard was the use of his discovery to describe a bull market in stocks that is only now concluding. But if Elliott was right about the Wave Principle, the bull market that he predicted implied changes in other human endeavors along the same line of progress. Indeed, on a Grand Supercycle basis, the bull market is more than 200 years old, so the over-arching impact of this positive social mood trend must have created some uniquely bullish institutions, endeavors and achievements. Over the years, *The Elliott Wave Theorist* has identified many of these manifestations.

This report focuses on one more: the game of basketball. As a seasonal activity that is played far less frequently and observed by fewer people than the stock market, basketball has its limitations as a register of mass mood. But basketball has a long history and is an intensely competitive enterprise. It is a field where performance is closely monitored and recorded. This examination of that history shows the dominant influence of social mood on an American sport. Basketball is a coincident reflection of the fluctuating but net-rising mood behind the bull market of the last century. The game's structure, rules and fortunes have developed in a manner that is totally consistent with the ebb and flow of the bull market in stocks. By linking the peaks and troughs of this professional game to the same junctures in the stock market, this analysis will shed light on the way a bull market operates in the cultural realm.

When the market is rising, optimism is growing and people express that emotion by attending basketball games. Owners express it by starting teams and leagues. This report also reveals surprising consistencies in the play itself by exploring the sport's propensity to crown the greatest teams and heroes at the most explosive points in the bull market as well as its regression to violence and chaos in bear markets. We will also speculate on just what it is about basketball that keeps it in time with the rhythm of the stock market. In the final analysis, we return to Elliott's original intent and examine ways in which this application of the Wave Principle can be profitably employed.

### Basketbull

In 1985, when *The Elliott Wave Theorist* presented the first in-depth dissertation on the link between cultural behavior and the direction of stock prices, included was a descriptive chart showing the "cultural manifestations" that could be expected at four different phases of "mood trend." In the box for the field of sports in a "rising mood," we associated bull markets with "clean, good guy sports." At the time, the current bull market was unfolding and baseball was still the undisputed national pastime, so baseball was labeled "supreme." The next box, for a sports manifestation of a "peak positive mood," was left blank. With the biggest stock market peak in history behind us, or very nearly so, we can now fill in that blank. Basketball is the ultimate bull market game. Its dependence on speed, height and jumping ability are all physical expressions of a bull market; its use of "fouls" to minimize contact make it the epitome of a "clean, good guy sport."

The game's long rise to prominence supports the case well. Professional basketball was born in 1896, the same year as the Dow Jones Industrial Average. In that year, the Dow put in a low of 26.08, which has never been challenged. Over the last 100 years, the basketball season has correlated precisely with what is on average the best seasonal 6-month stretch for stock prices. The November to April period, pro basketball's regular season, coincides with an average stock-market gain of 2.6%, almost twice the average semi-annual gain of 1.34% since

1896. Basketball's off-season is among the worst for stocks. Over the last century, May to October has produced a gain of just 0.5%.

The status of the game in the 1990s is the final indication of its status as the premier bull-market sport. As of 1993, *Professional Sports Team Histories* declared that professional basketball "had risen to the pre-eminent sport in America. ...Much to the distress of baseball and football, basketball was now the favorite sport of American children." Basketball cards are the fastest growing sector of the card market. Six of the top eight U.S. sports spokesmen are NBA players or former players. Michael Jordan and Shaquille O'Neal, with $38 and $23 million in endorsements, respectively, are the two most valuable names in sports. Jordan is the most valuable celebrity spokesman, period.

### Attendance

Figure 1 shows how NBA attendance from 1968 through the first half of 1996 has generally tracked the Dow. Its steady growth was interrupted by consolidation in the mid-1970s and early 1990s. The only major divergence from the Dow came in the 1970s, when attendance slowed only briefly in the early part of the decade, then expanded through a devastating bear market in 1974. In real terms, however, the market did not hit bottom until 1982, foreshadowing the NBA's attendance boom of the 1980s by a year. The Dow's correction of 1990 was followed by a season of falling ticket sales in 1990-91. Today, football is off 2% from 1995 and baseball attendance is down 14%, but basketball attendance has continued to rise with the bull market. In 1995-96, the NBA sold a record total of 21 million tickets.

### The Basketball Expansion

In its earliest days, professional basketball was far less organized than it is today. Every pro player was a free agent who jumped from one team to the next, sometimes on a game-by-game basis. There were 12 different pro leagues in the East up through the 1920s, but none gained any national recognition. They paid according to minutes played: $1 per minute for "good" players. According to *The Pro Basketball Encyclopedia*, it took the signing of the original Celtics to exclusive contracts in 1922 to "bring order out of chaos in basketball." That signing took place months after the end of a multi-year net-sideways period of chaotic movements in stock prices. In 1925, during the Roaring Twenties bull market, basketball's first major league, the American Basketball

THE DOW JONES INDUSTRIAL AVERAGE
AND
NATIONAL BASKETBALL ASSOCIATION
ATTENDANCE
(data through 1995-96 season)

NBA

DJIA

© 1996 Elliott Wave International
Source: National Basketball Association

millions

*Figure 1*

League (#2 in Figure 2), was formed. By all accounts, the economic disruption that followed the stock market crash of 1929 led to an immediate reversal of fortune for pro basketball. The league went out of business after the 1930-31 season (#3). During the Great Depression, pro basketball slipped back into a hodgepodge of industrial leagues and traveling squads that would go from city to city to get up a game.

Basketball history shows that the psychology of team owners is strikingly similar to that of stockholders. They can be counted on to lay their money on the line at the worst possible moment. Even more remarkable is that these errors of enthusiasm infect both the game and the stock market at precisely the same times. In 1937, the year of the Depression-era high in the Dow Jones Industrial Average, pro basketball formed a new league. Of course, by the time the National Basketball

1. First professional basketball game, 1896
2. ABL, basketball's first major league, formed
3. ABL folds
4. 13-team NBL formed
5. NBL consolidates into 4-teams
6. Rival BAA formed bringing total number of teams to 23
7. NBL and BAA consolidate to form NBA
8. ABL formed
9. ABL folds
10. ABA formed, NBA adds 8 teams in 5 years
11. ABA/NBA merge
12. NBA expands by four teams
    (two in 1988-89 and two in 1989-90)
13. NBA expands to a record 29 pro teams
14. ABL and WNBA formed

© 1996 Elliott Wave International

*Figure 2*

League (#4) was up and running, the Dow was back in a downtrend. The Dow slumped to a Cycle degree bottom at the still-unbroken low of 1942 (#5), and the number of pro basketball teams hit a simultaneous 54-year low of four. In 1946, the Dow hit another important peak, and basketball owners bought in at the top. The number of major league basketball teams increased to a new high of 22 with the formation of a rival league, the Basketball Association of America (#6). After the 1948-49 season, the owners of the two leagues consolidated to form the National Basketball Association (#7). Again, pro basketball reflected the correction in social mood perfectly, as this retrenchment came at a major bottom. In fact, on an inflation-adjusted basis, it was the end of a Supercycle correction from 1929 (see dashed lines in Figure 2). This bottom led directly to the relentless third wave rise in stock prices and the game's revolution from "an elbows out, feet-on-the-floor game" to the high-scoring, high-flying affair we know today.

After further consolidation in the early 1950s, the eight-team NBA enjoyed an era of unprecedented stability. The next expansion didn't come until 1961, when a minor rival league was formed. The American Basketball League (#8) concluded its first and last season with the Dow at all-time highs. The following autumn brought the "Cuban Missile Crisis" low in stocks and, apparently, enough of a washout in bullish sentiment to ground the ABL (#9). The larger degree of the Cycle degree top of 1966 was reflected by the ebullient mood of pro basketball owners. Starting with the Bulls in 1966, the NBA added 8 teams through 1971. The expansion mirrored the big top in stocks, as the Dow got within 5% of 1000 five times during that span. In 1968, at a major speculative peak in stock prices, the American Basketball Association (#10) was launched. Initially, the ABA expressed the festive mood of the time. With it came a red, white and blue ball and a wide-open offensive game that featured the three-point shot. It was the only serious challenge to the NBA. Ultimately, the ABA came to be viewed as a negative influence on the game. The new league divided fan loyalties while creating a fierce competition for talent that drove up team cost structures. By 1974, the expansion had diluted the overall level of play and fostered a style that focused more on individuals than the team game that characterized the Boston Celtics of the 1950s and 1960s and the Minneapolis Lakers before them. Unlike its predecessors, the ABA actually survived the bear market of 1974, but not by much. News articles later revealed that even established NBA teams were losing money by 1974. The ABA was consolidating by 1974 and finally shut down in 1976. Four of its teams survived in the NBA.

Despite the box office rebound in the 1980s, the NBA was hesitant to add new franchises, just as it was in its initial heyday, the late 1950s and early 1960s. By 1987, however, owners could not contain their optimism. They were confident enough to schedule the addition of four franchises. Two were added for the 1988-89 season and two more for the 1989-90 season, in time to catch the correction of 1990 (which featured a deep decline in the Value Line index and a 50% drop in the Dow Jones Transports) and the game's own recession in 1990. The last two teams were added in 1995-96 to create a record total of 29 major league basketball franchises. Like the most recent leg of the bull market, pro basketball's current expansion lacks the breadth of its predecessors, but it is unprecedented in terms of duration. Just as there has been no bear market in stocks since 1974, the number of major league basketball teams has not declined since 1976. Also, two new leagues of professional women players have been formed. The American Basketball League started in October 1996 and the Women's NBA will initiate play in 1997.

## Rules and Mores

Another big clue to the bullish essence of basketball has been the century-long evolution in how the game is played. Early on, the character and rules of the game had more bear-market characteristics. The tempo was slow. A score of 20-15 would be considered a fantastic total. In its earliest days, basketball was referred to as "basket football" or "football in a gym." A goal was called a "touchdown," and players wore padded clothing that resembled early football uniforms. When young children play basketball, observers have noted the resemblance to a rugby scrum. Photos of the early game played on dirt fields suggest that this may be a fair approximation of what basketball was like initially. The amount of physical contact was clearly closer to hockey or rugby than a modern NBA game. By Rule 5 of Naismith's original 13 Rules of Basketball, contact was not actually allowed, but referees seldom blew the whistle.

"When you were fouled, it was a real one," remembered Joe Lapchick, an early pro. "With only one referee, the guy who did the fouling usually got away with it. So you belted him back. Players practically tore their opponents' shorts and pants off when playing defense. Players were geared for almost any indignity." Not just from the opposing team. Fans' favored form of expression was open hostility. "Spectators invariably got into the act," Lapchick added. "A common annoyance in highly industrialized cities was the practice of 'fans' who would flip stove bolts at the 'out-of-towners.'"

Also missing from the modern game: the cage. Originally, pro basketball was played behind a wire enclosure. The cages came down in 1929, the year the Dow hit its great peak of 381. A second referee was also added that year.

After pro basketball crashed with the market, its first step toward rebuilding came in 1932, which is the same year the Dow hit its low of 41. One of the game's big problems was that instead of advancing toward the goal, outmanned teams would simply use the whole length of the court to keep the ball out of the other team's hands. The

10-second rule was established to prevent this stalling. Although the pro game was still unable to organize effectively, there were some signs of underlying strength. From 1932 to 1937, the market rallied and, as it did, the "faster, cleaner amateur game" swept the nation. By 1937, Madison Square Garden was featuring regular, highly popular college double headers and tournaments. "The greatest year for rule changes" was 1937, the year of the Dow's recovery high and the return of the pro game. The changes emphasized offense. They included the elimination of the center jump after each basket, the legalization of the laceless ball and a rule making it illegal for defensive players to touch the ball when it was on the rim of the basket.

The college game continued to flourish in the 1940s. Pro basketball gained momentum after the 1942 low, but it would not shed its "image as a slow sluggish sport until the 1950s," which is when the stock market emerged from its slow, sluggish sideways correction of the 1940s. Until that decade, fans still wanted a game that was more like a bear market sport, hockey. In fact, pro hockey at the time was a more established sport that served as a model for pro basketball owners. The National Hockey League was established 10 years before the first pro basketball league, and it survived the Depression when pro basketball fell into chaos. "Owners knew from their experience with hockey that a little fight now and then was good for business. Rough stuff was quietly encouraged." Fights were still common in the first half of the 1950s, and into the later half of the decade many teams still employed "enforcers," tough, lesser talents who were used to intimidate opponents, as is common in hockey.

The basketball establishment has generally displayed a willingness to experiment at the outset of a big move in the Dow. At the beginning of Cycle wave III, pro basketball really began to change following a 19-18 game in November 1950, the lowest scoring game in NBA history, one year after the end of a 20-year correction and two years after the smallest DJIA annual range in history up to that time. After this game, stalling, once again, came to be viewed as a problem, particularly in the fourth quarter, when fouling was also common. Teams would get a small lead, foul, get the ball back and play keep away until the final buzzer. A series of rule changes followed. Among the remedies attempted was a jump ball after every foul shot in the last 10 minutes. But this backfired when teams contrived ways to get their best leapers in on the jump ball.

The speed and scoring that typify the modern game came in 1954 as the 24-second clock was adopted. The shot clock, which was instituted at the top of Intermediate (3) of Primary ③ of Cycle III, the powerful midpoint of the Supercycle from 1932, accelerated the energy and excitement of the game by forcing teams to shoot the ball within 24 seconds of taking possession. In this third-of-a-third wave up, the shot clock did for basketball what the electric guitar did for popular music, and at the same time.

Rule changes since the 1950s have all been minor by comparison. Perhaps the most significant were the addition of a third referee and the three-point shot. Both continued the long tradition of reducing the level of physical contact and opening the game up for more offense. They came in the late 1970s, when the Dow had put in its lows and was slowly building a base for the bull market of the 1980s and 1990s. Perhaps the most significant change was to the tone of the game, in the late 1950s and early 1960s. The trademark soaring of Michael Jordan would never have happened if certain conventions restricting the defender from undercutting opponents near the basket did not become standard operating procedure during this period. Basketball is still a contact sport, but nothing like the early game or even that of the early NBA. Crowds don't throw things at players, fights are rare and the game basically moves too fast for lead-footed bruisers to keep up. These days "touch" fouls are called frequently, especially if the person being touched is one of the league's stars.

## The Dynasties, the Heroes and Their Magic

To an amazing degree, pro basketball has greeted every major stock market advance since the 1920s with "blue chip" talents. In the 1920s, the original Celtics were the first heroes of the hardwood. Like all the great bull market basketball powers, the Celtics took the game to a new level with a series of innovations. The original Celtics introduced the give-and-go, switching man-to-man defense, and the pivot play. In the pivot play, the ball is thrown to a taller post player who turns and shoots or passes it to an open man cutting to the basket. The Celtics effective introduction of the play foreshadowed the era of the great centers in Cycle wave III of the next Supercycle. In fact, it wasn't until the 1920s that height was even considered an important trait in players. The first tall talent was Francis Meehan, 6-foot-7 center who came into the game in 1919 as the Dow was nearing its run to 381 in 1929. Meehan earned the fantastic total of $100 a game in the 1920s. Joe Lapchick was considered the best of the new breed. At 6-foot-6, the Celtics star said he was considered something of a freak.

In the early 1930s, when the Dow collapsed, the pro game fell so hard that there were *no* champions during that decade. Still, the amateur game prospered. On the court, the big breakthrough was the one-handed shot. Hank Luseitti of Stanford University first awed the Madison Square Garden crowd at the stock market high in 1937. Joe Fulks introduced the jump shot at the next stock market high, in 1946. Fulks led his Philadelphia team to a title with a scoring average of 23.2 points per game. With this new weapon, opponents considered Fulks "unstoppable." But Fulks' performance was only a glimpse of the talent to come. At .305, Fulks' shooting percentage was half that of modern-day league leaders.

From the low of 1949 until 1954, George Mikan and the Lakers won five out of six championships. At 6-foot-10, Mikan was the first to approach the height of modern-day big men and became the NBA's first great center of attention. After his retirement in 1954, both the league and the stock market hit a four-year plateau. From the spring of 1955 to 1958, four different teams won the NBA title. Over the same span, the Dow gained just 30 points, a cumulative gain of 6% in a decade of otherwise steady advances. From 1958 to the Cycle wave III high in 1966, the Dow doubled and the Boston Celtics owned the NBA, with eight straight championships. In keeping with the market's move to a higher plane, the Celtics raised the skills of the game to a whole new level. They brought a combination of size, speed, dribbling ability and shooting that was previously unknown to the NBA.

Their perfection of the fast break helped lift scoring leaguewide. Scoring averages rose from 79 to a league record of 107 in the early 1960s. The introduction of a shot clock was only one reason for the scoring outburst. Others ranged from better shoes and balls to the jump shot's replacement of the two-hand set shot as the standard method of scoring from the outside. The Celtics star was Bill Russell, the first in a long line of athletic giants that would become the league's hallmark. Wilt Chamberlain followed Russell by three years. Chamberlain was the first 7-footer, and, by many accounts, the greatest player ever to play the game. Clearly, Chamberlain delivered the game's greatest all-around individual performances. All of them came during the stock market's waves ④ and ⑤, ending at Dow 1000. From 1959 to 1966, Chamberlain won seven straight scoring titles (1959-66). He also hauled in most of his record total of 24,000 rebounds. In 1961-62, he averaged

25.7 rebounds and 50.4 points per game. On March 2, 1962, at a major psychological peak in the stock market immediately preceding the 1962 crash, Chamberlain scored 100 points in a single game.

More than any other event, Chamberlain's rivalry with Russell and the Celtics drove the NBA to its new standing as the most popular winter sport. The clashes continued until Russell's retirement in 1969, five months after a 13-year high in the Value Line Composite index. The year also marked the official end of the Celtics' glory years, as the Russell-coached Celtics won just one more title.

On the court and in the market, the 1970s were a mixed bag. While basketball's talent pool was as deep as ever, the bear market in social mood manifested itself in another period of shifting fortunes at the top. During the decade, not one NBA champion team managed to defend its title successfully. After the arrival of Kareem Abdul Jabbar in 1969, 7-footers became more routine and overall player heights approached their peak. In 1968, the former Celtic and pro coach, Joe Lapchick, noted that players had nearly perfected the required skills.

By the most definitive measure, higher stock prices, the fifth and final wave of the Supercycle bull market began in December 1974. The fifth- wave character of the advance manifested itself as more of a re-finement in the style of play than the introduction of any fundamentally different skills or techniques. All it took was a liberation of sentiment for the game to literally take off near the lows of 1974. The high-flying slam dunks of Julius Erving revealed the new mood. "My game is in the air," Erving said. Or, as one of his first coaches said, Erving "was the first to fly; he did things with a basketball nobody else had ever done."

Few of the earliest players were even capable of dunking the ball. In the 1940s, many were able, but few did. "Back then it was showing a guy up," explained Alex Hannum, a player and coach who came into pro ball in 1948. "Today it's showtime." The dunk shot was popular in the 1950s and 1960s, but until Erving came along, it was an efficient way to score rather than a gravity-defying display. In the 1960s, players never took to the air with abandon. That era's greatest play maker, Oscar Robertson, displayed a more cautious approach. He urged players "never to go up in the air unless they knew what they were going to do with the ball."

In the later part of 1970s, however, a basketball writer noted that more and more young players were "choosing the pleasure and uncertainty of going up in the air to create a situation, deciding what to do when in full flight." After outlawing the dunk in 1967, the college game permitted it again in 1976.

As the constant-dollar Dow approached a 16-year low in 1982, basketball hit some rough spots. Basketball purists did not embrace the new freer style. The new trend toward "slam dunking," for instance, was considered a side effect of the consolidation with the ABA and not a particularly positive influence. "Although it showcased a player's pure athletic skill and made for some great highlight film clips, this wide-open individual play was antithetical to the structured team play" that had characterized the great teams of the past. A 1978 headline in a *Sports Illustrated* read, "There's An Ill Wind Blowing For the NBA." Television had "focused attention on spectacular slam dunks, the epitome of playground ball, running replay after replay of them and eschewing explanations of the intricacies of team play." In *Professional Sports Team Histories*, the second half of the 1970s is recorded as a period of "serious trouble" for the NBA. The problems were classic cultural manifestations of a bear market: "rampant selfishness," "violence" and "drugs." In 1980-81, 16 of 23 NBA teams lost money, and attendance fell by 1 million.

Julius Erving's rise as a basketball icon personified the slow emergence of the bull market. He entered pro ball during the 1971-72 season with a relatively obscure Virginia franchise in the less established ABA. 1972 was the year the Dow closed above 1000 for the first time. In 1976, when the Dow surpassed 1000 for the second time, Erving won a title for the ABA's New York franchise and then raised his profile to a higher orbit with the NBA/ABA merger and a move to the Philadelphia 76ers, an established NBA franchise. "We got the Babe Ruth of basketball," said the 76ers general manager. During the entire 1980-81 season, the Dow moved back and forth across the 1000 barrier and Erving won his first and only NBA MVP award. At the outset of the 1982-83 season, the Dow penetrated 1000 for good and Erving went on to his first and last NBA championship.

The dominance of the two major stars of the 1980s, by contrast, was apparent from the start, just like the bull market. Larry Bird and Magic Johnson graduated to the pros in 1979. While their rivalry "never approached" Russell/Chamberlain "for intensity and ferociousness," it is sometimes credited with saving the NBA. Here again, however, it seems to have taken a clear uptrend in social mood, as reflected in stock prices, to get momentum really going on the court. Three months after the Dow touched a low of 729 in March 1980, which is still intact, the Johnson-led L.A. Lakers won their first title. Bird's Celtics won in 1981. After the Lakers won again in early 1982, Erving had his title.

On the professional level, the Bird-Johnson rivalry was not officially consummated until the conclusion of the 1983-84 season, when the Lakers and Celtics, the two powers of the 1950s and 1960s, met in the finals for the first time since the glory days of the Celtics. The initial big-league showdown between Larry Bird and Magic Johnson drew the largest television audience in NBA history and defined the game in the 1980s. At 6-foot-10 and 6-foot-8, respectively, Bird and Johnson were the best passing big men in the history of the game. "One of the reasons Bird and Magic made such a difference to the league was the breadth of their abilities. They could score as well as dish the ball in ways once done only by the Harlem Globetrotters against patsy teams in exhibitions." From 1980 to 1988, the Lakers and Celtics won 8 titles (3 by Boston, 5 by the Lakers). The Lakers ultimately emerged as the team of the decade when they defeated the Celtics in the 1987 finals. That's when the "'showtime' game hit its peak," with the Lakers "playing the finest example of fast-paced Western Conference basketball the league had ever seen," according to *Team Histories*.

The stock market crash of 1987 was coincident with the emergence of a new force in the league, the "Bad Boys" of Detroit. The Pistons "played a rough physical game of basketball that harkened back to the old days." *Team Histories* describes a contrast in play that was as stark as the difference in the Dow in the five years before August 1987 and the three-and-a-quarter years thereafter (a 250% rise versus a 15% decline). "This rivalry between Magic and Bird and their teams had revitalized the game. Never ugly or bitter, the two teams battled with skill and brilliance and consistently displayed the sport at its best. The Pistons, however, displayed, to many, the sport at its worst." In 1988, Los Angeles beat the Pistons by three points in the final game of a grueling seven-game series. The following year, the Laker reign ended as the team fell in four straight. The "Bad Boys" ruled through the stock market correction of that year with another championship in 1990. The Pistons' reign effectively ended with the bottom in October.

The rising star of the Chicago Bulls eclipsed all others at the outset of the 1990-91 season. The Bulls finished the year 10 games ahead of Detroit and then swept to a 4-0 victory in the playoffs. In 1991, 1992 and 1993, the Bulls won all three championships, the first team to win three in a row since the Celtics' string of eight through 1966. (The only other team to win three championships was the Minneapolis Lakers. Their streak was through 1954, the year the Dow finally surpassed the 1929 high.) In the spring of 1996, the Bulls seemed to match the Dow point for point as they won at a record rate and ended the season with 72 victories, the most ever. The old record of 69 was set by the Lakers in 1972, also a year leading to new highs for the Dow.

For whatever reason, in every period of substantial and continuous new highs in the Dow, there has been a pro basketball power that has thrived on the high ebb of social mood. The Bulls' reign in the last great wave of the Supercycle degree bull market from 1932 shows how deep the link between basketball and the stock market goes. The very name, which has caused big red snorting bulls to be stamped on caps, t-shirts and bumpers across America, is a vibrant and ubiquitous symbol of the connection. Skeptics may say it is just another coincidence, but the history of pro basketball in Chicago suggests more than an arbitrary symbol. In the early 1960s, Chicago's NBA franchise was called the Packers. The team struggled, and the owners tried to repair fan apathy with a new name. The Zephyrs didn't last a season. In 1966, the year of the great Dow peak, the NBA returned to Chicago. As the *Bulls*, pro basketball finally survived there. Few, if any, fans see any relationship between their devotion to both the Bulls and their mutual fund portfolios. This is how it is with a collective psychological state: too pervasive—perhaps even poetic—to be recognized by most people.

### Michael in Microcosm

To put an even finer point on the athletic expression of social mood, consider the professional history of Michael Jordan. Jordan first entered the cultural consciousness in 1982, the year of the bull market's blast-off. As a freshman at North Carolina, he hit a shot in the last 16 seconds to win the NCAA college championship. In 1984, he joined the Bulls and was named Rookie of the Year. In 1987, the year of a substantial Dow high at 2723, he won his first MVP award and had a single-season scoring average of 37 points per game, which remains the highest since Wilt Chamberlain. His lifetime scoring average of just over 30 points per game is the highest ever.

As the highest-paid athlete in the world and Madison Avenue's most prolific endorser, Jordan's image is also locked to the stock market. In Figure 3, notice how the two fortunes expand and recede together. Plagued by gambling accusations and the death of his father, Jordan retired before the 1993-94 season. The sabbatical coincided perfectly with a correction in the market. Jordan came out of retirement in March 1995 and accompanied the Dow past 5000. The stinging personal

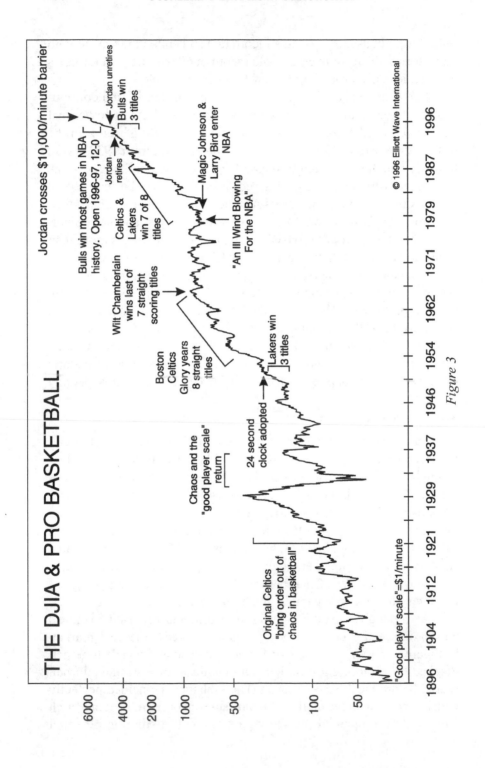

*Figure 3*

attacks that drove Jordan from the game two years ago have all but disappeared. It's not that Jordan is perfect; he's still accused of various shortcomings, but "criticism of Jordan doesn't stick," *Sports Illustrated* noted in a recent profile. Why? Because Jordan enjoys a "devotion that criticism can't touch." In the fall of 1996, as the Dow pushed past 6000 in a relentless succession of new highs, Jordan drove the Bulls to their best start ever, unveiled a new perfume and premiered as the star in a feature film that *The Wall Street Journal* calls the "ultimate commercial movie." "Michael is superman, plain and simple," concludes *Sports Illustrated.* "Dab on a little Michael Jordan and you're dabbing on the scent of success," claims a news article headlined "Smell Like Mike." Smell like a sweaty athlete? Only the hero factor can explain the depth of Jordan's popularity. *The Elliott Wave Theorist* has observed a cultural preference for heroes in bull markets. As the game's greatest hero, Jordan personifies the happiness and energy of the bull market just as George Mikan did in the early 1950s, Bill Russell in the 1960s and Magic Johnson in the 1980s, bull markets all.

**Waves and Means**

How does a wave of mass emotion express itself in the performance of a single individual? As the center for the Boston Celtics in the 1960s, Bill Russell was the most valuable player on the best team in basketball history. In his autobiography, he offers some observations that might explain how a bull market game might manifest itself in the actions of solitary participants. He describes the atmosphere of a big game as a kind of "spell" that "surrounded" fans, coaches, opposing players and "even the referees." "To me, the key was that both teams had to be playing at their peaks, and they had to be competitive. The Celtics could not do it alone...That mystical feeling usually came with the better teams in the league that were challenging us for the championship...It usually began when three or four of the ten guys on the floor would heat up; they would be catalysts, and they were almost always the stars in the league. If we were playing the Lakers, for example, (Jerry) West and (Elgin) Baylor and (Bob) Cousy or Sam (Jones) and I would be enough. The feeling would spread to the other guys and we'd all levitate. Then the game would just take off, and there'd be a natural ebb and flow that reminded you how rhythmic and musical basketball is supposed to be."

Russell says he never admitted it to his teammates, but, at such times, winning itself didn't matter to him as much as reaching that higher plane. "On the five or ten occasions when the game ended at that special level, I literally did not care who had won."

Players at substantially lower levels of play have reported similar sensations. Essayist and schoolyard ballplayer John Boe wrote, "It is popular to talk about rhythm and flow in basketball. And when playing basketball, you indeed feel the rhythm, flow with the group mind. I play basketball in order to experience those moments when I feel in rhythm, and it is more a matter of the rhythm having me than of my having the rhythm."

The structure of the game produces a "dance of ascendancy," wrote George Kovacs in *Hoops Zen*. "The obvious advantages of basketball over other sports as a medium of spiritual self-development is the idea—the ideal—of *upward striving*...(an) unrestrained yet disciplined challenge of the mortal entity against gravity and other oppressive earthbound limitations. James Naismith's notion of hanging a peach basket 10 feet off the ground to taunt and tantalize athletic pretenders was a stroke of genius in forcing hoopsters to elevate their endeavors and objectives as well. Thanks in considerable measure to 'upward striving,' no other sport, no other athletic activity—perhaps no other human activity—allows, encourages, enhances, necessitates the poetry, the poetic movement of the human body like hoops." That ideal of upward striving, we contend, derives from social mood and is manifest also in rising stock prices.

Another element in basketball's bullish essence may be the central importance of the ball. Boe once noted how newspaper photos of basketball games capture the ball frozen above the rim with the eyes of players and fans fixed upon it. "When the game is on TV, there are millions of eyes focused upon the same ball. This is a collective spiritual experience; the group consciousness is united by a single thing, the ball. The ball acts like the mandala of Tibetan systems of concentration and meditation, focusing the psyche of the individual, uniting the consciousness of the group."

According to the Wave Principle, we've been in a bull market at Grand Supercycle degree for more than 200 years, so it's hard to imagine what a bear market sport would be like. We envision something along the lines of boxing, where it's man against man. There is no ball to displace man's natural aggression and no hoop to make us focus on any loftier ambition than survival. As Russell tells us, basketball at its highest level doesn't pit men against each other. It's about technique and intelligence and working together to place a rubber ball through a round goal that is out of reach. Of a true bear market game, we suspect that it could never be said that winning didn't matter, as Russell said of his sport at its peak. Ball games have had their place in North American culture since before Columbus arrived. Various tribes played different games with round rubber balls. Black Elk, an Ogala Sioux priest, described a rite called "The Throwing of the Ball." He says it was born when a sacred ball was offered to the six directions—"North, South, East, West, *Up* and *Down*." The ball is a spirit that is "at every direction and is everywhere in the world." A buffalo calf then nudged the ball to a man and said, "This universe really belongs to the two leggeds, for we four legged people cannot play with a ball...It is the two legged men alone who, if they purify and humiliate themselves, may become one with—or may know" the ball.

### The Bottom Line

One of the great benefits of the Wave Principle is that it inspires such universal questions. Another is that none of them have to be answered for the speculator to take advantage of changes in social mood.

In November 1992, for instance, *The Elliott Wave Theorist* illustrated how cultural studies can be profitably pursued with the help of the Wave Principle, saying, "There is reason to believe that [baseball card] prices have just made a 'spike top' along with fans' emotions." Within three months, shares of The Topps Co., a producer of baseball cards, were halved, and the great baseball card bust of the 1990s was on. A July 1996 *Sports Illustrated* report on the card market described a textbook investment bubble. On the way up "there was this notion that sports cards were scarce," "the secondary market exploded" and "demand appeared insatiable." Next, "dozens of manufacturers sprouted, and hobby shops spread like pollen." A combination of oversupply, Wall Street hype and "greed by the leagues" are said to have pushed the market over the edge. Eventually, there came a "selling frenzy" and "a shake-out" of dealers across the country. "Crash is not too strong a word to describe what has happened."

This article and others through the fall of 1996 contend that baseball and the card market are bouncing back. They cite a rebound in baseball attendance, a new all-time high contract amount for a baseball player, the record purchase of a baseball card for $645,000 and a new labor agreement for Major League Baseball. While these items do reflect the continuing influence of the bull market, the top is behind us in the big picture. The November issue of *The Elliott Wave Theorist* noted that 1996 baseball attendance was still 14% lower than the all time high of 1993. In 1993, we showed a 90-year chart of baseball attendance and noted the completion of a clear five-wave structure. This pattern means that baseball's three-year-old high in popularity will not be exceeded by any substantial margin. Basketball's bull market, on the other hand, is still in force. *Sports Illustrated*'s anticipation of a turnaround in the card market was based partially on the fact that "basketball cards are the fastest growing sector." The evidence in this report suggests the opposite of the article's implication. Basketball, not the market for trading cards, is likely to reverse course, and in the other direction.

To paraphrase our advice to baseball interests in November 1992: If you're an investor, take profits on basketball cards. If you're a player, sign a long term contract. If you're an owner, sell your club. If you're a fan, prepare to gripe increasingly about the game of basketball after the stock market reverses to the downside.

The NBA's expansion to an all-time high of 29 teams, the addition of two new professional leagues, the total dominance and worldwide popularity of the Olympic Dream Team, the Bulls settlement of a suit with the NBA that will make "record numbers of Bulls games available on free television," the inauguration of a women's NBA, the likelihood of a long term peak in stock prices and the overall euphoria for the sport all say that a peak in basketball is at hand.

The elation surrounding basketball's brightest star is particularly telling. Last May, the aura of giddy excitement that encircled Jordan as the Bulls completed the greatest season in basketball history and sailed through the playoffs was exceeded only by that surrounding a small selection of NASDAQ stocks. A June 19 *USA Today* article was headlined "Michael Jordan's bigger than basketball: he's a pop icon." A sports sociologist said fans "worship Michael Jordan with much the same intensity as they worship religious figures." Another author invoked the name of the hero of Cycle wave III, calling Jordan a "black Elvis with wings." In the past, *The Elliott Wave Theorist* has successfully used milestone contracts (like Michael Jackson's March 1991 deal with Sony) to pinpoint a major trend change in the recipient's popularity. Jordan's $30 million contract for 1996 is the highest ever. Jordan negotiated the deal over the phone in a half hour. It pays him $5.8 million more than other teams are allowed to pay *all* their players and 10,417 times the original good-player scale of $1 per minute. Throw in $40 million more in endorsements, his top billing (over Bugs Bunny) in a $95 million movie and a $20 million investment in the new Michael Jordan "aroma," and the unrivaled extreme in popularity that Jordan represents is unmistakable and historic. Two other players recently signed long-term contracts valued at more than $100 million. History suggests that pro basketball's next consolidation could lag a Dow decline, but not by much. Salaries, attendance and the number of teams will unquestionably accompany the market down as people's attention moves away from this "bull market sport" and toward more violent fare.

This report on basketball is valuable from another perspective: Throughout this century, when enthusiasm for the sport has been unbridled, the stock market has fallen on hard times. "Top" signals in the sport are top signals for stocks.

As in the stock market, the euphoric sentiment for the sport masks signs of underlying fundamental weakness. They include the aging of the league's stars, a sudden decline in scoring and a crash in shooting percentages to 44.4% for so far this year, the lowest total in at least eight years. In another development that has baffled long-time observers, NBA referees are suddenly making the traveling call. A player travels by taking more than one step without dribbling. "For years, traveling in the NBA was like jaywalking—illegal but generally accepted. Not anymore. ...Even the unwritten rule that allowed superstars more liberty in regard to traveling no longer exists." The enforcement of this original rule is a subtle but profound change from the trend that began with the 10-second rule in 1932. It violates the long tradition of opening the game up by *restricting* rather than abetting the scorer. Others have observed a decline in the level of play. Expansion and the entry of players at younger and younger ages have thinned the talent pool appreciably. As one star, Charles Barkley, said recently, "There are only five good teams in the league. The rest are terrible." Finally, there has been a decline of gate receipts through the first 22 games of the 1996 season.

Non-fans should not dismiss these developments as trivial. The bull market in stocks has run so long that there are many outward examples of basketball's and the stock market's co-dependence on a rising social mood. One example was an editorial in *Pension & Investment* magazine urging Jordan to endorse a family of mutual funds that teaches kids how to invest in stocks. P&I suggested that Jordan entice children into the market by explaining that they could use the proceeds from their stock investments to purchase Nike sneakers. This spoon-feeding of the mania for stocks with the mania of basketball is based on the mistaken belief that the rising mood is a permanent fact of life. Fortunately for investors, it is so deeply entrenched that it has provided the means to profit by taking the hints of basketball's coming decline. First, it is a signal that an overall bear market in stock prices is not far off, a warning that could prove very valuable. More specifically, one might consider the implication for shares of Nike Inc. The firm recently paid $40 million for the rights to rookie golfer, Tiger Woods. It did so after a decade-long increase of more than 50 fold in its stock price, an increase that was built on the exploits of Jordan and other heroes of the bull market. Woods' contract represents an unprecedented willingness to *speculate* on the *next* bull market hero. "Air" Nike is a fiscal incorporation of the psychology of expanding expectations. When the bubble breaks, the next big profit will fall to the Nike short sellers.

### The Coming Changes in Trend

The Grand Supercycle degree of the current trend change in social mood suggests a big retracement in basketball. The game will probably survive the bear market, but not without regressing back toward its roots. The first and most noticeable sign of the trend change will occur when Michael Jordan and a host of other longtime stars retire or become less effective. Based on *The Elliott Wave Theorist's* observation of a rising demand for anti-heroes in bear markets, Dennis Rodman rather than Jordan is the role model for the NBA's immediate future. Rodman is not a scorer. His special talent is getting fouled by his opponents as they try to score. He sports fluorescent hair, tattoos and a penchant for cross-dressing and antagonizing opponents. Whereas Michael Jordan saves the NBA with teamwork in his new cartoon movie, Rodman's credo is that "individuality is the most important thing in life." After this season, clean-cut team players will be remembered as the heroes of a bygone era. Shortly thereafter, football, hockey, soccer or some other rough game will replace basketball as the No. 1 sport. Eventually, fans will turn hostile, and fights will be common. Ultimately, salaries will crash and player heights will fall. Finally, when the new leagues have consolidated or shut down and falling attendance and TV ratings have caused several NBA owners to fold or move, Michael Jordan's true heir will appear. As he rises, history says, the stock market won't be far behind.

## REFERENCES

Hill, Bob. (1988). *The amazing basketball book: The first 100 years.* Louisville, KY: Devyn Press.

Kovacs, George. (1968). *Hoops zen: The spiritual beauty of basketball.* Lewiston, NY: Edwin Mellen Press.

Lapchick, Joe. (1968). *50 years of basketball.* Englewood Cliffs, NJ: Prentice Hall.

Neft, David and Cohen, Richard M. (1989). *The NBA's official encyclopedia 1891-1989: Pro basketball.* New York: St. Martin's Press.

Pluto, Terry. (1992). *Tall tales.* New York: Simon & Schuster.

Rudman, Daniel. (1980). *Take it to the hoop.* Richmond, CA: North Atlantic Books.

Salzberg, Charles. (1987). *From set shot to slam dunk: The glory days of basketball in the words of those who played it.* New York: Dell-Dutton.

Kendall
*The Elliott Wave Theorist*
April 30, 1999

## Chapter 18

# *Fibonacci Glory Days for Sports Heroes*

It's striking that within a few weeks of each other, the giant, singular figures of three major sports—basketball's Michael Jordan, hockey's Wayne Gretzky, and football's John Elway—have retired. Only pro baseball was left out of this remarkable trend. Or was it? Baseball's Joe DiMaggio died in recent weeks and was eulogized as a legend among legends, a man of singular grace and style, the "classiest" player of them all. [Note: Ted Williams died with similar accolades in 2002.—Ed.] It's remarkable that this pattern is playing out now, with the stock market also suggesting the "glory days" are pretty much over.

— EWT subscriber Rick Peterson

This gentleman has learned a lot from reading *The Elliott Wave Theorist*, where we argue that these trends are not coincidence, but intimately related. These men and their stature are products of bull market social forces.

Getting out on top and *at* the top will not be the feat for which these heroes are remembered, but it may be the one that goes the furthest toward preserving their bright legacies. These guys played exactly the right number of seasons. For Jordan and DiMaggio, it was 13, and for Gretzky it was 21. Is the perfect career length a Fibonacci number? To come closer to an answer, we investigated the duration of other all-time greats in their respective sports and found a clear tendency for the number of years played to cluster around Fibonacci numbers. In baseball, for instance, the all-time top ten players (as identified by the *Sporting News*) had an average career length of 21.3 years. In hockey, Wayne Gretzky broke the scoring records of Gordie Howe, who played 35 seasons, one more than a Fibonacci 34. The career of the sport's other undisputed great, Bobby Orr, spanned 13 years. The all-time leading goaltender (in victories and shutouts) was Charlie Sawchuk, who played 21 NHL seasons. When Jordan retired, *USA Today* issued a list of the greatest basketball players. It showed that, plus or minus one year, all played a Fibonacci number of seasons. In order of greatness, they were Michael Jordan (13), Wilt Chamberlain (14), Bill Russell (13), Kareem Abdul-Jabbar (20), Larry Bird (13), Earvin "Magic" Johnson (13), Oscar Robertson (14) and Jerry West (14).

For the record, we found no strong Fibonacci correlations among the greatest football players other than a 13-year career by Walter Payton, the game's all-time leading rusher. EWT opined in 1985 that unlike baseball and basketball, football is a "bear market" sport. Therein may lie a reason for the difference.

Viewed against their productivity, some of the best athletes reveal an all-too human tendency to overstay their greatness. Babe Ruth is a prime example. After a Fibonacci 21 brilliant seasons with the Red Sox and Yankees, he jumped to the National League, where he had 6 homers and hit a measly .181 for the Braves in 1935. Hank Aaron broke Babe Ruth's home run record in his 21$^{st}$ season as a Brave. After that, he had two forgettable seasons with the Milwaukee Brewers. Willie Mays, who played 22 seasons with the Giants, is ranked right behind Ruth as the second best player on the all-time list. But the papers are still talking about what happened when he went back to New York and the Mets in his final season. "It was gut wrenching to see Willie Mays misplay flyballs in the 1973 World Series," said the April 26 issue of *USA Today*. This evidence indicates that when a great player chooses to play past his Fibonacci time, his abilities deteriorate rapidly, driving him to quit a year later.

Quitting at the top is the best move one can make. It may not seem as Herculean a feat as their scoring records, but Jordan and Gretzky wisely turned down enormous incentives to play one more season. Jordan's retirement cost the Chicago Bulls all hope of contention, the city of Chicago an estimated $1 billion and his heirs well over $30 million. Gretzky's own wife was reportedly trying to convince him to play one more season. The ability of so many of these heroes to resist such pressures is another display of the classic form that made them the great men that they are. (For guidance on how *you* can time your big exit, read pages 316-318 of *The Wave Principle of Human Social Behavior*.)

*[Note: Jack Welch retired from General Electric in his 34$^{th}$ year with the company and in his 21$^{st}$ year as CEO. The Beatles made hit recordings for 8 years, then broke up. Our observation with respect to Fibonacci durations for basketball celebrities, we suspect, probably extends to "bull market" celebrities of all types.—Ed.]*

*Chapter 19*

# Another Home-Run Year

For the first time since 1986 and 1987, the two seasons leading to the 1987 crash, a new record for the total number of homers (5,064 last year) is likely to be set in consecutive years. Home runs are running 11.1% ahead of last year's pace. On top of that, Mark McGwire and Sammy Sosa are replaying last year's home run race. But "there is no home run mania sweeping the nation—decidedly *unlike* last summer." "The homer has become commonplace," laments Bob Costas. The other day, when people barely even noticed that McGwire had "set yet another incredible" record by hitting his 50th homer for a fourth straight year, the papers even came up with a name for it, "chronic milestone fatigue. "Too many baseball records are falling in too short a period of time to keep the national interest." This is another cultural manifestation of the diverging social mood covered in the Cultural Trends section of the April *Elliott Wave Theorist*. This divergence actually extends back to 1992-1993, when we called for a reversal in baseball's attendance based on a five-wave, century-long pattern in attendance figures. On a per game basis, the highs of 1993 have not been exceeded.

The following graphic from *USA Today*'s cover story on the fans' "ho-hum" reaction to the greatest home-run display in history suggests that performance will eventually catch up to the slowly developing bear market in fan interest. It shows that measured in 10-year spans, the bull market in home runs has traced out a five-wave pattern of its own. The fact that the multiple from high to low is 2.618 strengthens the case for a peak this decade.

As we have said before, in the cultural realm, the completion of five waves leads to changes in style and performance simply because "it's time." Sluggers will tire and stop hitting home runs just as fans become tired of watching them. In April, EWT noted that the greatest athletes seem to have internal clocks that reflect mass changes in social mood to an almost uncanny degree. That's why they keep getting "out on top and *at* the top."

**DOES THIS PATTERN LOOK FAMILIAR?**

Home runs per 100 at-bats

© 1999 Elliott Wave International

Source: USA TODAY
* Data through August 5

August brought two additions to our list of retiring greats. Detroit Lions running back Barry Sanders and tennis champion Steffi Graf (easily one of the greatest female tennis players in history) "shocked" the sports world by calling it quits. Sanders retired even though he could have become the pro game's all-time rushing leader this year. Graf's decision came just two months after she had won her 22$^{nd}$ major tournament in May. Like Michael Jordan, Graf had turned pro in 1982 at the lift-off of the bull market and emerged as a dominant force in 1987 when she won her first major tournament. She was also ranked as the sport's No. 1 women's player for a Fibonacci 377 weeks, a record. But "when the fun stopped, Steffi Graf did what so many superstars have done in recent months. She said goodbye. 'I just feel the time is right to move on.'"

*[Just as sports achievements reach new heights in bull markets, so sports failures set records in bear markets. For example, the all-time record for hits against one pitcher occurred in a 17-inning game in which a hapless hurler gave up a whopping 29 hits. The time was July 1932, the month of the bottom in the biggest bear market in U.S. history to date.—Ed.]*

*Chapter 20*

# Pro Wrestling and the Bull Market

The February 7 *Newsweek* cover story asks *why* professional wrestling is "No. 1 in Cable, Videos, Toys & Books." *The Elliott Wave Theorist* answered this question fifteen years ago. Back in 1985, EWT explained that pro wrestling, "with its well-defined representatives of good and evil," is popular in bull markets. Definitive morals and heroes accompany a bull market; blurred morals and mixed heroes accompany a bear market. Indeed, the history of the World Wrestling Federation, as described by *Newsweek*, parallels that of the bull market.

The modern era began in 1982 (the year of the low in inflation-adjusted stock prices), when Vince McMahon took control of the company and started its expansion. "In the mid-1980s, it grew more popular than ever. For a 1987 show at the Pontiac Silverdome, the company sold 93,000 tickets. Then trouble struck." It lasted a little past the stock market's correction in 1990. Since 1996, "wrestle mania" and the stock mania have actually be indistinguishable in some ways. "Wrestle mania," with its good guys and bad guys, has exploded to become the dominant form of cable television entertainment, while the stock mania has exploded to become a dominant form of network television entertainment, with its "good guys" (bulls) and "bad guys" (bears). Combining the two trends, the WWF is now a publicly traded stock with a market capitalization of $1 billion.

On February 5, WWF president McMahon appeared on CNBC and in announcing a new plan to expand into professional football said, "I don't think we can fail." "Performers can make $5 million, plus stock options," *Newsweek* reported. In one insightful, behind-the-scenes note, *Newsweek* quoted a veteran wrestler boasting about his investment performance. Another wrestler, who plays the lovable Mankind and the redneck psychopath Cactus Jack, said, "When a new guy comes in, I try to give him financial tips." He has also written a book, which is No. 3 on *The New York Times* nonfiction list. His nemesis, the Rock, has a book, too, and it hit No. 1 on January 30. As Paul Montgomery (*Universal Economics*, Legg Mason Wood Walker, Newport News, VA) has noted, the standing of these books indicates "that public interest in pro wrestling could not get any greater than it is right now." That sentiment precisely reflects the stock market's level of popularity as well.

*Chapter 21*

# Top Tick for Basketball

In December 1996, *The Elliott Wave Theorist* released a Special Report, "Basketball and The Bull Market," which asserted, "Basketball is the ultimate bull market game." The largest part of that report was a four-page section called, "The Dynasties, The Heroes and Their Magic." It began, "To an amazing degree, pro basketball has greeted every major stock-market advance since the 1920s with "blue chip" talents." It traced out a 75-year history of precise correlations and ended with a long paragraph on Michael Jordan. "To put an even finer point on the athletic expression of social mood, consider the professional history of Michael Jordan. Jordan first entered the cultural consciousness in 1982, the year of the bull market's blast off." From that moment when he hit the game-winning shot to become a national champion, his career has kept an uncanny rhythm with the bull market.

On January 14, 2000, the very day of the all-time high in the Dow, Jordan added a final, perfect distinction to his unparalleled legacy as personal embodiment of "the happiness and energy of the bull market." He became a team owner. The world's greatest Bull is now the head Wizard, with complete control over the NBA's Washington franchise. In an analogy to today's stock market, Jordan may be a blue chip that is making a personal new high while the broader group is sinking. TV ratings are down 15% from strike-stunted levels a year ago. The first NBA all-star game without Jordan saw a 35% ratings decline. Apparently, blue-chip athletes, like blue-chip stocks, are the last to fall in with a downturn in social mood. Fall he will, though, and tying his fortune to a team will probably end up being a mistake.

The underlying trend in basketball's fortunes has been deteriorating for some time. The chart of Nike's stock on the next page tells the story. As we said in the "Bottom Line" of our 1996 basketball special, "'Air' Nike is a fiscal incorporation of the psychology of expanding expectations." Our recommendation at that time is shown on the chart.

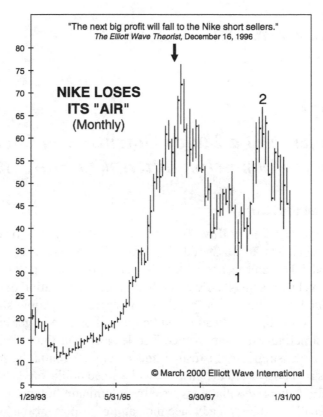

"The next big profit will fall to the Nike short sellers."
*The Elliott Wave Theorist,* December 16, 1996

**NIKE LOSES
ITS "AIR"**
(Monthly)

© March 2000 Elliott Wave International

Despite a decline in price of more than 50%, Nike stock appears to be in a third wave down, which means that it still has much further to fall. "People have kind of OD'd on big-name athletes, and there's definitely a trend to get away from them," says a sporting goods industry official. Shoe contracts have "always been the bellwether endorsement" for star basketball players. Still, the media and the players themselves seem merely puzzled by their fall from grace. They should be seriously concerned, because the chart of Nike actually understates what their sport is up against. Converse, Inc., the maker of Chuck Taylor All-Star canvas sneakers, is a better indicator because it is more of a pure play in the sport, and it has a deeper history with it. In the 1950s and 1960s, Chuck Taylors were "worn by 99% of NBA players." In the 1980s, its ads featured Larry Bird and Julius Erving, the brightest stars in the game, singing the praises of Converse shoes as "limousines for the feet." Converse stock reached its high of 28 two months after our special report. Since then it has declined an amazing 97%. This is a forewarning of the coming fortunes of professional basketball.

*Chapter 22*

# Evidence of a Major Downturn in Social Mood: Plummeting Interest in Ballgames

## A Baseball Forecast

In 1985, *The Elliott Wave Theorist*'s original study on "Pop Culture and the Stock Market" asserted, "Trends in sports reflect the prevailing mood." The emergence of a bull market produces an escalating energy level that is physically embodied in the organization of athletic competitions. As the rise in social mood progresses, people share the optimism of the time by heading out to the ball park in larger numbers and constructing elaborate events. The leagues and their champions become increasingly sophisticated and revered. Eventually, massive stadiums are constructed to house the widespread public obsession with sports. EWT theorized that a reversal by a dominant bull market sport like baseball could be "an advance indicator of important fundamental events." In late 1992, EWT put this theory to the test by publishing the following forecast for baseball:

> *A Top in Baseball?*
> Signs of a turn are there. If you're an investor, take profits on baseball. If you're a player, sign a long-term contract. If you're an owner, sell your club.

In early 1993, we counted a five-wave rise in total baseball ticket sales since 1901 and concluded, "At minimum, baseball faces its largest percentage drop in attendance since it became the national sport." The wave count from 1993 is displayed in Figure 1 with an updated version in Figure 2 showing that total ticket sales collapsed in 1994 then rebounded to a B-wave high. At 73.4 million, the 2000 total is slightly higher than the total for 1993, but it is labeled a bear market rally for several reasons. The key factor is that the implied attendance growth is illusory. First, observe in Figure 3 the lack of a new high in

Wave count in the January 29, 1993 issue
of *The Elliott Wave Theorist*

MAJOR LEAGUE BASEBALL
TICKET SALES
(prices shown in millions)

Source: Major League Baseball
© 1993 Elliott Wave International

*Figure 1*

MAJOR LEAGUE BASEBALL
TICKET SALES
(prices shown in millions)

Source: Major League Baseball
© 2001 Elliott Wave International

*Figure 2*

the *per-team* ticket sales. The number of tickets sold in the average major league city peaked in 1993, the season following EWT's forecast. Further, the sales totals shown in these charts represent tickets sold, *not actual attendance*. Brokers report that demand for seats has plunged. In fact, so many season tickets are not being used that scalpers sell some of the best seats in the house at "60% to 80% below face value." So in terms of reflecting popularity, the new high in Figure 2 is illusory and typical of B-wave personality (see *Elliott Wave Principle*, pp.79-81).

Another clue to the major change in the primary trend in baseball's fortunes is the plunge in television ratings for the All-Star game and the World Series. The total number of fans tuning in to baseball's two most important annual events actually topped the year before baseball's 1993 attendance peak, the same year as EWT's forecast. After successfully foreshadowing baseball's initial decline in ticket sales, TV ratings have continued to contradict a slight new high in total sales with a decline to their lowest level in history. This is a bearish non-confirmation of the new high in total ticket sales. The five-wave pattern of this decade-long trend announces the onset of a major bear market.

An interesting aspect of our forecasts is that they involve both classes of socionomic forecasting. *The Wave Principle of Human Social Behavior* defined the two types as:

1) predicting trends in social phenomena based upon waves within the phenomena themselves, and

2) predicting economic, political, social, cultural and other trends based upon the wave position of overall social mood such as the stock market.

We identified the 1992/1993 peak by the first method. The second method points to a B-wave high in 2000 or 2001, coinciding closely with the peak in stock prices. So, the B-wave rally has put EWT's forecast for a major trend change on track by both socionomic methods.

Two other measures of baseball's bull market, player contracts and team values, continued to climb with the stock market through the 1990s. These are less direct registers of grassroots demand for the game. They have continued higher through wave B, much as the "nifty fifty" stocks made new all-time highs in 1973 despite lower highs in breadth and the inflation-adjusted averages. Figure 4, showing the value of the top player contract per year since 1980 suggests a sharp reversal immediately ahead. Notice the similarity to the run up in tulip bulb prices from 1634 to 1637

*Figure 3*

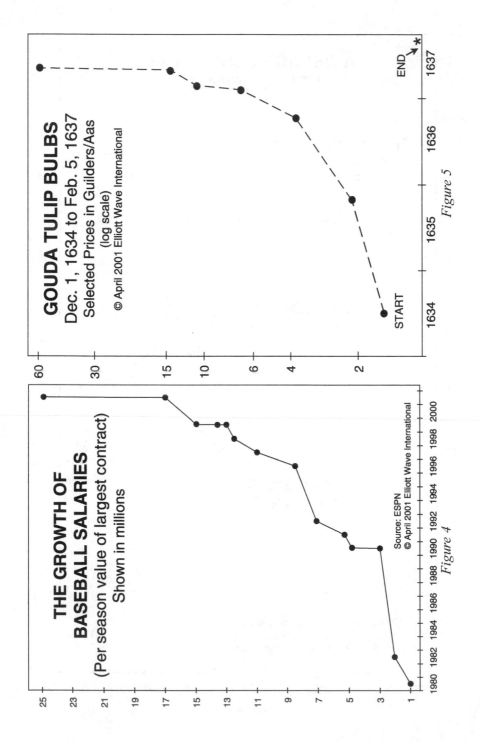

Figure 5

Figure 4

in Figure 5. The *Elliott Wave Theorist* has made very effective use of this simple "investment mania" pattern in recent months. The Texas Rangers added the last point on the chart when they signed shortstop Alex Rodriguez to the richest contract in the history of sports. The $252 million contract maintains a parabolic rise since 1980. Salaries of top players have now outstripped public demand for their services to an extent reminiscent of the Internet stock runup of 1999. If the classic pattern holds, the reversal in top salaries should be even more drastic than the drop in ticket sales. Based on the full retracement of past manias, a decline below the starting point of $1 million per year should follow.

### A Basketball Forecast

In 1996, *The Elliott Wave Theorist* relied on the second type of socionomic forecasting to anticipate the future of professional basketball. The correlation between the stock market and professional basketball identified basketball as "the ultimate bull market game." EWT's 11-page examination of basketball's history began, "The game's structure, rules and fortunes have developed in a manner that is totally consistent with the ebb and flow of the bull market in stocks." EWT noted that pro basketball and the bull market were born in the same year, 1896. Ticket sales, franchise growth and even the tempo of play have traversed a path that was virtually identical to the century-long expansion in stock prices. Using another socionomic forecasting tool, calling for reversals based on extremes in the fortunes of public icons (see *The Wave Principle of Human Social Behavior*, p. 314), EWT pinpointed the event that would mark the peak for basketball. The following excerpt is from a section on "The Heroes and Their Magic," which illustrated the sport's rich history of epitomizing each bull market era with very specific sets of idols:

> For whatever reason, in every period of substantial and continuous new highs in the Dow, there has been a pro basketball power that has thrived on the high ebb of social mood. The [Chicago] Bulls' reign in the last great wave of the bull market from 1932 shows how deep the link between basketball and the stock market goes. The very name, which has caused big red snorting bulls to be stamped on caps, t-shirts and bumpers across America, is a vibrant and ubiquitous symbol of the connection. To put an even finer point on the athletic expression of social mood, consider the professional history of [Bulls' star] Michael Jordan. Jordan first entered the cultural consciousness in 1982, the year of the

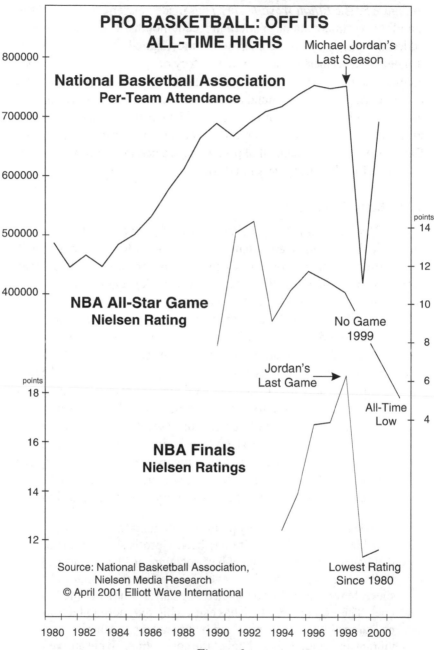

*Figure 6*

bull market's blast off. In 1987, the year of a substantial Dow high at 2723, he won his first MVP award. In the fall of 1996, as the Dow pushed past 6000, Jordan unveiled a new perfume and premiered as the star in a feature film. "Michael is superman," concludes *Sports Illustrated*. Only the hero factor can explain the depth of Jordan's popularity. As the game's greatest hero, Jordan personifies the happiness and energy of the bull market just as Bill Russell did in the 1960s and Magic Johnson in the 1980s.

EWT concluded, "the most noticeable sign of the trend change" would occur when Michael Jordan retired. Jordan retired in June of 1998. The euphoria of the moment was captured by a climactic NBA final in which Jordan made a last second shot to win the last game of the season and his last NBA title. Jordan's great finish marks the pinnacle of TV ratings for the National Basketball Association finals (see the bottom of Figure 6). A *Wall Street Journal* editorial said, "We were allowed up to Olympus." This Olympic peak was followed by the huge break in per-team attendance, as you can see at the top of Figure 6.

Taking the socionomic implication a step further, EWT added, "Top signals in the sport are top signals for stocks." The trend change clearly reflects the performance of the stock market, as it came just two months after the peak of a 24-year rise in the advance/decline line and thus the average NYSE stock, as shown in Figure 7.

Over the course of the last two years, every major index has followed suit, and the Chicago Bulls' dynasty has completely unraveled. Every single player from the championship era has left the team. Like the NASDAQ, the Bulls had the worst record in their history in 2000-2001. Back in 1996, EWT said, "Few, if any, fans see any relationship between their devotion to both the Bulls and their mutual fund portfolios." Now they feel as disgusted *at both* as they were elated during the mania, and they are no more aware of the principle that guides their collective emotional outlook than they were before. As we noted in 1996, this is the hallmark of "a collective psychological state—too pervasive to be recognized by most people."

### The Depth and Breadth of the Decline in Team Sports Viewership

The *extent* of the ratings plunge for televised sports is as enlightening as the timing. Ratings for the NBA's February all-star game were the lowest *ever*, plunging 17% from 2000, which was also an all-time

*Figure 7*

low. Since the start of the NBA season in November, regular-season NBA television ratings are down 28% from low levels in 2000. College basketball ratings have also fallen hard. As the NASDAQ broke from its all-time high in March, 2000, viewership for tournament games fell 20% to an all-time low. Ratings for this year's NCAA tournament were down still more.

Ratings for another highly organized athletic endeavor, the Olympic Games (which *The Elliott Wave Theorist* also linked to the long advance from 1896), fell off the table in 2000. Here again, the ratings were *never* lower. In fact, 2000 marked a clean sweep for the bear market in social mood, as every major sport experienced ratings declines. On April 23, *The Wall Street Journal* called the XFL, a new football league, "one of the biggest flops in television history." The breadth of the decline confirms that the long topping process that started with baseball ratings in the early 1990s has given way to a full-scale bear market in team sports viewership. (With a Grand Supercycle bear market in force, we should perhaps prepare for a prolonged fall from favor in team sports *per se*, which themselves may reflect the harmonious social relations typical of bull market.)

Ticket brokers report that the slack demand for seats extends to virtually every major sport. Another sign of exhaustion is that pent-up demand in many markets that were without teams, like Vancouver, Tampa and Miami, has been tapped as the big leagues expanded into just about every major geographic region. With the addition of new stadiums to most markets, sports in the 1990s attracted more marginal fans just as the stock market attracted more novice investors. The slumping per-team attendance figures shown at the top of Figures 3 and 6 show that the novelty is wearing off.

**Bull Market Sports on the Ropes: Expectations vs. Results**

As in the stock market, the raised *expectations* engendered by the preceding bull market have persisted through the first phase of collapse. Despite waning fan interest, values based upon *expectations*, such as salaries, stadium construction, the value of stadium naming rights and forward-sold advertising fees, continued to increase through 2000. Even new all-time lows in television ratings throughout 2000 could not dent the bullish expectations of participants. Table 1 shows how elevated official hopes have been on the eve of each recent sports event. The second headline shows that, in every case, a poor showing took television networks and sports authorities by surprise.

EWT has noted several times over the years that government is "the ultimate crowd." "It is always acting on the *last* trend, the one that is already over," it said in 1994. The following excerpt from the March 2001 issue of *Building Design & Construction* shows that the government commitment to the development of new stadiums is so deep that builders regard the spiraling growth in the costs and amenities of modern-day facilities to be a permanent condition.

**HIGH HOPES vs. THE NEW BEAR MARKET REALITY**
Despite one disappointing result after another, the media reflected bullish expectation
for baseball, basketball, and the Olympics in 2000.
© April 2001 Elliott Wave International

| Bull Market Expectations | Bear Market Result |
|---|---|
| **NCAA Tournament**<br>March 20, 2000<br>**CBS expects "improved ratings"** | April 5, 2000<br>**NCAA Tournament Ratings Hit an**<br>**All-Time Low** |
| **NBA Finals**<br>June 7, 2000<br>**NBC Expects Ratings Bump for Finals** | June 9, 2000<br>**NBA Finals Ratings Hit Low Point** |
| **Baseball All-Star Game**<br>July 10, 2000<br>**Baseball Banks on All-Star Game Ratings** | July 13, 2000<br>**NBC's Coverage Draws Lowest Numbers**<br>**Ever For All-Star Game** |
| **Olympics**<br>September 14, 2000<br>**NBC Expects Good Ratings, Good Profits** | September 20, 2000<br>**NBC's Ratings For Olympics Are**<br>**Worst Ever** |
| **World Series**<br>October 20, 2000<br>**Fox Sports Aims For Big Series Ratings** | October 28, 2000<br>**A Dubious Honor: Lowest Ratings Ever** |

# Sports Projects on the Dole

While building projects in many commercial sectors face uncertain futures, the sports niche is as robust as ever. Fueled by a
mix of technology, ebullient fans—and government support—the
momentum of sports construction is like that of the public sector: There is never a recession. Part of the reason is the use of
public funds and new taxes and bonds to pay for these projects.

Local and state authorities have taken on enormous financial
obligations to preserve the "major league status" that is on the cusp
of its biggest devaluation in history. Eventually, a public fury over the
stadium projects is inevitable. As the public thirst for ball games dis-
sipates, funds available for the real dole will be squeezed, and many
will cry, "What were they thinking?!" At this point, however, most are
still blinded by the emotional attachment to the erstwhile bull market.
Like governments, TV networks remain institutionally bound to the old
trend. Despite losses dating back to the early 1990s on contracts with
pro leagues, they continue to make long-term commitments based on

false hopes of a quick return to growth. After losing $40 million on the 1998 World Series and suffering through the worst ratings period in the history of baseball, Fox entered into a new contract that will nearly quadruple its yearly payout to the sport! The new contract runs through 2006 and will certainly cause Fox to lose a fortune.

### Home To Roost

2001 has produced the first inkling of the potential for a prolonged decline in the popularity of professional sports. In February, the record NBA all-star game ratings plunge joined a 45% decline for football's Pro Bowl and a 37% drop for the all-star hockey game. Fallout from the developing bear market was so pronounced that the media finally took notice. The first hint of recognition was signaled by headlines like this one from the *Detroit Free Press*:

## Are We Tired Of Sports?
### Early Sign Suggest Fans
### Are Losing Interest

*"Early sign?"* The true early sign was the Elliott wave count nine years ago. Now people are noticing the results. The press labeled the trend a "bedeviling, sociological change" and revealed that participation in most team sports fell through the 1990s. *Newsweek* disclosed on February 19 that after captivating America and verging on "global conquest" at the end of the 1990s, pro basketball "appears to have lost its magic." CNN Moneyline reports that one-time high-flying financial and technology firms that spent millions acquiring the naming rights to new professional sports facilities would love to get their names off these grand edifices. The problem is that no one wants the naming rights, at least not for the price they paid. An investigation of ticket prices by *The Wall Street Journal* found "enough to send a chill down the spine of the sports industry. Sports analysts say the industry could be sitting on a time bomb. The main reason fans don't renew their seats isn't the price or even the team's performance – but the number of times their tickets go to waste." An April 13 *USA Today* story reports that 25 of 30 major league teams lost money last year, and "teams are going deeply in debt to pay [player] salaries." "Baseball is in a golden era right now, but underneath all that is this huge problem," admitted the game's commissioner. Everything hinges on attendance and ratings growth

that has been waning for a full decade. "It's insane," says the general manager of the Cleveland Indians. Well, someone is insane, all right, but is it the fan, or is it the owner who signed the record high contract, or the banker who lent money to the team, or the government body that pledged taxpayers' millions for a stadium?

## Into the Teeth of the Bear

Most sports consultants say that fans are not tiring of sports; the prices of tickets and hot dogs just got a little too high. When prices come down, sports industry insiders insist that people will head back to the ballpark. But it does not cost anything to watch the World Series on television or to play baseball and basketball. A more reasonable explanation for the fallen interest is that the bull market in social mood has given way, just as *The Elliott Wave Theorist* predicted it would at the end of the Grand Supercycle bull market. The result is a reversal of the bull market trend described at the outset of this report. As the bear market emerges, a declining energy level has reduced participation and fan interest.

Eventually, more developed expressions of the long rise will unravel. In addition to the attendance shrinkage that EWT initially called for in 1993, the bear market should produce a retracement in every other aspect of these endeavors. The number of teams, leagues and viewers, the level of salaries and even the physical attributes and abilities of players should shrink substantially over the next few years. On and off the field, the games should be characterized by an increasingly rough tone. Player-on-player, fan-on-player, and fan-on-fan violence should continue a rise that has already begun. Formerly silent opponents will come forward to charge that sports are too violent, too commercial, sexist, racist or a corporate leech on communities. As the downturn in social mood accelerates, look for more revelations about the loss of passion on the part of sports fans everywhere.

To date, the lost interest in bull market sports and the psychology that surrounds them certainly support our case for an unprecedented downturn in social mood. These changes reveal the immense value of the Wave Principle and the concept of socionomics, which describe the psychology of crowd behavior. As we continue to demonstrate, these ideas allow for true forecasting at important junctures, when others' expectations are all pointed the opposite way.

*The Pittsfield Gazette*
May 24, 2001

*Chapter 23*

# Elliott Wave Analysis: Baseball Stadiums Now a Risky Investment

by Edward J. Baptiste

The Wave Principle is a tool of unique value, whose most striking characteristics are its generality and its accuracy. Its generality gives market perspective most of the time and its accuracy in pointing changes in direction is at times almost unbelievable. Many areas of human activity also tend to follow the Wave Principle, but it is best associated with stock market analysis. Wave analysis is useful in gauging markets from a longer-term perspective.

For example, Elliott wave analysis recognized the worthiness of gold at $35 an ounce, followed its move to $200, its correction to $101 in 1976, and then to its eventual climax in January 1980 to $875. By then, it was conventionally correct to own gold. The dollar was under attack, there was an oil crisis, Russian troops invaded Afghanistan and the gnomes of Zurich even had fears of their crossing over the Swiss Alps. Arab OPEC nations who sold their crude for years at $2 a barrel saw their earnings buying less in exchange value of other goods and services, reacted hawkishly. Amid rising commodity prices and concern over inflation, Elliotticians such as I clearly saw completion of a major wave movement and advised total liquidation of gold. Bullion within two months dropped to the $450 area and has since in this 20-year span been as low as $255.

Its most recent success was indicating a top of significance for the Dow Jones Industrials in January 2000, yet its signals for the Nasdaq were a trifle premature, as that index topped later in March of that year. Nevertheless, investors who listened to those signals were well served by avoiding the bubble collapse that followed. The Nasdaq 100 Index has dropped from 4816 to 1348. It has paid to heed Elliott wave analysis.

Now for wave analysis' relevance to baseball, stadiums and Pitts-field. Elliotticians see clear signals of a top in baseball and sports in general. We do not pontificate about such an observation and conclusion, nor do we rejoice in it. Had our conclusions indicated a major surge in baseball, it would have been reported as such.

My friends at Elliott Wave International in Gainesville, GA, in a piece dated April 30, 2001, have sounded the alarm for baseball in a seven-page single spaced report. This follows another report dated 12/16/96, "Basketball and the Bull Market." Both reports are available at elliottwave.com or 800-336-1618.

They wrote in 1993: "A Top in Baseball? If you're an investor, take profits on baseball. If you're a player, sign a long-term contract. If you're an owner, sell your club." Rest assured that baseball will survive, but prices change, as in gold. From 1901, there appears to be a clear five waves up in baseball game attendance, which has immediate implica-tions for a correction or downturn of secular proportions. A sharp drop in ticket sales is foreseen over the next few years, concomitant with a collapse in inflated baseball salaries. Such salaries (measured on a per season value of the largest contract in millions of dollars) have risen from $1 million in 1980 to an exponential $25 million currently. The Texas Rangers probably capped this bubble with signing of shortstop Alex Rodriguez to the richest contract in the history of sports akin to the Tulip Bubble in Holland of the 1630s. Succinctly put, salaries of top players have now out-stripped public demand for their services to an extent reminiscent of the Internet run-up of 1999. Supporting these conclusions are a sharp drop in World Series Neilsen Ratings since the early 1990s and ratings for the All Star game plunging to new lows. The total number of fans tuning into baseball's two most important annual events actually topped the year before baseball's 1993 attendance peak.

The five-wave pattern of this decade-long trend announces the onset of a major bear market. Nevertheless, two other measures of baseball's bull market have held firm, i.e., player contracts and team values, which continued to climb with stock markets of 1999 and early 2000. Fundamentals tell a different story. Growth in fan attendance and TV ratings both have been waning for a full decade, explaining why 25 of 30 major league teams lost money last year. The fact is that teams are going deeply into debt in order to pay higher and higher team salaries!

As EWI puts it, quoting the manager of the Cleveland Indians, "It's insane." They go on: "Well, someone is insane, all right, but is it the fan, or is it the owner who signed the record high contract, or the banker who lent money to the team, or the government body who pledged taxpayers' millions for a stadium?"

This change in social behavior can be replicated in what is happening to the NBA, Olympic Games and even the NCAA College March Madness finals, of which I am a devotee, having graduated from Duke. It is further exemplified by a *Wall Street Journal* article of April 23, which described the new XFL football league as one of the biggest flops in TV history!

This is as in stock market tops, where the majority of people buy just prior to and certainly after the peak. This is "Crowd Psychology" at its best. Elliott Wave International has noted several times over the years that government is the "ultimate crowd" as it is always acting on the LAST trend.

I leave the issue of eminent domain to others, location of stadium to still others. But I offer a genuine caveat to all concerned: The likelihood of a no-win, no-profit situation for baseball, challenging the idea of its being an economic engine for Pittsfield, is all too real.

*Part IV:*

# *CORPORATIONS,*
# *LEGISLATION*
# *AND*
# *SOCIAL CONFLICT*

*Chapter 24*

# A Dow-Stock Case Study: Coca-Cola

What is it about Coca-Cola? Is it the cola nut? The coca extract? The sugar? The answer, of course, is none of the above. In 1993's *For God, Country and Coca-Cola*, Mark Pendergrast actually published Coca-Cola's coveted 107-year-old secret formula. Since then, no one has cooked it up and successfully sold a reasonable facsimile of The Real Thing. In fact, Pendergrast reports that when he was researching his history, the company literally handed him the recipe. Coca-Cola executives were not concerned because they know full well that it is not the drink their customers are buying. As one put it, "We're selling smoke. They're drinking the image, not the product."

It is plain old sugar water, yet some call it the "essence of capitalism." How can it be? The answer appears on page 168 of *The Wave Principle of Human Social Behavior*. In a section called "Social Visioning as an Aspect of Herding," Prechter explains how social moods find expression in "shared fantasy images." As the chart of Coke from 1957 shows, it is a "social vision" that conforms nicely to the dictates of the Wave Principle. While Coke can stray from the Dow, it always finds its way back to the main trend.

The corporate history behind Coke's long rise shows that the company's old jingle is actually pretty accurate. *Things* really do go better with Coke. Unless, of course, the thing is a bear market. At such times, things don't go so well, not even for Coke. The firm's history is a living illustration of this passage from page 168: "Trends based upon subjective mental imagery undergo violent reversals when the imagery dissolves." Like the Dow Jones Industrial Average, Coca-Cola took off in the mid-1890s when its founders realized that there was more future in the beverage as refreshment than as medicine. "We found we were advertising to the few when we ought to advertise to the masses," said one of the firm's original leaders. By the turn of the century, the company was burrowing deep into the public psyche as it

THE REAL THING
Coca-Cola Stock
1957 - 1999

© December 1999 Elliott Wave International

"pioneered celebrity endorsements" to become "not simply a soft drink, but a phenomenon." The first big setback for Coke was the passage of the Pure Food and Drugs Act. Its date of passage was June 1906, five months after a Dow high that would not be materially exceeded until the 1920s. At the outset, Coca-Cola loyalists referred to proponents of the "pure food movement" as "cranks" and "misguided fanatics," but they had far more clout and staying power than expected. Their leader was Harvey Wiley, a man Pendergrast calls the Ralph Nader of the early 1900s. In 1907, Wiley took aim at Coca-Cola with the formation of a new "Poison Squad." Coke's annual report of 1907 reflected a coincident downturn in the company's prospects. As the bear market dragged on, Coca-Cola was beset by woes. In 1908, the U.S. government filed suit over its labeling and employment practices. "Even though Coca-Cola won the case in 1912, the publicity hurt the drink. D.W. Griffith put out an anti-Coca-Cola epic in which the inventor of 'DOPOKOKE' watched his son fall prey to the drink's cocaine. 'The drink no longer satisfies,' read one caption as the young man went on to hypodermic injections." Through the end of the 1910s, Coke was riled by rocketing sugar prices and a "civil war" for control of the company. After a "disastrous" year in 1920, as stock prices fell, Coca-Cola finally righted itself in 1922, a year after the Dow bottomed.

Pendergrast dates the start of Coca-Cola's "golden age" to 1923. With a push into global markets and a new age of mass media, Coke soared to heights of wealth generation previously unimagined for a maker of a 5-cent item. The real "secret," of course, was the company's primitive but powerful understanding of its underlying attractiveness. Ad man Archie Lee, "one of the first to realize that a product's image was more important than the product itself," came up with the "Pause that Refreshes" campaign in 1929. It is to that moment that anthropologist Clifford Geertz dates Coca-Cola's crossover from a soda fountain and syrup making company to "a system of symbols which acts to establish powerful, pervasive and long-lasting moods." The company "promotes a particular, satisfying, all-inclusive world view espousing perennial values such as love, peace and universal brotherhood. As a sacred symbol, Coca-Cola induces varying 'worshipful' moods, ranging from exaltation to pensive solitude, from near-orgasmic togetherness to playful games of chase."

With the help of its "social vision" and Prohibition, Coke held up better than most firms in the early 1930s, but by 1949, the end of the bear market in inflation-adjusted terms, it was experiencing the same anti-Coca Cola sentiment that had pulled it down in the 1910s. In Paris, mobs overturned Coke trucks, and "the level of hysteria reached such a pitch" that the wife of Coca-Cola's French president worried that her house might be bombed. "Coca-Cola faced similar threats and rumors at mid-century around the world." In Japan, the drink was said to sterilize women.

In the 1950s, the drink got back on track with the bull market. "Consumer behavior was often irrational, based on subconscious psychological motives," Pendergrast writes. "For the first time, the company attempted to plumb the depths of the subconscious mind." Coca-Cola was soon riding high again. In 1966, the end of Cycle wave III in the Dow and a long advance for Coke, the company "suddenly became a hot political topic" and nearly lost the Jewish market by refusing to grant an Israeli bottling franchise. The crisis was forestalled until late 1968 when the Dow topped and the resulting Arab boycott went into effect. In 1969, Ralph Nader himself surfaced with attacks in a hearing before the Select Committee on Nutrition and Human Needs. Shortly thereafter, "the Food and Drug Administration sounded another theme of the approaching seventies by revealing alarming results of tests on cyclamates." Coke's "perfect harmony" ad campaign of the early 1970s helped carry it to a final high with the Dow in 1973, but after that, it was all downhill as the company lost its long battle with the FTC, internal morale fell to an all-time low and "cozy relationships with dictators blew up one after the other." "No one would have guessed that a hopeful new era was about to commence." No one but a socionomist.

By 1995, Coca-Cola was the world's best known brand, with nearly half of the worldwide soft-drink market. The perfection with which the "peace and harmony" of its commercials reflected the public mindset is captured in the stock's price climb from 1982 to 1998.

Since its peak in July 1998, however, things have changed in ways reminiscent of past stock market tops. Coke has been shaken by a continuous stream of mysterious corporate crises that range from mold scares to the French government's rejection of its bid to buy Orangina to an assortment of unfavorable court rulings. In one case, the Belgian government successfully forced Coke to stop selling its beverages at a discount. In another, its own employees won the right to internal documents that they will use to mount a major discrimination case. As *The New York Times* said, the troubles have "revealed a different Coca-Cola," one that somehow manages to make unfortunate situations "even worse."

The true nature of Coke's problems is revealed by another recent snafu, an outbreak in which several Belgian school students reported feeling bad after buying Coca-Cola from a vending machine. Some were hospitalized, but no medical problems were ever diagnosed. Even though the company analysis showed "consumers were generally limited to subjective symptoms," massive recalls followed in Belgium and then France. "The pattern of this epidemic is consistent with a clinical entity which has been described as 'mass sociogenic illness.'" In socionomic terminology, this translates to "We're in a bear market."

## Food Fights and the Seattle Mob

As in 1906 and 1968, much of Coca-Cola's turmoil is rooted in emotional fears about food. The campaign against genetically engineered "Frankenfoods," which people have been consuming for years with no evidence of harmful side effects, started in Europe and has spread to the U.S. in recent weeks. As in 1908 and 1969, government hearings have been called to discuss the health risk in food. "The second of three FDA hearings on the safety and regulation of biotech foods is expected to be as contentious as the first meeting [on] November 18." "Growing resistance to new technology" has prompted the public forums. At the World Trade Organization conference in Seattle, protestors attacked a McDonalds, smashing its windows and unfurling a banner protesting the genetic engineering of food. Nobody seems to know what triggered the wave of irrational fears, but many are taking action. "Once Quick Converts, Farmers Begin To Lose Faith In Biotech Crops." Even when the "customer is wrong, the customer is right," says a farmer who has decided not to plant genetically modified seed next year.

In the middle of the unexpectedly explosive world-trade summit, Ralph Nader himself resurfaced and grabbed more public notice than at any time since the Naders' Raiders days. In countless other ways, the events of Seattle over the last few days have provided clear signs of a reversal in the long-term trend in social mood. What was supposed to be an inclusionistic *tour de force*, the biggest free-trade meeting in history, has been all but shut down by a well-organized amalgam of eco-terrorists, union agitators, food phobes, students and protectionists. With tear gas hovering over crowded streets, a call out for the National Guard, law-and-order types decrying the "mob tactics" of their adversaries, and the sudden labor unrest, a whole host of long-dormant cultural manifestations of a bear market have emerged. The National

Association of Manufacturers tried to head off the demonstrators by calling an army of Fortune 500 CEOs to the front. Before the WTO meetings even started, however, it was obvious that the world's corporate heroes would be powerless against the protestors. "We're never going to compete with thousands of Naderites rappelling and chanting," said a NAM spokesman. This is what happens in a bear market; the emotional forces of the crowd simply overwhelm the established order.

*Chapter 25*

# Is the Break in the Big Brand Names a Warning for the Overall Market?

Three months ago, the concept of the "old economy" barely existed. Now, it is the focus of daily speculation on the strength or weakness in the stock market. When the Dow falls, it is because the "bastions of safety are crumbling under this new economy." When the Dow rises, it's a "New Bull Market for [the] Old Economy." The chart below shows, however, that in lumping everything in the "old economy" into a single group, observers are missing an important distinction that could hold the key to the direction of the overall market. Figure 1 breaks the "old

*Figure 1*

economy" into two distinct sectors: companies that rely heavily on famous brand names and those that do not. Our Famous Brands Index consists of 21 stocks that generate their business from well-established brand names. It encompasses hundreds of different products that have built identities as major American brands dating as far back as the mid-1800s. Table 1 lists some of their key products and their year of establishment. Our Non-Brands Index consists of the 35 "old economy" stocks from the S&P 100 that are *not* dependent on branded products. Its membership includes established firms like Bethlehem Steel, Boeing and Columbia Healthcare.

| Company Name | Key Product(s) & Year Established | Date of Peak | Decline Through March 10 |
|---|---|---|---|
| 1) Kellogg | Corn Flakes 1906 Rice Krispies 1928 | 01/01/98 | 68% |
| 2) Campbell Soup | condensed soup 1897 | 03/23/98 | 53% |
| 3) Brunswick | recreational products 1874 | 03/25/98 | 56% |
| 4) Mattel | Barbie 1959 | 03/31/98 | 80% |
| 5) Sara Lee | cheescake 1949 | 04/07/98 | 54% |
| 6) Hershey | chocolate 1894 | 04/09/98 | 49% |
| 7) Fruit of the Loom | textiles 1856 underwear 1938 | 04/21/98 | 97% |
| 8) Disney | films 1923 theme parks 1955 | 05/04/98 | 17% |
| 9) Ralston Purina | cereal 1898 Purina Dog Chow 1957 | 06/30/98 | 37% |
| 10) Coca-Cola | Coke 1886 | 07/15/98 | 50% |
| 11) H.J. Heinz | ketchup 1876 | 11/17/98 | 48% |
| 12) Unilever | laundry soap 1885 Lipton Tea 1937 | 01/06/99 | 55% |
| 13) Gillette | Safety Razor 1903 | 03/26/99 | 53% |
| 14) Avon | perfume 1886 beauty products 1950 | 04/19/99 | 55% |
| 15) RJR Nabisco | Fig Newtons 1891 Oreo 1912 | 06/11/99 | 60% |
| 16) Anheuser-Busch | Budweiser 1876 | 09/08/99 | 33% |
| 17) McDonald's | fast food 1954 | 11/11/99 | 39% |
| 18) Quaker Oats | oatmeal 1901 | 11/12/99 | 35% |
| 19) Johnson & Johnson | BAND-AID 1921 Tylenol 1960 | 11/17/99 | 33% |
| 20) Procter & Gamble | Ivory 1879 Tide 1946 | 01/12/00 | 54% |
| 21) Colgate Palmolive | toothpaste 1873 | 01/13/00 | 39% |

*Table 1*

Without the drag of issues that rely heavily on brand names, stocks in the Non-Brands Index went to a new high in 1999. In recent days, this brand-free group also moved back above its high of April 1998. In contrast, the Famous Brands Index never exceeded its April 1998 peak and is now down more than 30% from that point. In the years preceding its all-time high, the index kept pace with the bull market, as you can see in Figure 2. One by one, however, each of these stocks has decoupled from the rising trend of the averages. Through March 10, the date of the NASDAQ's all-time high, all 21 had suffered serious declines. The numbers on the chart correlate to Table 1 to show the steady progression. Procter & Gamble, the granddaddy of American brand marketing, was one of the last to drop. It turned down two days before the Dow's January peak and has since lost 51%.

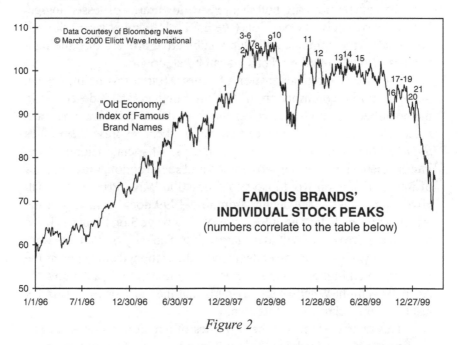

*Figure 2*

The exciting news is that the break in the brand stocks has established ideal conditions for a real-time test of a socionomic theory discussed in the chapter on "Impulsivity and Herding" in Prechter's book, *The Wave Principle of Human Social Behavior*. According to the idea of "social visioning," which Bob proposed on the basis of studies and observations from a host of social theorists (see Chapter 9), "it may be that shared fantasy images are an *intermediate step* between mood change and resulting action." When these images dissolve, he added, the trends they are "based upon undergo violent reversals." They may even "reflect mood quite immediately, before the public could mobilize itself enough to act in the economic and political arenas." This study takes the question to the market itself. Can a basket of equities backed by a broad cross-section of commercial fantasy images developed over the course of a bull market reflect the end of that bull market ahead of other major indexes? Since companies with major brands represent near-total investments in the techniques of crafting and maintaining icons that are amenable to the long uptrend in social mood, it seems quite possible. Their shares should be extremely sensitive to any loss of potency in the symbols, sayings, jingles, tastes or subliminal appeals they have created over the course of a long bull market. At downturns of lesser degree, EWFF's case study of Coca Cola (see EWFF December issue) showed how readily the complex and highly subjective process of building a business around a bull market icon can break down.

Only the market can answer, of course. But at this point, we can make an initial confirmation of "the intermediate step" described in the book because it also describes the form that social visioning must take. "Herding people feel a certain way and can express themselves *impulsively* to reflect those feelings," it says. "If social visioning is an intermediate step between social mood and social action, the dynamics of its manifestation would have to follow the Wave Principle, which governs its cause." The decline from mid-1999 does, in fact, bear the trademark of an Elliott impulse wave. Notice wave 3 on Figure 1. It is a clear five waves down within the larger five. The rally off that low went to a fourth wave of one lesser degree and then stopped cold even as the Dow rocketed higher and the Non-Brand Index moved back above its April 1998 high. What we are saying is that the Famous Brands Index has taken on a character of its own.

This character reflects the two sides of a major, major peak. The media have not noticed that the brand-name issues of the old economy have been rolling over one after another since the peak of the advance/decline line in April 1998. At the same time, the *idea* of branding has actually grown bigger than ever as the rationale for tolerating losses in the *new* economy. Rivers of red ink at Internet companies are not just tolerated but in fact *demanded* by investors who insist that "new economy" companies "need large marketing expenditures to build brand awareness." Proof of this assertion is that stocks of Internet companies that generate losses to build brand names have consistently outperformed stocks of Internet companies that turn a profit. Another indication that a historic extreme in brand awareness has reached its zenith is that in recent months, even individuals have become brand names. A number of them, including Dick Clark, Donna Karan, Tommy Hilfiger, Ralph Lauren, Martha Stewart and C. Everett Koop, have become publicly traded companies. All are down substantially from their closes on their first days of trading, but the effort literally to buy heroes continues to spread. The latest development is at the venture capital level, where numerous promoters are busily launching Internet investment funds with superstar athletes because "athletes have tremendous brand presence." Many venture capitalists and investors expect to get in on the ground floor of the "new paradigm," but the elevator is actually on the penthouse floor and starting down. If the bull market is topping as we assert, then these are the final death throes of brand name imaging *per se*.

*Chapter 26*

# A Socionomic Perspective
# on the Microsoft Case

How would you answer the question, "What effect will the Justice Department's antitrust lawsuit against Microsoft have on the overall stock market?" A fundamental analyst might write a thesis about it, pointing out the market's behavior after past antitrust actions and discussing why this time might be the same or different. He would remind us that we can draw no useful conclusions without knowing more about upcoming events. Many technical analysts would say that the market, digesting advance knowledge of the event, probably factored most of its impact into stock prices prior to the action. He would assure us that further events will be similarly discounted in advance. Again, though, we would be reminded that there are no useful conclusions to draw without anticipating upcoming events. Despite their differences, these responders would agree that events are causal to the stock market's behavior. The socionomic perspective is otherwise.

The report, "Socionomics in a Nutshell" (December 1999), demonstrated in brief that in the realm of economics, politics, demographics, war and even the threat of nuclear destruction, events are *not* causal to social mood and stock market trends. In every case, the direction of causality is the opposite of that generally assumed. The performance of the economy does not govern the stock market; the social mood as reflected by stock market trends governs economic performance. Politics do not govern the stock market; the social mood as reflected by stock market trends governs politics. Demographics do not govern the stock market; the social mood as reflected by the stock market regulates the overall rate of procreation. Changes in the threat of nuclear destruction do not affect stock prices; the social mood as reflected by the stock market affects the level of the threat. In each instance, social mood trends as reflected by stock market trends dictate the character of events,

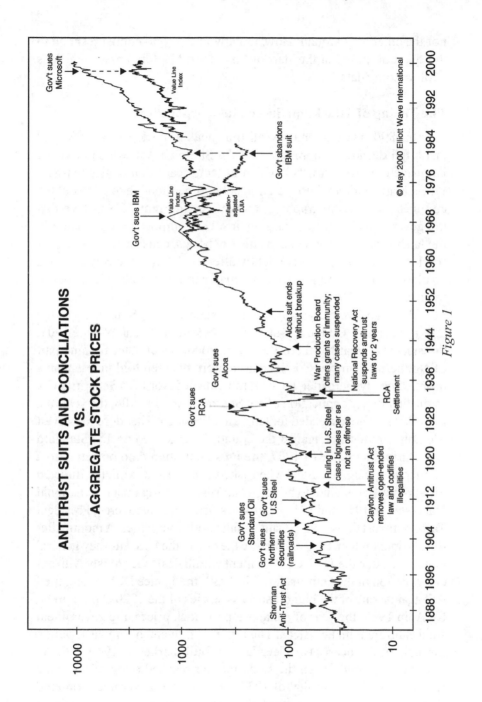

**ANTITRUST SUITS AND CONCILIATIONS
VS.
AGGREGATE STOCK PRICES**

*Figure 1*

© May 2000 Elliott Wave International

not the other way around. How, then, would a socionomist respond to the question posed at the start of this report? Before answering, let's explore some data.

## The Timing of Attacks on Successful Corporations

In 1890, a year after a new all-time peak in stock prices that would last a full decade, Congress passed the Sherman Act, which in vague language outlawed "trusts," which in fact means companies that service a large market without significant competition. Take a look at the comments above the graph of stock prices in Figure 1. Observe that the government's antitrust suits against U.S. corporations, particularly the landmark suits that make the history books, consistently come near stock market peaks, usually slightly afterward. Often the correlation is so close as to be within weeks of a major top that leads to declines in the averages of 50% or more.

Railroads were arguably the most successful U.S. industry in the late 19th century. On the run-up to the stock market peak of June 1901, the stock of Great Northern Pacific railroad, which later became part of Northern Securities Co., increased more than ten fold in less than a month. Shortly thereafter, the government sued Northern Securities Co. in the first major application of the Sherman Act. In 1906, the year of a peak that was not exceeded for ten years, President Theodore Roosevelt filed his famous suit against the country's largest company, Standard Oil. During the Panic of 1907, the President offered no objection to a merger involving U.S. Steel when asked to do so and explicitly directed his attorney general not to bring an antitrust action against International Harvester. In 1911 and 1912, after stock prices had recovered, President Taft's antitrust division filed suit against both companies. A month after the all-time high of 1929 and before the crash, the U.S. attorney general announced that the Justice Department would deal "vigorously with every violation of the antitrust law." In 1930, the Justice Department filed suit against one of the biggest success stories of the 1920s bull market, RCA. In 1937, the year of a major top in stock prices, the government sued aluminum maker Alcoa. The antitrust movement saw little action throughout the nearly two-decade long bull market of 1949-1966/68 until the very end, when the stock market reached a top of the same Elliott wave degree as that of 1937. In 1967, the government ordered Proctor & Gamble to divest itself of Clorox, and in January 1969, a single month after the most speculative bull market peak since 1929, the Justice

Department sued the country's most successful company, IBM. From 1982, antitrust activity again virtually disappeared during nearly two decades of bull market. On May 18, 1998, just one month after the final high in the advance-decline line and the Value Line geometric index, both of which had risen for 24 years, the Justice Department sued the world's most successful company, Microsoft. On April 3, 2000, a single week after the closing high in the NASDAQ 100 index, the court sided with the U.S. Justice Department in ruling that Microsoft had unlawfully violated the Sherman Act. Like his predecessors at prior historic turns, U.S. District Court Judge Thomas Penfield Jackson, representing "the people," has pursued and denigrated Microsoft with a fervor that borders on the evangelical. His desire to break up the most successful company of all time as measured by percentage gain in value per year is a passion born of the passing of a social mood peak of even higher degree than that of 1929. As you can see from this century-long history, major antitrust suits coincide remarkably consistently with the passing of major stock market tops.

### Direction of Causality

A conventional analyst would surely conclude from this evidence that antitrust suits *cause* stock market declines. This response does not answer the question of why the entire economy would be affected by a single suit, an idea bordering on the preposterous. Presumably, competitors would benefit as the target suffered, neutralizing any broad effect. The erroneous conclusion, moreover, is utterly negated by the fact that the target of the latest suit, Microsoft, saw its stock *triple in price* after the suit was brought. In fact, the last doubling took place after the November 1999 "finding of fact" in which Penfield ruled, "Microsoft Corp. is a monopoly with practices that wounded competition and consumers and hurt innovation."

More important, and typical of conventional explanations, the suggestion of a causative link between antitrust actions and falling stock prices goes against the assumptions of many other conventional analysts. Many economists believe (mistakenly) that "trust-busting" is good for the economy. If they were correct, and if their assumption that economic performance dictates stock market trends were correct, then stock prices should *rise* after an attack on a presumed monopoly, not fall.

Finally, this conclusion about causality fails to answer the question of why antitrust suits are typically brought after the stock market has climbed for years or even decades to a state of overvaluation in a climate of rampant speculation *rather than at any other time*. For the most part, the Justice Department leaves successful corporations alone near the end of bear markets and through 90%-100% of bull markets, even if it has to wait decades to do so. What is really going on?

The social mood shift that occurs at the transition from bull market to bear includes a change in general attitudes toward the financial success of others. Society moves from a feeling of support toward one of resentment. During a bull market, the social mood is directed toward rewarding achievement; during a bear market, it is directed toward punishing it. The bear market mood begins to creep into collective thinking late in a bull market. Democratic governments are instruments of egalitarianism. At some point, their representatives cannot stand watching some companies succeed wildly more than most others. When the bull market reaches exhaustion, the old supportive mood begins to crumble, and the new punitive mood bursts forth. One result of this metamorphosis in social character is governmental attacks against highly successful enterprises. In fact, they typically start with a major attack against *the* most successful enterprise of the time.

This socionomic perspective, moreover, is quite comfortable with the fact that Microsoft stock tripled after the suit was announced. The environment of stock market tops is one of rampant speculation fueled by a manic psychology. Reason and outside-event causality are not part of this landscape. Bullish fever among speculators and righteous anger among egalitarians can coexist for brief periods as major social mood tops are being formed, thus producing the anomaly of a soaring stock price for a company that is being attacked in court by its own government.

### The Timing of Permissiveness with Respect to Successful Corporations

Antitrust action typically continues throughout most of a bear market. As each bear market comes to an end, the old mood of resentment evaporates. The timing of this correlation is just as remarkable as that for tops, as demonstrated by the comments underneath the graph of stock prices in Figure 1.

At the 1914 low, the Clayton Anti-Trust Act reined in the broadness of the Sherman Act. In 1920, as the market was approaching the low from which the bull market of the Roaring Twenties would erupt, the Supreme Court "rejected the challenge to Andrew Carnegie and J.P. Morgan's formation of U.S. Steel, saying "mere size" is no offense. Near the 1932-1933 lows, the government settled its case against RCA, and the National Recovery Act suspended antitrust law for two years. Near the 1942 low, the War Production Board offered grants of immunity from antitrust action, and the government suspended many of its antitrust cases. A year after the 1949 low, the government settled its suit against Alcoa without achieving its objective of breaking up the company. In 1982, after a sixteen-year decline in real stock prices, the Justice Department abandoned its suit against IBM.

Like its attacks, the government's major acts of reconciliation and permissiveness typically occur within weeks or months of a major turn in the stock market, this time to the upside. In both cases, its acts are in response to, and part of, the changing social mood.

One could try to argue that once a stock market decline goes far enough, corporate fortunes in general are so poor that there is no longer any need to punish trusts. However, if the government's theory of monopoly power were correct, a contracting business environment would have no effect on a company's relative position. Further, this view does not explain why in some cases the government pulls back after stock prices fall 50% and the economy is in recession and in other cases after stock prices fall 90% and the economy is in depression. There is no mathematical "magic level" at which governments stop their attacks. *They stop when the social mood reaches bottom, wherever that may be.* The exact timing and level of *that* event are determined not by extent or time but by *form* as revealed by the wave pattern.

## A Socionomist's Response

With regard to the question posed at the outset, then, the answer from a socionomic perspective is this: The Justice Department's antitrust action against Microsoft has had, and will have, no effect whatsoever on the overall trend of the stock market (just as it had no effect on the price of Microsoft stock itself). The causality is the other way around: The exhaustion of an extremely positive social mood trend, as reflected by stock market statistics, affected the Justice Department's emotional mindset and caused it to capitulate to a desire to attack the most successful corporation it could identify, which was Microsoft.

**Forecasting**

In contrast to the predictive uselessness of conventional assumptions about the direction of causality between social events and mood (see opening paragraph), the socionomic perspective allows a basis for at least some limited probabilistic forecasting. With a knowledge of the Wave Principle, we can roughly anticipate the timing of major antitrust actions and later, their resolutions. For example, we can predict that no major government attacks on corporate success are likely from the time of a stock market bottom of Cycle degree or larger through most of the ensuing bull market. We can also predict continual government attacks on corporate success from the time of a stock market top of Cycle degree or larger through most of the ensuing bear market (the later attacks typically being of lesser import than the first one). We can state further that when a major antitrust action takes place after a long period of non-action, it is a sign that the social mood trend of at least Cycle degree is likely changing from bull to bear. We can also state that when a major antitrust action is resolved after a long period of conflict, it is a sign that the social mood trend of at least Cycle degree is likely changing from bear to bull. We can say these things because antitrust actions and resolutions do not occur randomly; they occur at *specific times* in response to a psychological environment involving a major extreme in social mood and its reversal.

**The Timing of Attacks on Monopolies**

First, we must define our terms. A monopoly is an entity that holds an economically preferential position due primarily to the use of force. Monopolies are maintained by the force of the state in favor of selected individuals, guilds, companies or state enterprises. European monarchs routinely granted monopolies on specific markets to individuals. Guilds successfully barred competition when the power of the state was behind them. Corporations and state enterprises such as the U.S. Postal Service, the Federal Reserve System and the U.S. Mint enjoy monopoly privileges. Persons attempting to provide services in competition with entities such as these are aggressively punished by fines and imprisonment.

A monopoly differs from an especially successful company in that the latter is *always* at the risk of competition. Monopolies have survived for *centuries* despite bad products and services. On the other hand, every non-monopoly company is subject to collapse if its products or services deteriorate, if it misses the next innovative trend in its field, or if the very field it is in becomes passé. Some people claim that an especially successful company can become a monopoly simply because its success gives it "power" to destroy the competition. It is true that immense success can allow a company to make deals with other businesses to induce them to deal with it exclusively. This condition is different from monopoly power, however, because the dealings are voluntary. Another business can always refuse to cooperate if it so chooses; there is no gun behind the deal. Further, such "power" is temporary. To the extent that any successful business engages in elaborate restrictive schemes, it will, in the long run, drain its resources and weaken itself, allowing future competitors to gain an edge. Competition, moreover, is not fixed to any number of firms existing at a particular time. A successful company frets as much over *potential* competition as over actual competition. It knows that the slightest slip in top quality goods and services will endanger it immensely. No matter how hard it may try, no company can keep a premier position forever. The natural order of things eventually reduces the relative success of every exceptional enterprise.

This distinction between actual monopolies and purported monopolies that are not is important for the purposes of our socionomic thesis regarding "trust busting." It allows us to see the essence of the commonality between the *suspension* of government's actions against successful *non-monopoly* corporations near stock market bottoms (shown below the graph in Figure 1) and its simultaneous *initiation* of attacks on *actual* monopolies.

Figure 2 shows times when the U.S. government has acted to limit or break apart the monopoly power of the original U.S. phone company, AT&T. Under the Communications Act of 1934, the U.S. government dubbed AT&T a natural monopoly and allowed the communications carrier to operate without competitive forces. In 1949, the year that a 20-year bear market pattern in real stock prices (not shown) ended, the U.S. Justice Department cited AT&T for "maintaining a monopoly" that violated the Sherman Act. On November 20, 1974, the month between the final lows in all the stock market averages following declines of 45% to 74%, the Justice Department sued AT&T for monopolizing the telecommunications industry. In 1982, the year that real stock prices bottomed, AT&T was ordered to divest itself of all seven of its local operating companies and cease offering local phone service, which it did in

*Figure 2*

1984. As a result of that action, the monopoly no longer existed, and the telecommunications industry exploded with innovation so dramatically that in just 16 years, many of the most successful and entrepreneurial companies on earth are those associated with telecommunications.

The more entrenched monopoly power of the U.S. Post Office survived the bear market of the 1970s, but it might not have if the decline had been one degree larger. In 1970, the two-century old U.S. Post Office was transformed from an agency of the executive branch of the U.S. government to a "quasi-independent postal corporation" modeled after a private-sector firm. At the same time, notes a "History of the Postal Monopoly in the United States" from the *Journal of Law and Economics,* the governors of the new U.S. Postal Service established a regulation allowing them "to surrender bits and pieces of their exclusive grant to preserve the substance of the monopoly." It adopted this policy to head off a rising chorus of public attacks on the Postal Service monopoly. As the law journal history notes, the attacks themselves "are extraordinary because ever since its original colonial times, the postal monopoly has seemed inviolable." In 1973, the House of Representatives convened hearings on mail delivery restrictions that had been in place for more than 150 years. In October 1974, the very month of the bottom in the S&P, the first official suspension of prohibitions on private carriage were put into effect for certain items. As a result, Federal Express, UPS and even the Postal Service itself brought a burst of innovation to the delivery industry. Congress was still debating a number of bills calling for the privatization of mail delivery as late as June 1982, two months before the final low of a 16-year decline in real stock prices. Things changed when the social mood trend turned up. In October 1982, as the Dow made its first decisive rise above 1000, the Reagan administration "decided for now to de-emphasize its opposition to the U.S. Postal Service's mail monopoly."

Monopoly privileges stifle innovation, so when monopoly power is removed, an industry is allowed to develop. In contrast, upon every single antitrust action against successful *non*-monopoly corporations (see Figure 1), innovation did *not* immediately burst forth. The reason is that each of these successful companies, in a climate of free competition, was precisely the one responsible for the immense innovation that had already occurred. These disparate results confirm the difference between the two types of entities.

We can now see that the principle behind the government's actions with respect to these disparate entities is the same: At tops, the government *initiates* force to stifle free competition and success; at bottoms, it *removes* force that has stifled free competition and success. This latter impetus takes two forms: withdrawing antitrust actions against successful non-monopoly companies and dissolving actual monopolies. With this knowledge, we again have the ability to do some limited probabilistic forecasting both in terms of predicting actions against monopolies and predicting major social mood changes when those actions occur.

**The Timing of Bailouts**

In the past three decades, the U.S. government has taken to bailing out losing enterprises. These actions derive from the same egalitarian impulse behind its attacks on successful companies at major social mood tops. Rather than acting to prevent *success*, though, the government acts to prevent *failure*. The overall economic result is still destructive, as saving one enterprise endangers its competitors and wastes both productive resources and tax money at the same time, but this fact is irrelevant to the socionomic observation that impulsive social mood is the engine of these actions.

*Figure 3*

When do bailouts occur? Bailouts occur near stock market lows, when the mood is the opposite of that near peaks. As you can see in Figure 3, Lockheed Aircraft and Penn Central Railroad applied for aid in March and May 1970, as the stock market was crashing into its biggest low in 28 years. (Aid was approved in December 1970 and August 1971.) In another bailout of Penn Central and several other northeastern railroads, Congress created Conrail in 1974, the final year of the biggest bear market since 1937-1942. (It took two separate "federal investments" of $2.1 billion in 1976 and $1.2 billion in 1980, as real stock prices continued falling, to keep Conrail on track.) The government's initial rescue of Continental Illinois bank came in May 1984, at the bottom of a fear-laden "wave two" stock market correction. (It was completed with a $4.5 billion FDIC package in late July.) Following the 1987 crash and the sluggish, mostly sideways year of 1988, Congress established the Resolution Trust Corporation on February 6, 1989 to bailout a slew of failed savings and loan institutions. Its creation marked the beginning of the biggest financial bailout in U.S. history. The crisis lasted through the 1990 bear market (which brought the Value Line index down to its 1987 low and cut the Transportation Average in half) and abated by mid-1993, when the RTC had liquidated or paid off the debts of 90% of the failed institutions it had taken over.

Although a bailout involves the use of force—taking tax money and using it to shore up an enterprise that no one will support voluntarily—it is *psychologically* the opposite of an attack. While free competition in fact requires allowing failure, the force wielded by the government is *intended*, however erroneously, to benefit competition by keeping the number of competitors in the marketplace higher than it would be otherwise. These actions, therefore, are consistent with the socionomic hypothesis that their origin is psychological.

### A Comment on the Breadth of Mood Causality with Respect to Pro- and Anti-Corporate Sentiment

Although the data available for this report pertain to government actions, results of social mood change with respect to the treatment of corporations are not confined to acts of the state. The changes in social mood that govern antitrust action are broadly experienced by the populace and have other effects.

During a major topping and declining mood trend, all kinds of sociological forces work against corporations that are visibly successful. Exactly which companies may be affected by the social mood change from bull to bear is probably unpredictable, but the mood will have its way with *some* entities or other.

For example, in the bear market environment of the early 1970s, countless people were apoplectic over an irrational fear that ITT (the International Telephone and Telegraph company), which had begun a program of taking over smaller companies, would "take over the world." It was considered an immense threat. College students fretted over it, and talk show hosts discussed it continually. ITT must have been mystified. In the end, it never threatened anyone but its own employees, as its fortunes flagged and its business focus narrowed to hotels and casinos. In 1998, ITT itself was taken over by a relatively obscure REIT.

As another example, in the past twelve months, Coca-Cola has experienced both widespread panic in Europe over a supposedly tainted product and protest marches in the United States over purported discriminatory hiring practices. The panic proved to be based primarily upon fantasy, and the hiring practices under protest have been in place throughout the bull market without similar consequence.

Evidence that mood change alone has compelled these actions in each case is the fact that they were based on *nothing new that was tangible*. The waxing negative social *mood* generated negative social *action*. ITT and Coke just happened to become targets. The stated reasons for public dissatisfaction were not actually *reasons* but *rationalizations* by frantic neocortexes that found themselves thrust into the position of having to objectify a mood that was forcing its way out of their hosts' limbic systems. (For more on this mechanism, see Chapter 8 of *The Wave Principle of Human Social Behavior*.)

When social mood is early in a positive trend, the same thing happens, but in reverse. Can anyone really justify the deeply sentimental mood with which flavored sugar water has managed to become associated in the minds of people around the world? (For a case study on the Coca-Cola phenomenon, see the December 1999 issue of *The Elliott Wave Financial Forecast*.) A socionomist recognizes that the waxing benevolent mood trend associated with the bull market appears first. The objects of its focus (whether it be pop drinks or pop stars) find themselves in the right place at the right time and exploit it.

## Practical Value in the Socionomic Perspective

Imagine the value of a knowledge of socionomics to enterprises designed *consciously* to harness the social mood trend. Even the one small observation presented in this paper would help the typical company. It would have a handle on when to increase its public presence and when to hold back. It would know when to push products and services attuned to the bull market mood and when to push products and services attuned to the bear market mood.

Let's try a practical application in our own small way. Now that we know the implication of major antitrust actions for the position of the social mood trend, we can anticipate that two to five years from now, the stock market is likely to be much lower than it is today. Conversely, when today's antitrust acrimony dissolves, the next bull market will be just around the corner. If we arrange our financial affairs to take advantage of this high probability, we stand an excellent chance of benefiting from it.

Kendall
*The Elliott Wave Financial Forecast*
July 20, 2000

*Chapter 27*

# New Assault on U.S. Corporations Confirms Microsoft Sell Signal

In May, *The Elliott Wave Theorist* analyzed more than a century of U.S. antitrust activity and found the government's case against Microsoft to be a socionomic confirmation of a significant stock market peak. Figure 1 in our "Socionomic Perspective on the Microsoft Case" shows the succession of antitrust actions at the start of major bear markets since 1889. The report explains that at the onset of a market top of Cycle degree or larger, a "new punitive mood bursts forth. One result of this metamorphosis in social character is governmental attack against the most successful enterprises. In fact, they typically start with a major attack against *the* most successful enterprise of the time." Within days of publication, Judge Thomas Penfield Jackson brought "the harshest penalty possible" against Microsoft, the dominant firm in the fastest growing segment of the U.S. economy. By ordering a break-up of the software giant, he "rubber-stamped" every aspect of the U.S. Justice Department's proposed penalty and issued one of history's most definitive long term stock market sell signals. The fact that the judge is a conservative Reagan appointee shows the power of social mood even over ideology.

In addition to signaling the start of a bear market, initial major antitrust cases mark a re-awakening in the antitrust movement as a whole. That's one reason that our May issue called for "continual government attacks on corporate success from the time of a stock market top." At this point, we should begin seeing an extension of the attack beyond Microsoft, and that is exactly what has been happening. Recent headlines have unveiled the gathering of anti-business forces in a wide range of social realms. In politics, the Vice President of the United States and Democratic candidate for President has adopted a "strategy of turning big business into [the] boogeyman" by launching a succession of attacks against drug, gun, HMO and oil companies. For the first time, a jury has reached "a reasoned and unanimous conviction to punish the tobacco industry." The $145 billion judgment is 30 times greater than the previous record and well beyond the companies' capacity to pay. The foreman explained the verdict as a matter of attitude and emotion. "It was insulting. It's just the tobacco industry's mentality, that they are beyond challenge. No one has ever challenged them and won." In another break from the former bull market mood, anti-trust authorities have set their sights on the electronic frontier. European and U.S. authorities have decided to scrutinize the "growing number of Internet business-to-business exchanges" for illegally colluding on prices and sharing purchasing services. The credit card industry has seen yet another milestone. The government is taking on card giants Visa and Mastercard for "collusion" in their control of 75% of the market. According to the U.S. Justice Department suit, the consortium of 7,000 banks that shares ownership of both groups is a "duality" that stifles competition. As *The Elliott Wave Theorist* noted with regard to recent attacks on Coca-Cola, this is further evidence of a waxing negative social mood because it is based on absolutely "nothing new that is tangible." According to the earliest market share data that we could find (from the Credit Card Management newsletter), Visa and Mastercard had the same 75% share of the industry in 1986. In fact, as the dominant credit card issuers since the 1970s, Visa and Mastercard have been the backbone of the consumer credit economy since the inception of Cycle wave V in 1974.

### Mergers and Mood

One way legal historians have quantified progress and regress in the U.S. antitrust movement is the amount of merger activity. Many have documented an inverse relationship whereby as antitrust activity rises, mergers "disappear." In our research for the May issue, we found the data on mergers for Figures 1 through 3 in a book on federal antitrust policy. The data for the most recent bull market is updated from the February issue of *The Elliott Wave Financial Forecast*. If you put each of these charts up against Figure 1 from the May *Elliott Wave Theorist* depicting antitrust suits and conciliations, you will see how beautifully they fill in the blank spots, i.e. the major bull markets.

## NUMBER OF U.S. CORPORATE
## MERGERS AGAINST THE DOW
© July 2000 Elliott Wave International

*Figure 1*

*Figure 2*

Figure 3

Figure 4

In light of this century-long correlation between the number of mergers and rising stock prices, another major confirmation of a reversal in social mood is a recent outbreak of anti-merger fever. Within the last few weeks, the U.S. authorities have blocked WorldCom's purchase of Sprint, H.J. Heinz's purchase of BeechNut Nutrition and the $6 billion combination of the Burlington Northern Santa Fe and the Canadian National Railway, which would have been the biggest railroad combination in history. Several other deals that would have met with no resistance in the late 1980s and 1990s, including United Airlines' buyout of US Air, AOL's merger with Time Warner and Bell Atlantic's bid for GTE, are now being challenged by various federal agencies. The SEC and Federal Accounting Standards Board have undermined the potential for *any* more record breaking deals with an attack on the "pooling of interest" accounting method that has allowed countless firms to make acquisitions with their inflated stock rather than with cash or debt. "During the topping and declining mood trend, all kinds of sociological forces work against corporations that are visibly successful," EWT said in May. Support, cooperation and synthesis give way to divisiveness and resentment. In the last two months, the speed and scope of this social change has clearly accelerated. Once the judge threw the book at Microsoft, it was as if he had declared "open season" on mergers and cooperative business relationships. This massive social change in attitude is consistent with the transition to a bear market in stocks.

*Chapter 28*

# The Land of Flint and Steel

Global conflict is a product of a downturn in social mood. The inescapable tensions between nations and distinct social groups that arise at such times is best illustrated by our long term chart of the "Political Results of Social Sentiment" (see page 337 of *The Wave Principle of Human Social Behavior* or the June, 2000 issue of *The Elliott Wave Financial Forecast*), which shows Hitler's rise to power, World War II, the Holocaust and the dropping of two atomic bombs on Japan between the bear market lows of 1932, 1942 and 1949.

Social clashes take myriad forms, but one bellwether rift that has an almost perfect record of erupting into open hostility right at the onset of major downturns is in the Mideast. Figure 1 shows that relations between Jews and Arabs in Israel (or Palestine before 1948) have been particularly responsive to the onset of important bear markets since 1929. In that year, says *The Year of the Great Crash*, "All hell had broken loose in Palestine. At the end of August, a series of relatively inconsequential disputes concerning the privileges of worship for Jews and Muslims erupted into an orgy of bloodletting." The violence came a few days before the Dow's final high.

If major hostilities are defined as wars or mob violence that result in mass killings, each of the headlines on the graph marks a significant outbreak. All were preceded by periods of easing tension (or at least an absence of bloodshed) and followed by further clashes. The greatest stretch of peaceful cooperation between the two sides is shown in the Era of Good Feelings table at the bottom of Figure 1. It started on September 13, 1993 with the famous handshake between the Prime Minister of Israel and the Chairman of the Palestine Liberation Organization. Historians said the handshake was a symbol of "a major breakthrough after a century of conflict." *The Elliott Wave Theorist* identified it as a product of the century-long advance in stock prices

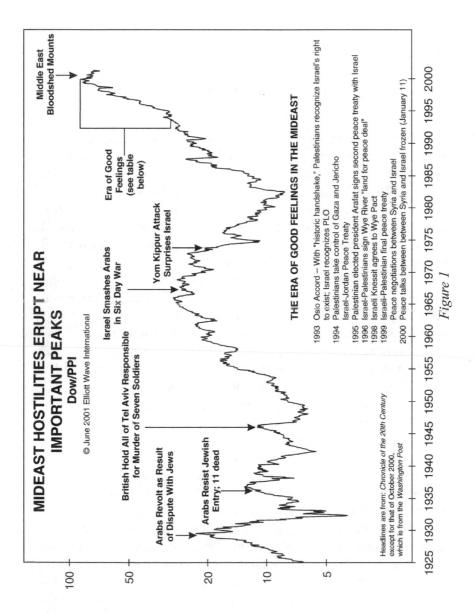

*Figure 1*

that would mark a long-term top rather than a great new era for Palestinian and Israeli relations. The next seven years of bull market yielded productive talks but no lasting peace. As late as January 30, 2000, the *Houston Chronicle* reported that the "tide of history" was moving the "Mideast toward peace."

In reality, however, the tide had already reversed. In July 2000, the same paper would mark the moment by reporting, "Syrian-Israeli peace negotiations have been frozen since mid-January." The exact date of the freeze was January 11, *three days before the Dow's all-time high.* By last summer, the anxiety level was clearly rising fast as the Palestinians threatened to declare statehood and another peace conference failed to produce a breakthrough for the first time since 1993. As stocks entered their September-October swoon, Palestinian sections of Israel exploded in a continuous wave of rioting. In December, this headline evidenced the depth of anger: "As Arafat Embraces Revolt, His Sagging Popularity Rises." Israel responded with the election of hardliner Ariel Sharon. In the first half of May 2001, the situation bordered on open warfare. "Is It War Yet?" asked one headline on May 20. On May 21, the Bush administration criticized Israel for using U.S. supplied warplanes against Palestinians for the first time since the 1967 war, which was a year after the peak of Cycle III. Finally, on May 22, the day of the Dow's secondary high, there was a "glimmer of hope" as Sharon talked of compromise and ordered Israeli forces "only to return fire if shot at."

Past signals have usually come at and after long term turns, although the 1967 outbreak was followed by a run that almost made a new high in 1968. Given that precedent, perhaps the unfolding crisis in the Mideast does not preclude a new high in the Dow. If the Dow goes to a new high, the conflict may ease briefly, but a historic sell signal for the stock market has clearly been issued by the open warfare. The Mideast's record as an *early* register of negative social mood suggests that a major bear market and thus the trend toward global hostility has only just begun.

Prechter
*The Elliott Wave Theorist*
September 11, 2001


*Chapter 29*

# Elliott Waves Guide Social Reality

*We here at EWI have lost dear friends in the World Trade Center attack. We grieve for them and for those of you who have suffered the loss of loved ones.*

As terrible as today's tragedy is, we must pause to point out another tragedy, which is that so few understand why it happened, what will happen next and what they can do about it. This issue of *The Elliott Wave Theorist* will try to present an unemotional account of these issues.

Sometimes it takes an appalling drama to stir people from lethargy and make them pay attention to matters of grave importance. If your friends and family have yet to wake up to the Wave Principle's crucial message, please do your part to help them realize where we are in the social cycle and why it matters. For this issue, we will suspend our ban against re-transmission so that you may distribute it to others as you see fit.

Comfort and safety come from *understanding.* If you can see the big picture clearly, both past and future, you will be able to make fruitful decisions calmly.

As this issue is being composed and issued in a single day, please excuse any passages that appear rough or incautious.

### Understanding the Engine of Social Trends

The radical thesis of *The Wave Principle of Human Social Behavior and the New Science of Socionomics* (New Classics Library, 1999) was unmistakably manifest in the raucous social comedy of the 1990s, and now it is playing out in the first act of a developing worldwide social tragedy that will last years. The primary thesis of this book is that *changes in social mood **cause** and therefore **precede** changes in the character of social events*. In contrast to this idea, most people erroneously try to divine the implications of events in attempts to forecast financial markets and people's collective feelings. Their approach *cannot* work because *markets are driven by natural trends in mass psychology*, and events resulting from those psychological trends come *afterward*. It is the changes in such trends, as indicated by turns in the stock market, that signal a coming change in the tenor of social events.

An equally radical thesis underlying socionomics is that *social mood is patterned, and it is patterned according to the Wave Principle.* Since these patterned mood trends precipitate social events, you can *forecast the character of social events* by tracking the trends and patterns in the primary meter of social mood, the stock market.

*The Wave Principle of Human Social Behavior* explained why global atrocities *followed* the 1929-1932 crash and continued during most of the rest of the bear market pattern, which ended in 1949. It also explained why the worldwide peace initiatives and unprecedented acts of reconciliation of the 1990s *followed* nearly half a century of social mood uptrend. The dramatic, historic pictures shown in Chapter 18 of that book convey the power of these moods were not placed there simply for academic purposes. This is real life we're talking about. You have to live near those events to sense that fact.

### Forecasting the Tenor of Social Events

Such observations have not simply been reflections on the past. In 1982, *The Elliott Wave Theorist* forecast a rising stock market, boom times and "no war for at least ten years."[1]

*At the Crest of the Tidal Wave* (1995) then forecast the next major change, saying in no uncertain terms that severe social unrest would follow the onset of what was then the approaching—and is now the developing—Grand Supercycle bear market. Here is the book's introduction to that topic:

> **SOCIAL IMPLICATIONS** [excerpted from *At the Crest of the Tidal Wave*, pp.432-433]
> While the Wave Principle is the single best method for anticipating the behavior of markets, its value at times goes way beyond even that great benefit. As explained in Chapter 12, the effects that a change in market trend will have on society are not in evidence at the start of the trend. They become intensely manifest by the time of its termination. Is it too early to begin projecting events that will result from the approaching bear market in social mood? To be sure, this book contains dozens of very specific financial

forecasts, which are at root social phenomena. Forecasting social events outside that realm, however, is an even more complex and less exact science. Nevertheless, a few observations appear suited to the limited scope of this book.

A long term trend toward a positive social mood always leads to times of peace and political cooperation, such as we enjoy today. An extreme trend change in social mood toward the negative always leads to calamities. The average level of conflict during the bear market will be far greater than it was during the bull market and will lead to periods of turmoil, not just in financial markets, but in society. Indeed, the trends now implied by long term market patterns have *always* produced dramatic social upheaval. The last time a bear market of the currently projected magnitude took place was 1720 to 1784, a period that began with a market crash, ended with the Revolutionary War, and led to a deep and global five-year depression.

The developing trend of negative social psychology will be characterized primarily by polarization between and among various perceived groups, whether political, ideological, religious, geographical, racial or economic. The result will be a net trend toward anger, fear, intolerance, disagreement and exclusion, as opposed to the bull market years, whose net trend has been toward benevolence, confidence, tolerance, agreement and inclusion. Such a sentiment change typically brings conflict in many forms, and evidence of it will be visible in all types of social organizations. Political manifestations will include protectionism in trade matters, a polarized and vocal electorate, separatist movements, xenophobia, citizen-government clashes, the dissolution of old alliances and parties, and the emergence of radical new ones. Tariffs will become popular, regardless of the fact that virtually everyone knows they are dangerous and wrong, because they are a consequence of an increasingly negative psychology involving fear, envy and a misguided attempt at self-defense. Xenophobia will be practiced regardless of people's generally good intentions, because fear and hatred become pervasive in major bear markets regardless of whether or not they are justified. There will also be a danger that governments will impose police-state type controls as a consequence of the bear market. Such periods often end with emotional political oustings, whether by vote, resignation, impeachment, coup or revolution.

The worst economic and social programs are years away, but advance planning is incalculably better than trying to react when it is too late.

## Forecasting Styles of Social Events

Here is another esoteric point but one of great value. A section on "Nuances" in Chapter 15 of *The Wave Principle of Human Social Behavior* explains that negative social themes due to appear in any approaching bear market first express themselves in milder form in the preceding fourth wave of one lesser degree. Stop for a minute until you get this idea. Here is a more detailed explanation: Social mood repeatedly traces out five waves up followed by three waves down. The negative themes in "wave four" within the "fives waves up" presage those that will dominate, *more dramatically and on a much bigger scale*, in the ensuing "three waves down."

This is true of the styles of cultural trends. For example, *Psycho* came out in 1962, at the end of a fourth wave correction of Primary degree. In the larger bear market of 1966-1982, slasher films (the *Halloween* and *Friday the 13th* series) were a dominant theme.

It is also true of the character of social events. In an earlier fourth wave from 1916 to 1921, collectivists took over Russia. In the larger fourth wave that followed, from 1929 to 1949, collectivists took over nearly half of the earth's population, in Germany, Italy, Eastern Europe and China.

In the current case, the most recent fourth wave of Cycle degree or higher took place from 1966 to 1982, roughly, "the '70s." Aside from a slew of terrorist incidents in the 1910s,[2] a decade dominated by a long bear market in stocks, *the idea of "terrorism" as a social force began with the 1966-1982 bear market*. A 10-volume chronology of American social history over the last 100 years (*American Decades*, Manly, Inc.) lists *no* acts of terrorism in the 1920s, 1930s, 1940s, 1950s or the 1960s. In early 1970, when the Dow was in year four and the Value Line Composite in year two of a Cycle-degree bear market, the age of terrorism began. An Arab terrorist strike killed one person and injured 23 in Munich. On February 21, 1970, another group of suspected Arab terrorists hijacked a Swissair flight and crashed it. On September 6-9, 1970, Palestinian terrorists hijacked five planes and blew up three. Unlike the earlier period of "scattered terrorist bombings" in the 1910s, this era was distinguished by the frequency, extent and organization behind the attacks. As the bear market continued, the events grew in size and complexity. The increasing sophistication of terrorist tactics and their rising political power is revealed by the progression from the scattered strikes in 1970 to the PLO raid on the Olympic Village in Munich in 1972 and eventually to a state-sponsored takeover of the U.S. embassy in Iran in 1979. The worst of it ended approximately when the bear market did, as Iran finally released its U.S. hostages in January 1981. In those first terrorist acts committed against the United States, we caught a glimpse of the style of conflicts that we would have to endure when the bear market of next bigger size arrived, which it certainly has.

Neither is this point made only in retrospect. Our recent publications have speculated as to specific social actions that will take place during Grand Supercycle wave ⒾⓋ, and *The Wave Principle of Human Social Behavior* listed events typically associated with major bull and bear markets. Two excerpted comments summarize the scene that has just come to pass:

> "Foreigners will commit terrorist acts on U.S. soil...."
> — *At the Crest of the Tidal Wave* (1995)
> Chapter 21, p.435

> "The impulse to build shows up in the construction of record-breaking skyscraper buildings at social-mood peaks. At troughs, few buildings are built, and many of those already in place may be burned or bombed out of existence."
> — *The Wave Principle of Human Social Behavior and the New Science of Socionomics* (1999)
> Chapter 14, pp.229-230

Here is a summary of today's event, which truly is "more dramatic and on much bigger scale" than those that occurred during the previous fourth wave of the 1970s:

> New York, Sept. 11 (Bloomberg)—The attacks on the World Trade Center and Pentagon today are the worst acts of terrorism ever on U.S. soil and change the scope of foreign policy, experts say.

> Never before has a large-scale terrorist attack on the U.S. been coordinated successfully in more than one U.S. city. At this point, no organization has taken responsibility.

"It's just an attack of extraordinarily sophisticated planning," said Michael R. Fischbach, a professor of history specializing in the Middle East at Randolph-Macon College in Ashland, Virginia. "The world that we know has now changed."

"Americans' whole attitude about daily life, about foreign policy will be forever changed," Fischbach said.

"The world that we know has changed" is a correct statement, but it did not change "now." It changed between January 14 and March 24, 2000, a two-month period during which the three major U.S. stock indexes signaled the end of a Grand Supercycle uptrend that had been in force for *216 years*. We are only now beginning to feel the lagging results of that change.

The 1966-1982 period had many other unfortunate characteristics that we will see again to a larger extent in the current bear market. At *Grand Supercycle degree*, however, the "preceding fourth wave" actually refers to 1929-1949. As the Grand Supercycle bear market pattern unfolds over the next few generations, eventually it will bring on the kinds of conflicts that ruled *that* correction.

Do you recognize the value of this information? Most people understandably fret over whether or not an action is "a one-time event" and speculate on whether "the worst is over" without *any idea* of how to answer these questions. Socionomics can answer them, and it does. Right now, we can say with confidence, *we are at the beginning of a long period of social unrest, and while it will wax and wane with the waves, overall it will intensify*. The best time to prepare was two years ago, but it is *not too late* to do so now.

## Symbols as the Focus of Anger

During the 1990s, we studied the history of skyscraper construction and issued several reports on the correlation between the erection of tall buildings and the late stages of positive long-term social mood trends. As EWT stated in April 1996, "Of all the cultural relationships we consider here, the link between stock prices and the tallest buildings is one of the most fascinating because it is literally etched in stone." We concluded that skyscrapers are "monuments to peaking social mood." Some people take such studies as frivolous. They are not. Now that we are in a negative social mood trend of greater magnitude than any since the construction of the first skyscrapers in the 1890s, we should hardly be shocked that the forces expressing the emerging downtrend in mood have aimed their sights at these towering structures, symbols of the productive optimism of Grand Supercycle wave Ⓘ.

## Why Now?/What's Next?

Generally speaking, the most shocking news in the social context comes in two places: in declining *fifth* waves and in declining *C* waves. The stock market is not in a *C* wave. Since the all-time high, it has been in wave **a** of what will eventually be an **a-b-c** decline. *Within* wave **a**, it is almost certainly in wave 5.

If the stock market is indeed in wave 5 down, then this wave will end within days or weeks and lead to a substantial A-B-C rally (or perhaps a triangle) for wave **b**. Then wave **c** down will begin. If this assessment proves correct, it is good news for the short term. If instead, the "big crash" is upon us, we should know shortly after the markets' reopening. Rest assured that *The Elliott Wave Financial Forecast* (perhaps with an Interim Report) and the *Short Term Update* (to be published next on Wednesday night, whether markets are open or not) will keep you abreast of all our conclusions regarding the stock market, and bonds, gold and the U.S. dollar as well.

## A Long Term Development

Today's terrorist focus on the United States is *not* an isolated, inexplicable situation. The founding fathers, notably George Washington and John Adams, warned our new country against foreign entanglements. They begged us, in Washington's words, "in regard to foreign nations... to have with them as little *political* connection as possible." (Source: http://www.virginia.edu/gwpapers/farewell/transcript.html.) Contrary to this advice, many U.S. presidents of the twentieth century, usually citing altruistic motives, have insinuated our government into foreign hives to such an extent that we have finally stirred one set of bees into reacting. Though no one has yet "taken credit" for today's atrocities, the actions of the perpetrators are surely irrational, perhaps based on dreams of global domination or the hope of a glorious reward in the next world. That is, generally speaking, what the founding fathers feared: the mire of foreign political irrationality. The environment in which we are currently beginning to suffer results from decades of redirected government policy, and the underlying cause of *that* change is the initially brave but ultimately reckless set of shared emotions underlying the magnificent ascent of Grand Supercycle wave ⓘⓘⓘ. This is not to affix blame on "us." Many everyday Americans have decried our "police the world" policies, and our leaders' penchant for well intentioned meddling has just been part of the social pattern. Its outcome was therefore predictable. Tens of times during the past decade, we at EWI cringed as our president issued yet another threatening ultimatum to various other countries' governments (at least seven, which we documented in EWT at the time). We thought, *"Does he know what this attitude will lead to, how many Americans it will ultimately endanger?"* All the while, and in keeping with the waxing mood of invincibility, our "fundamentals"—in terms of national intelligence, security and military preparedness—were going to seed. Don't let anyone tell you that these attacks and our lack of preparation are a surprise. They are the result of feelings of complacency and overconfidence born of the final decades of GS ⓘⓘⓘ. Ironic as it may seem, the suffering in bear markets is greatly the consequence of cavalier policies adopted late in bull markets.

**The Utility of Socionomics**

Are Elliott waves and socionomics purely academic toys? They are not. Like good philosophy, they are not just *theoretically* correct; they are *practical* and useful in everyday life. At major junctures, understanding the change at hand can mean the difference between success and failure, life and death. The people who started successful businesses in 1949 and 1982 or went bankrupt in 1933 and 1975 understand the first point. The people who got out of Europe in 1938, or who stayed there, would understand the second.

In coming months and years, others will be repeatedly shocked over "surprising" single events, which they do not understand as being part of a larger pattern. At least you will know *that* we are in a pattern and even, most of the time, *where* we are in it. From that, you can make important decisions that will guide your life.

**Getting the Word Out**

In response to a question about how EWT's long-term stock market forecast would be remembered, the February 2000 issue responded as follows:

"Most people will not be paying as much attention to the stock market after it falls, so in a few years, *most of today's investors will not care who predicted what. Their focus will be on other things.*"

People have also asked me in the past two years why I have stayed off television. Forecasting unrest during good times is like singing to rocks. Nobody's listening. Then once the unrest begins, you can't be heard over the cacophony. Everyone's singing, and most of it is off key. Besides, you cannot communicate a book's worth of analysis and advice like *The Wave Principle of Human Social Behavior* in 2½ minutes. You have to sit down and read them.

## NOTES

[1] Prechter, Robert R. (1982, October 6). *The Elliott Wave Theorist*

[2] The first act of terrorism listed in *American Decades* is the explosion of the Los Angeles Times Building in October 1910, which was linked to organized labor. The last one of note was a bomb that rocked Wall Street on September 16, 1920. The scars of that blast can still be seen in the façade of 23 Wall Street, then as now the offices of J.P. Morgan Inc. The financial attack centered on Wall Street became physically manifest. Almost the same thing has happened today.

*Chapter 30*

# World Peace, World War, Fibonacci and Elliott

U.S. President George W. Bush made two statements that, taken together, may turn out to be meaningful to history. He called the September 11 attacks "an act of war" and, speaking to all the governments of the world, said, "You are either with us, or you're with the terrorists." Taken together, these statements conjure the image of world war. Will this inference prove to be hyperbole or reality?

The 20th century was one of the most violent and deadly in history. Most of the deaths were not due to war, however; they were due to governments slaughtering their own people, primarily in China, the Soviet Union, Germany and Cambodia (in that order). Nevertheless, the mortality rate in the 20th century's two world wars was substantial and dwarfed that of most previous wars. The last time that a war was as deadly for Americans as World War II was the Civil War. These wars followed the bottoms of Supercycle bear markets, waves (IV) and (II) respectively. (See Chapters 16 and 18 *The Wave Principle of Human Social Behavior*.)

Many are saying that the attack on the World Trade Center and the Pentagon is analogous to the Japanese attack on Pearl Harbor in 1941. It is alike both in the element of surprise and in causing about an equal number of deaths. But perhaps it will eventually turn out alike in also having sparked world war.

So is the world headed for war, and if so, has it begun? This issue will explore a time progression that suggests that a world war has begun. It will also give reasons, based on the history of wars and their usual position in the Elliott wave pattern, for believing that the greater risk lies several decades in the future.

## A Fibonacci Progression in War and Peace over the Past Century

As detailed in *The Wave Principle of Human Social Behavior*, the Fibonacci sequence governs many of the forms and processes within animate objects. It also governs aspects of aggregate human interaction, as indicated by the patterns of the Wave Principle. A growing body of evidence suggests that the *timing* of social change is governed to some degree by the Fibonacci sequence as well.

A Fibonacci number of days or years often separates major turning points in the stock market. Such durations are often tempered, slightly exceeding or falling short of precise Fibonacci numbers. Any difference is only one unit in durations up to 55 and expands thereafter accordingly. For example, the advance from the lowest point of Supercycle wave (II) in 1842 to the high of Supercycle wave (III) in 1929 took 87 years, which is **89** (-2) years. Within those parameters, the periods of world war and periods of relative world peace since 1914 seem to be governed by a Fibonacci progression, as detailed in Figure 1.

The assassination of Archduke Ferdinand of Austria in 1914 sparked World War I. World War II began when Hitler seized Austria in 1938 (but was not officially declared until 1939 upon the invasion of Poland). From their sparking points, these two wars lasted four years and seven years respectively, which are a Fibonacci **3** (+1) years and **8** (-1) years. The periods of world-scale peace that followed these wars lasted twenty years and fifty-six years (so far) respectively, which are a Fibonacci **21** (-1) years and **55** (+1) years. As shown in Figure 1, the two world-war durations skip a Fibonacci number (5), and the two peace durations (to date) skip a Fibonacci number as well (34).

Notice that each set of numbers alternates between +1 and -1 in the war durations and -1 and +1 in the peace durations. These differences cancel each other out in a sense, so that an idealized progression arrives at the same year, 2001. To illustrate, *if* the following durations had occurred, we would have ended up at the same point from 1914: World War I lasting **3** years to 1917, peace lasting **21** years to 1938, World War II lasting **8** years to 1946 and peace lasting **55** years to 2001. In other words, the Fibonacci progression 3+21+8+55 covers the ground from 1914 to 2001. The turn dates in history were off by one year each time, alternating between "long" and "short" periods.

# WORLD PEACE, WORLD WAR AND FIBONACCI
© 2001 Elliott Wave International

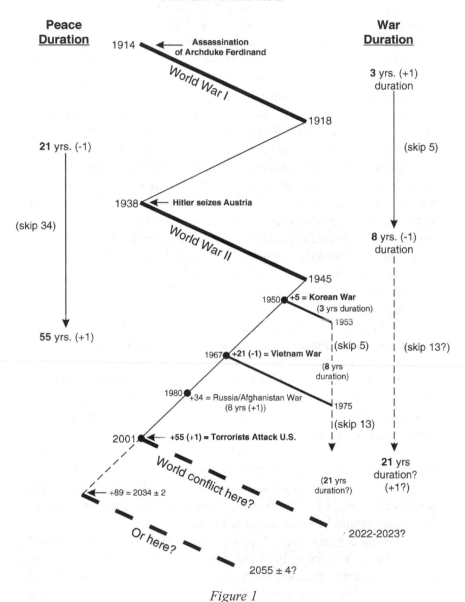

*Figure 1*

**Subordinate Fibonacci Progressions in War Since 1945**

The long period of relative worldwide peace from 1945 to 2001 was hardly benign. Lesser conflicts erupted that involved the United States. As you can see beside the "bullet" points in Figure 1, those conflicts occurred on a Fibonacci progression from 1945. The Korean War began **5** years after 1945, and the U.S. sent troops to begin the Vietnam War **21** (-1) years after 1945. (Also, the Indochina War began **1** year after 1945 and was a precursor to the Vietnam War. Russia invaded Afghanistan **34** years after 1945, which is a precursor of the current conflict.) Now after **55** years, a "War on Terrorism" may have begun.

Notice that the progression of U.S. involvement in important wars skips some of the Fibonacci numbers in this sequence. U.S. involvement begins with the Korean War after **5** years, skips 8 and 13, returns with the Vietnam War after **21** (-1) years, skips 34 and returns again with last month's terrorist attack after **55** (+1) years. Conflicts that did *not* fall on the Fibonacci progression, such as the Cuban Missile Crisis, the war in Grenada and the Persian Gulf War, caused very few U.S. casualties.

There is another progression. Each of these interim wars involving the U.S. lasted a Fibonacci number of years (+ or − 1). The Korean War lasted **3** years, and the U.S. fought the Vietnam War for **8** years. (Russia also fought Afghanistan for **8** (+1) years.) Notice that these durations—**3** and **8**—are the same as those for World Wars I and II. Like the first progression, this one also implies a **21**-year duration for the next global conflict.

**The Combined Picture**

As you can see, the attack that took place in September 2001 is doubly significant in terms of Fibonacci time progressions. It occurred at the culmination of a Fibonacci progression of peace durations from 1918 and a Fibonacci progression of war commencement from 1945. The smaller progression implies that 2001 is a year to be concerned about the onset of U.S. involvement in a war. The larger progression implies that 2001 is a year to be concerned about the onset of U.S. involvement in a *world* war.

**The Presumed Outlook from Figure 1**

The suspected Fibonacci progressions are hardly extensive enough to demonstrate statistically that they are real. The larger progression does not extend back into the 19th century. These progressions could be no more than an imposed construct.

*If* these Fibonacci progressions continue, then a significant war has begun. *If* the progression on the left of Figure 1 is valid, then a *world* war has begun. Regarding its duration, *if* the skipping of Fibonacci durations continues, as implied by *both* progressions of "war duration," then one would expect the current conflict to last twenty-one years. *If* the progression of plus and minus one year continues, that duration would last an extra year. 2001 + 21-22 years comes out to 2022-2023.

Given the fact that the genesis of the current conflict is less the product of the designs of political states and more the product of radical elements within a religion that has millions of adherents in numerous countries around the world, the suggested worldwide scope and extended duration of struggle should not be lightly dismissed.

**Update for 2015**

On November 13, 2015, Pope Francis called the terrorist attacks in France part of a "piecemeal third World War,"[1] and on November 28 a Huffington Post headline wondered, "Has World War III Already Started?"[2] While the U.S. has been involved militarily in the Middle East since the 1950s, the beginning of the period of continuous conflict began with the retaliatory jihadist attack of September 11, 2001, fitting our forecast made the month after it occurred. The progress of this war is reminiscent of that of the Vietnam War, which simmered for years before erupting into full-scale engagement. Its intensity should continue to wax and wane with the stock market.

**NOTES**

[1] Serrano, Richard A. et al. "As Paris reels, investigators piece together the attackers' stories," *The Los Angeles Times*, November 14, 2015.

[2] Micallef, Joseph V., "Has World War III Already Started?" *The Huffington Post*, November 28, 2015.

Prechter
*The Elliott Wave Theorist*
June 1, 2002

*Chapter 31*

# The Socionomic Insight vs.
# The Assumption of Event Causality
# The Enron Scandal

## The Socionomic Insight

The socionomic insight is that the conventional assumption about the direction of causality between social mood and social action is not only incorrect but the opposite of what actually occurs. Socionomics is based on a principle developed by deduction from the existence of the Wave Principle and by induction from the chronology of market behavior and other social actions. The principle is that *social mood determines the character of social events.*

As previous studies demonstrate, rising stock trends do not improve the public mood; an improving social mood makes stock prices rise. Economics do not underlie social mood; social mood underlies economics. Stock trends do not follow corporate earnings; corporate earnings follow stock trends. Politics do not affect social mood; social mood affects politics. Demographics do not determine stock market trends; the social mood that determines stock market trends determines demographics. Styles of popular art and entertainment do not affect the social mood; the social mood determines the popularity of various styles of art and entertainment. War does not impact stock market trends; the mood that governs stock market trends determines the propensity for war. And so on. All economic, political and cultural developments are shaped and guided by the Wave Principle of human social behavior. It is the engine of everything from popular fads and fashions to the events of collective action that make history.

Conventional belief is the opposite of the above insight. It is solidly entrenched and pervasive almost to the point of ubiquity. It is deeply intuitive and utterly wrong.

The conventional mind sees social events as causes of social mood. Few ever ask the causes of the events themselves. Those who do simply assign the causes to other events.

## The Counterintuitive Nature of the Socionomic Insight

I continually marvel at how counter-intuitive the socionomic insight is. For the entire time of my professional career, I have been comfortable with the central implication of technical analysis, which is the primacy of market form over extramarket events such as economics and politics. (I eventually discovered to my dismay that technicians rarely accept this implication and believe that various random, unpredictable "fundamentals" are behind the market's patterns, which is a contradiction.) Yet even I find myself upon occasion having to work hard at dispelling old contradictory thought patterns in order to re-establish mental integrity on the more difficult challenges of the socionomic insight. My first real challenge came from the claim that "demographics" determined stock price trends. I knew the claim had to be incorrect, and it took only a few days of research to debunk it. But it was only during the course of that pursuit that I began to formulate the proper response: that if indeed there were any correlation at all, *the causality had to be in the other direction*. The result was the 1999 study, *Stocks and Sex*, which shows exactly that. My latest—and greatest—challenge to date has been the proper conception of the Federal Reserve Bank's role in the causality of monetary trends, which I will discuss in an upcoming report. [See Chapter 13.—Ed.]

The average person's resistance to the socionomic insight is so formidable that it compares to having one's view of existence challenged. I believe that the reason for this resistance is the easy naturalness of the idea of event causality: It works in physics, so people assume that it must operate in sociology. This deeply rooted assumption is stronger than piles of evidence to the contrary.

Let me give you an example of how strong this resistance is. On April 25, 2002, I was pleased to address a conference on the psychology of investing sponsored by an arm of Harvard Medical School. Attendance ran the gamut from academics and psychiatrists to Wall Street professionals and private investors. It was a great group of people. After presenting the Wave Principle of social mood and explaining its social effects, numerous attendees kindly told me that the presentation had changed their perspective on markets and social causality.

The following day, I attended the event's final half hour, in which attendees were given the opportunity to ask questions of that day's panel. The final question was, "The Enron scandal has deeply discouraged investors; what can we do to remove this black cloud hanging over the stock market?"

Respondents from both the panel and the audience dealt with the question as if it were valid. Not a soul in the room challenged the questioner's assumption. An earnest discussion followed. I was upset but remained silent. Clearly I hadn't made a dent in anyone's thinking.

A week later, *USA Today* and doubtless countless other newspapers and magazines trumpeted the same theme. "Scandals Shred Investors' Faith," declared a front-page headline. Begins the article, "A drumbeat of corporate misdeeds has helped crush stock prices and eviscerate pension plans."[1]

If you recognize the socionomic insight as a *principle*, you need know nothing about the details of the situation. You can formulate the proper response immediately. Before reading further, would you like to give it a try? Remember, the socionomic insight is that the conventional assumption about the direction of social mood vs. event causality is the *opposite* of what actually occurs. I will make your task easy by re-stating the assumption that the questioner held: "The Enron scandal discouraged investors." Can you state its opposite in terms of causality?

### The Significance of the Enron Scandal

Did the Enron scandal discourage investors? *No, discouraged investors precipitated the Enron scandal.*

Many readers undoubtedly will balk at accepting the principle behind this formulation without their own tedious process of induction via repeated examples. To aid in that process once again, we must disprove the questioner's and media's false premise and demonstrate the validity of the socionomic stance.

First, let us define scandal not as misdeeds themselves, which can occur in secret. Scandal is the recognition of misdeeds, the outcry of recrimination and the public display of interest and outrage.

The premise is revealed as utterly false when we observe, despite virtually everyone's *feelings* to the contrary, that (1) investors in general knew nothing about Enron's malpractice prior to or anytime during the stock market's decline, and (2) *throughout the drama of the Enron scandal, the market advanced, and related psychological indicators improved*. Figure 1 shows the stock market's progress, two measures

*Figure 1*

of optimism and the key events surrounding the Enron scandal. It is abundantly clear that as the Enron scandal developed, *investor and consumer psychology improved, and stock prices rose.* Therefore, it is utterly false that the Enron scandal "discouraged investors."

Anyone who posits event causality in this instance is boxed into a corner. Given the facts before our eyes, he has no choice but to conclude that the Enron scandal was bullish for stock prices and that it caused investors' mood to improve![2]

I would like to proceed directly to what would seem to be an obvious statement: that such a conclusion is ridiculous. Incredibly, though, I cannot say it. Why? Because conventional analysts *actually proceed directly to such absurd conclusions repeatedly as a matter of course.* For example, *The Wave Principle of Human Social Behavior* relates a news report of an analyst who watched the stock market rally despite revelations of President Clinton's misbehavior and came to the conclusion that presidential sex scandals are bullish! Economists have reviewed the temporal proximity of war and economic recovery, and they assert, almost to a man, that war is good for the economy. If economists can argue that the most destructive activity of man is a positive force for economic well being, then conventional thinkers will have no trouble devising an argument as to why financial scandals are bullish. I can do it myself; such rationalization is easy.

The only antidote to such perversity is the socionomic insight. War is not causal to any aspect of social mood; it is a *result* of a deeply negative social mood. Likewise, the Enron scandal was not causal to any aspect of social mood whatsoever; it was a *result* of a change in social mood.[3]

Figure 2 demonstrates the chronology that supports this statement. As you can see, the stock market fell for many months prior to the scandal breaking. This meter of social mood showed increasing negativity—involving conservatism, suspicion, fear, anger and defensiveness—all of which went into precipitating the Enron scandal. As the CEO later explained, increasing conservatism affected the company's derivative positions, bear markets triggered "exit clauses" that allowed partners to their deals to withdraw their funds, and increasing fear and suspicion prompted them to do it. Throughout 2001, the company's stock retreated, removing support for financing. The house of cards built upon confidence collapsed.

*Figure 2*

By the time the *results* of that negative mood trend brought the Enron scandal to light, the negative mood trend was already over. The S&P 500 completed five waves down on September 21, and it was time for the largest rally since the high in March 2000 (as forecast in *The Elliott Wave Theorist* on September 11). During that rally, these particular consequences of the downward mood trend became manifest.[4]

Now we know for sure: The Enron scandal did not "discourage investors" or "shred investors' faith" *one bit*. Their level of faith *rose* during the scandals. It did not "crush stock prices and eviscerate pension plans," either. Stock prices *rose* during the scandals. All the hand wringing and ink spilling on this presumption has been a waste of time and energy.

To make a subtler point, "corporate misdeeds" are not even to blame for the bear market that *preceded* the eruption of the Enron scandal. Corporate misdeeds were in full flower throughout the 1990s, yet no scandals erupted. In fact, those very misdeeds—Ponzi-like accounting practices—could be credited with *raising* stock prices and *fattening* pension plans during the 1990s to the same extent that they could be blamed for crushing and eviscerating them now.

Yet the proper amount of credit to assign to suspect accounting practices for both trends in stock prices is zero. The credit goes to a change in mass psychology. Various accounting irregularities were an *effect* of the psychological environment. They were in place for years, and they were reported from time to time, sometimes in major journals, *but during the bull market, few cared.* Corporate *misbehavior* persisted for a decade, but there was no *scandal* until well after the trend changed. While the trend was up, people ignored the phony accounting; when the trend turned down, they began to investigate it. When the trend was up, psychology supported both actual and illusory corporate health; when the trend turned down, psychology caused both actual and illusory corporate health to deteriorate rapidly. Again, the formulation of causality is the opposite of the conventional belief: Corporate misdeeds did not crush stock prices; crushed stock prices finally drew back the curtain on corporate misdeeds. What, then, caused corporate misdeeds to expand so greatly in the first place? The mass psychology of the stock mania, which was unskeptical to an extreme, invited and even rewarded companies for "creative accounting." It was the psychological environment of the bull market that led companies to dare to mislead investors in the first place.

**The Power of Socionomic Prediction**

Figure 2 at least sets the chronology of the true cause and effect with respect to the Enron scandal. It falls short of proving it, of course, as the other option regarding causality is that the two events (and all the others we have explored) are unrelated. Let's see if we can dismiss that hypothesis.

An important aspect of science is the ability of a hypothesis to *predict*. Using the socionomic insight, could anyone have predicted the flood of accounting and corporate scandals that has so far climaxed with the revelations regarding Enron?

The answer is yes. Moreover, someone did.

At the height of the stock mania and during the months thereafter, Peter Kendall of Elliott Wave International went on record in *The Elliott Wave Theorist* and *The Elliott Wave Financial Forecast* identifying the end of the line for what we dubbed "bull market accounting standards" and forecasting a climate of scandal and recrimination. As we now know, that emerging climate decimated images of all kinds of heroes, from corporate CEOs to economists to brokerage firm analysts to accountants, to name just a few. The ensuing commentary[5] shows the predictive advantage of the socionomic perspective in the area of corporate scandal (emphases added):

*September 16, 1998*

> The discovery of "fictitious revenue" at Cendant Corp. [first reported just 13 days after the all-time peak in the advance-decline line on April 3, 1998] is part of a slow awakening to the realization that the fundamentals of many companies, weak as they have become, are not even what they purport to be. Financial improprieties at Sunbeam, Oxford Health, Green Tree Financial, Boston Chicken and Mercury Financial have also been reported.... The emerging shift in social mood is beginning to shatter the collective financial delusion. *These stories can "now be told" because people are disposed to listen to them. As the bear market unfolds, many more "scandalous" cases will be revealed.*

*October 1, 1999*

> Accounting standards have eroded as the bull market has aged. The flip side of these papered-over cracks in the fundamentals is that in a bear market they will be an enormous weight on growth. Combined with the unprecedented global economic dependence on a rising U.S. stock market, the likelihood is that they will exert their drag with stunning speed.

*February 25, 2000*

> *The bull market's attendant accounting gimmicks will get a lot more ink as the blinding light of the new era gives way to sober reflection and recrimination.*

*May 26, 2000*

> **Financial Shenanigans Coming to Light:** Some of the lame excuses for optimism are being outed. As *The Elliott Wave Theorist* noted in our 1998 Special Report on the relative weakness of the fundamentals in Cycle V vs. Cycle III, *"the enduring psychological coercion of the bull market"* has compensated for Cycle V's obvious fundamental shortcomings with the general acceptance of accounting standards that overstate the quality of companies' financial performance. The exposure of fallacious bull-market bookkeeping has been a subject of ongoing discussion in EWFF. For our purposes, the importance is not the transgressions themselves but the timing of their discovery and repudiation. This process has accelerated in the wake of the NASDAQ's retreat. There is now "growing concern among accounting professionals that many companies are relying on financial alchemy to burnish their results." Instead of peripheral corporate players and outright fraud, the charges of "financial engineering" are now being leveled against stalwarts like Microsoft, Dell and Cisco Systems *for accounting practices that have been known to be in place for years*. Less than a month after Cisco was tabbed as the new stock-market bellwether, its aggressive acquisition strategy was profiled as a "modern house of cards" in *Barron's*. Days later, Cisco's reported earnings, which surpassed analysts' expectations by one cent for the 12th straight quarter, failed to produce the usual upside pop.

*June 30, 2000*

> Last month, we reported that the exposure of slack bull market accounting standards and outright frauds was worth watching as an indication that the "return to sobriety" was gaining ground.... It turns out that *Cendant's accounting shenanigans date all the way back to its initial public offering in 1983*. As columnist Floyd Norris notes, "For investors, the most interesting question is not whether [the firm's founder] will go to jail. It is how this fraud managed to go on so long." The answer, according to a

professor of accounting who has studied a report on Cendant's bookkeeping practices, is that *"auditors were fooled because, in some measure at least, they wanted to be fooled." This, at bottom, is the thesis of socionomics. The social mood dictates how people treat real data. From 1983 through 1999, public mood was in a bull market. This year, it all changed, and so has the socially perceived reality.*

A steady stream of big-time financial scams gave the world its first hard look at the scale of financial fraud that bull market psychology had refused to expose. On June 15, reports revealed the "largest securities fraud sting in history," as the FBI arrested 120 people and broke up "a ring of organized crime on Wall Street" that has been operating for *five years.* When the Royal Bank of Canada was charged with stock manipulation, a Toronto paper said, the "practice of manipulating stock prices and pension fund performance *has been suspected for so long,* the only real surprise is that Canada's largest bank got caught first." *This acceleration in the size and scope of fraud exposure is exactly what* The Elliott Wave Theorist *has said we should expect in a post-mania environment.*

## September 1, 2000

Many of the bull-market accounting gimmicks that we have covered in recent issues of EWFF are also alternate forms of financial leverage…. The trend poses "systemic, long-term risk" to companies' debt ratings, says one specialist. *All it took was a two-month decline of 16% in the Dow to expose this weakness. The same practices that goosed the numbers on the way up will drag them down in a bear market.*

## December 1, 2000

It turns out that GE massages its numbers. *Money* magazine even reported in November that GE's earnings consistency is "a charade." Even "fans" are asking about the "confusing but apparently legal gimmicks" GE has used "to achieve its vaunted consistency." As *The Elliott Wave Theorist* pointed out in September 1998, this "discovery" of questionable bull market accounting standards is exactly what we should expect in the early stages of the bear market. In reaching GE, the last of the original Dow companies, *the emerging financial skepticism goes a long way toward confirming that the stock market's long-term topping process is behind us.*

## March 28, 2001

Considering the size of the NASDAQ's bubble and its inexorable, year-long decline, the attacks on Greenspan, CNBC and Wall Street analysts constitute a relatively serene response so far. Ironically, a rally might never be accomplished by an escalation in the attacks. The preliminary breaks from the mania in 1997 and 1998 illustrate how this delayed response works. In 1997, many emerging markets actually peaked in the first half of the year and fell out of bed in October as the U.S. market joined in. Once the bottom was actually in, the IMF became the focal point of an international backlash. On December 2, 1997, *The Wall Street Journal* reported on a sweeping wave of "resentment." "From Thailand to South Korea, casualties of the region's market meltdowns are casting blame far and wide." In October 1998, after the worst of another selling wave was over, we were treated to criticism over the bailout of Long-Term Capital Management and a Congress that roiled with demands for the regulation of hedge funds. As the market rallied on, the storm dissipated. [Perhaps one] reason for the delay is that the economy lags the stock market, and people don't reach their peak of anger until they are buffeted by the economy. [*Note: This is the same chronology that attended the Enron scandal, as revealed in Figure 1.—Ed.*]

## June 29, 2001

**The Witch Hunt Takes Flight:** In matters of survival, particularly those that are defined by highly subjective human interactions, the rational faculties of the neocortex are no match for the emotionally based survival instincts that inhabit the limbic system. The expanding controversy over accounting standards is a perfect example of the same brains later taking the opposite of a previous view in response to the demands of survival. As of late 1990, many thousands of analysts altered the tenets of the profession to a point where book value, dividends, profits and total earnings *did not matter*. Contending otherwise was grounds for dismissal; in fact, some analysts lost their jobs because they refused to adopt the new standard. Now, however, succeeding in the same job requires a single-minded devotion to judging earnings. The change revolves around a very specific event at a very specific time. On March 10, 2000, the direction of the NASDAQ switched from up to down, and the influence of social mood on millions of limbic systems reversed. On the approach to that high, the accountants themselves were consumed with hope and denial. Afterward, the essence of the job became to doubt the numbers. *USA Today*'s June 22 story notes, "accounting experts, analysts and academics" all agree, "companies are twisting the numbers to show better results." Numerous bull market instruments, like corporate stock buybacks, splits and stock options, which EWFF and *The Elliott Wave Theorist* said would have "an equal and opposite effect in a downtrend," are now getting all sorts of bad press (see March 1999 EWT and May and June 2000 issues of EWFF). Within the last few weeks, newspapers report, "Share Buybacks Hit a Wall of Fear," and stock options have "turned the investing world upside down." In an unexpected twist, "re-pricings" have created "a perverse incentive" for employees to "hold stock prices down."

It is no coincidence that as the backlash gathers steam, analysts and other economic thinkers are a special point of focus. In 1999, economists—scratch that; we mean *bullish* economists— emerged as the new "superstars of academia." Now a *Newsweek* column calls economics "the illusion of knowledge" and reveals, "Economists are clueless." In June, Congressional hearings were conducted to dissect the inaccurate opinions of securities analysts. A team of professors from four major California universities produced a paper showing that the stocks analysts liked the most fell 31% in 2000, while their least favorable recommendations rose 49%! The detailed analysis calls into question the "usefulness of analysts' stock recommendations." As we said months ago, this is not news. Has there has ever been a time when *average* Wall Street analysis has been useful as anything more than a contrary indicator? The news is how much of the academic and media firepower that supported Wall Street notions is now directed against Wall Street. This defrocking appears to be an inevitable response to the reversal of a mania. As *The Wave Principle of Human Social Behavior* points out, people tend to "live in the limbic system, particularly with respect to fields such as investing where so few are knowledgeable and the tendency toward dependence is pervasive." This was at least doubly true in the mania, as even the most highly developed neocortex was at a loss for prior experience to draw upon. The failed images of the previously bullish social mood now induce jilted investors to destroy the advisors upon whom they have grown so dependent. It is fascinating to see how much sense the neocortexes of the attackers can make as this limbic-based process plays itself out.

### *November 30, 2001*

Enron Corp.'s imminent [bankruptcy] will easily be the largest bankruptcy ever, topping the old record (Texaco in 1987) by almost 70%. The "forensic accountants" have been called in to sort out a mess that will lead on to a *seemingly endless series of financial catastrophes.*

### *February 1, 2002*

**All Enron, All the Time:** "Twenty minutes ago, the only topics on the nation's radar screen were Afghanistan and terrorism. Now there's Enron," says a *USA Today* column on "How Enron Stole Center Stage." One of the big mysteries is why the public suddenly cannot get enough dirt on Enron. *"A few years ago, it would hardly have seemed possible," Business Week* notes. "The nation's attention, from the halls of Congress to Main Street, has been riveted on an accounting scandal, a subject so abstruse it rarely makes the front page." *But there it is on page 1, day after day after day.* The Enron scandal and its recent "spread to other large, complex companies" shows that *investors are waking up to what they did not want to know during the bull market.*

### *March 1, 2002*

**What's Beyond Enron:** Last month, we showed how perfectly the Enron scandal fits the blueprint for a Grand Supercycle-degree bear market. This month, the river of recriminations broke its banks. The potential for a flood of Enron-style revelations into virtually any sector of the economy is signaled by word that the Federal Reserve is "stepping up" its scrutiny of securitized credit-card debt and mortgages as well as a *Fortune* expose that offers investors "More Reasons to Get Riled Up." *Fortune* points out that Enron's $63 billion in market losses is nothing compared to the $155 to $423 billion in market cap that disappeared from 10 other firms. *"Let's get mad at them, too,"* says the magazine. "Let's put *our anger and righteous outrage* in all the places they belong."

> *Meanwhile, Enron has evolved into what one Washington attorney called "an eerie financial witch hunt" that is comparable to the Salem witch trials.* The still-expanding demand for dirt on Enron is apparent by its arrival on the cover of the *National Enquirer*. The tabloid claims to have the "untold story" in its latest issue. When it comes to Enron, however, the only story the media has left untold is what's driving the fascination.

Mr. Kendall thus predicted in no uncertain terms that the conse-quences of the approaching—and then the developing—bear market would result in accounting scandals increasingly hitting the newspapers. (Note that this is a double forecast: both for a bear market and some of its social results.) Thus, socionomics once again predicted the character of upcoming events, events that have since led to dramatic congressional hearings, anguished public outcry and of course, the classic conventional error in assigning causality.

Thanks to an intrepid writer of the above-quoted article of May 2, 2002, Kendall was provided space in *USA Today* to summarize the correct stance on the rash of scandals and recriminations. Here are the relevant excerpts:

> Peter Kendall, co-editor of newsletter *The Elliott Wave Financial Forecast*, says a bear market often reveals the worst excesses of a bull market. "Everything that was revered on the upside is a target in a bear market." Those excesses have to be corrected before the public regains its confidence. Typical features of the so-called recrimination phase: reviled CEOs. "Those who had Teflon in the bull market have Velcro in the bear market," Kendall says. In 1929, the chief target was Richard Whitney, president of the New York Stock Exchange. Kenneth Lay, former CEO of Enron, may be the current target.
>
> Reform and regulation are one step to regaining the public's confidence. But that often happens well after much of the damage is done to investors' trust. "The government takes steps after the horses have left the barn," Kendall says.[6]

We socionomists are few in number. Were this a developed science with many practitioners, an astute socionomist might have listed Enron specifically as being one of the companies likely to explode in scandal. One financial ratings firm in April 2001 placed Enron on its "Corporate Earnings Blacklist" and cited the company as being "highly suspect of manipulating its earnings reports," so the hints were there.[7] An alert socionomist who knew, as we did, that corporate accounting scandals were rising in a flood might have filled in the blanks and anticipated this specific manifestation of the socionomic dynamic, although certainly not its ultimate position as the premier poster-child of manipulative accounting.

## Toward a New Understanding

People have a tendency to ask questions such as, "Are you saying that had the trend in social mood *not* changed, the Enron scandal would not have come to light?" The short answer is yes, but the questioner is missing an important point. It is crucial to understand that while the precipitation of Enron's financial meltdown and the revelation of its shaky accounting practices were due to forces behind the new negative social-mood trend, the precondition of their very existence was the psychological forces behind the old *positive* social-mood trend. Had the rose-colored glasses of optimism not clouded investors' vision in the first place, no company would have been able to survive practicing such shenanigans. During the 1990s, countless companies practiced them, and they were actually *rewarded* for it.

Socionomists were able to predict the eruption of scandals for three reasons: (1) because we knew that the euphoric optimism of the positive social-mood trend was inducing individuals and corporations to take huge financial risks and simultaneously inducing observers to turn a blind eye to improprieties, (2) because we knew that the qualities of a negative social-mood trend would reverse both of those forces and (3) because, knowing that social mood change would be the determining factor, we researched past major downside reversals in the stock market to glean some of their social characteristics, one of which was the rapid eruption of scandals, recriminations and Congressional investigations into corporate malfeasance. Believers in the conventional assumption of event causality, in contrast, were caught blindsided, as usual.

While the conventional error of thought regarding social mood causality is nearly ubiquitous, a few thinkers in history have derived the correct posture on this question, at least to a limited degree. For instance, Thomas Paine observed, "Panics bring things and men to light, which might have lain forever undiscovered." In other words, panic is causal; scandals are a result. It is time for social scientists to accommodate this view and to embrace the greater socionomic insight that lies behind it.

Corporate accounting scandals are only one area of social behavior among dozens that we at Elliott Wave International have successfully predicted. To cover them all would take several books. While this report details just a single example of what socionomists can do, it also elucidates a principle of social forecasting that anyone can learn to apply. A practiced artisan in this field can predict the headlines in countless areas.

## Quiz

You can do this. On May 2, 2002, the same day that newspapers blamed the Enron scandal for shredding investors' faith, another front-page article about arson and a gun battle at the Church of the Nativity in Bethlehem (West Bank) declared, "Church Battle, Fire Inflame Passions."[8] What is the socionomically inspired, i.e., the causally correct, formulation for that headline?

Now that you have formulated the correct headline, you should be able to see the value of the socionomic perspective not only in understanding what is going on in the world but also in forecasting. Had you been privy to a meter of the local social mood in this instance, you could have predicted the character of the events that resulted.

## NOTES

[1] Waggoner, John and Fogarty, Thomas. (2002, May 2). "Scandals shred investors' faith," *USA Today*, p. 1

[2] Any economist who bothers to view the relationship between the U.S. trade deficit and the stock market or the economy faces the same dilemma. The two trends move together in near lock step, opposing the ubiquitous presumption to the contrary. For chart and discussion see Prechter, Robert, *The Wave Principle of Human Social Behavior and the New Science of Socionomics*, pp. 377-380.

[3] Likewise, the social mood downtrend of 1974 forced the Watergate scandal to become a national obsession, crushing President Nixon's approval ratings and causing him to resign. The social mood uptrend of the 1990s, in contrast, allowed President Clinton to maintain his popularity despite lying in court and to the public about an adulterous affair with an intern.

[4] Further evidence of the power of social psychology to rule social events and social visioning is the amazing fact that the aspect of the scandal over which investors and politicians were most enraged was phony. Newspapers reported endlessly that the "big shots" at Enron got out of the stock while the poor employees were "locked in." In truth, employees could have gotten out whenever they wished, except for a brief period of 16 days during which the stock slipped an additional four points from 13 to 9, on its year-long descent from 83 down to 0.57, at which time it was de-listed in January 2002. The restriction, moreover, was not a punitive policy but a technical consequence of the company's turning over management of its pension plan to another firm. Investors in Enron stock, employees included, lost a lot of money because they were imprudent and foolish, just as countless other investors have lost money. The psychological desire of investors to redirect blame for their decision not to sell is stronger than facts.

[5] Prechter, Robert R. (1998, September 16). *The Elliott Wave Theorist* Special Report. Also Hochberg, Steven and Kendall, Peter. (1999, October 1; 2000, February 25, May 26, June 30, September 1, December 1; 2001, March 28, June 29, November 30; 2002, February 1, March 1). *The Elliott Wave Financial Forecast*.

[6] See Endnote 2.

[7] Weiss Ratings, Inc.; www.weissratings.com

[8] Gee, Robert W. (2002, May 2). "Church battle, fire inflame passions." *The Atlanta Journal-Constitution*, p. 1.

*Chapter 32*

## Challenging the Conventional Assumption about the Presumed Sociological Effect of Terrorist News

There is probably not one person in a million who would disagree with the conventional view, espoused everywhere, that the attacks of September 11, 2001 and the subsequent deliverance of anthrax-laced letters to individuals shattered the confidence of Americans. Yet that conclusion flies in the face of the facts.

Figure 1 shows every one of those events in the context of stock market behavior, consumer confidence and market psychology. As you can see, social mood and confidence *bottomed* five trading days after the 9/11 attack and continued to improve for months, throughout the reports of anthrax-laden mail deliveries, throughout the spectacles of men covered from head to toe in protective suits testing offices and other facilities for deadly anthrax spores, throughout reports of six deaths by anthrax, throughout the reports that al-Qaeda was running rampant and planning to poison water supplies, blow up bridges, release smallpox into the population and detonate a nuclear bomb in major U.S. cities. The conventional belief, which is an utter assumption, is that these reports would and did cause and instill increased fear and pessimism in society. This belief is the way people think, probably because they assign the type of causality that exists in the world of physics, the realm that humans have greatly learned to manipulate and control, to that of sociology. The facts contradict this notion.

Pundits who make the claim of news causality *never* check the data. Now we can see that social mood actually *improved* throughout the time of the anthrax news reports. Proponents of the conventional view of social causality (i.e., virtually everyone) are now obliged to ignore this fact in order to maintain that incorrect view.

*Figure 1*

Does that mean that social events and mood are random? Is there no causality at all? No, the socionomic hypothesis explains the proper causality. Social mood had deteriorated for eighteen months prior to the outbreak of these attacks. The negative mood permeating society by September 2001 had served to cause government agencies to become sloppy, missing cues to al-Qaeda's plans. It gave al-Qaeda's members the emotional trigger to decide that then was the time to strike. It caused someone either aggressive or unbalanced to choose that time to kill people through the mail and others later to perpetrate anthrax hoaxes.

Now observe the aftermath: A few months after the trend changed toward the positive, as evidenced by all the graphs in Figure 24-1, what happened? *There were no more attacks from al-Qaeda, and the anthrax mailings ceased.* The improving mood supported coordinated efforts to deal with these events and suppressed the forces that triggered them.

Whether or not you accept the idea that the changes in social mood effected these changes in social actions, the fact is that the chronology supports this case while simultaneously *decimating* the conventional view of causality. At minimum, an honest thinker has no choice but to abandon the conventional view. Whether he accepts the socionomic insight is another question, but he may no longer without contradiction espouse the old way of thinking. In fact, any objective person who bothers to check the chronology of various such assertions will be forced to abandon the conventional view.

*Chapter 33*

# The Timing and Character of Investment Legislation

## Introduction

Until now, no researcher outside Elliott Wave International and the Socionomics Institute has applied the socionomic insight when investigating relationships in social data. I am proud to say that just prior to the completion of this book, two academics have made a pioneering mark in being the first outside researchers to test and apply the socionomic hypothesis.

Washington State University finance professor Dr. John Nofsinger, an expert on the psychology of investing, and his colleague, Kenneth Kim, have been writing a book characterizing the stock mania of the 1990s. Nofsinger was considering recommending laws to temper investors' behavior to prevent the bubble and crash cycle from repeating. He wondered, for example, whether incentives would work better than regulations.[1] Implied in this line of inquiry was the idea that regulation is causal to investor behavior.

Gordon Graham, Director of our Socionomics Institute, contacted Nofsinger for a discussion. Graham suggested that he consider viewing financial laws not as *causes* of social behavior but as *products* of social behavior. Intrigued by this statement of causality, Nofsinger reviewed all major investment legislation from the 1920s to present. He found that the character of each new investment law reflected the direction of the stock market *prior to* its enactment. Moreover, the relationship held every time; there were no exceptions. As I would hasten to add, these results suggest, per the hypothesis, a process of *cause and effect*.

This is another example of how a socionomic perspective leads one to search for the right relationships. It does not take social actions as "givens" independent of human thought but rather ties preceding thoughts to resulting actions, in this case government legislation related to investing. A simple change in perspective shed the light. Nofsinger's work would support an assertion that the socionomic insight is a prerequisite for understanding the social forces behind the making and unmaking of financial legislation, and their timing. Expansive legislation is a symptom of a maturing or completed positive mood trend, and restrictive legislation is a product of a maturing or completed negative mood trend.

Consider the implications were economists and politicians to take the unlikely path of viewing most legislation primarily as products of social mood. The endless debates about which new policy should be adopted in response to a preceding trend would end. A wiser tone and a longer term perspective would prevail, unleashing resources available for more productive purposes. It would be real progress.

Nofsinger has provided a model for other academic economists to work from. We encourage all to take note and follow his lead in considering the socionomic perspective when investigating social history.

— Robert Prechter

## PROTECTING INVESTORS (NOT)

by Dr. John Nofsinger and Kenneth Kim[2]

The government continually tightens and loosens its laws regarding the investment industry just as it continually raises and lowers income taxes. After each major bear market or scandalous period, the government enacts new laws to protect investors. Consider the new laws

| MAJOR LAWS CREATED TO PROTECT INVESTORS | | |
|---|---|---|
| **Act** | **Purpose** | **Preceded By** |
| **1933 and 1934** Banking Act and Securities Exchange Act | Separates commercial and investment banking, creates SEC as market regulators | Stock market crash of 1929 and ensuing bear market removes nearly 90% of Dow value |
| **1940** Investment Company Act and Investment Advisors Act | Regulates investment companies and advisors | Market decline of 25% from October 1939 to May 1940 |
| **1970** Securities Investor Protection Act | Creates Securities Investor Protection Corporation and insurance from broker defaults | Market decline of 30% from April 1969 to June 1970 |
| **1974** Employee Retirement Income Security Act | Regulates pension funds | Long bear market from December 1972 to September 1974 takes the Dow down 40% |
| **1988** Insider Trading and Securities Fraud Enforcement Act | Increases penalties and liabilities for insider trading and fraudulent activities | Stock market crash of 1987 takes Dow down over 40% |
| **2002** Public Company Accounting Reform and Investor Protection Act | Increases regulation of auditors, lengthens punishment for white collar crimes, and creates more corporate fraud laws | 2½ year bear market reduced Dow by 35%, Nasdaq declines 75% |

Excerpts from *Infectious Greed: Restoring Confidence in America's Companies*
By John R. Nofsinger and Kenneth A Kim

*Table 1*

shown in Table 1. The securities acts passed in 1933 and 1934 followed the corporate governance problems of the late 1920s, the 1929 stock market crash, and the beginning of the Great Depression. The investment company and advisors acts in 1940 followed a bear market that took 25% of the value of the stock market. The late 1960s experienced a 30% bear market. In 1970, the government created the Securities Investor Protection Corporation (SIPC). Investor protection laws also followed the bear market of the early 1970s and the Black Monday market crash of October 19, 1987. And, of course, the recent corporate scandals combined with the severe stock market decline spawned the 2002 Public Company Accounting Reform and Investor Protection Act.

Unfortunately, the laws that are enacted to protect shareholders and investors are often repealed during times of economic strength and stock market euphoria. The 1920s and the 1990s had many similarities. Both decades experienced strong economic expansions and powerful bull markets. Indeed, investors at the end of each decade could have been called irrationally exuberant. In the middle (or toward the end)

| REPEALS OF SOME INVESTOR PROTECTION | | |
|---|---|---|
| Action | Purpose | Preceded By |
| **1927**<br>Government agency policy allowing commercial banks to issue securities | Allows commercial banks into investment banking activities | Stock market rose over 200% from 1925 to 1928 |
| **1995**<br>Private Securities Litigation Reform Act | Limits the ability and available damages of investors suing for corporate fraud | Dow increased 60% between 1993 and 1995 |
| **1998**<br>Securities Litigation Uniform Standards Act | Precludes plaintiffs from bringing securities actions in state courts | Dow increased 125% from 1996 to 1999 |
| **1999**<br>Financial Services Modernization Act | Allows the combining of commercial and investment banking activities | Dow increased 125% from 1996 to 1999 |

Excerpts from *Infectious Greed: Restoring Confidence in America's Companies*
By John R. Nofsinger and Kenneth A Kim

*Table 2*

of the excitement over stocks, the government changed its laws that protected investors.

Consider the examples in Table 2. In 1927, the stock market was toward the end of a bull market that increased values over 200%. There were many new companies conducting IPOs that were not really strong enough to be offered to investors. Investors did not seem to care and rushed in to snap them up. The commercial banks were prevented from getting into the investment banking activities to share in the lucrative fees. They lobbied the government to change the rules and succeeded. Commercial banks began helping companies issue securities. Unfortunately, the stock market crash of 1929 left commercial banks with many losses that jeopardized people's bank deposits. The people panicked and demanded their money back. Of course, banks did not have the cash to return all the deposits at once. That cash was loaned out. So, the banks had to close their doors.

Now, examine the three law changes in the 1990s. The Private Securities Litigation Reform Act limited the ability of investors to sue companies and executives for damages due to corporate fraud in federal courts. This law was enacted in the midst of a strong bull market that increased the value of the Dow Jones Industrial Average by 60%. It was followed three years later with a similar act that applied to state courts. The Financial Services Modernization Act allowed commercial banks to associate themselves with investment banks again. This is similar to the 1927 capitulation. Again, this reduction in investor protection occurred toward the end of a market rally that increased the Dow 125%.

Another recent example is not listed in the table. In 1997, the SEC proposed new rules that would have severely limited the ability of shareholders to introduce corporate resolutions. The procedure for the SEC to enact new rules is that the regulator proposes a new rule and then provides a time period in which people can comment on the rule. A consortium of investor activists lobbied strongly against the new rule. In the end, the SEC decided not to enact the new limitations. Even though it was defeated, this is still an example of how investor protections are often reversed or limited during an extended bull market.

Our point is that laws are frequently made to protect shareholders and investors. This usually occurs after people become angry over scandals and a bear market. However, these protections can also be reversed in the midst of good times. A strong economy and good bull market lead to pressure on lawmakers to loosen restrictions on corporate participants. The loosened restrictions have the potential to help push the stock market from a bull market to a bubble market.[3] When a bubble occurs, a crash will inevitably follow. This leads to more scandals and more investor protection laws. We need to avoid this cycle.[4]

Yet, the social mood can be represented by stock prices. The level of the stock market indicates what kind of mood the people are in. This dictates the tone and character of the resulting action by government, regulators, and investors. The relationship we show between how the stock market has performed and the resulting legislation[5] illustrates this point.

---

**EDITOR'S NOTES**

[1] This thinking reflects the conventional viewpoint, not the socionomic perspective.

[2] Excerpted from Nofsinger, John and Kenneth Kim, *Infectious Greed: Restoring Confidence in America's Companies*, Financial Times Prentice Hall, forthcoming 2003, January.

[3] Socionomists would maintain that loosened restrictions do not "push the stock market from a bull market to a bubble market" but rather that the shared psychology of a late-stage bull market pushes investors, CEOs and regulators to loosen restrictions.

[4] Bull and bear markets can neither be avoided nor changed. Whether the behavior of lawmakers can change may be open to debate, but we are skeptical.

[5] The August 1, 1997 issue of *The Elliott Wave Theorist* also cited the SEC's adoption of "Rule 144a" in 1990/1992, which loosened reporting laws for restricted securities in order to induce foreign corporations to sell bonds—typically "junk" bonds—to U.S. institutions. *The Wave Principle of Human Social Behavior* cites related legislation, the Monetary Control Act of December 1980, which was enacted in response to the preceding entire decade's accelerating inflation, which had in fact already ended in January of that very year.

## A Graphical Summary of Nofsinger's Observations

We always find graphics instructive. Figure 1 summarizes Nofsinger's observations, with some added notes and instances. The upper arrows mark the timing of expansive legislation, and the lower arrows mark the timing of restrictive legislation. The former type occurs late in bull markets, the latter type late in or after bear markets. It is particularly impressive that the essentially identical laws of 1927 and 1999 combining commercial and investment banking (see the asterisks on the graph) occurred late in a stock mania within a wave V of Cycle degree (for wave labels, see Figure 1 in Chapter 13).

*Figure 1*

*Mr. Graham concurrently expanded upon this theme in response to an article in* The New Republic.

*The New Republic*
October 21, 2002
Letter to the Editor

In the first part of "Busted,"[1] George Soros deftly outlines the nature of boom and bust market behavior. The theory of reflexivity is a step in the right direction, but it misses the big picture. Soros's article sounds like an echo of the sentiments expressed in 1932. Then, as now, many prescriptions for controlling the behavior of market participants were implemented. Indeed, shortly after each bear market dating back to the Depression —1933, 1934, 1940, 1970, 1974 and 1988—legislation was introduced to protect investors with the intention of producing a more stable investment environment. What happened?

As stocks broke out of their slump in the early 1980s, an increasingly positive social mood brought forth a new set of "values": market fundamentalism. After the 1987 hiccup, the markets, propelled by social mood, gained a full head of steam, and the "protections" offered in the previous bear markets were altered, ignored and ultimately scoffed at, reflecting the blossoming euphoria and the desire for "financial gain irrespective of how it is achieved."

Bear markets produce regulation in response to the public's demand for protection, and bull markets dissolve them. As Mr. Soros points out, investors in the bull market had put a premium on management's ability to massage the numbers; the euphoria driving outrageous stock valuations drives equally outrageous social events.

From this perspective, the concept of equilibrium seems mighty strange, for the market is in constant flux. Mr. Soros's search for just the right amount of legislation and the proper values hints at "equilibrium seeking." However, no such thing exists in society or has ever existed. The fluctuating patterns of social mood are fundamental and ceaseless. One silver lining of the current bear market may be that it will cause a paradigm shift away from the search for market equilibrium(s) and toward a model that reflects an obvious reality: Social mood is never at "equilibrium," and its constant flux drives social action, including actions designed—futilely—to stop it.

—Gordon Graham
The Socionomics Institute
Gainesville, GA

## NOTES

[1] Soros, George. (2002, September 2). "Busted." *The New Republic.* http://www.tnr.com.

*Part V:*

# *TOWARD A REVOLUTION IN FINANCIAL AND MACROECONOMIC FORECASTING TECHNIQUES*

Prechter
*Adapted from a speech to the International Conference on the Wave Principle, Buford, GA, September 21, 1991, which was adapted from an essay in The Elliott Wave Theorist, September 4, 1984*

*Chapter 34*

# Understanding Technical vs. Fundamental Analysis

What differentiates technical from fundamental analysis in the realm of finance? What is the proper role of each method in investment selection, market timing and asset allocation? What is their relative value and utility? I think you will find my answers different from those you would commonly receive from other sources.

The questions posed above are critically important to investment success because they pertain to an analyst's proper intellectual orientation when undertaking the task of anticipating market valuations, a task that every investor faces whether he chooses to acknowledge that fact or not. Clearly it is preferable to face the task head-on, consciously and deliberately, in an effort to lower the risk of loss and increase profit potential. The advantage gained thereby could mean the difference between consistent success and continual frustration, confusion and anguish.

### Definitions

The available literature disagrees on definitions, so I have distilled the essence of each term to formulate definitions that clearly reveal the dichotomy between the two approaches. These definitions are crucial in providing a proper understanding of the essential nature of all approaches to market analysis and forecasting.

Technical analysis is the study of *market* data, i.e., data generated by the action of markets and by the behavior and psychology of market participants and observers—that is, events, conditions and processes relating to financial market behavior. Its goal is to predict the probable direction and extent of price change in a financial market or an investment item.

Fundamental analysis is the study of *extramarket* data, i.e., data generated by events, conditions and processes outside the marketplace with the same purpose of predicting the probable direction and extent of price change in a financial market or an investment item.

Some people who call themselves fundamental analysts may not see their particular approach in my definition. It may be because their approach is properly understood as a hybrid, as explained below. Similarly, some people who call themselves technical analysts will discover that by my definition they too are practicing a hybrid approach.

It is not so much my definitions that depart from traditional views but my stance on the relative value of each type of analysis.

## Categories of Technical Analysis

Within the technical analysis approach, there are three main areas of study: sentiment, momentum and price patterns.

*Sentiment* measures report investors' psychological disposition toward a market, specifically, whether in the aggregate investors are optimistic (bullish) or pessimistic (bearish) about future prices, meaning whether they expect prices to be higher or lower, respectively. The analyst compares the present extent of bullish or bearish conviction in the market in question to that in other available investment items and to historical levels in the same market. Evaluation is based upon two observations: (l) sentiment and prices tend to rise and fall concurrently, and (2) high and low levels of optimism are associated with probabilities of trend change.

*Momentum* measures report absolute and relative increases and decreases in the rate of change of prices, breadth (the number of component issues, groups or indexes that are participating) and volume, all with respect to such developments in the past. Evaluation is based upon two primary observations: (1) markets trend, and (2) trends usually slow and/or fragment (i.e. the breadth of stocks, groups, sectors and indexes' participation in the trend narrows) before reversing, and degrees of such conditions are associated with probabilities of trend change.

*Patterns* of prices (and occasionally volume) imply states of market psychology, which in turn imply probabilities for subsequent market behavior. Patterns catalogued in various empirical studies include Dow Theory, point & figure charting, standard chart analysis (as catalogued by Edwards and Magee), Wyckoff analysis, candlestick charting, time cycles and the Elliott Wave Principle. If financial market dynamics follow laws, or at least tendencies, assessing patterns can help an analyst anticipate future trends.

All three approaches help determine the psychological state of the market. From that knowledge, an analyst can interpret the data in the light of precedent and estimate probabilities of future courses of action for a market or investment.

### Applications of Fundamental Analysis

To assess the probable direction of the stock market, fundamental analysts study factors such as interest rates, the inflation rate, political developments and business conditions. To assess the potential price behavior of a single stock, fundamental analysts study the performance of and conditions within the associated company. To assess the potential price behavior of a commodity, fundamental analysts look at the available supply of the commodity and the outlook for production and consumption. To assess the future trend of interest rates, fundamental analysts look at the economy, central bank behavior, and trends in credit expansion or contraction. To assess the future trend for the price of gold, fundamental analysts look at mine production, net demand from major buyers and sellers, and the inflation rate. And so on. In every case, the analysts assess data outside the market in question to reach a conclusion.

Under the umbrella of the term fundamental analysis, there are two main methods of application: pure fundamental analysis, which uses only extramarket data; and a hybrid approach, which considers the price of the investment item in light of extramarket data (and which is often called fundamental analysis). We will keep our definition for the following discussion and then address the hybrid version.

### Which Is Best: Technical or Fundamental?

The primary goal of financial analysis is to decide whether to be long, short or out of a market, in other words, to determine whether a particular investment will rise or fall in price sufficiently to profit. Which approach is superior for this task? Or, should analysts employ them both in a comprehensive approach?

My answer is that technical analysis is not only superior but is also required for any financial analysis to be valid. Fundamental analysis by itself is not merely inferior for the purpose stated, it is invalid. This presentation will attempt to demonstrate that invalidity and also to present in very limited scope the essential reasons why some degree of technical analysis is unavoidable in any financial analysis.

## False Assumption

Fundamental analysis is invalid for one simple yet counterintuitive reason, which is that outside events and conditions rarely cause market movements. Prices are primarily determined by collective mental states, i.e., the psychology of the crowd. Outside conditions and events do not change that psychology, but rather the psychology shapes the tenor of crowd action and therefore of social events.

Many of you know that I have a theory of causality of social events by social psychology, which is the opposite of the widely accepted view. A full discussion is beyond the scope of this presentation,[1] but I'll give one brief dramatic example. When Adolf Hitler took power in Germany at the global stock market low in 1933, stock indexes both in Germany and around the world immediately soared for four years. Absent other data, a fundamental analyst would be forced to conclude that Hitler's ascendancy was a bullish event for Germany and the world. Instead, I argue that the negative social psychology, as evidenced by the record collapse in stocks that began in 1929, reached such an extreme in 1932-1933 that the result was popularity for Hitler and his views. His placement in power was the consequence of society's psychological state. The reversal in social psychology that followed was a normal, leading dynamic, not a consequence. The historic bear market fore-shadowed Hitler's rise, but his rise in itself said nothing about the next move in the stock market. The inversion of this truth is behind some economists' conclusion that World War II—which in fact destroyed capital and productive capacity on a monstrous scale—was "good" for stocks and the economy. They assumed that the event caused the subsequent market advance of 1942-1946. But the war did not cause the uptrend; rather, the natural shift toward positive social psychology beginning in 1942 fueled the stock market rise and also foreshadowed the end of both the war and Hitler's influence.

## The Autonomy of the Crowd

Crowd psychology has its own dynamic. The causal primacy of this dynamic is the reason that the market so often ignores events and acts in ways that most people judge perverse. It also explains why most people lose money in markets: They operate under the assumption that outside events and conditions dictate market movements. This false yet widespread conviction is as unmovable as Mount Everest. It is also wrong, as one can observe time and again in real life.

At times, the market will soar upward week after week in the depths of recession, defying the headlines. At other times, it will lose a third of its value in a two-month crash right in the middle of an economic boom. No bad news can transform an ongoing bull market into a bear or vice versa.

The market will often ignore news in favor of its technical condition, but it will not ignore its technical condition in favor of news. In 1932, the stock market's declining trend was exhausted amid extreme pessimism, so its technical condition was long term bullish. News continued to worsen into 1933, but the market took off on the upside anyway. In 1969, humans walked on the moon for the first time; but stocks were in a bear market and did not care.

### Mental States Precede Events

Society's mental states produce, and therefore precede, social events, so news is the ultimate result of psychological trends that are already in place. Changes in mental states immediately produce changes in areas where people can act quickly, such as stock market prices and leading-edge cultural expressions. Other social actions—such as expanding or contracting businesses or mobilizing Congress to pass a law—take time to materialize, and news of them results from trends in social mood that have already occurred. To summarize, news is not unrelated to the market; it merely lags the market.

Since mental states and the actions they motivate both trend, lagging social actions, which are reported in the news, eventually catch up with the market's trend and become consistent with the market's direction. The positive correlation that thereby often does exist fools people into believing that there is empirical support for their assumption that news causes markets to move. But the disassociation of markets and events immediately following major market turns belies that assumption.

Because markets and events trend together much of the time, a fundamental analyst who predicts a continuation of the past—such as continued earnings gains or losses or continued economic expansion or contraction and thus a continuation of the market's trend—may be right for a while simply because trends persist. But because the fundamental

analyst waits for events to change in order to call for a change in the
trend of a market, he will always predict trend continuance right through
and past major market turns. The reason is that he is analyzing and
forecasting lagging data. Fundamental analysis based on extramarket
data may appear benign when the two trends are in sync, but at turning
points it fails. It *must* fail, because psychology changes before events.

Perhaps you're not convinced. Let's examine the two types of
fundamental analysis, first the pure and then the hybrid, and discuss
their implications.

### The Essential Error of External Cause

Purely fundamental analysis, as defined above, attempts to determine the future direction of a market by postulating a specific reaction to
specific outside factors, which are deemed "the fundamentals behind the
market." Examples include asserting that a stock has a bullish outlook
because of a determination that a company's earnings will rise next
quarter, or concluding that stocks in general should be sold because
the economy is expected to deteriorate, or deciding that gold should
be bought because of a determination that inflation will increase. No
thought is given to the psychological state of the market in question as
revealed by price or any other evidence. The causality is simply assumed,
so the analyst does not ask, as a technician would, whether the price
of the investment item already reflects the expected future earnings,
economic performance or inflation rate. It does not concern itself with
the market's own dynamics. It even necessarily ignores many so-called
fundamental factors as too numerous to consider.

Though this kind of analysis is as common as the daily newspaper
and equally blithely accepted, I would challenge the basic assumption
underlying pure fundamental analysis that outside events move the
market. As far as I can determine, no proposed external cause has any
reliable correlation to market movement. Numerous analysts relying
on such causes make their claims without studying history thoroughly
and without bothering to verify their assumptions. They imply that the
correctness of their causal assumption is obvious.

The pervasiveness of this approach is the reason why a recent
newspaper cartoon was funny. It depicted a TV newscaster. The caption read, "On Wall Street today, news of lower interest rates sent the
stock market up, but then the expectation that these rates would be

inflationary sent the market down, until the realization that lower rates might stimulate the sluggish economy pushed the market up, before it ultimately went down on fears that an overheated economy would lead to a reimposition of higher interest rates." We have all heard every one of these causal arguments separately, but it took putting them together to reveal the absurdity of the external-cause approach to financial analysis. Anyone who takes the time to study the history of the market, or tries to make money from the market, eventually must come to grips with the fact that common assumptions of external causality are contradictory and of no value in predicting the future course of prices. Let's review some specific examples.

Is it true that inflation causes gold and silver prices to rise? Suppose you had decided to act upon that assumption at gold's peak in January 1980. Ever since that time, inflation, as evidenced by an increasing money supply and rising consumer prices, has continued for an entire decade, albeit at a lower rate relative to the rate at gold's peak. Yet the price of gold and silver have declined. In fact, at today's prices, gold has lost 60% of its peak value and silver is down over 90%. Obviously gold and silver do not rise automatically in response to monetary inflation. Gold and silver prices in 1980 had reached an extreme as a result of the dynamics of investor psychology, and their bull market was over regardless of continued inflation. At the extreme in price, investors envisioned endless monetary inflation and presumed it would cause endlessly higher metals prices. Inflation did continue, but the expected result failed to materialize.

Paradoxically, yet profoundly, we can attribute the failure of investors' vision of a continuing bull market in gold and silver in large part precisely to that very expectation, which in turn prompted private and public behavior that thwarted it. Mines stepped up production of gold, and exploration resumed, increasing supply; and manufacturers sought alternatives to using gold, decreasing industrial demand. After the bear market in the metals began, the Fed became more hawkish in its orientation toward interest rates, and voters expressed their dismay over inflation at the polls. All this behavior resulted from the mental state of the very crowd that produced high metals prices. In simpler language, the bull market in gold and silver ended in 1980, period. As there is no mention of inflation in that statement, it constitutes a technical observation. As such, it addresses the essence of market and social behavior.

was run by communists and communists don't change because they are idealists and their totalitarian ideals preclude change. All the comments about communists were true, yet profound and dramatic change happened in the country anyway, and it was logical. But it resulted logically from the laws of human social *change*, not those which apply to stasis or linearity. An analyst with a knowledge of social behavior might have said, for instance, "The potential for change in the Soviet Union is inevitable, and it is inevitable because the country is run by communists. Communists are idealists who ignore human nature. Their policies ruin incentives for production. Such a governmental system has to collapse from privation. Today there is evidence that the desperation point is closer than ever." This example illustrates the difference in thinking when one takes into account social dynamics rather than assuming stasis.

A final example is the fundamental analysis of companies. Fundamental analysts in brokerage firms spend the bulk of their time trying to predict corporate earnings over a one-month to one-year period. The record shows that such predictions are often wrong; but, more important, when they're right they rarely correlate with future stock price behavior. The dismal track record of this approach has hardly deterred the activity, because those involved will not abandon their premises.

The technician sees earnings reports in a different light. Here's a true story, which I'll read from an account in a magazine:

> A man in Indiana was taking a soothing bath when his wife burst in to tell him there was a snake in the bedroom. He jumped out of the tub and ran into the bedroom, getting down on his hands and knees to look for the snake. At this critical moment, the family dog padded quietly up from behind and poked him with its nose. The man fainted. Thinking her husband had been bitten by the snake, the wife phoned for an ambulance. As the man was being placed on the stretcher, the snake reappeared, the wife yelled 'snake,' and the ambulance attendant dropped the patient, breaking his collarbone.[2]

This man became a physical wreck, yet the snake never touched him. The people around the victim—his loving wife and a professional trained to handle emergencies—only wanted to help him. What caused havoc is that people are afraid of snakes. Likewise investors and their advisors' hopes and fears about a corporate earnings matter more than the earnings, which merely provide a referent for expressing those emotions.

### Fundamental Analysts Must Predict Their Indicators

There is an even more profound flaw among the requirements of fundamental analysis: *Fundamental analysts are forced to predict their indicators*. They have no alternative.

Even if it were true that inflation always coincided with rising gold prices, the fundamental analyst would have to predict the trend of inflation. Even if it were true that falling interest rates were always bullish for stocks and vice versa, the fundamental analyst would have to predict interest rates. Even if it were true that corporate earnings affected stock prices, the fundamental analyst would have to predict earnings.

To expand on this point, let's suppose that a sophisticated fundamental analyst makes an exhaustive study of the behavior of interest rates, the inflation rate, commodity prices, the economy and the stock market, and determines that certain relationships in behavior are reliable. You've heard it a million times. "If interest rates continue to do X, then stocks will do Y"; or, "If inflation does X, gold will do Y." But we must interrupt the discussion to say, "Fine, *if*. But how do you know whether the present condition or trend of the predictive component will continue?" Typically the analyst will offer another fundamental cause: "This will happen because that will happen." "How do you figure that?" "Well, because such-and-such will happen," etc. In every case, he must predict his causal indicator with reference to yet another cause. If he stops, he must admit he has *no idea* how the indicator components he has cited will behave going forward, which means he cannot predict the market in question.

Consider the example of the gold market discussed above. A fundamental analyst might well assert that if inflation goes on long enough, it will eventually force gold prices higher. Unfortunately, that statement is of no value in making investment decisions. How can one predict whether the required inflation will continue, and at what rate, and for how long? No answer can be reliable without predicting the indicator. A fundamental analyst might offer a bullish opinion based on the fact that there has been monetary inflation for fifty years. Yet that fact does not indicate whether inflation will continue. Deflation may even be possible. Whoever bet on long term inflation by buying gold ten years ago or even four years ago faces a gut wrenching decision today, as his gold and silver continue to decline in dollar value. Suppose the fundamental analyst were to assert, "Government will always inflate the money supply eventually." He's still predicting his indicator, and his basis is unreliable. While one might agree that governments typically inflate their currencies, history provides exceptions which last for half a century or more. Governmental change is dependent on the psychology of voters and leaders. What if an anti-inflation government were to assume power? Then the basis of the projection would evaporate. Fundamental analysts would shift to debating what the new government means for gold prices ("Should we finally sell?"). Meanwhile, technicians would be assessing the psychology of the market to determine if it had reached historic extremes of pessimism, thus providing a buying opportunity.

### Technical Analysis is Ultimately Unavoidable Regardless of the Method Employed

The only way the fundamental analyst can finally stop the chain of causal claims from external factors is to base his opinion on how one of the indicator components, that is, interest rates or commodities or stocks, *itself* typically behaves. *Now he is engaging in technical analysis*, which at some point is always required if the causal chain is to be finite and if a forecast is to have any basis at all.

If a fundamental analyst were indeed to have discovered a reliable coincident external indicator of market behavior, he must state whether he thinks the causal factor will continue trending in its current direction. If he concludes it will, it can only be because of another so-called fundamental factor or because "the indicator tends to trend," which, if true, is a technical fact. Ultimate closure, then, must come from technical analysis. The technical analysis may be simple trend-following, one of its least sophisticated forms (which nevertheless has been shown to work, most recently in a *Journal of Finance* paper by William Brock, Josef Lakonishok and Blake LeBaron[3]), but it is technical analysis nevertheless.

In contrast to the fundamental approach, the technician many times can look at a set of indicators and say, "These measures of investor behavior unequivocally indicate a high probability of a continuation of (or termination of) the longstanding trend of prices," period. This is not to say that a market always does the probable, but at least the technician is not reduced to predicting his indicator. The indicator speaks to the future, and that's that. The difference between this simple formula and fundamental analysis is glorious.

To conclude, there are two possible ways a fundamental analyst can answer the question, "Why do you think your causal fundamental factor will persist?" He can refer to yet another so-called fundamental ad infinitum, or he can resort to technical analysis.

### Intrinsic Value; People as Machines

External-cause logic fails in finance because it rests on three false assumptions: (1) that actual value is intrinsic and based upon specific factors; (2) that people are emotionless machines reacting to changes in these factors; and (3) that the benchmark of value is some present, computable value, not future potential.

If there is an improvement in the company's earnings, dividends, book value, debt level, balance sheets, management technique, product sales potential, dividend rate, etc., says the fundamental analyst, then the intrinsic value of the company's stock rises and people will pay more for it. Inversely, if there is deterioration in such measures, the stock price will fall.

Market behavior invalidates this view. Even when companies' fundamentals are accurately determined, stocks do not act as if those factors represent intrinsic value. The marketplace, if it is valuing earnings, cash flows and balance sheets at all, places wildly differing valuations upon them. Earnings of a company are at times valued infinitely high, if the company has no earnings or is losing money, or very low, if they are expected to drop, or anywhere in between. Dividend value can be infinitely high, if a company pays none, or very low if there is fear that the dividend will be cut because the company has negative growth potential, or anywhere in between. Bond yields have been valued twice as highly as stock yields in the psychological environment of the 1940s, while in another psychological environment, stock yields can be valued at quadruple the value of bond yields, as they are now. Is it not instructive that in 1987 the price of Nippon Telephone reached a level at which it was worth more than all the stocks on the West German stock exchange combined? How can it be argued that there is an intrinsic standard for stock prices? Intrinsic value is valid as a concept only if human beings, who actually determine value and price, are omitted from the equation, but then there is no market.

The wild history of stock valuations relative to company-valuation criteria confirms that people do not respond mechanically to such factors. Instead they change their minds, sometimes radically, with respect to them. The endless discussion of future prospects confirms that current fundamental values don't matter much in determining stock prices.

Equally suspect is the same approach applied to commodities, where the fundamentals involved include the existing supplies of the commodity, production schedules, demand schedules, weather prediction, and so on. In the first place, the number and elasticity of all these fundamentals make evaluating them little better than a guessing game, and in the second place there is no evidence that commodity prices adhere to these factors.

## The Real Fundamentals

The pure fundamental analyst ignores human emotions fluctuating by crowd dynamics, which is the most important factor in pricing. This omission has proved so troublesome to theoretical constructs that it has finally caused the entrenched ideas of Random Walk and the Efficient Market Hypothesis (EMH),[4] after decades of acceptance, to lose face. EMH postulates that all the market's valuations are the result of cold decision-making by rational investors. So, both high and low P/E multiples are rational. As a recent *Wall Street Journal* article lamented, however, "the lists of high P/E stocks from 1972, 1981 and 1986 are full of names that once seemed invincible. Many are fine companies, but most have disappointed investors. That's because investors' expectations were so high it would have taken a superhuman performance to live up to them."[5] Precisely. A technical analyst would have said exactly that, but he would have said it at the time, not years and decades later. Some changes in valuation are blindingly swift, and no shift in fundamentals explains them. Objective observers of market behavior, when hit over the head with the Crash of 1987, could ignore the truth no longer: that Random Walk and EMH are faulty models.

The latest twist on this idea is Stanford economist Mordeci Kurz's theory of "Rational Belief Equilibrium,"[6] which states that yes, investors all act fully rationally, but they reach different conclusions due to varying degrees of knowledge and wisdom with respect to markets, and specifically, to different mental models of how the market operates. While this formulation may have a big future in academia and is more insightful than EMH, it, too, fails to explain satisfactorily why millions of fully rational and independent people with no clear event motivating them would suddenly change their approaches to investment decision making all at once, producing a near-vertical rise or drop in the market.

The answer is that most people are not rational in their investment decision making but rational*izing*. They offer logical arguments mostly in order to justify emotionally motivated conformity with the herd.

To the extent that an investor is rational, independent and wise in investment decision making, he must take human non-rationality into account. When carrying out an investment decision making process, he must consciously consider the fact that the engine of investment price movement is at least to some degree the shifting, subjective value judgments of market participants, and those shifts are governed primarily not by cold reason but by crowd psychology.

One cannot reason with a crowd. A crowd is not rational but emotional and impulsive. Experts on crowd behavior throughout history have made the observation that something in human nature makes people behave in coordinated ways when they are members of a crowd in a supercharged social setting. Financial behavior is coordinated because it fits this condition. Uncertainty produces an emotional state compelling investors to disengage their rational faculty and adopt the view of others.

When the herding impulse dominates the rational faculty in a group of people, patterned behavior results. That's why the technical analyst focuses on pursuing ways to measure the psychological state of the crowd with the goal of recognizing extremes and therefore times of high potential for change in the perception of value in the marketplace. This is the truly objective, rational basis upon which to approach the task of forecasting market trends.

In conclusion, the actual fundamentals of financial market forecasting are not what the pure fundamental analysts say they are. The term *market fundamentals* instead properly applies to sentiment, momentum and the behavioral patterns of crowds.

**A Valid Use of Fundamental Analysis: Venture Capital Investing**

Some investors have fared well by investing in stocks of promising start-up companies. In this limited realm, the extramarket information with respect to a company's vision, its management quality, the state of the competition, the potential size of the market for the company's products, etc., matters a great deal. The marketplace has yet to consider the company, so crowd psychology with respect to its stock value is at a minimum. This overriding technical fact makes the fundamental-analysis approach valid.

Even so, the approach is not immune to crowd psychology. Even a successful evaluation can be overwhelmed by a technical event that pushes around the values of many start-ups, such as a major bull market that ushers in a boom that rescues precarious companies that looked like good shorts, or a major bear market that brings on a depression that destroys promising companies that looked like good buys. So, even this type of analysis fares better if the analyst pays some attention to market psychology. This is especially true when the overall market already displays extreme optimism or pessimism. New ventures undertaken near a frenzied market peak can overwhelm fundamental analysis, because investors' shared vision of the most positively imaginable scenario is what brought the new stock to market in the first place. The crowd has already wholly embraced IPOs that open at huge price premiums and new start-up companies that join in an aging sector boom.

Determined efforts to seek out future corporate successes in the marketplace is a major justification for having a stock market in the first place and is the proper place for consideration of extramarket factors. The approach takes more work than most people are willing to do. Once analysts and investors follow a company to any great extent, extramarket factors no longer have reliable predictive value. Favorable or unfavorable prospects for established companies, even if accurate, are virtually irrelevant compared to the question of whether the price of the stock reflects high optimism or pessimism about such prospects.

Pure fundamental analysis is never reliable for a market index, commodity or any seasoned stock, all of which are governed by psychological trends. A fundamental analyst who offers an opinion on inflation, the economy, wheat production or the outlook for sales of an established company's new product is predicting inflation, the economy, wheat production and a sales outlook, *not stock prices*. He may claim to be predicting stock prices as well, but there is no established connection.

## A Hybrid Approach: Company-Valuation Analysis

A hybrid practice of individual company valuation, often called fundamental analysis, is more entrenched among successful professionals. The approach is also called value investing, a more accurate term except that it pre-empts a more appropriate wider application of the term *value*, which should include the work of technicians, who also discern value but by different criteria.

Valuation analysis is based upon the external-cause idea that there is some intrinsic value for a company determinable by a list of corporate health factors. Practitioners commonly call such factors "fundamentals," equating with our definition. Before making an investment decision, however, the value analyst takes a crucial additional step and considers the *stock price* against his list of valuation factors. After calculating the supposed "intrinsic value" of a number of companies' stocks on this basis, an analyst determines whether to buy, hold or sell shares by identifying either stocks priced above or below a fixed standard of value based on historical parameters or stocks with high or low current valuations as compared to the other stocks. This approach, pioneered by Graham and Dodd,[7] has been useful in the marketplace, sometimes for prolonged periods. But where does its validity come from?

The validity comes from the fact that the valuation analyst is now introducing a technical component to his work. The fact that one can find apparent bargains among stocks and short-sale opportunities on this basis in certain market environments proves that a powerful technical factor is making investors ignore supposed fundamental values. This type of analysis is a hybrid of fundamental and technical analysis, because the analyst judges each calculated company valuation *relative to the stock price*, thus providing some insight into the psychological state of investors in the stocks under consideration.

A value analyst is actually assessing changing states of optimism and pessimism as measured by a specific set of criteria. This fact often enables competent practitioners of company valuation analysis to place bets before psychology changes. Since market psychology is always in flux, the chance that psychology will reverse rather than become more extreme is significant. The result is that company valuation analysts can be positioned months or years ahead of news that pure fundamental analysts will later view as important.

Many value analysts claim to reject technical analysis while practicing it. By considering only factors outside the market as a basis of their analysis, they exclude other valuable clues to an impending change in market valuation. Despite this constraint, the approach can work for long periods, and when brilliant minds pursue it with commitment, it can bring substantial rewards.

While the valuation approach often works because it has incorporated technical analysis, its self-imposed restriction puts the effectiveness of the analysis at great risk. For one thing, the assumed standards of value can fluctuate as dramatically as the price. Major shifts in social psychology can result in booms or depressions, dramatically impacting the company-valuation measures upon which these analysts depend. "Value" investors who bought IBM "cheap" at 110 are wondering what to do with it at 50 now that earnings have plummeted and the dividend has been cut.

Theoretically speaking, a value analyst could arrive at an accurate opinion about the future stability of his measures—earnings, dividends, and so on—only by correctly assessing all factors impacting the future potential for the success of a company, a forbiddingly complex task. The task, moreover, ultimately necessitates some form of technical analysis, as established above.

Many value-oriented portfolio managers stay heavily invested and assert that their primary goal is to invest in stocks that will outperform others, not stocks that will go up. As a result, they rarely concern themselves with whether a bull or bear market is in progress. This omission is benign during a bull market, but it places their value conclusions in occasional jeopardy of being overwhelmed, as holding stocks in a major bear market while the value analyst's adopted standards fall ever lower can cause disaster to a portfolio. While managers may keep their jobs if they lose less money than their brethren during a modest decline, make no mistake about it: The true goal of investing one's *own* capital is but one thing: *making money*, not losing less money than somebody else. In 1929 and 1968, the fact that a bear market was imminent should have overridden all other considerations, and even portfolios that lost a bit less than others were devastated. Ironically, many managers who outperformed on the upside underperformed on the downside, erasing the previously presumed advantage.

Valuation analysis may not even work on a relative basis. A practitioner might accept the idea that even a stock appearing to provide an opportunity for gain because it was priced below its supposed corporate intrinsic value could go down in a bear market, or conversely that an apparently expensive stock could continue to rise substantially in a bull market. It happens all the time. He might even agree that a particular stock that is apparently expensive or cheap on a relative basis might not follow an expected relative price appreciation or depreciation. Nevertheless, he would probably maintain that, at minimum, the value approach is a good way to predict *relative* performance among stocks. Much of the time, it is; but sometimes even relative values are irrelevant for no clear reason. In the 1980s, the universal utility of the value approach was quite emphatically challenged. *The Wall Street Journal* offered this description of the inefficacy of value investing by mutual funds in an article on September 17, 1991: "The common denominator is that all these funds were looking for stocks that were cheap relative to the supposed value of the company on some basis: on private market values, on cash flows, on earnings, on assets, or even on intangible things such as the franchise value of the companies." The shocking news in the article was that for the past six years, these "value stocks...have underperformed the rest of the market" relentlessly, year after year, by a huge margin. Value investing in fact was one of the worst possible ideas upon which an investor could have based his decisions during this entire period. Obviously investors were determining the value of *stock* by some criteria other than the calculated value of the *company*.

That the market could ignore company values over a full decade pretty much proves that the theoretical basis of value investing is false; investors do not in fact determine the attractiveness of stocks by valuing earnings, dividends and other corporate statistics. Whatever method they do use produces the statistical artifact that stocks are sometimes valued reasonably with respect to value-investing measures and sometimes not. The only aspect of the theory that remains valid is that sometimes psychology makes stocks cheap and sometimes it makes them expensive. The assumptions of value criteria in this case were worthless, if not dangerous. Mental orientations change. Value investing does not take that fact into account.

Empirics fit this conclusion. It seems evident when talking to most investors that they rarely use measures of corporate value as their primary reason for investing. Most investors buy and sell on tips, rumors, greed, fear, visions of the future, the desire for thrills, the greater fool theory and the exhortations of the crowd, not because of a careful consideration of the current value of the investment item.

As the preceding example implies, a period of success for an approach is not by itself proof that the premise of the approach is sound. Some trends and tendencies in markets can go on for decades, and some people can be successful despite an error of premise.

This hybrid approach can be productive for long periods. The reason is that it provides an insight into one measure of market psychology, and in some market environments, that's enough to produce success.

To summarize my position on this type of analytical hybrid, it is useful under certain technical circumstances, that is, in certain styles of markets but not in others. Predicting the style of the next bull or bear market requires a study of long term technical patterns, i.e. patterns of social and financial behavior.

## Hybrid Approaches by Technicians

Some technicians argue that fundamentals do determine stock prices but that the market somehow discerns and then "discounts" these factors in advance. I am unaware of any evidence, however, that investors know the future at all, much less well enough to price it into the present.

Some technicians believe that extremes in market psychology develop in response to fundamental news: Good news makes people optimistic, and bad news makes them pessimistic; when optimism or pessimism gets too extreme, the market is set up for trend change. But if news were the rational basis for market pricing, it could not be a rational basis for the radical swings in optimism or pessimism that myriad indicators objectively display. Each current price would reflect all knowledge, period. There would be no basis for an opinion about future trends, which is what "optimism" and "pessimism" mean. The efficient market hypothesis, which proposes that investors in the aggregate price financial markets entirely by rational evaluation of extramarket information, characterizes the market in exactly this way, and it is consistent in doing so.

If I were to try to rescue this theory, I would propose to add the hypothesis that people suffer under a mental flaw by which they non-rationally project trends in news into the future. So, they do not price stocks according to news but according to past trends in news that they have projected for months or years into the future. If that were the case, natural fluctuations in good and bad news would be enough to cause the shifts in optimism and pessimism that sentiment indicators record.

This would be a technical claim about fundamental causes, producing a hybrid approach. While this theory has the advantages of not being self-negating or subject to limitless regression, it fails to account for why there is so little evidence that news drives the market and plenty of evidence that it doesn't.

## Crowd Behavior

The idea that crowds have a nature all their own is not new. The basics have been known for decades, if not longer. In the 1920s, Cambridge economist A.C. Pigou connected social dynamics to booms and depressions.[8] As R.N. Elliott phrased it, Pigou maintained "that an error of optimism tends to create, throughout the community, a certain measure of psychological interdependence until it leads to crisis. Then the error of optimism dies and gives birth to an error of pessimism."[9] The key phrase in this summary is "psychological interdependence." An investor is drawn into the crowd dynamic when his opinion about a market or investment item is primarily dependent upon others' opinions rather than on independent research and the independent judgment of his own mind. This dependence is nearly universal. Paradoxically, then, it is not a confirmation of your correct posture when you look around and can comfortably say, "Gee, everybody out there agrees with me." It is a warning. As John Spooner said, "If you sit in on a poker game and you don't see a sucker at the table, get up, because you're the sucker."

Agreement with others does not involve only positive emotions. Professor Irving Janis of Yale University, after studying at length the dynamics of group decision making, concluded, "In general, the greater the number of those in the decision maker's social network who are aware of the decision, the more powerful the incentive to avoid the social disapproval that might result from a reversal."[10] When the best time to buy or sell is at hand, even the person who thinks he should take action experiences a strong psychological pressure to refrain from doing so. He thinks, if only half consciously, "When my neighbor or advisor or friend thinks it's a good idea, then I'll do it, too. If I do it now, and I'm wrong, they'll all call me a dope, and I'll be the only dope." Pressure from, and influence by, peers is at least one reason why most people can't bring themselves to change their portfolios from a bullish to bearish orientation or vice versa if to do so would go against the ideas of their associates and contacts. It also explains why trends can continue for a long, long time and why valuations can become so extremely high or low as to appear outrageous to those who believe that people ought to base their decisions upon some calculable fundamental value.

These dynamics are immutable. The reason is that they are not the province of our rational faculty but of the pre-rational areas of the brain.[11] According to MacLean,[12] the nerves in the primitive brain stem, called the basal ganglia, control the ancient, pre-human brain functions, those that are often termed instinctive: the desire for security, the reaction to fear, the desire to acquire, territorialism and the selection of leaders. This bunch of nerves also controls the flocking and herding instinct, in other words, the social tendency to desire incorporation into the group. All these brain functions ensure lifesaving or life-enhancing action under most circumstances and are fundamental to animal motivation. Due to our evolutionary background, they are integral to human motivation as well. They are rooted so deeply in the human psyche that in many circumstances their impulses can overwhelm the higher brain functions. This knowledge is critical to market analysis. The ultimate value of being alive is protected substantially by the primitive portion of the brain, which generates powerful herding urges that overwhelm rational thought. These herding urges are detrimental to investment success.

Pre-rational areas of the brain rule prices even when a market appears reasonably valued by fundamental analysts' external criteria, as it is merely a transitional condition along the continuum between extremes of optimism and pessimism. The lower brain stem also rules investors when the market is calm, just as herding animals are often calm for long periods when grazing in a quiet field. When one of them starts to run, however, panic throughout the group is a hairsbreadth away from erupting.

### Desires in Financial Markets Differ from Desires in Markets for Goods and Services

Those who buy in bull markets are following a desire to enhance their sustenance (often called "greed"), while those who sell in bear markets are following the desire to survive (often called "fear"). These desires per se are rational, and in markets for goods and services, they enhance life. Consumers desire low prices, while producers desire high prices, for the same fundamental reasons, survival and self-sustenance. As a result of these polar goals, prices reach natural, objectively determined balance. In financial markets, however, the buyer of the investment item (akin to a consumer) and the initial seller of it (akin to a producer), both desire high prices. Consumers become motivated to buy goods and services when prices fall and avoid buying them when they rise, but investors become excited to buy investment items as prices *rise* and are pressured by unconscious herding impulses to sell when they *fall*. This situation occurs uniquely in financial markets and leads inevitably to subjective valuation for investment items. Investors who desire to be objective face the inescapable requirement of understanding that fact and its implications.

The same dynamic rules chain letters. Both sender (seller) and receiver (buyer) have visions of riches and want the chain to continue. No participant wants it to stop. But it will stop some time, and it is the objective person who knows it and acts accordingly.

In the product marketplace, the human goal of surviving and thriving leads to objective pricing and price stability. In the investment marketplace, the very same survival instinct leads to herding, which produces subjective pricing, price volatility and trends that lead to overvaluation and undervaluation. Investors generate subjective mental imagery to justify their feelings about future prices, and they effect violent price changes when their feelings change and those images dissolve. Such images are governed mightily by the pre-rational portions of the brain.

**Successful Investing**

At minimum, successful investing requires that you be independent in your thinking. Thinking independently of the crowd, however, does not mean always fighting the crowd. "Contrary opinion" is sometimes viewed as the correct orientation to markets because it reflects fierce independence. Yet the tendency to fight every trend with a contrary view is just as destructive to success as the lemming-like desire to jump on trends after they are well aged. To succeed, you must avoid both a lazy willingness to conform to the group and the curmudgeonly desire always to fight it. You must also be knowledgeable, which is one point of this presentation. Finally, you must be as objective as possible at all times. Even if you have all these traits, it is still impossible to be truly mentally independent of the crowd, because the crowd's feelings and actions rule financial markets, and you can't avoid dealing with them.

What factors enable you to be objective? First is the knowledge that the essential dynamics of crowd psychology are immutable because human beings have a fundamental nature with respect to herding in situations where uncertainty is pervasive, such as when engaging in financial speculation. Next, it is necessary to understand that you also have this trait; your own herding impulses are going to be powerful and at times overwhelming. From that solid foundation, success in markets then demands a tremendous effort, the goal of which is nothing less than training the rational cerebral cortex to override, to the extent possible, the powerful emotions and unconscious motivations produced by herding impulses serving the survival instinct.

One must understand with crystal clarity that buying in a high and rising market is not the same as putting food on the table. The "food" in this case is a mental construct, not a reality. Similarly, selling in panic as the market falls is not equivalent to running from a wild animal on the attack; indeed, the more dangerous the animal appears, the greater the overall panic, and the closer to a bottom the market will be. The "wild animal" is an ephemeral image, a mirage. Only by resisting the urge to flee can one maintain an advantageous position in the berry field, picking the best of the crop after others have fled. When a trained investor senses a wild animal on the attack in the financial marketplace, reason may dictate embracing it rather than fleeing, i.e., buying rather than selling. Cultivating such paradoxical thinking in the investment marketplace and then acting upon it provides a survival advantage over those who instinctively join rallies and flee declines.

So, in order to think and act objectively in the marketplace, you must pit your reason and knowledge against your deeply inbred emotional tendencies. It takes a tremendous effort first to understand how it feels when the primitive part of your brain tries to compel you to take specific action in certain circumstances, such as the "fight or flight" reaction when you see a tiger ten feet away or the herding instinct when the group packs up to leave for another location, and then to override these tendencies with calm and independent reason in the cerebral cortex when the fear is created not by the presence of a tiger but by a powerful consensus opinion of your peers.

It should now be clear why so few people excel at the task of successful investing. Intelligence is not enough. Knowledge is not enough. Independent thinking is not enough. You also need the ability to recognize, and then to overcome, your deepest and most powerful impulses. This skill is difficult to obtain because it requires negating the unconscious assumptions upon which the "primitive" area of the brain has based its commands. Yet it is unavoidably required for success in the field of speculation.

### Inescapability of Opinion

While investors have some leeway in their choice of methods for forming an opinion on the prospects for an investment item, one thing is for certain: Every investment posture requires a market opinion.

People try to evade responsibility for having a market opinion in numerous ways: by owning many investment items for the sake of diversifying a portfolio (ignoring the possibility of a deflation that could bring down all assets), by depending on the idea that a market always goes up long term (an opinion usually adopted about stocks, gold or real estate after the market has risen for a long time), or by claiming that allocating money to government bonds, the bank or the mattress is risk-free (overlooking possibilities, however remote, of bankrupt governments, bank failures, hyperinflation or confiscatory laws).

No investment approach is safe or guaranteed, and therefore each one requires an opinion. Since as an investor you cannot escape having an opinion, you might as well obtain a good one. The best way to do that is by objective thought and knowledgeable analysis.

### The Wave Principle

The Wave Principle is unique in postulating that there is a patterned social dynamic involving impulses of creation and destruction, expansion and contraction, and hope and fear. Not only does it describe that dynamic comprehensively and in great detail, but it is also the only approach that includes a hypothesis of why such patterns exist.[13] Indeed, today it is being demonstrated by the new science of fractal geometry that the Wave Principle reflects the most fundamental laws of growth and order in nature, just as R.N. Elliott concluded sixty years ago. Perhaps the most comforting aspect of the Wave Principle is that the detailed explanation of how market dynamics operate provides a solid basis for decision making. By providing a meticulous list of rules and guidelines for interpreting that behavior, it provides the investor a basis for exercising reason and objectivity when approaching the task of market analysis.

**Not Always Right**

While this presentation has affirmed that there is a sound basis for technical analysis, it does not mean to imply that all specific conclusions or methodologies based thereon are valid. On the contrary, there are incompetent technicians, unknowledgeable technicians and non-objective technicians. A few people who call themselves technicians rely on techniques that are little more than numerology. Many technicians are closet fundamental analysts and are therefore subject to the widespread errors of external-cause thinking. There are dependent technicians, who conform to group opinion, which is why polls of technicians' opinions sometimes reveal consensus opinions that turn out to be wrong.

Will competent technicians always agree? No. Will competent technicians using the same method always agree? Not necessarily. Market forecasting involves probabilities, not certainties. While reasonable analysts might agree that the probabilities are nearly even for two outcomes, they might disagree as to which side the advantage belongs.

Sometimes the probability is high for a particular outcome, and competent analysts using the same method should agree on that fact. Unfortunately, even when the probability of a particular outcome is high, that does not mean that the outcome will occur. It means that even given that fairly reliable circumstance, sometimes your investment decision will still be wrong. Even knowledgeable technicians are often wrong on the outlook for a market. I've helped prove that point numerous times.

Finally, the science of market forecasting is young and undeveloped. There is so much more to learn. Lack of knowledge increases uncertainty, and uncertainty triggers impulses to herd. Technicians are therefore nearly as prone to herding as everyone else. But at least they know there *is* a herd.

If you come to a wrong conclusion about the market, does that necessarily mean your method is flawed? Read this article[14] from the Associated Press about an occurrence in New Orleans.

> New Orleans (AP)—Although 100 lifeguards were present, a fully clothed man drowned at a party to celebrate the first summer in memory without a drowning at a city pool, officials said yesterday.
>
> Jerome Moody, 31, was found on the bottom at the deep end of a Recreation Department pool at the end of the party Tuesday, said Madlyn Richard, department director.

Moody, a guest who was not a lifeguard, was fully dressed, she said.

Four lifeguards were on duty and more than half the 200 people there were certified lifeguards, she said.

The body was found as the pool was being cleared. It was not known when Moody got in the water or how he drowned.

Lifeguards attempted to revive Moody until emergency attendants arrived. An autopsy confirmed Moody had drowned, said Coroner Frank Minyard.

—August 2, 1985

How many of you would have assumed that pool to be relatively safe? I would have. Did the outcome prove our thinking invalid? No. Sometimes less probable events occur. The only way to achieve a successful record over the long term is to accept the fact that you will be wrong sometimes. You cannot deviate from an objective application of your approach just because your last market call was a bad one. If you do, you'll ruin your long term ability to take advantage of probability and anticipate market direction correctly much of the time, which is all that good analysis promises. In other words, some percentage of error is a requirement for overall success, and trying to avoid it or achieve perfection by overriding your proven methodology will ruin your chances for success.

Even when you have substantial knowledge and employ the right hypotheses, acting only on favorable probability is difficult, because the unavoidable feeling of uncertainty that accompanies taking even a rational risk heightens the motivation to join the herd. Most people are better off avoiding the urge to speculate altogether and picking the safest storage vehicles for savings. But if you think you can overcome your counterproductive impulses, at least go after your dreams armed with the right premises.

## NOTES

[1] Prechter, Robert R. "Popular Culture and the Stock Market." *The Elliott Wave Theorist* Special Report, August 22, 1985.

[2] [missing reference]

[3] Brock, William A., Lakonishok, Josef and LeBaron, Blake. (1992, December). "Simple technical trading rules and the stochastic properties of stock returns." *Journal of Finance,* Vol. 47, No. 5.

[4] Fama, Eugene F. (1965). "The Behavior of Stock-Market Prices." *Journal of Business*, Vol. 38, No. 1, 34-105.

[5] [missing reference]

[6] Kurz, Mordecai. (1994). "On Rational Belief Equilibria." *Economic Theory*, Vol. 4, 859-876. Springer-Verlag.

[7] Graham, Benjamin and David Dodd. (1934). *Security Analysis.* New York: McGraw-Hill.

[8] Pigou, Arthur C. (1920). *The Economics of Welfare*. London: Cass. As quoted in *Business Cycles: The Problem and Its Setting*. (1927) Ed. Wesley Clair Mitchell, 18-19.

[9] Elliott, R.N. (1943, April 20). "Educational Bulletin Q—Psychology." Reprinted in *R.N. Elliott's Market Letters, 1938-1946*. Edited by Robert R. Prechter. Gainesville, GA: New Classics Library, 1993, pp. 182-184.

[10] Janis, Irving L. (1972). *Victims of Groupthink*. Boston: Houghton-Mifflin.

[11] Montgomery, Paul M. "The Logical Primacy of Mental States in the Price Structure of Investments," reprinted in *Market Analysis for the New Millennium*. (2002) Gainesville, GA: New Classics Library.

[12] MacLean, Paul D. (1990). *The Triune Brain in Evolution: Role in Paleocerebral Functions*. New York: Plenum Press.

[13] Frost, Alfred John and Robert Rougelot Prechter, Jr. (1978). *Elliott Wave Principle—Key to Market Behavior*. Gainesville, GA: New Classics Library.

[14] Associated Press. "Man Drowns at Party for 100 Lifeguards." AP News Archive, August 1, 1985.

*Chapter 35*

# Predicting Economic and Monetary Trends

How does one apply socionomic techniques to economic forecasting? A socionomist knows that the stock market is a meter of social mood, which is the engine of social progress and regress. Therefore, the current-time change in the stock market is an immensely useful indicator of upcoming economic change. With a knowledge of the Wave Principle, a socionomist has two further advantages over conventional approaches. First, he can often anticipate and recognize the *degree* of the trend change and therefore the probable extent and severity of the new trend. Second, he can refine his timing in certain cases with respect to the *label* of the corrective wave, for example expecting only one recession in an (A)-(B)-(C) correction of Primary degree, as a response either to wave (A) or wave (C), as explained in Chapter 16 (p. 262) of *The Wave Principle of Human Social Behavior.*

There are three supporting elements to socionomic forecasting: the wave patterns in economic data, the momentum of stock market and economic data (involving rates of change and divergences) and the psychological state of the professionals and the public. These factors provide evidence either that an analyst has correctly interpreted the wave patterns or that he has done so *incorrectly*, forcing a re-examination of his outlook.

Some of what follows in this section may be found in Chapter 17 of *The Wave Principle of Human Social Behavior* and Chapters 1 and 5 of *Conquer the Crash*. This seems a good opportunity to chronicle the highlights of the record in one place. It also provides an opportunity to include some recent additions to it. The purpose of this chapter is not to claim a track record for economic forecasting (because I gave it so little thought and effort) but rather to show some ways that a socionomist might approach the task.

*Figure 1*

### Some Success in Forecasting Near-Term Economic Trends

Figure 1 shows that from 1975 through 1979, the U.S. economy was recession-free. Then it underwent two recessions, which lasted from January through August 1980 and from July 1981 through November 1982, respectively.

The following quotations show how *The Elliott Wave Theorist* navigated the expansions and the recessions from the publication's inception in April 1979 through 1983's developing boom.

*November 4, 1979*

In the September 9 letter, I reproduced from the *Wall Street Journal* a chart of durable goods orders, which then stood at $72b., under the title, "Is the Recession Over?" Here is an updated chart, and as you can see, the a-b-c reaction in mid-1979 has already produced a rebound. A headline on the front page of the

Journal on October 31 read, "Surprising Surge—Third Quarter Profits Topped Expectations." Elliott waves appear to be useful even with fundamental data, as Elliott claimed.

In a normal wave pattern, the current rise would constitute wave B upward, to be followed by a downward wave C. If this pattern occurs, a steeper downturn in the economy might be expected between now and early next year.

### Weekly Earnings

AVERAGE WEEKLY PAY of factory workers in November rose to $275.37 from a revised $274.85 the preceding month, the Labor Department reports.

### January 6, 1980

The chart of weekly earnings shows five upward waves separated by corrections, which follow the rule of alternation (wave two is simple, wave four complex). Close scrutiny shows hints of five wave subdivisions within each broad upwave. The wave appears to channel well, also. This chart suggests that, unless an extension is building, the first quarter of 1980 may show an a-b-c downswing of greater proportion than any of the past three years (see durable goods orders chart in November issue). Does that mean stock prices have to come down? Not if the recession is discounted, and if you haven't discounted this recession in your own portfolio, you haven't been reading the papers for the last three years....

### February 9, 1980

In the past several issues, I have featured charts of fundamental economic data that seem to display an Elliott pattern. So far, I have included charts of durable goods orders and weekly earnings of factory workers, both of which show

### Construction Spending

SPENDING for construction fell in November to a seasonally adjusted annual rate of $235.3 billion from a revised $238.5 billion in October, the Commerce Department reports.

five waves upward. Now comes another data series, construction spending, which shows exactly the same pattern. Taken together, the charts of the economy suggest a marked slowing of economic activity some time in 1980, unless of course an extension forms. A "slowing" may indeed mean a recession by the official definition, but even if it occurs, it will take a lot more than that to frighten the stock market, since whatever slowing we do get has been more than discounted over the last three years.

### April 6, 1980

Not once since I began these letters have I said anything about the economy except "Forget the Recession." Now, as you can see on the front page table, I fully expect one to occur. The reasoning is simple. The market, for the first time since 1973, is predicting a recession. How deep it will be depends upon the severity of the decline in the market..

Based on the Elliott counts of economic data (see previous letters), a recession now appears to have its best excuse for occurring since the economists began predicting one three years ago. This chart of durable goods orders looks like it's right at the top of the "b" wave of an a-b-c correction following a five-wave advance. The "c" wave should carry under the 72 level.

*June 10, 1980*

From the time I began writing these reports to the March 9, 1980 issue, my front-page conclusion regarding the economy was "Forget the Recession." Since last November, however, I have been displaying all sorts of charts of fundamental economic data that were counting out complete "fives," from the average weekly pay of factory workers to construction spending to durable goods orders to the number of new incorporations. We knew we were close to that recession, but two pieces were missing. The first was the contrary opinion aspect, which finally fell into place when the WSJ headlined: "As the Heralded Slump Still Doesn't Show Up, Firms Disregard Threat—Analysts Explain Mistakes, Now See Mild Recession and Still More Inflation." The other indicator which had yet to "click in" was the stock market, and the performance in March supplied the missing piece. The Elliott conclusion was then clear as crystal: SEVERE RECESSION 1980-1981.

As the two charts below indicate, the economy, which has been weakening ever so slightly, absolutely collapsed in April and May, and may still be collapsing. The leading indicators dropped 4.8% for the month of April, their largest drop since the series began in 1948. That drop compares to a 3% drop in the worst month (September) of the 1974-75 recession. The incredible slide in short term interest rates indicates that the demand for funds is practically zero. The charts of the fundamental data mentioned above are well into their a-b-c declines as well. O.K., score one for Elliott analysis, which not only saw the turn in the economy developing, but recognized "the top" as well.

| *Unemployment Rate* | *Leading Indicators* |
|---|---|

Percent of Labor Force
Seasonally Adjusted

Index: 1967 =100

1977 1978 1979 1980

COMPOSITE of key indicators of future economic activity fell in April to 126.3% of the 1967 average from a revised 132.6% in March.

*July 6, 1980*

The economy has remained on its downward course as per expectations. These charts of retail sales, new incorporations, durable goods orders and construction spending illustrate the Elliott influence since 1977.

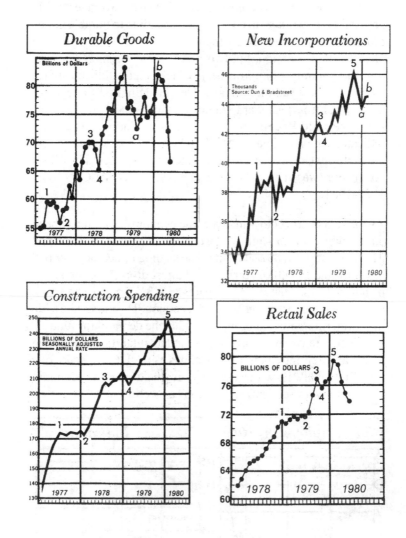

Since the Elliott guideline for a normal bear market is the low of the previous fourth wave of lesser degree (or the second wave of lesser degree when the first wave is extended), we might expect a bottom in the recession quite soon. "Normal" targets for these economic indicators are as follows:

Retail Sales: $71b.
Construction Spending: $207b.
Durable Goods Orders: $65b.
New incorporations: 42,000.

### August 10, 1980

Elliott Wave analysis caught the "top" in the economy just weeks before the economic indicators tumbled. Last month I displayed four charts of economic data and commented that based on the normal expectation of wave retracement, "we might expect a bottom in the recession quite soon." I also gave downside targets for the four fundamental factors. The only follow-up data yet available is for durable goods orders, for which a normal Elliott guideline projected a bottom at $65b. The chart at right shows the latest data, and the slowing down in the rate of descent could indicate a bottom right on target.

### September 9, 1980

In the July 6 letter, I put "RECESSION ENDING" on the front page table and showed charts of four different measures of economic data, with target points for each. As you can see, durable goods orders bottomed at $66b. (target $65b.), while retail sales (target $71b.), construction spending (target $207b.), and new incorporations (target 42,000) appear to have a bit more to go. Based on these charts, we could have a "pullback" (as part of a W pattern) in some areas of the economy, with retail sales the most vulnerable area.

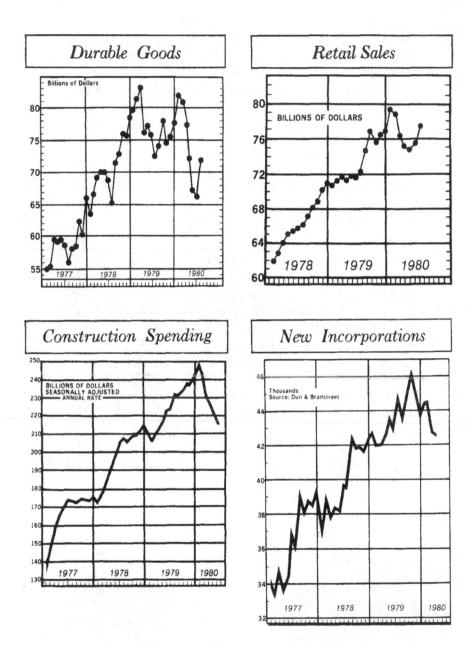

*October 3, 1980*

July was my first letter marked "RECESSION ENDING." Along with many other economic indicators, the chart of industrial production shows a July low, as you can see from the accompanying chart.

As for the current recovery, I expect that it will peak out in the first quarter of 1981 and show a second dip into the latter half of the year. This projection is based on the Elliott outlook for the stock market and the bond market, as well as an expected tightening of monetary policy after the election no matter who wins.

*January 9, 1981*

The economy rebounded right on schedule from the Elliott-based forecast, as the accompanying chart of industrial production illustrates. Last month I indicated that I expected a "second dip" some time during 1981. That second dip should not be a full-fledged recession, but only a month or two of weak statistics.

The most important point I can make is that I think the "second dip" has been entirely discounted during the corrective wave of the past four months, so it's not something to worry about from a stock market standpoint.

*April 12, 1981*

Starting on the front page of the December 14 issue of *The Elliott Wave Theorist*, I indicated that the economy should undergo a "SECOND DIP EARLY 1981." This "second dip" was not (and still is not) expected to become a new full-fledged recession. These quotes from the WSJ's front page summarizes what has occurred since the robust economic rebound that began last July started slowing down.

**THE ECONOMY** slowed in February on the effects of inflation and high interest rates, and new government figures support economists' predictions of sluggish performance this year. Housing starts plunged nearly 25% to an adjusted annual rate of 1,218,000 units, while industrial output fell an adjusted 0.5% after six consecutive gains. Personal income rose an adjusted 0.7%, its smallest gain since June, and the savings rate in January, at 4.4% was the lowest in three decades.

For two years now, I've had excellent success in calling the turns in the economy, and I don't mind revealing my secret. But don't hold your breath; it's one that's been known for decades: If you can define what the stock market is doing, then you can anticipate the economy with a precision as yet unmatched by any other method. A Cycle degree decline precedes a severe recession. A Primary degree decline generally precedes a moderate or short recession. An Intermediate degree correction, such as we have undergone since August, should precede a "softening" in the economy. These "forecasts" are often possible only with a knowledge of the Wave Principle, since many sideways periods might not be defined as corrective "declines" under another method of analysis. Furthermore, one must employ a flexible definition of recession, not the economist's rigid definition of X number of months of decline in GNP.

*August 2, 1981*

I don't comment on the economy very often because it isn't necessary. In the July 6, 1980 letter the front page comment was "RECESSION ENDING." That changed to "REBOUND IN PROGRESS" until December 1980, when it changed to "SECOND DIP EARLY 1981." Following a marked slowdown in economic activity in the first quarter, I changed the

**THE ECONOMY** contracted at an adjusted 1.9% annual rate in the second quarter, and many analysts see continued weakness through the fall. They attributed the decline largely to high interest rates. Price increases in the period slowed to a 6% annual rate, down sharply from the 9.8% pace of the preceding quarter.

**Durable-goods orders** fell 0.8% in June to an adjusted $87.46 billion.

heading in the April 12 letter to "SECOND DIP OCCURRING."
The data for April-May-June are now in and show these results:

Even though I put very little effort into it, I've had no trouble
forecasting the general trend of the economy in these letters.
My methods were explained in the April 12, 1981 letter and
can be used by anyone who prefers to avoid digesting reams
of statistics in order to reach a conclusion. Since no method of
forecasting is perfect, one of these days I'm bound to get a false
signal, but I expect that the overall record will continue to be
highly successful.

*September 8, 1981*

As these paragraphs from the WSJ indicate, the economy is still
on track with a "second dip" in progress. The chart of housing
starts displays the double dip profile quite clearly. I fully expect
to be changing the front page comment on the economy next
month from "SECOND DIP OCCURRING" to "SECOND DIP
ENDING." [Note: This change was not made.]

**C**ORPORATE PROFITS after taxes fell 11.3% in the second quarter, the Commerce Department said, indicating the economy was weaker than had been thought. Gross national product declined at an adjusted 2.4% annual rate after allowing for inflation. The department has estimated the decline at a 1.9% pace.

\* \* \*

**The economy deteriorated** in July as production, employment and new orders plummeted, according to a survey of purchasing agents.

*Housing Starts*

*January 11, 1982* through *October 4, 1982*

"RECESSION IN PROGRESS."

*November 8, 1982*

I haven't said much about the economy lately, being satisfied to leave "RECESSION IN PROGRESS" on the front page of the letter. Until now, the market had not given an adequate indication that the economy was truly about to turn, so I had no reason to change it. Now it's given a powerful signal: the current very deep recession is ending. Economic recovery will begin soon.

The correlation between the stock market and the economy is so consistent that it is by far the finest tool for forecasting the economy, as long as you don't restrict yourself to "official" definitions of recession. It is extremely instructive to note the precision with which the March-May rally gave an advance indication of the subsequent moderate improvement in some economic indicators. The May-August slide then correctly preceded a "mysterious" backsliding in the economic figures once again. I've waited for the stock market to give an unmistakable major turn signal by roaring ahead before placing "RECOVERY BEGINNING" on the front page of the letter. Now it's done it, and the Elliott counts on economic data (see charts) agree. By waiting for the full signals, I haven't been wrong on the economy since *The Elliott Wave Theorist* began. Let's see how this one works out.

*March 7, 1983*

Even while administration officials were still sending out gloomy messages as recently as January, the economy has been roaring into life. Finally, as this recent report shows, the data can no longer be ignored.

At this point, I feel it warranted to change "RECOVERY BEGINNING" to "ECONOMIC BOOM" on the front page table. This is somewhat of a change in my thinking regarding the environment for the 1980s. The *monetary* environment should be one of stability, but the economy itself, if my outlook for stocks is correct, really should enter a full-blown boom, similar in many ways to the 1920s. The rise in stocks, the drop in the price of oil and overall monetary stability for the first time in ten years should provide the fuel. By the way, if someone (as *Time* magazine did recently) is still telling you to worry about an imminent banking collapse, you should ask them why bank stocks have just begun to take off on the upside.

**T**HE **INDEX** of leading economic indicators rose 3.6% in January, the largest one-month gain since July 1950. The increase confirms that the recession has ended. But Commerce Secretary Baldrige warned that the index's strength shouldn't be perceived "as a sign of a coming economic boom."

Indeed, April 1983 saw the start of the longest uninterrupted economic expansion since 1961-1969.

*August 9, 1983*

On the front page of the March 7 issue, I changed the comment on Economic Conditions from "RECOVERY UNDERWAY" to "ECONOMIC BOOM" based entirely on the performance by the single best indicator of economic trends, the stock market. 4 1/2 months later, the news is out. The accompanying comments appeared under the headline, "Economy Surges to 2-Year High":

**JULY 22, 1983 – USA TODAY**

The economy's growth has hit a two-year high, the government said Thursday, setting a "stunning" 8.7 percent pace that President Reagan called "the surest route to more jobs."

Gross national product—the total output of goods and services—soared by an inflation-adjusted $31.3 billion in the April-June quarter. Consumer spending increased by $23.8 billion.

The surge is much higher than the government's early estimate of 6.6 percent, and higher than virtually all private forecasts.

From that point forward, my interests shifted, and I ceased analyzing economic statistics. Unfortunately, my lack of rigor in this area from that time forward eventually led to numerous premature warnings about the depression that was expected to follow wave V. For an explanation of why I was so early in my concerns, see Section Two of *View From the Top of the Grand Supercycle*.

### "Getting It" from the Point of View of Macroeconomic Causality

Having studied the typical results of Primary degree corrections (see *The Wave Principle of Human Social Behavior*, Chapter 16, p. 262), I was able to make this statement on August 4, 1986:

> Primary wave ④ will precede an outright recession in economic activity, much as Primary wave ④ in 1926 led to the 1926-1927 recession.

This exposition anticipated what did happen, as the final months of the 1987-1990 (1991) wave ④ produced a recession, as you can see in Figure 2.

For the record, I did not recognize wave ④ for what it was in real time. When the time came to announce a new phase of boom, I instead expected an imminent downturn. While the Japanese economy followed the script relentlessly, the U.S. economy sailed through the 1990s unscathed.

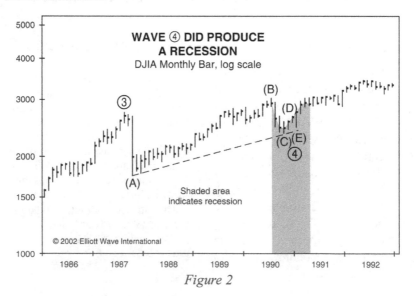

*Figure 2*

**Forecasting the Relative Strength of an Economic Expansion**

Fifth waves are weaker than third waves, both in terms of their breadth of stock participation and their economic results. This simple truth has immense value in macroeconomic forecasting.

The idea that there is a difference in quality between the macroeconomic trends that manifest from a *third* wave and those that manifest from a *fifth* wave has been a part of the Wave Principle for over twenty years. *Elliott Wave Principle* describes third waves as "wonders to behold" as they deliver on the promise of rising stocks with "increasingly favorable fundamentals." In contrast, "the fifth of the fifth [wave] will lack the dynamism that preceded it." This description is useful because contrasting periods of economic performance can confirm or contradict a wave interpretation. However, it can also provide a basis for forecasting the *quality* of economic trends. For example, by labeling the March 1942 to February 1966 bull market wave III, Frost and I in 1978 established the extramarket vitality of the 1950s and early 1960s as a standard that the forecasted wave V bull market would not surpass. *The Elliott Wave Theorist* reiterated the expected relationship between the two periods with this description in the August 1983 report (reprinted in the Appendix to *Elliott Wave Principle*) on the upcoming "superbull market":

> This fifth wave will be built more on unfounded hopes than on soundly improving fundamentals such as the U.S. experienced in the 1950s and early 1960s. And since this fifth wave, wave V, is a fifth within a larger fifth, wave (V) from 1789, the phenomenon should be magnified by the time the peak is reached.

This is an unusually specific forecast. The very idea of commenting on the relative strength of a projected multi-year recovery is so unusual that no economist has ever attempted anything of the kind. Once you understand that economic trends fit the overall Elliott wave structure, you can understand how I could presume to do it. How has this prediction fared?

Each of the two great post-Depression expansions accompanied a bull market in stocks that lasted a quarter-century, from 1942 to 1966 in the first instance and from 1974 to 2000 in the second. The percentage gain in the DJIA during the latter period was nearly *double* what it was during the former (1930 percent vs. 971 percent). On that basis alone, one might assume that wave V should have produced a stronger economy than wave III. On the contrary, an objective contrast of the quality of the macroeconomic and fiscal aspects of waves III and V shows that wave V has been a weaker performance in terms of *every relevant measure*, as shown in Figures 3 and 4. Combining the GDP and Industrial Production figures, we may generalize that the economic power of wave V was two-thirds of that of wave III.

## Balance Sheet Items at the End of Wave III vs. Wave V
### (scales at left)

*Figure 3*

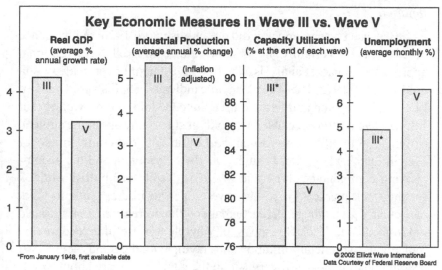

*Figure 4*

The forecast included this phrase: "The phenomenon should be magnified by the time the peak is reached." In other words, the economic expansion would wane even further as wave ⑤ of V progressed and further as wave (5) of ⑤ progressed. True to expectation, the economic expansion slackened further in the latter stages of wave V.

Probably because background conditions in the 1980s and 1990s were so much better than those in the *1970s*, conventional observers miss this very important long-term distinction. In contrast, the Wave Principle provides the basis for a profound insight regarding the relative character of the economic environment of the 1980s and 1990s. What's more, it is available not only as a useful latter-day observation (which even today is utterly lacking in current conventional economic discourse) but as a *prediction*, published four years into the second quarter-century expansion. (Had you been a practicing socionomist at the time, you could have presented that outlook in 1975 or even earlier.)

### Some Success in Forecasting Monetary Trends

Socionomics is hardly a perfect tool for forecasting long-term monetary trends, but in its brief history of application, it is already unparalleled in that role. We have records of successful forecasts of inflation, disinflation and deflation.

*Inflation*

Because I was young and did not publish until 1976, our evidence here is weak but certainly shows some value compared to conventional approaches to market analysis. The first investment I ever made was in gold stocks in 1972. The Wave Principle indicated a bullish gold market. I bought West Rand and Orange Free State Geduld, but only partly for Elliott wave reasons because I was only just learning about the subject. (From 1976 to 1979, I published market-timing gold commentary for Merrill Lynch.) Figure 6-11 in *Elliott Wave Principle* and the accompanying commentary show that in 1978, despite our bullish outlook for the stock market, Frost and I were open to further gains in gold, particularly given the sizeable "expanded flat correction" that it traced out from 1974 to 1976. So the Wave Principle was useful in recognizing indications of monetary inflation and staying with the trend—or at least accommodating it—until very late in the game, as we are about to see.

*Disinflation*

Elliott wave analysis has proved useful in forecasting a major trend change from accelerating inflation to disinflation (i.e., decelerating inflation). The spiraling inflation dating from 1967, after weathering two setbacks, finally culminated in January 1980 in an atmosphere of long term financial panic. Two months before, in November 1979, *The Elliott Wave Theorist* spelled out expectations for the major sea change that was at hand. *Commodities* (now *Futures*) magazine published some of EWT's comments in its January 1980 issue. Here is an excerpt:

> The incredible conjunction of "fives" in different markets [gold, silver, interest rates, bonds, and commodities] all seem to point to the same conclusion: *The world is about to begin a phase of general disinflation*. As I see it, a pattern of several disinflationary years leading to a deflationary trend later on would be a perfect scenario for the Elliott outlook for stocks. A gradual disinflation would create an optimistic mood in the country and lead to the conclusion that we may have finally licked the inflation problem. This sentiment would support a bull market in stocks for several years until the snowballing forces of deflation began to take over. At that point, a major deflationary crash would be impossible to avert, and the Grand Supercycle correction would be underway.

The inflationary trend that had accelerated for a Fibonacci 13 years ended abruptly, as indicated by gold and silver prices, the very next month. Indeed, the above paragraph spelled out, just weeks before the reversal of trend, the experience of the ensuing two decades.

The onset of the new trend was as exciting as the termination of the old one. The 1980 peak was followed by a brief two-year period of extremely rapid disinflation that shocked the markets. From a peak of $850 per ounce in January 1980, gold collapsed to $296.75 (basis London fix) in June 1982. From its long-time resistance area just above 1000, the Dow fell back to 777 in August 1982, reaching its lowest real value since World War II. The bond market was scraping bottom, having been ravaged by both the inflationary period, which stoked fears of ever-rising interest rates, and the recessions of 1980 to 1982, which kindled default worries. The next monetary event appeared to be anyone's guess. The most popular competing opinions were (1) that inflation would accelerate into hyperinflation, and (2) that deflation and economic contraction would bring about financial collapse. These opinions were so popular that they were called "The Great Debate" at financial conferences, which attracted thousands of people.

In contrast to the two prevailing opinions, the September 13, 1982 issue of *The Elliott Wave Theorist* offered ten points supporting the forecast for the Dow to quintuple to 3885. (For details, see the Appendix to *Elliott Wave Principle*.) Two of those points pertained to the expected monetary environment:

> — Fits the idea that the Kondratieff cycle plateau has just begun, [supporting] a period of economic stability and soaring stock prices. Parallel with late 1921.

> — Celebrates the end of the inflationary era [and] accompanies a stable reflation.

Specifically, then, *The Elliott Wave Theorist* forecasted a mild *reflation* relative to the crunch of 1980-1982 that would occur within the longer term trend of *disinflation*. Monetary stability was the last thing on most people's forecast list. Yet, the period of stability and reflation began right then. That the Wave Principle could be applied to recognize the onset of such a period was of immense value to investors, particularly in the stock and bond markets, which began historic advances.

Four months later, in January 1983, *The Elliott Wave Theorist* added to its case as follows: "Quietly behind the scenes, despite all the return-of-inflation rhetoric, the utility stocks have scored a major breakout, providing [another] strong foundation for the 'continuing disinflation' argument." That November, EWT further bolstered the case that the slackening in the rate of inflation was not just a brief respite but was of multi-year significance:

> Two years ago, I used the percent change in the PPI to show a massive momentum divergence against new highs in the index in 1980. That lower peak in the rate of change was essentially a "sell signal" on inflation. Since then, the inflation rate has not only declined substantially, but its rate of change has fallen beneath the long term uptrend line from 1949. That break...does seem to support the claim that there has been a change over the last three years that is larger than just a cyclical disinflation due to recession.

In June 1984, as stock prices slipped to an intermediate-term low, *The Wall Street Journal* published a five-page special report on the financial outlook, which included interviews with many distinguished economists and statesmen. The consensus was overwhelming that the country's economic and monetary problems were insurmountable and about to get worse. (Page 128 of *The Wave Principle of Human Social Behavior* provides some details of this report.) Yet the benign disinflationary trend was already underway, supporting the bull markets in stocks and bonds that continued for another decade and a half.

## Deflation

As you have read, the forecast for disinflation issued in late 1979 spelled out the expected sequence of events, calling for "several disinflationary years leading to a deflationary trend later," which would resolve with "a major deflationary crash." In 1995, it appeared that outright deflation was imminent, worldwide. Japan had been experiencing deflation for five years. Countries in Southeast Asia underwent deflationary crashes in 1997 and 1998. Argentina's deflation hit bottom in 2001. Hints of deflationary pressures have continued to build in the United States and Europe, particularly after early 2000. For more on my outlook for deflation, see *Conquer the Crash*. The outcome of this forecast remains to be seen, but I believe that signs of accelerating, developing or approaching (depending on your locale) deflation are now more legion than ever.

## A Basis of Value for Macroeconomic Prediction

There are two ways to look at the performance of conventional economists vs. what socionomists can do. One is to assess how right they both are in terms of a percentage of the time that they make predictions. On that basis, conventional economists do pretty well, being right about whether the economy will expand or contract in the next quarter as much as 70 percent of the time. Their opinions, demonstrably in the aggregate and (based on my observations) in almost every individual case as well, simply lag the actual economy. Thus, after they finally recognize a new trend that has been in force, their extrapolated predictions can be correct for awhile thereafter when the economy trends that way for a long period of time. In terms of time, socionomists would probably do about as well. The second way to assess performance gives a far different result. If one presumes that economists' job is to anticipate change, then they are virtually never right. Economists' views lag the economy, which lags the stock market. Socionomists anticipate the stock market, which anticipates the economy, so they are often way ahead of coming changes. Even when they fail to anticipate the stock market, they can observe the stock market in real time and forecast economic change quite reliably thereby. Most conventional economists get something close to a zero for performance, a lower score than one would get flipping a coin annually to call economic expansions and contractions. Socionomists, on the other hand, can be trained to read the indicators of approaching or concurrent trend reversal, so they can anticipate change correctly fairly often (although there are as yet no data addressing the rate of success). To be sure, sometimes they anticipate changes that do not occur, and sometimes they miss changes that do. Still, they often *do* anticipate change, and conventional macroeconomists do not. On this basis, there is no comparison between the two approaches; socionomics wins hands down.

December 2001

*Chapter 36*

# Toward a New Understanding of Growth and Recession, Boom and Depression

by Hernán Cortés Douglas

"This expansion will run forever."[1] So said an MIT Professor of Economics in *The Wall Street Journal*. Think about it. A respected leader in the field comes to a conclusion about economic behavior that defies the entirety of history. Since that article appeared on July 30, 1998, we know that its breathless conclusion also failed to accommodate the future. Nor was this opinion unique at the time. Ninety-eight percent of economists in *The Wall Street Journal's* New Year's poll of 2001 said they expected continued expansion throughout the year.

This type of forecasting error is hardly a first for academic economists. Examples of our profession's failure to anticipate economic contractions are legion and span its entire history. *The Economist* reiterated in its November 29, 2001 issue, "Economists have a dismal record in predicting recession." Some instances have been so glaring and instructive that they beg retelling.

## A Brief Review of Major Failures in Economic Forecasting

To most famed and respected economists of the 1920s, the crash that preceded the Great Depression was utterly unexpected. Fourteen days before Black Tuesday, October 29, 1929, Irving Fisher, America's best-known economist and Professor of Economics at Yale University, declared, "In a few months I expect to see the stock market much higher than today." Fisher, a consummate theoretician, a founder of econometrics, and a pioneer in index number analysis, was also a successful capitalist, having invented the c-kardex file system, which he sold for a staggering sum. He had such faith in his economic analysis that he is reported by his son to have lost an estimated 140 million of today's dollars in the crash.[2]

British economist John Maynard Keynes, a renowned father of macroeconomics who had amassed fortunes in the financial markets for both himself and Cambridge University, was caught unprepared, shedding a million of today's pounds sterling of his net worth.[3]

Days after the crash, the Harvard Economic Society reassured subscribers, "A severe depression such as 1920-21 is outside the range of probability. We are not facing a protracted liquidation." In 1932, after a string of failed optimistic forecasts, the Society closed its doors.

New societies—at universities, central banks and independent "think tanks"—have since sprung up. Do they know any more about macroeconomic forecasting than their predecessors?

Since the Great Depression, we have had immense improvements in science and technology. Given seven additional decades of data collection and progress in econometric techniques, one might presume that the forecasting tools of macroeconomics have become vastly more effective than their predecessors of 1929. Yet as recently as 1988, some leading economists went on the record about the profession's lack of progress. Writing in *The American Economic Review*, the journal of the American Economic Association, Kathryn Domínguez, Ray Fair, and Matthew Shapiro reported that a modern economist, armed with the latest and most sophisticated econometric techniques, and even using voluminous data that was unavailable in 1929, would have had no idea in 1929 that the Great Depression lay around the corner.

Real results continue to bear out the implications of this conclusion. For example, as one writer observed, "It is hard to imagine any article with worse timing than, say, 'Asia's Bright Future,'"[4] which appeared in the November/December 1997 issue of *Foreign Affairs*. The article, by two Harvard professors, appeared as East Asian economies were already melting down and as Japan was staggering through one of the three recessions it has suffered in a decade of financial difficulty. Consider its disutility in light of the fact that the year 1974, a full 23 years earlier, would have been the best time for such a forecast, while 1997, *late* 1997 at that, was the worst time since the onset of World War II to have made it.

President Herbert Hoover, reflecting in his Memoirs on economists' consensus prior to the Depression for which the public so often blamed him, complained, "With growing optimism, they gave birth to a foolish idea called the 'New Economic Era'. That notion spread over the whole country. We were assured we were in a new period where the old laws of economics no longer applied." Seven decades later, our MIT professor's prognostications about the "New Economy" echoed those same follies. The justification once again was that we had conquered the business cycle: "As we have the tools to keep the current expansion going," he wrote, "we won't have [a recession.] We have the monetary and fiscal resources to keep one from happening, as well as a policy team that won't hesitate to use them for continued expansion."[5] If that were true, then Japan, with its own dedicated "policy team" of macroeconomists and its world-class kit bag of macroeconomic "tools," would have prevented the prolonged stagnation that was as evident in 1998 as it still is now.

## Mysteries Loaded with Suspects

The Minneapolis Fed, in October 2000, invited some sixty noted economists to a conference to present research papers on the Great Depression. The event attracted a number of macroeconomist luminaries, including University of Chicago professor Robert E. Lucas Jr., the 1995 Nobel Laureate, and professors from the University of Minneapolis, UC Berkeley, Princeton, Carnegie Mellon and other top universities. All that talent brought to bear notwithstanding, the report on the conference in the Minneapolis Fed Review, *The Region*, concludes on a rather disappointing note. When economists review the facts surrounding the Depression, it says, they "each time come up with another explanation. The Great Depression is…a mystery that is loaded with suspects and difficult to solve, even when we know the ending." [6]

By and large the explanation of this failure is that economists have been leaning on so-called macroeconomic fundamentals to attempt such predictions. Have they ever succeeded? The historical data say that they *cannot* succeed; financial markets never collapse when things look bad. In fact, quite the contrary is true. Before contractions begin, macroeconomic flows always look fine. That is why the vast majority of economists always proclaim the economy to be in excellent health just before it swoons. Despite these failures, indeed despite repeating almost precisely those failures, economists have continued to pore over the same macroeconomic fundamentals for clues to the future. If the conventional macroeconomic approach is useless even in retrospect, if it cannot explain or understand an outcome *even when we know what it is*, has it a prayer of doing so when the goal is assessing the future?

Apparently not. As Lucas candidly observed years ago, "Economic reasoning will be of no value in cases of uncertainty."[7] We have learned from Nobel laureate Friedrich von Hayek, his mentor, Ludwig von Mises, and from Frank Knight, a Professor of Economics at the University of Chicago who taught several Nobel Laureates, that uncertainty is normal and pervasive. Given that the future is always uncertain, is Lucas saying that "economic reasoning" has no forecasting value whatsoever? Reasoning *per se* is not at fault; more and more, it appears that the flaws reside in the *conventional economic premises* upon which that reasoning is founded. There is a different but correct set of fundamentals.

**Toward a New Understanding**

What are economists missing? What did they once learn but later forget or neglect? What new studies shed light on the subject? For answers, I suggest looking to the following three subsets of empirical observations that have emerged from disparate sources.

*1. Debt drives the business cycle.*

Well-known to economists but oddly ignored is the fact that large, sustained increases in money and private sector debt accompany economic booms. Conversely, important contractions in money and private sector debt accompany economic contractions. Fluctuations in private debt levels correlate with stock indices and economic activity in general, especially with respect to trends lasting years or decades. These observations are consistent with the monetary (Milton Friedman) and Austrian (Mises and Hayek) theories of the business cycle, but economists have ceased putting them to practical use. In 1933, Irving Fisher highlighted the correlation in an article in *Econometrica*, "Debt-Deflation Theory of Depressions," which most economists have neglected. Similarly, in a lifetime of work ignored by mainstream economists, post-Keynesian economist Hyman Minsky focused on the financial instability created by expanding indebtedness. In the major boom that ended with the 20th century, private sector debt accumulated at a blistering pace and hit very high levels, especially near the end. Economists again paid scant attention to this phenomenon and again paid the price by missing the reversal.

*2. Market indices trace patterned paths.*

Ralph N. Elliott, author of *The Wave Principle* in 1938 and succeeding works,[8] established in the mid 1930s that financial markets trend and reverse in recognizable patterns. Their structures are clear and definite in form, although not fixed in time or amplitude. Market movements have different degrees. Patterns of smaller degree link together to form similar patterns at larger degree. Thus, Elliott established that markets are hierarchical. In recent years, physicists who have studied financial markets have discovered aspects of market behavior that are compatible with this insight.[9,10]

For the past three decades, Robert R. Prechter, Jr. has applied and extended these principles to a wide variety of social phenomena.[11] Perhaps most important, his latest book, *The Wave Principle of Human Social Behavior and the New Science of Socionomics*, has established that markets are "robust fractals," (termed quasi-fractals by physicists Arneodo *et al.*[12]). The existence of self-affinity in price patterns at all scales indicates fractal ordering, but if Elliott is right, they are intermediately ordered fractals in contrast to the indefinite fractals described by Mandelbrot. They have "a qualitative specificity of form akin to that of self-identical fractals such as nested squares as well as a quantitative elasticity akin to that of indefinite fractals such as clouds and seacoasts,"[13] says Prechter.

Because of the form specificity of robust fractals, there is an element of predictability in markets, not in spite of, but because of, their complexity. As one recent example, physicists Anders Johansen and Didier Sornette found that markets proceed unabatedly toward a crash, "anticipating [it] in a subtle self-organized and cooperative fashion, releasing precursory fingertips observable in stock market prices."[14] Yet at such times, everything looks rosy to mainstream macroeconomists because stocks have been rising persistently, and output, employment and other standard indicators appear healthy. Economists relying on such "fundamentals" invariably extrapolate the good times into the future ("the crudest form of technical analysis"[15]), rather than recognize their true import in a patterned world.

If we economists are to advance our craft, we will have to abandon the widespread illusion that financial markets are random walks, as many top business schools, unfortunately, continue to preach, against formidable evidence such as that reported by Andrew W. Lo and A. Craig MacKinley.[16] Markets proceed relentlessly according to a robust fractal, whose components or phases Elliott designated as "waves." The new theoreticians and social physicists find themselves in good company with classical analysis: Pythagoras's doctrine called for inquiry into pattern rather than substance to determine the essence of things.[17] Such inquiry is now bearing fruit in the macroeconomic field.

*3. Changes in economic variables follow stock market fluctuations according to degree.*

Changes in the stock market indices precede—they do not follow—changes in economic fundamentals or news about them. Thus, they are a leading indicator of economic activity. Eight decades ago, Wesley Mitchell and the National Bureau of Economic Research recognized this phenomenon, but an inability to recognize different degrees made the breakthrough less helpful than it might have been.

If the changes in markets are hierarchical, then so are the economic changes that follow. This explains why declines in stock indices of very high degree anticipate depressions, while drops of lesser degree anticipate recessions and milder downturns. Paul A. Samuelson, 1970 Nobel Laureate, famously quipped, "The market has anticipated five out of the last three recessions," completely missing the hierarchical nature of markets. It was a clever but inaccurate remark. Understanding the hierarchy and chronology of stock market and economic events will allow macroeconomists more accuracy in prediction.

**A New Basis for Theory and Modeling**

Only two academic economists—Friedrich August von Hayek and Ludwig von Mises—correctly forecast the market break of 1929 and the ensuing Depression.[18] Did economists adopt their Austrian theory? Alas, no. They adopted the economics of Keynes, and not the best economics of Keynes.[19]

In a world of uncertainty, expectations are a critical variable in most financial decisions. Some notable economists have acknowledged that the mental variability of human beings in this regard is missing from the conventional model. "It is acutely uncomfortable," 1987 Nobel Laureate Robert M. Solow wrote recently, "to have so much in macroeconomics depend on how one deals with a concept like expectations, for which there is (inevitably?) so little empirical understanding and so much room for invention."[20] If you know where to look, though, you will find a growing body of new work that displays an impressive empirical understanding of aggregate expectations, so its lack is in no way inevitable if we put our minds to it.

As Solow intimates, a solid concept of expectations is crucial. We may be close to that goal. Certainly if stock markets are patterned, so must be the causal forces driving them. Citing the prior work of Paul

Montgomery of *Universal Economics* and Paul MacLean of the National
Institute of Mental Health, Prechter presents an intriguing hypothesis
regarding the forces behind expectations. He proposes that this key
macroeconomic variable may derive from pre-rational thought patterns
that drive the fundamental impulse of human social cooperation in a
context of uncertainty.[21] The emotions that govern expectations, he
says, are essentially a "first cause," generated by impulsive portions of
the brain associated with herding. Yale economics professor Robert J.
Schiller, a leading voice in the new field of Behavioral Finance, con-
curs at least to the extent of saying, "Solid psychological research does
show that there are patterns of human behavior that suggest anchors
for the market that would not be expected if markets worked entirely
rationally."[22] If so, consider an alternative to mainstream macroeconomics' idea that each individual is a "representative agent" with rational
expectations, responding mechanically to exogenous changes in news
about economic fundamentals to create in the aggregate a random walk
in the stock market and the economy. Perhaps we should entertain the
contrasting assumption that endogenous changes in aggregate expectations—in confidence and mood, in optimism and pessimism—are at least
a force, if not *the* driving force, behind stock prices and the economy.[23]
The economy expands and contracts not because of random shocks, as
suggested by mainstream business-cycle theory, but because optimism
and pessimism in societies naturally trend and reverse in the form of
a robust fractal.

   With this new insight, we may begin to suggest a consistent theory
of business cycles: Naturally expanding optimism during a boom stimulates hiring, expansion, investment and speculation. Euphoria in the
latter stages encourages excessive credit extension and cavalier financial
risk-taking. When optimism reaches a natural extremity, the boom ends
and pessimism takes over. Companies lay off employees, investors recall
their capital, lenders recall loans, banks tighten credit, bankruptcies accelerate and a major contraction ensues. When pessimism has run its
course, debt has been liquidated to low levels, financing has become
conservative, the stock market has reached its nadir, the society is ready
for recovery.[24] There are no "new eras" or "new economies" and no
conditions upon which the patterns of social behavior will disappear.

   The indication that a major change is actually beginning comes
with a major trend change in the stock market, which is a proxy for a
major change in expectations. The model has some predictive value

because the necessary precursors for a major change in trend are a state of extremity in the volume of debt and a potentially completed wave pattern of changes in expectations at high degree.

Recall the sweeping certainty of the quotation that begins this article, the guarantee in 1997 of "Asia's Bright Future" and the Harvard Economic Society's assertion in 1929 that "A severe depression such as 1920-21 is *outside the range* of probability" and will "*not*" happen. As it happens, our new model also explains why conventional macroeconomists are so certain just before they are most wrong. Because economists lack useful tools to guide them, they are powerless to resist getting caught up along with everyone else in the optimism at the peak or the pessimism at the bottom. Or, as Prechter asserts, "the prevailing social mood has full rein to affect the tone of their conclusions."[25]

**Conclusion**

Nobel Laureate James Buchanan, in his "Economics and Its Scientific Neighbors," stated, "Precisely because it has divorced itself from the central proposition relating to human behavior, [Keynesian and Post-Keynesian] macroeconomic theory is really no theory at all."[26] In contrast, the new model provides a consistent theoretical framework with strong predictive implications. For the linear extrapolation of the present commonly used by macroeconomists, it substitutes the nonlinear framework of markets' robust fractal patterns. This framework, in turn, offers compelling evidence that, to a first degree, changes in optimism and pessimism, measured by changes in stock market indices, are exogenous—independent of changes in economic variables, which simply follow. By understanding the nature and hierarchy of stock market changes, we economists can improve our predictions for the economy in terms of form, magnitude and timing.

*Hernán Cortés Douglas is Professor of Economics at Catholic University of Chile. He is a former Deputy Research Administrator at the World Bank and Senior Economist at the International Monetary Fund. Professor Cortés Douglas has taught at American, European and Latin American universities. For the 2002-2003 academic year, he will serve as the Luksic Scholar at Harvard.*

## NOTES

[1] Dornbusch, Rudi. (1998, July 30). "Growth forever." *The Wall Street Journal*.

[2] Based on nominal figures provided by Irving Fisher's son and biographer, Irving Norton Fisher and adjusted by the U.S. CPI.

[3] *Ibid*. Figures provided by Keynes' biographer, Professor Skidelski.

[4] Grabbe, J. Orlin. (n.d.). "And now, financial apocalypse." www. aci.net/kalliste/Apocalyp.htm.

[5] See endnote 1.

[6] "Something unexpected happened." (2000, Dec.). *The Region*. Minneapolis Fed.

[7] Lucas, Robert. (1977). "Understanding business cycles." In K. Brunner and A. H. Meltzer, (Eds.) *Stabilization of the domestic and international economy*. North Holland, p. 15.

[8] Elliott, Ralph N. (1938). *The wave principle*. Reprinted (1980/1994) Robert R. Prechter, Jr. (Ed.) *R.N. Elliott's masterworks*. Gainesville, GA: New Classics Library.

[9] Arneodo, A. *et al*. (1993). "Fibonacci sequences in diffusion-limited aggregation." In J.M. García-Ruiz *et al*. (Eds.) *Growth patterns in physical sciences and biology.* New York: Plenum Press.

[10] Discrete scale invariance, as developed by D. Sornette (1997, October 15). "Generic mechanisms for hierarchies." *InterJournal complex systems,* 127. And (1999). "Discrete scale invariance and complex dimensions." *Physics Reports,* 297.

[11] Prechter, Robert R. (1999). *The wave principle of human social behavior*. And with Frost, A.J. (1978). *Elliott wave principle.*

[12] Arneodo *et al*. put it this way: "There is room for 'quasi-fractals' between the well-ordered fractal hierarchy of snowflakes and the disordered structure of chaotic or random aggregates."

[13] Prechter, Robert R., email in response to inquiry.

[14] Sornette, Didier and Johansen, Anders. (1997). "Large financial crashes." *Physics A*, 245, 3-4.

[15] Prechter, Robert R. (1999). *The wave principle of human social behavior*. Gainesville, GA: New Classics Library.

[16] Lo, Andrew W. and MacKinlay, A. Craig. (1999). *A non-random walk down wall street*. Princeton University Press.

[17] Bateson, Gregory. (1972). "Form, substance and difference." *Steps to an ecology of mind*. Chandler, p. 449. Also Collingwood, R.G. (1945). *The idea of nature*. Oxford.

[18] Hayek in February 1929 wrote in the *Austrian Institute of Economic Research Report*, "The boom will collapse within the next few months." Mises foresaw a worldwide depression in the 1930s, as reported by Fritz Machlup, Mises' assistant at the time. Mises' wife, Margit, wrote in her husband's biography that, in the summer of 1929, he declined a high-ranking position in Kredit Anstalt, then one of the largest banks in Europe because "a great crash is coming and I do not want my name in any way connected with it." Within two years, Kredit Anstalt was bankrupt.

[19] Keynes' *opus magnum*, *The General Theory of Employment, Interest and Money*, contains not one but several theories. The profession, unfortunately adopted the Hicks-Samuelson version.

[20] Solow, R. (2000, Winter). "Toward a macroeconomics of the medium run." *Journal of Economic Perspectives*.

[21] See endnote 15.

[22] Schiller, Robert J. (2000). *Irrational exuberance*. Princeton University Press.

[23] Early in the century, some economists were well aware of the importance of these waves of optimism and pessimism. Pigou, Arthur C. (1927). *Industrial fluctuations*. London: Cass; Also (1920). *The economics of welfare*. London: Cass. And, yes, Keynes, John Maynard. (1936). *The general theory of employment, interest and money.* London: Macmillan, chapter 12.

[24] An expanded treatment of this process applied to the present situation appears in Douglas, H. Cortés. (2001, January). "Forewarnings." *processed*, Catholic University of Chile.

[25] See endnote 15.

[26] James, Buchanan. (1979). *What should economists do?* Liberty Press.

*Part VI:*

# CONTROVERSY
# AND
# VALIDATION

Mr. Prechter:

If you haven't done it yet, hop on down to the local newsstand and pick up the February 1999 issue of *Scientific American*. Contained therein is an article called "A Multifractal Walk Down Wall Street," by none other than Benoit Mandelbrot. I read this and my jaw dropped—it is very similar to the Wave Principle.

—J. Gregory Wharton, AIA Project Architect
February 1, 1999

Prechter
*The Elliott Wave Theorist*
March 4, 1999

*Chapter 37*

# Controversy

I urge you to obtain the February 1999 issue of *Scientific American*. Its cover article is entitled "A Fractal Walk Down Wall Street." In it, a famous scientist purports to present the "new" idea that financial markets may be modeled as variable hierarchical fractals. Illustrations depict markets as having patterns that subdivide into identical sub-patterns. Credit for this idea belongs to R.N. Elliott. The author of the article knows this, as he took pains to read Elliott's works thoroughly so as to find bits of writing that enabled him to denigrate Elliott in a 1997 book. When you look at the illustrations and read the text of this article, you cannot help but consider the idea that Elliott was ripped off. Get the magazine and make up your own mind.

After you read the article, you might send *Scientific American* a letter to the editor at 415 Madison Ave., New York, NY 10017 or by e-mail at editors@sciamer.com. I have composed a brief response, which the magazine says it will publish probably in its June issue, due out in mid-May. In a coming issue of EWT, I will alert you to a more detailed response, which will be available on our web site.

# ...and Affirmation

The good news, as we have seen in recent years, is that cutting-edge scientific work is converging toward the Wave Principle. We are coming very close to having Elliott's ideas confirmed and verified by the scientific community. It is in fact evidence of further validation that a renowned scientist has decided that at least one implication of Elliott's work is so important that he wants credit for it. Whether that credit is taken properly or otherwise is a question for the scientific community to decide. Proponents of the Wave Principle can take heart that these ideas are rapidly becoming viewed as *important*.

Prechter
Letter to the Editor of *Scientific American*
June 1999

## Chapter 38

# *Fractals and Finance*

I am impelled to point out that most of the ideas presented in Benoit B. Mandelbrot's article, "A Multifractal Walk Down Wall Street," [February] originated with Ralph Nelson Elliott, who put them forth more comprehensively and more accurately with respect to real-world markets in his 1938 book, *The Wave Principle*. Figure 1 shows an illustration from Elliott's literature depicting the [hierarchical] multifractal nature of markets; Figure 2 shows Mandelbrot's exposition. Slight differences in the specific pattern used in these diagrams are irrelevant because Mandelbrot is not arguing a specific form, just multifractal self-affinity. For a detailed response to Mandelbrot's article, please visit http://www.elliottwave.com/response.htm on the World Wide Web.

—Robert R. Prechter, Jr.
President, Elliott Wave International
Gainesville, GA

Prechter
*The Elliott Wave Theorist*[1]
May 1999

***Personal Note****: In 1985, it was with pleasure that I watched Benoit Mandelbrot receive adoring news coverage for his case that fractals permeate nature. It was in a cooperative spirit that I sent him material describing R.N. Elliott's original 1938 discovery of the same thing in finance. He did not respond. Out of deference to a great scientist, I chose to keep quiet about Mandelbrot's libelous treatment of Elliott in his 1997 book. However, his claim to a substantial portion of Elliott's work in the February 1999 issue of Scientific American has forced me to address these issues. If it is a sad day when one's hero falls short of expectations, then this day for me is grievous.—RP*

*Chapter 39*

# Credit Where It Is Due

Benoit Mandelbrot's cover article in *Scientific American* (February 1999, "A Multifractal Walk Down Wall Street")[2] is a good read and contains important knowledge. His only omission is in properly crediting most of the ideas presented therein to Ralph Nelson Elliott, who put them forth more comprehensively, and more accurately with respect to real-world markets, sixty-one years ago in his book, *The Wave Principle*.[3]

**A Study in Similarity**

Figure 1 shows R.N. Elliott's depictions from 1938 of the fractal nature of markets. Figure 2 shows Mandelbrot's from 1999. Figure 3 shows an illustration traced directly from Elliott's literature. Figure 4 shows *Scientific American's* depiction of Mandelbrot's thesis, from a figure he provided.[4] It is important to understand that slight differences in the specific pattern used in these diagrams are irrelevant to the matter of proper credit because Mandelbrot is not arguing a specific form, just multifractal self-affinity.

# ELLIOTT'S FRACTAL
# GENERATOR MODEL (1938)

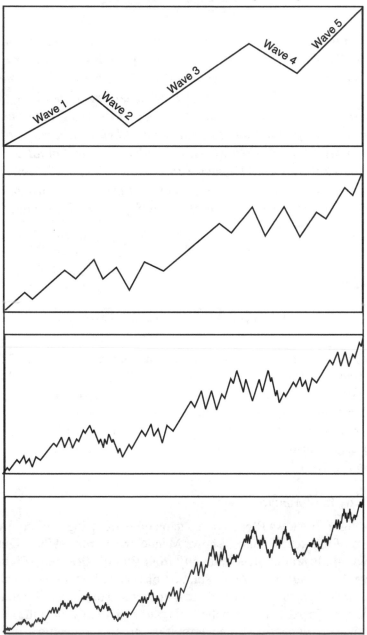

*Figure 1*

## MANDELBROT'S FRACTAL GENERATOR DEPICTION (1999)

*Figure 2*

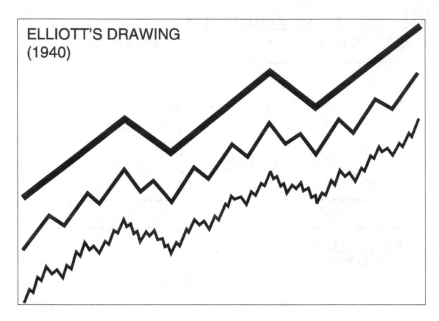

**ELLIOTT'S DRAWING (1940)**

*Figure 3*

**MANDELBROT'S DRAWING (1999)**

*Figure 4*

The similarity between these figures is undeniable, yet Mandelbrot lists only four references for his article: Mandelbrot, Mandelbrot, Mandelbrot and Mandelbrot.[5] His article includes the following self-references:

"*I claim* that variations in financial prices can be accounted for by a model derived from *my work* in fractal geometry."

"These...*new modeling techniques* are designed to cast a light of order into the seemingly impenetrable thicket of the financial markets."

"*My own work* [contradicts modern portfolio theory and random walk]."[6]

In fact, it was R.N. Elliott in 1938[7] who meticulously described the fractal self-affinity of market patterns. It was a 1978 book, *Elliott Wave Principle*, that included among the implications of Elliott's discovery that it "challenges the Random Walk theory at every turn."[8]

The ideas displayed in Figures 1 through 4 are over six decades old, and Mandelbrot knows it. This is clear because in dismissing Elliott in 1997[9], he quoted from a volume[10] that includes all of Elliott's major work as well as the illustrations contained in Figures 1 and 3.

Far from incororating "new modeling techniques," every aspect of Mandelbrot's general model, as presented in *Scientific American*, fits Elliott's specific model, and no aspect of Mandelbrot's general model contradicts Elliott's specific model. Mandelbrot's work is compatible with, and therefore provides support for, Elliott's more detailed description of financial market behavior. We must concede the possibility—remote, in my view—that Elliott's specific model will be proven false and that financial markets will ultimately be shown to be indefinite fractals, which is Mandelbrot's claim. At minimum, though, it may be said that for the time being Mandelbrot's studies have dramatically increased the probability that R.N. Elliott's model is in fact valid and accurate.

Mandelbrot's long-delayed response to years of questions about the significance of Elliott's work was to pen a brief condescending dismissal of Elliott's discovery. As you will see in an upcoming discussion, Mandelbrot's summary of Elliott is half *ad hominem* attack and half misrepresentation, the net effect of which is to malign Elliott both by innuendo and omission. Worse than the condescension, however, is that Mandelbrot appears to have effected it, if his *Scientific American* article is any indication, in order to ignore the man and claim his predecessor's breakthrough as his own.

Even in his dismissal, Mandelbrot himself could not avoid stating the obvious truth that "Elliott's diagrams are qualitatively reminiscent of certain self-affine generators [in my book]...."[11] Mandelbrot knew this before he wrote his article for *Scientific American*, yet it still reads, "The *novelty* (and *surprise*) is that these self-affine fractal curves exhibit a wealth of structure—a foundation of both fractal geometry and the theory of chaos."[12] This is no novelty or surprise, but rather an observation with sixty years of history involving six major authors,[13] who have produced a nearly continuous stream of literature on the Wave Principle since 1938. If, as Mandelbrot says, these curves indeed reveal the foundation of both fractal geometry and the theory of chaos, then according to Mandelbrot's own formulation, Elliott deserves the credit for discovering and elucidating it.

Although Mandelbrot's words (and lack thereof) imply that in the scientific world, Elliott is a nonentity, this is not the case. Physicist Didier Sornette of the Department of Earth and Space Science and the Institute of Geophysics and Planetary Physics at the University of California at Los Angeles, who has been systematically conducting pioneering studies in the fractal nature of markets, along with colleagues Johansen and Bouchaud stated three years ago in their 1996 study, "Stock Market Crashes, Precursors and Replicas," which appeared in France's *Journal de Physique*: "We speculate that the 'Elliott waves'...could be a signature of an underlying critical structure of the stock market."[14,15]

As honorable scientists should, Sornette *et al.* cite a proper reference source (*Elliott Wave Principle*) in this and several other studies. Here is how Mandelbrot phrases his only mention that other knowledge preceded his "new modeling technique":

> ...this concept is not a rootless abstraction but a theoretical reformulation of a down-to-earth bit of market folklore—namely, that movements of a stock or currency all look alike when a market chart is enlarged or reduced so that it fits the same time and price scale.[16]

In that statement, Mandelbrot alludes to a supposed real-world foundation for what truly is his otherwise "rootless abstraction" yet omits referring to the empirical work that R.N. Elliott undertook over two decades in order to lay that foundation. Mandelbrot ascribes the empirical foundation he invokes to "market folklore," which it emphatically is not, either in its origin or in the implication that the idea is widely accepted. Folklore is an oral or fable tradition with misty origins, whereas the original source of this idea is on the written record. As for his term's implication that market self-affinity is common knowledge, most economists and even most financiers assign the cause of long term trends to economics and politics and of near term trends to "psychology." They neither espouse nor accept the idea of financial market self-affinity in either cause or appearance. (I have personally fought that lonely battle for 23 years.)

If circumstances were as Mandelbrot describes, then his article would have been mostly superfluous, not the "novelty" it claims to be. Which is it, then, a "novelty" or "down-to-earth market folklore"? In trying to have it two ways, Mandelbrot renders false both sides of his contradictory characterization. It is neither a novelty nor folklore. The truth is that in the financial world, the idea that market movements at all scales look alike has been entirely the domain of the Wave Principle. Elliott recognized the originality of his idea, calling it "a newly discovered phenomenon."[17] He wrote two books, twelve articles and four essential essays on the subject, all of which are contained in the volume from which Mandelbrot quoted. This "folklore" comment, absent any other reference, from someone who knows the true source of the idea, appears to be designed to avoid crediting the man who discovered that financial market patterns are a variable, self-affine, hierarchical fractal.

Regardless of what one thinks of Elliott's occasional unscientific incaution, which gave Mandelbrot ammunition for his dismissal, it does not diminish his achievement. One cannot concede as much to Mandelbrot's incaution. It is one thing to dismiss another's work as valueless. It is another to claim someone else's work as one's own. To combine the two acts is hypocrisy.

Mandelbrot claims in his article to present a "theoretical reformulation" of the idea of market self-affinity, which it is not. It may be a reformulation only of his own thinking, in which case exposure to Elliott's work appears to have prompted it. Allowing for differences in terminology and form, there is nothing in his model "fractal generator" that writers about the Wave Principle have not already proposed, either in the same way or in a better way.

Mandelbrot persistently ignores (and has derided, as we shall soon see) Elliott's seminal discovery of the fractal nature of markets, but in this article he appears specifically to desire credit for the potentiality that the market might be *discretely hierarchical*. In no uncertain terms, Elliott elucidated his conviction in this regard, both as an *actuality* and as a theoretically defensible model. Mandelbrot, in contrast, has never argued that financial markets are anything but indefinite fractals, like clouds and seacoasts. If Mandelbrot has decided that Elliott's model—or a variation of it—*might* be true, it would explain why he attempts to capture this aspect of it for himself via his fractal generator depicted in Figures 2 and 4.

Mandelbrot cites his "new modeling techniques" and states:

> On a practical level, this finding suggests that a fractal generator can be developed based on historical market data. The actual model does not simply inspect what the market did yesterday or last week.... The charts created from the generators produced by this model can simulate alternative scenarios based on previous market activity.[18]

This is hardly a "new modeling technique" that can now arise from Mandelbrot's "finding." Developing a "fractal generator based on historical market data" is exactly what Elliott did. Numerous published practitioners have used it to produce "alternative scenarios based on previous market activity" as an ongoing exercise over six decades. Mandelbrot uses virtually the same language employed years earlier in *Elliott Wave Principle*, which specifically describes "ordering the relative probabilities" to develop an "expected scenario" from among the "valid alternatives."[19] In 1986, my firm employed the Lockheed Corporation to begin developing a computerized expert system that applies Elliott's model to the task of stock market forecasting. It considers stock market data going back to the start of the century and ranks alternate counts by the degree to which they fit the ideal model. (For details, see Chapter 4 of *The Wave Principle of Human Social Behavior*.) In other words, we have been *doing* for years what Mandelbrot is simply *proposing*.

In 1993, a correspondent wrote to my firm in response to an article about physicists pursuing chaos in financial markets and said, "Like Alexander King's story of the man in the isolated village in Switzerland who unknowingly reinvented the typewriter, it looks like these people are about to rediscover the Elliott wave."[20] Rediscovery in isolation may be excused. Knowing about a previous discovery and claiming it for oneself may not.

## Pattern Recognition

In the latter 1980s, James Gleick made Professor Mandelbrot famous in a glowing *New York Times* article and his national best selling book, *Chaos*. Gleick, an unabashed fan, was nevertheless compelled to include this frank discussion of what fellow scientists saw as a chronic and disturbing propensity of Mandelbrot's:

> Mandelbrot['s]...book...rings with the first person: *I claim...I conceived and developed...and implemented...I have confirmed...I show...I coined...."* Wherever chaos led, Mandelbrot had some basis to claim that he had been there first.... Even an admirer would cry with exasperation, "Mandelbrot didn't have *everybody's* thoughts before they did." [emphasis in the original][21]

Whatever the extent of his proclivity, in this latest article, he has overstepped the bounds of courtesy and honesty by an unforgivable margin. This transgression is particularly glaring given Mandelbrot's own lifelong passion for demanding proper credit when it is warranted. Gleick describes this ardor:

> At the height of his success, he was reviled by some colleagues, who thought he was unnaturally obsessed with his place in history. They said he hectored them about giving due credit.... Sometimes when articles appeared using ideas from fractal geometry he would call or write the authors to complain that no reference was made to him or his book.[22]

Because R.N. Elliott is safely dead,[23] he is unable to exercise the same privilege. It is fortunate for the integrity of the history of scientific discovery that some of us know the facts.

In an inset to his article, Mandelbrot asks us to "pick the fake." This is a tempting invitation that I will avoid answering out of deference to a brilliant mathematician who has given the world so much in advancing the science of fractal geometry. Yet after giving the world so much, is it really necessary that he claim even more? The 1993 book, *Classics on Fractals*,[24] sets the record straight regarding much of the history of work involving fractals. My 1999 book, *The Wave Principle of Human Social Behavior*,[25] which discusses the vast implications of Elliott's work, credits Mandelbrot with his inarguably great achievements. Can he not bring himself to do the same for his predecessor?

## Prechter's Response to Mandelbrot's Dismissal of Elliott

Mandelbrot's brief dismissal of R.N. Elliott was emailed to our website in 1998 by a concerned reader, who requested that I respond. I held off in deference to a famous scientist, but because the article in *Scientific American* makes it appear to be part of a larger injustice, I can no longer do so. Here is the citation in full from his book, *Fractals and Scaling in Finance—Discontinuity, Concentration, Risk* (1997):

> Elliott Waves: This section devoted to miscellanea is as good a place as any to mention Ralph N. Elliott (1871-1948). A former peripatetic accountant and expert on cafeteria management, he studied Fibonacci, the Secrets of the Great Pyramid and the prophecies of Melchi-Zedik, and in 1938 announced a great "discovery," a "Wave Principle" that "really forecasts." A claim that he was a precursor of the use of fractals in finance prompted me to scan Elliott [in] 1994. It is true that some of Elliott's diagrams are qualitatively reminiscent of certain self-affine generators of the kind studied in Section 4 of Chapter E6. That is, they embody the wisdom present in Swift's qualitative metaphor quoted earlier in this section, but nothing more. Elliott's work fails the requirements of objectivity and repeatability: in his own words, "considerable experience is required to interpret [it] correctly" and "no interpretation [is] valid unless made by [him or his direct licencees]."[26]

Below are numbered phrases constituting Mandelbrot's full commentary, followed by my responses.

(1) "This section devoted to miscellanea is as good a place as any to mention Ralph N. Elliott (1871-1948). A former peripatetic accountant and expert on cafeteria management..."

This is pure condescension. Elliott is not tangential to Mandelbrot's field but its originator. A grab-bag of *miscellanea* is hardly "as good a place as any" to discuss a pioneer unless one's object is to bury him. Why is Elliott a *former* accountant, because he is dead? Or because after pursuing the accounting profession as a business reorganization expert for four decades, he published a book on the stock market at the age of 67? If Mandelbrot were to publish a book on music at age 67, would he be a *former* mathematician? Mandelbrot's term *peripatetic* implies that Elliott was some kind of itinerant semi-professional who worked out of a suitcase. Elliott was not just an accountant but the chief accountant for several major corporations and national railroads and even administered the finances of Nicaragua as an appointee of the Coolidge administration's State Department during the U.S. occupation. For a brief period of two years, he did author several articles and a book on cafeteria management to cash in on the nationwide tea-room craze of the 1920s (whose counterpart today is the trendy coffee shop). Mandelbrot's subtly precious citation of this aspect of Elliott's entrepreneurship appears designed to characterize him as being beneath the discovery of fractal geometry in finance.[27]

(2) "...he studied Fibonacci, the Secrets of the Great Pyramid and the prophecies of Melchi-Zedik and in 1938 announced a great 'discovery'..."

The fraud behind this calculated composition is appalling. The parts of this phrase that matter are utter invention, extrapolated from a few words on two pages in Elliott's second and final book.[28] Elliott did not study or even cite "secrets" of the Great Pyramid or the prophecies of anybody. What he did was to credit a book with the unfortunate title, *Prophecies of Melchi-Zedik*, as the source of a tidbit of information regarding the height of the Great Pyramid that suggested to him that its builders knew about Fibonacci numbers. In Frost's and my 1978 book *Elliott Wave Principle*, we similarly quote Peter Tompkins, author of *Secrets of the Great Pyramid* (1971), as confirming that the dimensions of the structure are related by *phi*. Our collective point is simply that knowledge of Fibonacci numbers and ratios has been around for a long time. At most, Elliott was (as perhaps we were) guilty of ignorance of scientific sensitivities, but that's all there is to it. While scientists rightfully reject anything that hints of the mystical, Elliott's reference in this regard was not of that nature. More important, this reference, along with two associated comments in all of Elliott's writing that derive from religion, is tangential and conceptually irrelevant to the nearly 300 pages that precede and follow it. Mandelbrot concocts his phrasing to imply that central to Elliott's thought was an error of magical thinking, which is false. What's more, to have located this obscure sentence in a 300-page book makes it clear that Mandelbrot painstakingly searched for any tidbit he could find that would serve to belittle his predecessor, even if doing so required both omissive and commissive misrepresentation.

Mandelbrot further implies by his sentence structure that the "studies" he imputes to Elliott preceded, and therefore were the basis for, Elliott's discovery and its announcement. In fact, Elliott explored Fibonacci mathematics in botany two years after he published the fractal illustrations in his first book. The cited brief reference occurred eight years after the publication of his first book. Given the fact that Mandelbrot possesses Elliott's literature and knows its chronology, his false implication is clearly deliberate.

Mandelbrot's putting the word "discovery" in quotes is more conde-scension. Mandelbrot credits *himself*—again and again and again—with great discoveries, yet he does not put his self-credits in quotes.

Up to this point, Mandelbrot's introduction reads in the same manner as if he were trying to claim that he had recently concocted the theory of evolution while dismissing Darwin as "an indecisive, wandering globetrotter who suffered from chronic nausea and who could barely be bothered to write about his own incompletely formed ideas." There may be some truth to the words, but as a summary, it is a misrepresentation tinged with obfuscation and meanness.

(3) "…a 'Wave Principle' that 'really forecasts.'"

In the *Scientific American* article, Mandelbrot says this about his model:

> These techniques…*provide estimates of the probability of what the market might do and allow one to prepare for the inevitable sea changes*…. The actual model *does not simply inspect what the market did yesterday or last week*[, but] charts created from the generators produced by this model can *simulate alternative scenarios based on previous market activity*.

In other words, he claims in no uncertain terms to have discovered a technique that "really forecasts." He makes the same claim as Elliott, yet he mocks Elliott for it.

Mandelbrot cites no fact to justify his mockery of Elliott's claim to having provided a basis for prediction. Is it true or false? If false, why so? Far worse from a scientific standpoint, Mandelbrot does not describe any method for using his own model to achieve his dramatic claims of "providing estimates of the probability of what the market might do" or allowing one to "simulate alternative scenarios based on previous market activity," much less to "prepare for the inevitable sea changes." These bold assertions are highly misleading, as a close read of the article reveals that all Mandelbrot can offer is a catalogue of past market volatility, which any market student may glean by casually perusing a historical chart. What forecasts can Mandelbrot show to justify his claim to his model's predictive ability? *There are none*. Nor will there ever be, given his model's assumption of specific event randomness, not to mention his proposed generator's unnatural 3-wave-3-wave construction. Mandelbrot's model can simulate only "the same patterns of variability" in the sense of volatility, power laws and indefinite fractals, which offer no basis for forecasting specifics. He coyly demurs, "multifractals do not purport to predict the future with certainty," as if they can predict the future at all. In truth, indefinite fractals cannot be employed to predict any specific future event even to a useful probability. The title of his article, "A Multifractal Walk Down Wall Street," is a play on Burton Malkiel's *A Random Walk Down Wall Street*, but for practical forecasting purposes, it may as well be the same title.

James Gleick confirmed in a 1985 article, "Mandelbrot's mimicking of stock market and river charts *does not help in predicting* particular rallies and floods."[29] That is still true, fourteen years later, because Mandelbrot has mimicked only one very rough aspect of stock market and flooding patterns: the extent of their fractal irregularity. He has not even considered, much less discovered as Elliott did, that their behavior might exhibit forms. While Mandelbrot's claims to forecasting and practical utility stand unsubstantiated either by a forecasting model or by any attempt to predict anything, R.N. Elliott and later writers elucidated how to do exactly these things with the Wave Principle.

Mandelbrot's assertions of predictability appear as a desperate bid to claim Elliott's territory yet without the substance necessary actually to capture it. In contrast, Elliott made some of the most remarkable stock market forecasts ever, and they are on the record.[30] The chief difference between the two men with regard to their claims of forecasting value is that Elliott made good on his claim.

> (4) "A claim that he was a precursor of the use of fractals in finance prompted me to scan Elliott in 1994."

Let us first note from this sentence that some observant people *do* recognize that Elliott pioneered "the use of fractals in finance." This very recognition must irritate Mandelbrot to the point of prompting the behavior that is the focus of this discussion. The term *precursor* is misleading and condescending. Elliott did not *predate* the use of fractals in finance; he originated the idea and developed it in detail. What's more, his model actually did effect—extensively, in fact—"the *use* of fractals in finance," which Mandelbrot's has not and cannot.

Additionally, if Mandelbrot did not "scan Elliott" before 1994, I will eat my hat. Because I sent them to Mandelbrot (to no response), he had in his possession *Elliott Wave Principle* (1978) and my essay, "The Fractal Design of Social Progress," (1986)[31] at least as early as 1986. It is difficult to accept ignorance on the subject of the Wave Principle on the part of someone who has been interested in finance and fractals for his professional lifetime. He could even have known about it prior to 1962 when he first investigated the distribution of cotton prices.[32] The well-known editor of *The Bank Credit Analyst*, A. Hamilton Bolton, who served as president of the Financial Analysts Federation, published widely read "Elliott Wave Principle" supplements annually from 1953 to 1966 from his office in Montreal, Quebec and wrote a book on the subject in 1960 entitled *The Elliott Wave Principle—A Critical Appraisal*, which further popularized the Wave Principle on Wall Street. Gleick says that it was in the same year of 1960 when Mandelbrot first had "...a ghost of an idea, a faint, unfocused image..."[33] that started his search for fractals. This chronology might explain why Mandelbrot's studies of nature's fractals began with the financial markets (specifically the cotton market, to which Elliott referred in his 1946 book as following the Wave Principle) rather than coastlines, mountains or clouds. Alternatively, he should at least have heard about it some time after 1978, when *Elliott Wave Principle* was published and waves in the market began making waves in the press, particularly after 1983.

Now consider Mandelbrot's flip declaration that he bothered to *scan* Elliott. His unearthing of the obscure bits of information quoted in citations (1), (2), (3) and (8) belie this characterization and reveal that in fact he *scoured* Elliott from cover to cover. Mandelbrot seems to want to present a disinterested front, but that is not what we observe. His meticulous hatchet-job and careful claims for credit show that he is on a mission.

> (5) "It is true that some of Elliott's diagrams are qualitatively reminiscent of certain self-affine generators of the kind studied in Section 4 of Chapter E6."

Well, that is a key concession. Even here, though, Elliott's diagrams cannot be *reminiscent* of generators that *postdated* them. "Reminiscent" also carries connotations of only the vaguest recollective similarity. This carefully selected word thus appears designed to steer the reader's mind into thinking that Elliott was an after-the-fact dabbler. Chronologically speaking, it is some of Mandelbrot's illustrations that look like Elliott's, not the other way around, and that is the way it should be stated if proper credit is to be given.

> (6) "That is, they embody the wisdom present in Swift's qualitative metaphor quoted earlier in this section..."

Here Elliott is depicted as embodying *Jonathan Swift's* wisdom, as if the poet's brief line about fleas had scientific weight or even (in the context of the larger poem) addresses self-affinity at all, which it does not.

> (7) "...but *nothing more*."

Elliott discovered so much more than Mandelbrot (forget Swift) about financial market behavior that the gulf is unbridgeable. If there is any difference between Elliott's and Mandelbrot's formulations of their models, it is the relative richness of the former and the thinness of the latter. Elliott's body of work shows that there is much more to the stock market than general fractality. It details the formal characteristics of the actual financial market fractal, while Mandelbrot's only new offering in the area of modeling is an artificial construct. His main thesis in the article, that financial markets may be modeled as any number of mechanical fractals and multifractals, manipulated along one axis or the other—not by nature but by the modeler—is arbitrary, primitive and random compared to Elliott's robust[34] fractal model, which he uncovered in his meticulous cataloguing of the intricate details of pattern formation.

Elliott spent the better part of a decade studying actual market price movements before coming to a conclusion regarding the essential patterns that repeat at higher scales. He observed that in the real world, rising trends typically subdivide into five waves and falling trends into three. His detailed model is thus consonant with the real world, while Mandelbrot's fractal generator is truly, to use his words, a "rootless abstraction." Mandelbrot proposes no specific pattern while nevertheless being forced to invent one for his depiction. He just draws three lines (he calls them "pieces") in each direction to simulate market fractality. Mandelbrot reveals the arbitrary nature of his model when asking us to "imagine a die on which each side bears the image of one of the six permutations of the pieces of the generator. Before each interpolation, the die is thrown, and then the permutation that comes up is selected." (Then the one chosen is available for infinite manipulation!) The 65-year history[35] of uniquely successful Elliott wave forecasting would not exist if the market fluctuated according to random die-throwing instead of the Wave Principle.

Mandelbrot's multifractal model is, as he says, better than Modern Portfolio Theory, which isn't saying much. The only way that the multifractal model improves on MPT is to add a warning that large or swift moves can occur at any time at any scale, a fact that portfolio managers may just as easily glean from a brief review of market history. Elliott's robust fractal model takes these simple implications of the multifractal model into account. In fact, it does so far better since it elucidates when to expect changes in the slope and rate of ascent or descent in the market and at what degrees to expect them. The market is in fact *not* a multi fractal but a robust one, so while the multifractal model may simulate market *volatility*, it does not simulate the market. Mandelbrot concedes as much when he refers to the actual market as obeying "unknown rules." Whether the Wave Principle correctly reveals those rules is open to debate, but that does not change the fact that Mandelbrot has said nothing novel, and, if the Wave Principle is true, he has modeled the market at a level way beneath Elliott's.

Elliott's fractal generator is also more coherent that Mandelbrot's. Two aspects of human social endeavor are *fluctuation* and *net progress*. Elliott's model accommodates both aspects in a natural way. To achieve fluctuation, a wave model must have at least three waves in each direction, which Mandelbrot recognizes. To achieve net progress, however, it must have, absent additional assumptions, at least two more waves in one direction than the other. Elliott's depiction, then, provides both fluctuation and progress in the simplest possible model, which reflects nature's efficiency in achieving goals. In contrast, Mandelbrot's assignation of three "pieces" in each direction is arbitrary because it omits net progress from its essence. His model entreats one to ask, "Why should the rising lines be longer than the falling ones?" With no theoretical justification for an upward bias, the same number of waves up and down *should* imply a cycle producing no net progress. The only way that Mandelbrot can depict net progress is to lengthen the waves in one of the two directions, which he does without explanation. Mandelbrot does not claim to have done so because the market in *reality* does so, because he disclaims that the market actually follows his fractal generator depiction. Therefore the lengthening of waves in one direction is an *ad hoc* concession to the truth that the stock market—like mankind—makes progress over time. Elliott's alternating 5-3 concept, in immense contrast, is *logical* in terms of more naturally implying progress and *objective* in having been developed from real-world observation.

Mandelbrot has made historic contributions to science: He elucidated fractal dimension, developed the mathematics of measuring roughness, recognized the wealth of variety that fractal rules can produce and discovered that fractals permeate the world. These are seminal achievements. Unfortunately, they are of no use in creating an accurate, practical, predictive model of financial market behavior, so his claim to this territory fails. Elliott's claim, backed by empirics and 65 years of application, is a demonstrable success.

Mandelbrot's belittling of Elliott's hypothesis cannot be born of ignorance, as he possesses the literature. A scientist of financial fractals may attempt to dispute Elliott's work in cataloguing the forms that appear in the real world, but he may not dismiss it or ignore it. If he disagrees with either Elliott's detailed observations or his wider conclusions, he should say so and explain why, not simply mock them as a phony "discovery." I cannot help but wonder if he is *wishing* them away because (at least in my opinion) they are so profound and, if proven true, will dwarf even the great Mandelbrot's contribution to our knowledge of finance.

(8) "Elliott's work fails the requirements of objectivity and repeatability: in his own words, 'considerable experience is required to interpret [it] correctly' and 'no interpretation [is] valid unless made by [him or his direct licencees].'"

Elliott wrote this "warning" on the title page of his first book so that readers would guard against inept forecasting from opportunists who might wish to make a fast buck without studying the subject. It was simply a business decision meant to establish his planned stock market publication as the authoritative one on the Wave Principle. He never claimed that knowledge of the Wave Principle was proprietary to any one person's brain. In fact, he explained his work repeatedly in two books in 1938 and 1946, a series of 12 articles for *Financial World* magazine in 1939 and even via a course on the subject taught in New York City, information that is covered in the biography published in the very book that Mandelbrot used as his source. These facts, along with the entire remainder of Elliott's writing, contradict Mandelbrot's depiction via this out-of-context quotation. We might ask whether Mandelbrot's own (unsubstantiated) claim to useful probabilistic forecasting can be exploited by someone who lacks "considerable experience" with fractals. If not, will he write that he has proved his own model's non-objectivity and non-repeatability? Of course not; it would be irrelevant.

A man with Mandelbrot's obvious intelligence knows that culling one line from Elliott's books and articles to assert the grand damnation of non-objectivity and non-repeatability shows nothing of the sort. Quoting these few words out of context is a smokescreen that skirts the question. *If Mandelbrot can show that Elliott's work fails the require-ments of objectivity and repeatability, then he should do it. Otherwise, he has no business stating it as if it were a fact.* The expression of the Wave Principle is objective, as there are books that spell out the ideas. I, for one, reject subjectivity as having any place in the field. Whether the Wave Principle is true is another question, but Mandelbrot's lifetime work supports the case that it is. Mandelbrot's dismissal is, simply stated, a blanket assertion that is utterly unscientific in failing to address the point at hand and dishonest in pretending that it does.

### Elliott on His Discovery

In citation (5), Mandelbrot concedes only that R.N. Elliott's *dia-grams* are "reminiscent" [sic] of self-affine generators. He avoids saying that Elliott's *words* on the subject of self-affinity in social processes, which are in the book he quotes, also predate all modern commentary on the subject. Here is some of Elliott's commentary introducing what at the time was a revolutionary concept, derived completely independently of others' influences:

> Extensive research in connection with what may be termed human activities indicates that practically all developments which result from our social-economic processes follow a law that causes them to repeat themselves in similar and constantly recurring serials of waves or impulses of definite number and pattern. It is likewise indicated that in their intensity, these waves or impulses bear a consistent relation to one another and to the passage of time.
>
> The expression "human activities" includes such items as stock prices, bond prices, patent (application)s, [the] price of gold, population, movements of citizens from cities to farms and vice versa, commodities prices, government expenditures, production, life insurance [purchases], electric power produced, gasoline consumption, fire losses, price of seats on the stock exchange, epidemics, real estate, business, politics [and] the pursuit of pleasure.[36] It is particularly evident in those free markets where public participation in price movements is extensive.
>
> Those who have attempted to deal with the market's movements have failed to recognize the extent to which the market is a psychological phenomenon. They have not grasped the fact that there is regularity underlying the fluctuations of the market, or, stated otherwise, that price movements in stocks are subject to rhythms, or an ordered sequence. The wild, senseless and apparently uncontrollable changes in prices from year to year, from month to month, or from day to day, link themselves into a law-abiding rhythmic pattern of waves. The same rules apply to the price of stocks, bonds, grains, cotton, coffee and all the other activities previously mentioned.
>
> The student should recognize that there are cycles within cycles. Major waves subdivide into intermediate waves[, which] subdivide into minor waves. One cycle becomes but the starting point of another, or larger, movement that itself is a part of, and subject to the same law as, the lesser movement. This fundamental law cannot be subverted or set aside by statutes or restrictions.

Current news and political developments are of only incidental importance, soon forgotten; their presumed influence on market trends is not as weighty as is commonly believed. Underlying this progression, in whatever field, is a fixed and controlling principle, or the master rule under which nature works. This treatise has made use of price movements in stocks to illustrate the phenomenon, but all the principles laid down herein are equally applicable to the wave movement in every field where human endeavor is registered.[37]

—R.N. Elliott, 1938, 1939, 1940, 1946

Clearly, Elliott was fully conscious of the facts, to use Mandelbrot's own words (cited at the outset of this paper) that he had created "a new modeling technique" that "cast a light of order" on market behavior from his own original "work in fractal geometry." Not only did Elliott draw fractal diagrams but he also understood their meaning and implication. That the markets' fractal is robust rather than self-identical or indefinite, along with Elliott's recognition that Fibonacci mathematics govern its behavior, ultimately establishes an intimate kinship between mankind's pattern of progress and countless other growth forms in nature. These observations predate the same implications of Mandelbrot's discovery of the ubiquity of fractals. In fact, it was decades later before words such as those quoted above emerged as a result of studies in fractal geometry. I believe that, especially along with his diagrams, they are more than sufficient to credit Elliott with having introduced the idea that fractal self-affinity governs social processes and is fundamental to nature. Indeed, with his dedicated empiricism, mathematical insights, encompassing hypothesis and universal perspective, I think that Elliott, though a business professional unaccustomed to scientific protocol, was worthy of the title "scientist."

## A Bifurcation in the Road

Whenever Mandelbrot knew about Elliott's work, he must have decided to ignore it in hopes that it would go away. It didn't. It seems that by the late 1990s, he could no longer resist or postpone staking his claim to Elliott's territory. Given Mandelbrot's obsession for taking credit, he would have no choice but to avoid depicting a financial market's fractal generator as five waves and three waves because his place in history would then be reduced to confirming and furthering work originated by R.N. Elliott. He came as close as he dared, depicting his financial market fractal "generator" in the same way as Elliott did but with three waves in each direction. In his 2002 book, he asserts that his "newly coined" term, "tile self affinities," provides pictures "of almost every basic fractal or multifractal," presumably thereby including Elliott's Wave Principle.

At least we know, given Mandelbrot's 1997 comments cited above, that he knew of Elliott's work before penning his *Scientific American* article. At an inadequate bare minimum, he should have cited Elliott among his sources, because that's where he got the idea for the illustrations of his fractal generator. But to do so would have been to admit that Elliott invented the idea. He was between a rock and a hard place. In my opinion, morally speaking, which means practically speaking as well, he chose the wrong way out.

Anyone who wishes to make up his own mind on this subject, as well as on the credit Elliott deserves, need only read one of these three volumes:

(1) *R.N. Elliott's Masterworks* (1980/1993), which includes all of Elliott's original books, articles and major essays, as well as a biography.

(2) *Elliott Wave Principle—Key to Market Behavior* (1978/1998) by Frost and Prechter, a concise presentation of Elliott's work.

(3) *The Wave Principle of Human Social Behavior and the New Science of Socionomics* (1999) by Prechter.

These books are published by New Classics Library, which has also published the historical works of every other major practitioner of the Wave Principle. For a list, visit www.elliottwave.com/books or use the following contact information: Address: P.O. Box 1618, Gainesville, GA 30503; phone: 770-536-0309; fax: 770-536-2514; e-mail: customercare@elliottwave.com.

## Postscript

Mandelbrot may also have incorporated and claimed some original ideas and expressions of other Elliott wave practitioners. The preceding pages discuss, for example, the wording of Mandelbrot's claims to his model's forecasting value that mirror expressions appearing in *Elliott Wave Principle*. Perhaps the following quotations will serve further to demonstrate that Mandelbrot has read and absorbed the expressions in that volume. Compare this quote:

> Can we both theorize and observe that the stock market operates on the same mathematical basis as so many natural phenomena? The answer is yes.... *In its broadest sense, the Wave Principle suggests the idea that the same law that shapes living creatures and galaxies is inherent in the spirit and activities of men en masse.*[38]
> —Frost and Prechter, *Elliott Wave Principle,* 1978

with this one, which opens Mandelbrot's article:

> *The geometry that describes the shape of coastlines and the patterns of galaxies also elucidates how stock prices soar and plummet.*[39]

This idea is repeated in the article, as follows:

> *Fractal patterns appear not just in the price changes of securities but in the distribution of galaxies throughout the cosmos* [and] in the shape of coastlines....[40]
> —Mandelbrot, "A Multifractal Walk Down Wall Street," 1999

While I am prone to quip that all these lines could be part of the same fractal object, I will leave it to you to judge their similarity.

Cynics have often objected to comments such as the one quoted above from *Elliott Wave Principle* on the grounds that its implications are too grand. As you can see, one of the most renowned scientists in the world is now saying essentially the same thing.

## A Market Forecast?

Mandelbrot's article ends with this line: "The new modeling techniques…also recognize the mariner's warning that, as recent events demonstrate, deserves to be heeded: *On even the calmest sea, a gale may be just over the horizon.*" One might take this as simply a general comment about the suddenness of major movements within the financial fractal except that its imagery is specific to market panics. Thus, in conjunction with the magazine's table of contents introduction saying, "When will the Dow top 10,000? When will it crash?", it stands as a sentence that Mandelbrot would probably love to have quoted when the stock market does crash. It would seem so *prescient.* Yet Mandelbrot's method provides no basis for anticipating any such thing. Any implication that it does is false. Only the Wave Principle—or perhaps some other specific market model—can do that. If his closing line is to be accepted as a knowing hint of coming events, as an indication that Mandelbrot was *bearish on the stock market,* then we would have to ask him on what basis he held such an opinion. One hopes that he did not simply purloin Elliott wave analysts' long term stock market outlook, which has received worldwide publicity through countless books and articles.

## NOTES

[1] This chapter is an expanded version of the original exposition.

[2] Mandelbrot, Benoit. (1999, February). "A multifractal walk down wall street." *Scientific American*, p.70.

[3] Elliott, Ralph Nelson. (1938). *The wave principle*. Republished: Prechter, Robert (Ed.).(1980/1994). *R.N. Elliott's masterworks—The definitive collection*. Gainesville, GA: New Classics Library.

[4] Mandelbrot projected Figure 4 from a slide during his lecture at Emory University on May 11, 2002.

[5] Mandelbrot, Benoit. (1982). *The fractal geometry of nature*. W.H. Freeman & Co. Also (1997). *Fractals and scaling in finance: Discontinuity, concentration, risk*. Springer-Verlag; And (1997). "The multifractal model of asset returns," discussion papers of the Cowles Foundation for Economics, #1164-1166, Yale University; And (1999). *Multifractals and 1/f noise: Wild self-affinity in physics*. Springer-Verlag.

[6] See endnote 2.

[7] See endnote 3.

[8] Frost, Alfred John, and Prechter, Robert R. (1978). *Elliott wave principle—Key to market behavior*. Gainesville, GA: New Classics Library, p.184.

[9] Mandelbrot, Benoit. (1997). *Fractals and scaling in finance—Discontinuity, concentration, risk.* Springer-Verlag.

[10] Prechter, Jr., Robert Rougelot (ed.) (1980/1994). *R.N. Elliott's masterworks—The definitive collection*. Gainesville, GA: New Classics Library.

[11] See endnote 9.

[12] See endnote 2.

[13] They are R.N. Elliott, Charles J. Collins, A. Hamilton Bolton, A. John Frost, Richard Russell and Robert R. Prechter, Jr.

[14] Sornette, D., Johansen, A., and Bouchaud, J.P. (1996). "Stock market crashes, precursors and replicas." *Journal de Physique I France* 6, No.1, pp. 167-175.

[15] The ellipses in this quotation replace the unfortunate phrase, "... so strongly rooted in the financial analysts' folklore...." Sornette, *et al.* may perhaps be excused for having referred to the Wave Principle in this fashion even though the "folklore" terminology is false because at least they conscientiously credited a *proper source* from which interested parties may glean the truth. Further, Sornette today more accurately refers to the Wave Principle as "a market model hypothesis." No person fully informed of Elliott's orginal work, as Mandelbrot is, may be excused from using the term "folklore."

[16] See endnote 2.

[17] See endnote 3, p. 87.

[18] See endnote 2.

[19] See endnote 8, p. 87.

[20] (1993) Personal letter to R. Prechter from J. Barnes, Wetumpka, Alabama.

[21] Gleick, James. (1987). *Chaos: Making a new science.* New York: Penguin Books, pp. 111-112.

[22] *Ibid.,* p. 111.

[23] This is not the first time a famous researcher has claimed Elliott's work for his own. Edson Gould, writing under the pseudonym Edson Beers, presented a pack of Elliott's original ideas in a *Barron's* article on May 19, 1941, eight months after Elliott published them. Gould, an inventive and rising star in the market forecasting field, apparently recognized the seminal importance of Elliott's work and wished himself into the originator's chair. (Does that sound familiar?) In that instance, Elliott was alive, so he could lodge his own well justified protest. For more on the story, see "A Biography of R.N. Elliott" in *R.N. Elliott's Masterworks.* (1980/1994). Prechter, Jr., Robert Rougelot. (Ed.). Gainesville, GA: New Classics Library.

[24] Edgar, G.A. (ed.) (1993). *Classics on fractals.* Reading, MA: Addison-Wesley.

[25] Prechter, Robert. R. (1999). *The wave principle of human social behavior.* Gainesville, GA: New Classics Library.

[26] See endnote 9.

[27] With multi-million dollar corporations and universities to support him, Mandelbrot, to be sure, has not had to stoop to commerce to make a living. His sniffy attitude on this topic reveals an intense annoyance— fueling what appears to be denial—that someone outside of the scientific world, someone who had to work for a living in the commercial world— originated the idea of fractals in finance and made many of the biggest discoveries in the field. Being miffed is hardly sufficient justification for this ungracious response.

[28] Elliott, R.N. (1946). *Nature's law.* Republished: (1980/1994). *R.N. Elliott's masterworks—The definitive collection.* Prechter, Jr., Robert Rougelot. (Ed.). Gainesville, GA: New Classics Library.

[29] Gleick, J. (1985, December 8)."The man who reshaped geometry." *The New York Times.*

[30] For a good summary, see Chapter 5 of *The Wave Principle of Human Social Behavior.* For Elliott's full record, see *R.N. Elliott's Masterworks* (1980/1994) and *R.N. Elliott's Market Letters* (1993) New Classics Library.

[31] Reprinted in this book as Chapter 7.

[32] Mandelbrot, Benoit. (1962). Sur certains prix spéculatifs: faits empiriques et modèle basé sur les processus stables additifs de Paul Lévy. *Comptes Rendus* (Paris): 254, 3968-3970. And (1963). The variation of certain speculative prices. *Journal of Business*: 36, 394-419. Reprinted in Cootner 1964: 297-337. University of Chicago Press.

[33] See endnote 21, p. 83.

[34] Chapter 3 of *The Wave Principle of Human Social Behavior* explains this term.

[35] Dating from Elliott's first letter to Collins in 1934, in which he made a brief, general market forecast.

[36] Elliott showed graphs of these activities in *The Wave Principle* (1938).

[37] These sentences are collected from pp. 92, 147, 157, 183, 192, 217, 218, 228, 229 of *R.N. Elliott's Masterworks* (1980/1994), which includes *The Wave Principle* (1938), The *Financial World* articles (1939), "The basis of the wave principle" (1940) and *Nature's law* (1946). I have omitted ellipses and one-letter brackets for reading clarity.

[38] See endnote 8. p.114, 121.

[39] See endnote 2.

[40] *Ibid.* p.71.

## Chapter 40

# *Reply and Response*

### Mandelbrot's Reply...

In the June 1999 issue of *Scientific American*, Mandelbrot replied to the storm of response to his article (see next section) as follows:

> At some point Ralph Elliott's "principle" and my cartoon simulations both use recursive interpolation in which each part is a reduced-scale version of the whole. The idea is ancient, but his use and mine stand in absolute contrast. Elliott drew a certain nonrandom "wave" that he claimed "really forecasts" every real-world market; however, this simplistic wave was first stretched, squeezed or otherwise adjusted by hand. In contrast, fractal or multifractal models must follow firm mathematical rules that allow quantitative developments throughout, as mine do. In any event, the random or nonrandom cartoons themselves are of no interest; they serve only to introduce the subtle quantitative properties and tools of my model of price variation—fractional Brownian motion in multifractal time. The rules of this model are not recursive but fully specified mathematically and can be adjusted to fit the historical financial data.[1]

### ...and Prechter's Response

Prechter posted the following response on the Elliott Wave International website:[2]

> "At some point Ralph Elliott's "principle" and my cartoon simulations both use recursive interpolation in which each part is a reduced-scale version of the whole."

That's our point. It is more accurate to say, though, that Elliott did not *use* recursive interpolation but rather *reported* it in the actual stock market. Mandelbrot condescendingly uses quotes and lower case for "principle," but the model has a *name*, which he knows full well, and the idea is grand enough fully to deserve it.

"The idea is ancient…"

Please. The idea of recursive interpolation (for art and so forth) may be ancient, but the use of it to describe and model the stock market is not. It originated with Elliott.

"…but his use and mine stand in absolute contrast."

That they do.

"Elliott drew a certain nonrandom 'wave' that he claimed 'really forecasts' every real-world market…"

The Wave Principle is indeed substantially non-random. Its specificity is what makes it useful. In probabilistic terms, and with varying degrees of success, it can indeed be employed to forecast most real-world markets.

"…however, this simplistic wave was first stretched, squeezed or otherwise adjusted…"

In this comment we find both error and irony. Elliott did not model the market as a certain simple picture and then stretch, squeeze or adjust it. He was describing reality, and reality itself is diverse. This accusation is akin to saying that someone who sketched pictures of a dozen types of trees and then proposed a composite model to depict tree-ness "started with a simplistic tree model and then stretched, squeezed and otherwise adjusted it." It's backwards.

There is irony in Mandelbrot's depiction because in fact it describes precisely what he himself is doing in creating his "multifractal model." He begins with a simple fractal generator and then *adjusts* it by *stretching* it on the vertical axis and *squeezing* it on the horizontal axis, all quite on an ad hoc basis, as you can clearly see in Figure 1, taken directly from his article.

"…by hand."

Was Elliott supposed to have used a computer? In 1934?

"In contrast, fractal or multifractal models must follow firm mathematical rules that allow quantitative developments throughout, as mine do."

# Stretching, Squeezing and Adjusting

(Mandelbrot's fractal model, as shown with attending commentary in *Scientific American*, February 1999)

MOVING A PIECE of the fractal generator to the left ...

... causes the same amount of market activity in a shorter time interval for the first piece of the generator and the same amount in a longer interval for the second piece ...

... Movement of the generator to the left causes market activity to become increasingly volatile.

*Figure 1*

*Must* they? It is important to distinguish between a model that we can manipulate precisely and a model of reality. The ability to model with precision requires mathematical rigidity, but a model of reality requires a commitment to truth, which may preclude mathematical rigidity, at least in the model's formative stages when knowledge is limited. This result seems particularly applicable to living systems and even more especially to human behavior. A model with firm mathematical rules that purported to predict your friend Charlie would be absurd, and one that allowed for Charlie to do *anything* would be useless, yet we get both of these things from Mandelbrot's model with respect to financial markets. One could certainly build a useful model of Charlie's past and potential behavior, but it would have neither that basis nor that outcome. Consider the question of whether trees follow "firm mathematical rules." Perhaps they do, but no currently known model using such rules would be useful for forecasting the final outcome of any particular tree. On the other hand, a robust model based on detailed empirics—using mathematical rigidities and probability statements—might help you anticipate much of it. Elliott's model is of this type.

The above discussion is in no way a concession to Mandelbrot's claim that only his model can be described mathematically. Elliott's model *can* be quantified with firm mathematical rules. That is why we were able to create our EWAVES computer program[3] to label data series according to Elliott's rules and guidelines. I have no illusions, though, that the resulting program has captured every possible nuance of market behavior, perfectly assigned its ranges of probability, eliminated all impossible patterns or completely encapsulated the robust Wave Principle model, about which there is surely more to learn.

Neither is this discussion a concession to Mandelbrot's claim to having modeled the stock market in the first place. Although he claims that his model "follow(s) firm mathematical rules," it doesn't follow any *useful* rules of form but rather allows for infinite manipulation. Can you imagine the dismissive response to R.N. Elliott had he claimed that markets can do anything at all as long as they fluctuate up and down? What kind of model is that, and of what practical value are such "firm mathematical rules"? Do you want a model that admits random "quantitative developments throughout" *if that's not what happens in reality?* Random walk theorists can describe their model with mathematical precision, too, but it is not therefore relevant to the stock market. Elliott's model and Mandelbrot's model both allow for an infinite variety of quantitative developments, except that Elliott's model *limits aspects of the variety that may occur,* making it useful in real-world forecasting. Mandelbrot's model eliminates no potential market event (except that prices cannot move backwards in time!). The incorporation of infinite possibilities for price behavior in Mandelbrot's purported model in fact makes it no different from a random walk and thus, for practical purposes, *no model at all*.

> "In any event, the random or nonrandom cartoons themselves are of no interest..."

In his 1997 book, Mandelbrot presents drawings like those in Figures 2 and 4 in the preceding chapter, as well as a few others, that utilize a specific pattern (such as 3-up, 3-down, using certain lengths) in order to display the idea of multifractal self-affinity. He calls these illustrations "cartoons," an apt word in this case, perhaps, because with respect to the actual patterns of financial market behavior that Elliott elucidated, they represent either arbitrary constructs or potentialities, not actualities. As we can see by Mandelbrot's inclusionary use of the term above, he means to include Elliott's drawings among such "cartoons," which may be why he chose such a diminutive word. Elliott's illustrations, however, are no more cartoons than a detailed painting by a realist. Elliott drew aspects of reality, not abstract constructs. For this reason, Elliott's *nonrandom* cartoons are of interest to thousands of people. Indeed, they are fascinating both in their reliable reflection of reality[4] and in their theoretical implications. Mandelbrot's *random* cartoons are of far less interest. (Having seen Paree, I would extend that judgment to his entire model.)

If Elliott's depictions are of no interest to Mandelbrot, that's fine. He has placed this fact on the record to his great detriment if and when the Wave Principle model is vindicated. Yet shouldn't Mandelbrot be thrilled to discover that someone who set out to depict actual stock market behavior recorded a structure that his model accommodates? Apparently, the problem with his recognizing this feat is that Elliott did it decades ago. Had someone come up with this depiction ten years into the future, Mandelbrot could claim that his model, however vaguely, anticipated it. Given the true chronology, admitting Elliott's Wave Principle into the academic discussion places Mandelbrot in the position of being a latecomer who is either giving Elliott's model some added justification or proposing a broader derivative umbrella under which to consider market fractality, which may have theoretical value (though still no practical value) only if Elliott's model is disproved. That must be why to him, the Wave Principle is "of no interest."

If Mandelbrot were to undertake a theoretical modeling of the automobile, perhaps he would take credit for having invented "carness." The mere fact that people have already *built* cars would presumably have no bearing on his claim. He could dismiss them as "non-random cartoons of no interest."

We should further note that Mandelbrot never created any cartoons—or used that term—until *after* he saw R.N. Elliott's illustrations depicting the Wave Principle. Mandelbrot's cartoons and his related commentary may have some value apart from the Wave Principle, but their timing and presentation appear designed at least partly with the hope of enveloping Elliott's model within the scope of his work while simultaneously relegating it to near insignificance. When Elliott's specific observations become accepted in the scientific community, this strategy, if that's what it is, will be revealed as inadequate to the task and turn the tables on the implied relative significance between the contributions to financial market modeling.

> "...they serve only to introduce the subtle quantitative properties and tools of my model of price variation—fractional Brownian motion in multifractal time."

That's what *Mandelbrot's* cartoons do. Elliott's model does not depict *Brownian* motion; it depicts *stock market* motion. They are very different categories.

> "The rules of this model are not recursive..."

Mandelbrot's model may not be recursive, but his fractal generator is; that's what Figures 2 and 4 imply, and that's what he himself says: "...my cartoon simulations...use recursive interpolation...." If there is no recursion, then what is the point of the illustrations other than to muscle in on Elliott's territory? Elliott's model is not *rigidly* recursive; there is great variety within the Wave Principle. Finally, the stock market *is* robustly recursive, so a model that is *not*—like Mandelbrot's—does not capture the essence of the stock market.

> "...but fully specified mathematically and can be adjusted to fit the historical financial data."

To repeat, of what value is a model that is "fully specified mathematically" but whose result is no different from saying, "The stock market can do anything"? Elliott's model describes what aspects of stock market movement are certain *and which are not*, and therein lies much of its value.

Mandelbrot says proudly that his model *"can be adjusted* to fit the historical data." Did we not just read a few sentences ago that Elliott's model is a joke because it was *"adjusted"* to fit actual market behavior, i.e., historical data? Aside from noting the hypocrisy, observe this crucial difference: Elliott *derived* his model from "historical financial data." People applying it do not have to *adjust* it to fit new data. Indeed, his model is adequate for anticipating *future* financial data.

Regardless of one's opinion on these matters, *Mandelbrot's claim to full mathematical specification is utterly inadequate to the goal of discrediting or dismissing Elliott's discovery*. That there is a difference between their models does not reduce Elliott's achievement, much less obliterate him from the scene. So what if Elliott did not work out all the mathematics of his model? Darwin did not work out any of the mathematics of evolution. At least Elliott worked out an important portion of the math, for example the crucial governance by Fibonacci, which Mandelbrot has yet to discover or acknowledge. Because Darwin's model of evolution—a fractal process after all—did not include "firm mathematical rules," was it therefore unimportant or not a model? No. His model made a quantum leap in our understanding of reality. Does a successor to Darwin get credit for *originating the idea of evolution* because he figured out some of the math involved? No. The credit goes to the person who had the ground-breaking insight that all others had missed. With respect to social behavior, that man is R.N. Elliott, who uncovered the fundamental truth that group behavior creates a fractal dynamic of waves. Does a successor to Darwin get credit for modeling evolution because he invented a mathematical construct that can't predict a single evolutionary trend? No. The credit goes to the person whose model can anticipate events in reality. It was R.N. Elliott who described the Wave Principle and formulated rules and guidelines for anticipating coming trends. Both of these achievements are on the record for all to see. Readers of *Scientific American* were right to recoil at Mandelbrot's glaring omission, and I am right to challenge his derogation of Elliott's achievement.

## NOTES

[1] Mandelbrot, Benoit. (1999, June). Letters to the Editor. *Scientific American*, p.6.

[2] The original text has been lost, so I have re-created it to the best of my recollection. I would appreciate hearing from anyone who downloaded the original comments.

[3] See Chapter 4 of *The Wave Principle of Human Social Behavior.*

[4] This email from a professional portfolio manager, who began following the market closely in 2002 after learning the Wave Principle, arrived yesterday: "I'm a born again waver!!!! Seriously, this is the most amazing tool I've ever seen. I sit on the board of the James Madison College at Michigan State University, a liberal arts school that encourages students to read all the great works of western thought. I'd like to get some of the professors acclimated to the Wave Principle." I get messages like this all the time because the Wave Principle does model reality, and it does it well.

*The June 1999 issue of Scientific American begins, "Benoit B. Mandelbrot's article 'A Multifractal Walk Down Wall Street' in the February issue elicited myriad responses from readers." Among those addressing the Elliott question, only Prechter's letter was published. Fortunately, a few of the many letters not published in the magazine were cc'd to our web site's Bulletin Board, so we can reproduce them here.*

## Chapter 41

# Letters to the Editor of Scientific American

Today, I read Benoit Mandelbrot's article, "A Multifractal Walk Down Wall Street." In it, he does a good job of arguing against the prevailing assumptions at the heart of Modern Portfolio Theory. (Those assumptions remain dear to the heart of academic economists even though the person on the trading floor knows them to be false.) He also furthers the understanding of stock prices as fractals with his method for modeling them. Unfortunately, the model bears a large number of similarities to work that precedes his by years, even decades. Mandelbrot's model borrows heavily from R.N. Elliott's work during the 1930s. This work has since been refined by Robert Prechter and A.J. Frost. The similarity becomes very striking when comparing Mandelbrot's article side-by-side with previously published work. For example, Mandelbrot's Figure 1 is little more than a simplified version of Figures 1-2 to 1-4 in Frost and Prechter's *Elliott Wave Principle*, published in 1978. That's twenty-one years ago! In 1978, Frost and Prechter did not yet refer to market prices or the wave model that describes them as fractals. The term fractal was still new, and fractal methods and concepts were still too arcane. However, now writers, investors and analysts such as Prechter, Bill Williams and others have understood, discussed and published on the fractal nature of the market and waves for over a decade. Yet nothing is mentioned in Mandelbrot's article, and ALL items in the further reading refer to his work and his work ALONE. I never anticipated referring to a genius of Mandelbrot's caliber as unprofessional, but I find the need now. Had a graduate student of mine written a paper that only referred to his own work, he would quickly find himself sent to do more research in the library! I look forward to Mandelbrot's future work, which should add greater mathematical rigor to our understanding of the fractal nature of market prices and the tendency of markets to trend with waves of various duration. It will help advance the field. But it will advance a field that already exists, whether he acknowledges it or not. I know that I can respect the integrity of *Scientific American.* I look forward to an editorial comment in a future issue correcting the false impressions left by an otherwise useful article.

— James J. Donovan, PhD
February 15, 1999

This message is about the article "A Multifractal Walk Down Wall Street" by Benoit B. Mandelbrot in the February 1999 issue of *Scientific American.* I am sending this message for two reasons: (1) To say well done for putting the above article on your cover and (2) To protest that Mandelbrot did not give credit to R.N. Elliott as the first person who modeled financial markets using multifractals. It is appropriate that in these times of a high profile to the stock market that a scientific point of view is published. Mandelbrot is right in saying that the current models do not perform well and that better models are required. His fairly simple model of markets using fractals quickly shows how fractals model the market much more closely than modern portfolio theory. His article and reputation bring much needed credibility to this fascinating area of investigation. However, while Mandelbrot is providing this benefit to financial modeling, he is subtracting from his own integrity. Mandelbrot states on the second page of his article the following: "I claim that variations in financial prices can be accounted for by a model derived from my work in fractal geometry." Notice how Mandelbrot states, "my work in fractal geometry." The reader can imply that Mandelbrot is the first to use fractals to model financial prices. It is true that the model Mandelbrot uses can model the variations in financial prices, but it is NOT true that Mandelbrot was the first to do so.

Mandelbrot should have been scientifically honest enough to cite R.N. Elliott as being the first person to publish a fractal approach to analyzing financial markets—way back in the 1930s. The word "fractal" was not coined at that time, but it is clearly the contribution that Elliott made. Even the diagrams that Mandelbrot shows in illustration 1 in the article are strikingly similar to many diagrams published in Elliott's writings. Examples of Elliott's diagrams are Figures 3 and 4 in *The Wave Principle* (1938) and Figures 5 to 13 in *Nature's Law* (1946). Elliott's publications are still available in *R.N. Elliott's Masterworks,* published by New Classics Library, which contains these and other Elliott publications. Mandelbrot has published a book that criticizes Elliott, so we know Mandelbrot is aware of Elliott's work. The book is *Fractals and Scaling in Finance: Discontinuity, Concentration, Risk*—listed under "Further Reading" in the article—so Mandelbrot cannot excuse himself out of ignorance. Mr. Mandelbrot is deservedly famous for his work on fractals and chaos but is less than professional in his attitude to Elliott's contribution.

*Scientific American* has a valuable opportunity to further its contribution to science by pursuing this debate further. Scientific debate is always healthy, especially when it affects something at the foundations of our way of life—money. Your magazine could publish an article about R.N. Elliott to present a balanced view. Mr. Robert Prechter Jr. who heads Elliott Wave International in Gainesville, Georgia is appropriately knowledgeable about Elliott to provide such an article.

— Eugene Morrow, Sydney, Australia
April 4, 1999

Down Wall Street again!

An investor's principal question is: "How can I make money tomorrow?" In "A Multifractal Walk Down Wall Street," Benoit Mandelbrot has woven a chaotic pattern of claims and self-defeating counterclaims. There is an incorrect implication that, by employing the principles of fractal geometry, the investor's question has been answered. In the process he has borrowed generously without citations and incurred the ire of many proponents of Elliott's Wave Principle. Perhaps the same is true of supporters of Burton Malkiel, one of his colleagues at my old Alma Mater, who authored *A Random Walk Down Wall Street*. One is hard-pressed to succinctly unscramble such a tangle of short threads.

Mandelbrot labors to force his multifractals to resemble a specific period of price history. With that as his only guiding rule, unfortunately, any other technique, including a kid drawing freehand with a crayon, should accomplish the same minimum noise result. Logically, he first reasons that stock price fluctuations are governed by rules which he does not know. He demonstrates that he can replicate a period of reality from a stock chart using a sequence of 3 vectors divided into multiply nested 3-vector offspring. But then he incorrectly assumes that the rules of reality automatically apply equally to both representations and that through some magic of fractal geometry, his model somehow contains new and valuable information not contained in the original price chart.

By his own admission, his simulation has essentially no predictive power. In a two-part article entitled "Pseudo Securities for Technical Analysts," which will soon be published in *Technical Analysis of Stocks and Commodities* (www.traders.com), I graphically illustrate a basic problem in modeling to which Mandelbrot's replicas are subject. In essence, one may make numerous radically different mathematical models that over a limited time span appear to accurately mimic reality. However, such models for the investor are valid only if, when allowed to run in time beyond the limits of the analysis span, they continue to accurately mimic both previous history and, more important, the future. The rules of cause and effect still appear to be ignored at one's peril.

His stress test is to compare his "model" to the original data source he copied. There's little surprise that he might subtract the two and get the small difference noise signals in his illustrations, regardless of the degree of volatility involved. It is unclear how a portfolio manager might profitably stress test a portfolio (or a security) by comparing it to a purposely inaccurate approximation of itself over the time span selected.

Finally, Mandelbrot suggests that with further work, his invention may become a useful predictor of future stock prices. Indeed, your readers should be informed that it already has! R.N. Elliott in the 1930s recognized that the markets follow a succession of zig-zag "waves" consisting of a 5-up then 3-down core structure. If, as seems logical, Elliott considered the simpler 3-wave structure, he rejected it as not being valid when he formulated his final model of market behavior. Both Elliott and Mandelbrot recognized that the basic patterns in real life are fractals, being composed of smaller repetitions of themselves, and multiples of themselves being the building blocks for larger look-alike structures. The word fractal had, of course, not been coined in Elliott's time. The Elliott Wave Principle subsequently has been widely studied and applied, somewhat refined, and made available in several software applications that run on a modern home computer.

Elliott's fundamental approach was exactly opposite that of Mandelbrot's. His theory, with its hundreds of rules and guidelines, was developed from a meticulous combing of historical records to find the real basis for the bits and pieces of the fractals and to determine painstakingly the myriad ways the market fits them together. That's just what Mandelbrot hopes to accomplish in the future.

—Charles E. Miller, Carlisle MA
March 5, 1999

I purchased a copy of *Scientific American* today and read the article. I find it interesting, especially in light of the fact that Mandelbrot wrote about Elliott's discoveries in 1997, that he gave no credit [to him] at all. I also found it interesting that the article gives a hint of how "multifractals" might be used to approximate action in the financial markets, but it is very frustrating to attempt to make much sense out of his graphs and relate them to real-world events.

— Andy MacKenzie
February 16, 1999

I read the February article, "A Multifractal Walk Down Wall Street," by Benoit Mandelbrot, with interest, amusement and disappointment. I found the topic interesting and timely since the U.S. stock market has been in a historic bull trend that has become of manic proportion recently. I was amused because Mandelbrot acts as if he has discovered something new. In fact, the essence of his thesis has been known and described for years. R.N. Elliott talked about market patterns of this type from observations he made and published in the 1930s and 1940s. I was somewhat disappointed by Mandelbrot's failure to credit Elliott for his work but hugely disappointed that Mandelbrot didn't prove his hypothesis with examples and discussion. I don't think his examples prove a thing, and his description of them is inadequate.

But there is good news for those who might want to pursue this line of reasoning and actually apply it to present day financial markets. The works of R.N. Elliott have been collected and published by Elliott Wave International, easily contacted at www.elliottwave.com or 1-800-336-1618. In fact, Elliott Wave International has developed summary and detailed descriptions of the Elliott patterns (free) and prints daily and monthly newsletters (for a fee) that interpret and predict United States and world market movements on the basis of them.

A short list of pertinent titles that Mandelbrot might have quoted include the following:
R.N. Elliott's works:
*The Wave Principle* (1938)
The *Financial World* articles (1939)
*Nature's Law—The Secret of the Universe* (1946)

*Elliott Wave Principle—Key to Market Behavior*
by A.J. Frost and Robert R. Prechter (1978, revised 1998)

— Jay Ham, MD
February 4, 1999

To a person with a deep interest in financial theory, just reading the title of Mr. Mandelbrot's paper indicates that it must have something to do with the Elliott Wave Principle first described almost 70 years ago. But as the reading continues, curiosity and enjoyment begin yielding to astonishment, which turns into outright dismay at the end of the paper: No mention of R.N. Elliott, Robert Prechter, A.J. Frost and others? How can that be? Is Mr. Mandelbrot so arrogant that he believes nobody else matters, or is he so ignorant that he has never heard of the books and papers in which others described the fractal geometry of financial markets? As it's hard to imagine that Mr. Mandelbrot would be unaware of these other contributions, one arrives at the conclusion that arrogance may be the engine at work. Mr. Mandelbrot's attitude to acknowledge the work of nobody and to recommend only himself for "further reading" appears to be an ego trip that lies outside the standard deviation of decent scientific behavior. It seems that scientific self-centeredness can run away in a manic pattern, just as the behavior of market participants occasionally bursts out in "irrational exuberance." Mr. Mandelbrot is not the first scientist who fell deeply in love with himself. The knowledge of this phenomenon prompts raising another question: Does *Scientific American* have something like a peer review? If the answer is no, then maybe the magazine should learn from this experience and consider establishing such a system—just to protect its own reputation. If the answer is yes, and if Mr. Mandelbrot's paper was indeed reviewed, shouldn't a flag have gone up at the realization that all recommended "Further Reading" bears the author's name? Credentialism is a perpetually recurring and non-eradicable quirk in the realm of investment, where the misdirection of capital to those "who have done it before" recently pushed the world to the brink of a financial meltdown. Credentialism in the scientific field may be less hazardous to the general population, but it is no less upsetting to the few who are affected by it. More likely than not, credentialism was the mechanism that prompted the rubber stamping of Mr. Mandelbrot's paper: If the theme has something to do with fractal geometry, can anybody dare lecture the man who wrote the book about fractals? To be a good reviewer, it is not enough to have an in-depth understanding of the pertinent field of science. One must also be able to understand that even the most accomplished individuals, be they scientists, artists, statesmen or whatever, remain humans and can frequently not conquer to the most basic human instincts and emotions. Consequently, good reviewers must be able to stand up to the big names of their field when ego, pride and other ingredients of human nature threaten to overwhelm the established rules of decent scientific demeanor.

— Eduard J. Botz
February 16, 1999

Your article on Benoit Mandelbrot's "discovery" that markets exhibit fractal like price behavior prompts a sharp response, since Professor Mandelbrot's insight was predated by decades by R.N. Elliott. His "Wave Principle" has been in the public domain since the 1940s and has been used with enormous success by such high profile market operators as Edson Gould.

Long disparaged by mainstream investment theory and academia, Elliotticians within the broad discipline of technical analysis could have told Professor Mandelbrot how to apply his mathematics to the marketplace. Technical analysts generally welcome academics' growing awareness that the skilled use of tools within our trade produce a level of success in forecasting market movements. However, it seems rather ironic that having derided technical analysis and Elliott in particular, that the academic establishment should suddenly decide that it works and take credit for it.

I write to you as a practitioner using Elliott's theories to forecast daily movements in the interest rate and currency markets. With a consistently high degree of accuracy in my daily work for major institutional clients, I can assure you that I have known and used Professor Mandelbrot's so-called insight for years. His assertion of novelty is ludicrous. Should you wish to take a balanced view in the matter, I suggest you inquire with Robert Prechter of Elliott Wave International. Bob is the foremost Elliottician in the world and since the 1970s has been the torch bearer of Elliott's work to the next generation of market analysts.

— Nina G. Cooper, President, Pendragon Research Inc.
February 22, 1999

In the February 1999 issue of *Scientific American,* you included an article by the above author entitled "A Multifractal Walk Down Wall Street." You probably need to know that your inclusion of that article has worked to tarnish the image of *Scientific American,* as the author, in writing his article, appears to have borrowed heavily from the ideas of others without giving credit where credit is due. In fact, it is rather pathetic that the author has previously chosen to dismiss the work of

R.N. Elliott while at the same time borrowing heavily from Elliott's theories about the market. Before including future articles on the same subject, you may want to become familiar with the works of R.N. Elliott and Robert Prechter. It is my hope that you will then be able to ferret out the Elliott-Wannabes like Mr. Mandelbrot or at least force such authors to give credit where credit is due. P.S. Please pass this on to Mr. Mandelbrot, as his ego should not be spared knowledge of the consequences of his actions and inactions.

— E.L.

February 16, 1999

Dear Editor, I am appalled that a publication as respected and as well read as *Scientific American* would publish such a blatant piece of plagiarism as was written by Mr. Mandelbrot. It's very surprising to me that a journal such as yours, which I have always immensely enjoyed consuming, would insult all who have studied the Elliott Wave Principle by condoning dishonesty among writers who are supposed scientists in the pursuit of truth. Disappointedly,

— Dr. Rashid A. Buttar, Emergency Medicine, Preventive
Medicine
February 16, 1999

To the Editors of *Scientific American*: That Dr. Mandelbrot coined his own word for "self-similar" points to an overactive ego. Your February article supports this [conclusion]. It may be impossible to say whether Mandelbrot knew of Ralph Elliott's 1930s discoveries before he verified them in several complex systems, but by now he ought to be objective enough to share credit with his remarkable predecessor. This especially so in an article dealing with Elliott's venue, the financial markets. That you allowed such an omission is an unfortunate collaboration in the mis-writing of history.

— Andrew Robin, Center Sandwich, New Hampshire
February 15, 1999

There's no getting around the insight and brilliance, not to mention just plain truth, embodied in Benoit B. Mandelbrot's piece in the February issue of *Scientific American*. But the omission of any reference to the work of R.N. Elliott, A.J. Frost, and R.R. Prechter, et al. is just too glaring to pass unremarked. Market technicians have used fractal analysis since Elliott introduced it in the 1930s, though to my knowledge the term fractal may have been first [connected to the Wave Principle] in Prechter's 1986 report "The Fractal Design of Social Progress."

Mandelbrot's analysis is best regarded as a refinement of this prior work. This point is strikingly and most graphically brought home by a quick comparison of the four diagrams in illustration 1 with Figs. 1-1 to 1-4 in Frost and Prechter's 1978 book, *Elliott Wave Principle* (New Classics Library). This financial classic certainly merits a place on the recommended reading list.

— William E. Terrell, Stafford, VA
January 30, 1999

I find it appalling that R.N. Elliott would plagiarize the work of Professor Mandelbrot decades before Mandelbrot created it.

— Pete Shamlian
May 24, 1999

### Follow-Up Correspondence Directed to Elliott Wave International

I am a scientist, and it has always irritated me when "credit is not given where it is due." As I have moved through my career, I have come across scientists who only reference themselves, who will not recognize others' work, and (fortunately only seldom), who steal others' ideas and claim them for their own. As these behaviors are carried out in the public arena, refutation and condemnation should also be carried out there. I urge you to submit the material in your "Special Report" to *Scientific American*. They should be willing to air both sides, I would hope.

— Jodie V. Johnson, Ph.D., Chemistry Department, University of Florida
May 21, 1999

I think this is a non-issue and that no one benefits by the argument. In mathematics, it is the mathematical characterization that counts, so—as Mandelbrot first defined fractals mathematically—Mandelbrot did indeed discover fractals, and fractals in finance. I myself have seen firsthand the hostility accorded Mandelbrot in having done so (in economics departments and in finance).

With respect to Elliott, an analogy with respect to Brownian motion may be illuminating. Brownian motion is named after Robert Brown because he first observed the phenomena in a *general* context in 1827 even though Brown himself cites at least one earlier observation of the phenomena in a specific context of fish eyes.

However, the first mathematical descriptions of Brownian motion were given independently by Louis Bachelier in 1900 and Albert Einstein in 1905. So it might be said the latter two individuals "discovered" Brownian motion. But, of course, the mathematicians wanted a much more rigorous development, which didn't come along until Norbert Wiener in 1923. So maybe Wiener created Brownian motion (the "Wiener process").

In the same spirit as Brown, Elliott clearly observed fractals in financial markets and can be said to have "discovered" financial fractals. But in the same spirit as Bachelier and Einstein, Mandelbrot "discovered" fractals because he defined the term and gave a specific mathematical characterization. It is only because of Mandelbrot that most in an academic environment would pay any attention to Elliott. (This approach to truth may not be justified, but that's the way it goes anyway.)

When I first encountered Robert Prechter (in 1984 on FNN, channel 64 in the Philadelphia area), and then the term "Elliott Wave," I immediately recognized it as a fractal approach to financial markets—although it was an open question in my view whether the structure of these fractals necessarily followed the form specified by Elliott.

So I have no problem with your (Robert Prechter's, whoever's) statement that Elliott discovered fractals in financial markets. Clearly Elliott did. Clearly Prechter was justified in adopting the name "fractal" as a description of Elliott's description. Nor do I have any problem with Mandelbrot's saying he discovered fractals in financial markets, because he created and popularized the entire mathematical concept. If you read Mandelbrot's books, you will see that he goes out of his way to point out predecessors. And if Mandelbrot doesn't think Elliott is that interesting, he—of all people—should be allowed that right. But I think you should feel quite free (and not defensive) about ignoring Mandelbrot on this point.

— J. Orlin Grabbe, Ph.D.
June 11, 1999

*Prechter replies: Perhaps it would indeed be a non-issue if it were generally acknowledged that both Elliott and Mandelbrot discovered fractals in markets but with differing amounts of qualification and quantification. The only reason there is a controversy is because Mandelbrot wants it all. I believe that is way too much credit to give. Look at Figures 1 through 4 again. Can you imagine the howl that would arise were someone today to write an article featuring a replica of the Mandelbrot Set and call it a "novelty," a "surprise" and the result of "my own work"? Mandelbrot has described his multifractal* market model *mathematically, but that is not at all the same thing as having described the* stock market *mathematically. The fact is that he has applied mathematics (brilliantly, to be sure) to only one aspect of the financial market fractal: a measure of its roughness. That is the aspect* he *has pursued and elucidated, but that may be only a small aspect of all there is to say about it. If one describes the circumference of an elephant with mathematical precision, it does not mean he has described the elephant. So it is far too much to say that Mandelbrot has* defined *the financial market fractal. According to Elliott, there is an immense amount of information about its form—its very definition—of which Mandelbrot is unaware. Elliott modeled the financial markets' fractal form in 1938 and in 1940 described the Fibonacci mathematics governing his model and, if the model is accurate, therefore the form of the market. It is unfortunate if others have been hostile to Mandelbrot for his achievements. In this case, though, it is Mandelbrot's hostility that requires a response. Regarding "pointing out predecessors," one scientist's email,[1] listing five sources, says, "Several groups in the world have noticed previously that more precise models of self-affinity and multi-self-affinity (loosely called multifractality by Mandelbrot) can better describe the real stock market." Also, defensiveness is hardly the issue when it is Elliott whom I am defending; ignoring attacks and omissions would be an injustice.*

I haven't spoken to you for many years, but I wish to congratulate you on your response to the *Scientific American* article on Mandelbrot. I have read a number of articles and books written by Mandelbrot over the years, and I endorse your overall rebuttal of his recent article wholeheartedly. I was in fact very lucky to have subscribed in May (having read Mandelbrot's article in the *Scientific American*), not knowing that you would refute his claims but delighted that you took him so head-on.

In some of my own research over the years and in business practice in general, I have found a tendency for people to claim all sorts of innovations as their own. This practice is so disturbing to the investigative mind (which of its nature is non-defensive) that your rebuttal is all the more pleasing. In fact, I think that the way you analysed the article and carefully went through each passage was first rate.

— Stephen Barrett
June 11, 1999

Thanks for your well-documented and thorough essays regarding Benoit Mandelbrot's intellectual theft of the ideas, even the principles, of R.N. Elliott's seminal works. I, too, am appalled at the use of perjorative terminology by Mandelbrot, whose only intent can be to denigrate and dismiss the pioneering works that so definitely preceded his "tinkerings." I find it refreshing that someone, anyone, would stand on the principle of "credit-where-credit-is-due," one of many concepts I'd thought had left the planet or at least the small corner in which I reside....

— K. Skinner, pclv.com
May 21, 1999

First and foremost, *Scientific American* is not a scientific journal. I have never submitted anything to this magazine myself, but I believe it does not perform pre-publication peer review. I know of no scientific or mathematical journal which publishes without expert review, nor do I believe a journal would publish any paper accompanied by literature references restricted entirely to the author's prior publications. I have never seen one yet, and I have read and reviewed thousands of physical chemistry papers during the last 60 years. Nor have I ever seen the phrase, "I claim that," used! At the most, one could accept "I propose...." My point is simply that if you have a worthwhile contribution to make, why publish it in *Scientific American*? The answer is that no self-respecting journal would accept it without review. Having been subjected to similar failure to acknowledge (my) prior contributions in chemistry, I can empathise with your disappointment that Mandelbrot failed to recognize Elliott's original work and the developments of it which you and Frost have made.

— Harry Godfrey Oswin
May 31, 1999

He must have studied Elliott quite closely to be able to fabricate this:

"2) He studied Fibonacci, the Secrets of the Great Pyramid and the prophecies of Melchi-Zedik and in 1938 announced a great 'discovery.'" I share your outrage.

— Joseph F. Joyce
May 21, 1999

I like Bob's car inventor analogy [posted on the EWI's Bulletin Board and used in the text cited in this chapter], but I have a better analogy. Remember when Vanilla Ice (the rock star) came out with the song, *"Ice Ice Baby"?* It had a real catchy tune (bass riff). It was really good, and became very popular, very quickly. Only thing is, he happened to steal the basic tune from the song by Queen (with David Bowie) called *"Under Pressure"* (it was a music video, also). Well, one day at the height of Vanilla Ice's fame and fortune, he was being interviewed on television (MTV, I think), and he was asked about it. The interviewer came right out and said, "Didn't you steal that from Queen? Do you know what Vanilla (Mandelbrot) Ice said? He said, "No I didn't, mine is an original tune. The tune in Queen's *'Under Pressure'* went like this:" *Doo doo doo...da..da do do...do do...Doo doo doo...da..da do do...do do...* "But mine went like this: "Doo *doo doo... da da do do...do do..... Doo doo doo... da da do do...do do.....* The interviewer looked at him somewhat incredulously, but you know something, Vanilla was serious as could be. He really believed that that infinitesimal little pause [between "doo doo doo" and "da da do do"] actually made that song his. Needless to say, his popularity plummeted over the coming years.

— Rich DeRosa
May 21, 1999

[Regarding] Mandelbrot, I have seen it before. He is ripping Elliott off and knows it.

— Steven W. Poser, President, Global Market Strategies, Inc.
May 14, 1999

I have a comment to make about the controversy surrounding Mandelbrot and R.N. Elliott. I am 16 years old attending Upper Dublin High School in Pennsylvania, and we are studying fractals in math. There is not very much information in our textbook, so our teacher uses programs and recent articles to teach our class about fractals. We have been taught that Mandelbrot was a genius, pioneer and ten steps short of a Mathematical God in the Twentieth Century. I sat down to write a quaint four-page paper on fractals. My unimaginative topic was the history of Mandelbrot and his cotton prices. I am rather busy, and that seemed to be the easiest topic at hand. After finding a nice webpage about Mandelbrot's childhood and a brief history on fractals, I returned to the search engine only to uncover a controversy. I honestly do not know what to think. I have the image of a small Frenchman with Einstein hair and a nice IBM computer smiling maniacally while rewriting Elliott's book for a *Scientific American* article. Can this be true? Certainly not. I understand the need for citing sources. Plagiarism means expulsion from school. I simply cannot understand Mandelbrot's motives, and even fractals cannot clearly represent this man's reality! I am confused, so I hope someone could answer my question. Has Mandelbrot fooled himself into the belief that he "invented the car" seventy years after the inventor made the first model? Or is Mandelbrot actually a genius who compiled these images and predictions using strict mathematical procedure?

—David Wengert
May 25, 1999

*Prechter replies: Mandelbrot is certainly one of the mathematical gods of the twentieth century. He discovered the ubiquity of fractals and revealed their mathematics, thereby fundamentally and immeasurably expanding the world of geometry, an accomplishment on a par with Euclid's. So he is indeed a genius; he is just not the* only *genius.* **Elliott discovered the hierarchical nature of financial markets, catalogued their quasi-geometric forms, explained their mathematical base, linked the entire process to universal forms, and then developed a fractal model of market progression, all on his own in a decade and a half, after his 60th birthday, without the aid of computers.** *Is that genius, or what?*

*Elliott's and Mandelbrot's financial models are different. Elliott claimed (rightly, in my opinion) to have discovered the pattern behind financial markets, which is a specific (robust) fractal. Mandelbrot has not explored pattern but proceeds as if markets are indefinite fractals. Mandelbrot's mathematics do not contradict Elliott's model; they support it.*

Mandelbrot derides Elliott the man with obvious bias, as if to head off anyone's exploring the man's work, and summarily dismisses Elliott's pattern model without any contrary evidence or discussion. Regardless of one's views on the specificity of the financial market fractal, Elliott did come first, and Mandelbrot did read his work. Perhaps Mandelbrot (as some colleagues appear to believe) recoils from the possibility that the reverence he enjoys might be partially parceled out to another. If Elliott is wrong, science will tell us. If Elliott is right, his genius is comparable to Mandelbrot's. Were Elliott alive, he would be urging his primacy with vigor, though with far more courtesy than Mandelbrot has shown.

Mr. Prechter, you cleared up my confusion concerning Mr. Mandelbrot, and I ended up writing my paper on financial fractals. I appreciate you taking the time to answer. Thank you.

— Sincerely, David Wengert

## NOTES

[1] Several scientists responded with like dismay and emailed us with comments of support. They declined to have their comments published due to their perception of risk in opposing such a renowned figure.

## Chapter 42

# *More of the Same Over the Ensuing Decade*

### A Lecture at Emory

At 4 p.m. on Saturday, May 11, 2002, I attended a lecture by Benoit Mandelbrot in Room 208 of White Hall at Emory University in Atlanta. That evening, the university was to present him with an honorary doctorate. It was a rare opportunity to hear the famous mathematician speak.

Mandelbrot ran through a list of the pioneers of fractals, being careful to point out their shortcomings. For example, he noted with a wry smile that George Cantor, inventor of the Cantor Set, had the "unfortunate fate that his papers were not destroyed," since they reveal that he believed his fractal compositions "had nothing to do with the real world."

Though Mandelbrot cited half a dozen figures in the history of fractals, and despite the response to his *Scientific American* article, he omitted any mention of R.N. Elliott. It is disappointing to discover that this great scientist continues simultaneously to ignore Elliott and to claim territory that belongs to him.

In his lecture, Mandelbrot showed slides of the drawings presented in Chapter 39 as Figures 2 and 4. Figure 2 also appears on page 51 of his new book for 2002, *Gaussian Self-Affinity and Fractals*. In that book, Mandelbrot comments,

> This is a very special family of constructions for which Chapter H2 will propose the (newly coined) term, "tile self-affinities." For many purposes, however, this very restricted family proves to be sufficiently versatile. In particular, it includes – hence relates to one another – special examples that provide "cartoons" of almost every basic fractal or multifractal behavior examined in M 1997E, M 1999N [i.e., his papers], this book, *and elsewhere*.[1]

Presumably, that wide net captures Elliott's "cartoons" as well. As far as Mandelbrot is concerned, that is all that needs to be said.

## Mandelbrot Dismisses Wolfram

Later that year, pioneering scientist Stephen Wolfram wrote a review of Mandelbrot's autobiography, *The Fractalist*, for the November 24, 2002 issue of *The Wall Street Journal*. In a gracious appraisal of Mandelbrot's achievements from a self-professed supporter, Wolfram nevertheless had to touch on his own experience with Mandelbrot's treatment of him:

> In 2002, my book "A New Kind of Science"—in which I argued that many phenomena across science are the complex results of relatively simple, program-like rules—appeared. Mandelbrot seemed to see it as a direct threat, once declaring that "*Wolfram's 'science' is not new except when it is clearly wrong; it deserves to be completely disregarded.*" In private, though, several mutual friends told me, he fretted that in the long view of history it would overwhelm his work.[2]

That Mandelbrot was driven to dismiss the work of the great Stephen Wolfram elevates the status of Mr. Elliott to being a comparable threat to Mandelbrot's desire for lone eminence. Wolfram's seminal book post-dated books by Mandelbrot, who could have tried to claim somehow that his own work inspired it. That Mandelbrot went to greater lengths to stifle Elliott's work implies that he saw him as the greater threat. This is undoubtedly true, as Elliott's work on the structure of financial prices pre-dates by decades Mandelbrot's initial work in the very same field, thereby opposing his claim to the discovery of fractals.

## Erasing Pioneers of the Mandelbrot Set

In March 2009, *Scientific American* republished its article from April 1990 discussing controversies over Mandelbrot's claims to originality in discovering the Mandelbrot set. Here is a taste of what the article says other mathematicians have experienced:

> Mandelbrot claims that he and he alone discovered the Mandelbrot set—which has fractal properties—about a decade ago. Three other mathematicians have challenged his claim.

Douady now says that he and other mathematicians began to think that Mandelbrot took too much credit for work done by others on the set and in related areas of chaos. "He loves to quote himself," Douady says.

Krantz introduced a new element into the debate by stating that the Mandelbrot set "was not invented by Mandelbrot but occurs explicitly in the literature a couple of years before the term 'Mandelbrot set' was coined." A subtly different claim of precedence has been made by Hubbard, who...began using a computer to map out sets of complex numbers generated by an iterative process known as Newton's method. In late 1978 one of Hubbard's graduate students, Frederick Kochman, approached Mandelbrot at a conference and showed him Hubbard's pictures. [S]hortly thereafter Mandelbrot wrote a letter to Hubbard inviting him to IBM to discuss his work. In the letter, which Hubbard kept, Mandelbrot wrote: "When sampling the works of Fatou and Julia, I had thought of doing these things myself, but had not mustered the courage. Nevertheless I can claim that I was awaiting your pictures for a long long time." ...Hubbard says he was and continues to be "outraged" that Mandelbrot did not give him credit in the 1980 paper and later writings. "It was a breach of mathematical ethics," he asserts.[3]

*(excerpts only; the entire article is posted at http://www.scientificam-erican.com/article.cfm?id=mandelbrot-set-1990-horgan)*

In the above-cited article, one mathematician is quoted saying that Mandelbrot "is reluctant to quote others who aren't dead." But the record shows that he treats dead pioneers just as badly as those living.

One of the mathematicians quoted in the article said politely, "I just wish Mandelbrot were a little more gentlemanly." Little did I know that his behavior was about to get even worse.

### Strong-Arm Tactics in 2009: The Sad Case of *Colours of Infinity*

A film titled *Colours of Infinity*, released in 1995, celebrates the beauty of fractals and discusses their ubiquity in the world. This knowledge was described mathematically and made manifest by Benoit Mandelbrot. In 2004, Clear Books decided to create a book of the same title, and the editor asked me to contribute a chapter to it. I submitted a chapter on Elliott waves of social mood and their socionomic effects in social action. Designed for the general public, it was hardly profound, but it served to expand the scope of the book to discuss fractals in the realm of social causality, an area Mandelbrot never addressed. The editor and publisher were pleased enough to include it in the book.

In 2009, the publisher decided to reprint the book. Apparently it had not originally secured the rights properly for reprinting, so it asked the editor to secure the chapter writers' permissions for republication.

When the editor contacted me, of course I said yes. I spent a few days improving upon the original version and was ready to send it. Then a strange thing happened. On December 8, 2009, he sent an email, apologizing for the disappointing news that Mandelbrot had submitted a new chapter, titled "Fractal Financial Fluctuations," and that he was going to substitute that new chapter for mine.

I called him to find out what was going on, and he said he was concerned that Mandelbrot's chapter and mine did not "mix." This was not true in an aesthetic sense, since the book was wide-ranging enough to include a chapter on the work of M.C. Escher. I assured him that a discussion of the first model to propose fractal fluctuation of financial prices, and my extension of it to describe fractal fluctuations in social mood was completely different from Mandelbrot's treatment and did expand the scope and interest of the book. We had a 20-minute chat, and he said, "Thank you. I have decided to keep your chapter in the book." That same afternoon, I received another email from him. It read,

> Oh dear, Robert. I am in a really tough place. If I keep you in Mandelbrot will withdraw both his papers, which will leave me nothing.
>
> A rock and a hard place! As you can appreciate he does not leave me any choice. Without him the whole project – THE COLOURS OF INFINITY – becomes meaningless. I am, as we say, stuffed. Sorry. I did try.
>
> I will attempt a revised edition in due course. In the meantime I would appreciate your support and good will.
>
> Many thanks.[4]

So, Mandelbrot insisted that the editor delete my chapter and replace it with a new one by him. If the editor refused, he would deny permission to include any of his material and withdraw from the project, thereby killing it. The editor is a pleasant person who simply felt he had no choice in the matter.

I informed the editor that I would play the gentleman and not get in the way of his business decision. Having seen Mandelbrot replace Elliott's seminal proposal with his own claims in *Scientific American*, I added, "I suspect that his new chapter will substitute his own wave illustrations, as if Elliott's work from 1938 never existed."

My suspicions proved founded when the second edition came out. Indeed, Mandelbrot's substitute chapter stakes his *Scientific American* claim once again, without the inconvenience of my chapter's testimony. So, by gutting Elliott's model from this record, Mandelbrot maneuvered to keep his name on the deed to Elliott's property.

Most scientists would have dealt with the issue, not railroaded it out of the way. There was room—physically at least—for both chapters.

On October 31, 2012, David Pennock, co-author of Chapter 6 in the book, posted an article on Yahoo.com on the approaching presidential election and included the case for socionomic causality of election outcomes. He kindly noted that I had been a "co-contributor" with him and linked readers to *Colours of Infinity* on Amazon. Little did he know my contribution had been erased. The contents pages from the two editions are reproduced on the following two pages.

Copies of the original edition are still available on Amazon. You can get a feeling for my banned chapter by reading Chapters 1, 2, 3, 8 and 20 in *The Wave Principle of Human Social Behavior*, from which it was condensed.

### And When Did He Know It?

Mandelbrot's failure to credit Elliott may be more egregious than it already appears. It is clear from Mandelbrot's initial abstract for a 1963 paper on financial fluctuations that he already knew about technical market analysis. On page 371 of his 1997 book, *Fractals and Scaling in Finance*, he reproduced the initial abstract, which states, "The [random walk model of the stock market] is contradicted by facts in four ways, at least: ... (3) Successive price changes ... exhibit a large number of recognizable patterns, which are, of course, the basis of the technical analysis of stocks.... I shall show that there is a simple way to solve difficulties (1), (2) and (4), and – to some extent – difficulty (3)." In other words, he intended to propose a model that would somewhat account for patterns in real data that technical analysts had observed,

## ORIGINAL TABLE OF CONTENTS, 2004:

# Contents

**REVISED TABLE OF CONTENTS, 2010:**

# Contents

as opposed to academic models assuming full randomness, which do not account for such patterns. Since then, he has distanced himself from technical analysis, but he cannot delete from the record the fact that he knew about it.

As to the specifically proposed "recognizable patterns" of which he was aware, Edwards and Magee's book, *Technical Analysis of Stock Trends* had been published in 1947. But it is unlikely that Mandelbrot would have taken inspiration from isolated, independent "head and shoulders," "flag" and "scallop" patterns, none of which are fractal. R.N. Elliott's all-encompassing, self-dependent, iterative model is another matter, and Mandelbrot's theoretical "fractal fluctuation" pictures (see Figures 1 through 4 at the start of this chapter) are nearly identical to Elliott's. Elliott's work was also quite well known at the time, thanks to published analyses beginning in 1953 by A. Hamilton Bolton of *The Bank Credit Analyst*, and especially because of his widely distributed 1960 book, *The Elliott Wave Principle—A Critical Appraisal*. (This book is reprinted in *The Complete Elliott Wave Writings of A. Hamilton Bolton*.) Mandelbrot's comments in 1963 about technical patterns suggest that he was aware at that time of Elliott's model, probably via Bolton's book from three years prior.

### Elliott's and Mandelbrot's Differences May Ultimately Matter

For the record, one thing is clear from Mandelbrot's writing: He does not endorse Elliott's specific model of financial behavior, either generally speaking, in terms of its 5-3 wave construction, or specifically speaking, in terms of Elliott's detailed observations about the real-world fractal form of financial markets. On the contrary, he maintained that financial markets fluctuate as random, or indefinite, fractals. Edgar Peters, following Mandelbrot, summed up his mentor's view: "Coastlines are good examples of random fractals. Stock prices are comparable to coastlines."[5] In 2004, Mandelbrot confirmed a necessary consequence of his model: "*I agree with the orthodox economists that stock prices are not predictable in any useful sense of the term.*"[6] We should remember Mandelbrot's dismissal of Elliott and his hierarchical-fractal model if and when the scientific community finally accepts the validity of the Wave Principle.

New discoveries in the field of complexity theory as well as natural fractal forms, particularly in biology (see Parts I and III of *The Wave Principle of Human Social Behavior and the New Science of*

*Socionomics*), are rapidly yielding more and more knowledge bolstering the case that the Wave Principle is a correct description of financial reality. In our opinion, there will be no escaping this juggernaut of discovery. Time and science are on our side. In the end, truth will out, and Elliott will get his due. I call on every concerned scientist to help assure that R.N. Elliott is properly credited with having originated the idea of fractal modeling in finance and pioneering its utility.

## 2011 Obituary in *Physics Today*

The June 2011 issue of *Physics Today* published an obituary on Benoit Mandelbrot by University of Oregon physicist Richard Taylor. Nearly a decade earlier, Taylor had been invited to write the announcement for the *Proctor Prize* when it was awarded to Mandelbrot in 2002. A respectful piece in every way, it reads, "Mandelbrot will be best remembered for his epic book *The Fractal Geometry of Nature* (W.H. Freeman, 1982), which changed the way that many of us view the mathematical structure of the world." Taylor naturally omitted mention of Mandelbrot's objectionable behavior, but he knew the history and properly cited Elliott as the first person to recognize the fractal form of financial pricing:

> Although Mandelbrot invented the term in 1975, he didn't actually discover fractals. In the late 19th and early 20th centuries, scientists such as Karl Weierstrass, Helge von Koch, Waclaw Sierpiński, and Giuseppe Peano explored the exotic consequences of building complexity from fractal shapes. However, they saw no connection between their mathematical creations and the physical world around them. Mandelbrot criticized such pure geometry as being "cold and dry." His interests were instead closer to those of Ralph Elliott, who in 1938 showed that the temporal patterns in stock market variations repeat over different time scales. Mandelbrot extended his own explorations of the stock market to show that similar repetitions occur in other temporal patterns, such as the rise and fall of the Nile River. His broadening horizons triggered a thirst for understanding the complexity of physical phenomena rather than the cleanliness of pure mathematics.[7]

We can be thankful not only for scientists of genius but also for those of integrity.

## NOTES

[1] Mandelbrot, Benoit. (2002). *Gaussian self-affinity and fractals*. New York: Springer, p. 52.

[2] Wolfram, Stephen, "The Father of Fractals," *The Wall Street Journal*, November 24, 2002, p.C7.

[3] Horgan, John, "Who Discovered the Mandelbrot Set?" *Scientific American*, April 1990 and March 2009.

[4] Lesmoir-Gordon, Nigel, email dated December 8, 2009.

[5] Peters, Edgar E., *Chaos and Order in the Capital Markets* (1991), p.51.

[6] Benoit Mandelbrot, *The (Mis)Behavior of Markets* (2006), p.6.

[7] Taylor, Richard, "Benoit Mandelbrot," *Physics Today*, June 2011, p.63.

# Part VII:

# SOCIONOMICS
## AND
# QUANTUM PHYSICS

*Chapter 43*

# Parallel Revolutions in the
# Physical and Social Sciences

**Preface**

My favorite books are ones that dispel decades, centuries or millennia of misconception in one brilliant stroke. Intricate, long-standing
misconceptions are called "error pyramids." Perhaps the greatest error
pyramid ever constructed in the hard sciences was the one built around
the false premise of a geocentric universe. Some planets appeared to act
weirdly as a result of this error, such as Mercury moving "retrograde"
with respect to Earth. Astronomers produced complicated calculations
and theories to account for the motion of the planets in a perceived
geocentric solar system, even to the point of perfect prediction. Yet
Copernicus' 1543 book on celestial mechanics, *On the Revolution of
the Heavenly Spheres*, wiped away the entire vision. Not atypically, the
collective "Oops!" took over a century to occur. I have read only a few
books that have accomplished a similar feat, but each one was a pleasure.

One comparable achievement is J. Thomas Looney's *Shakespeare
Identified*.[1] This 1920 book attacks the problem of identifying who
Shakespeare really was in the manner of an open-minded detective
interested in facts and where they lead, not in presumption. It presents
a coherent picture of the true author. The collective "Oops!" has taken
80 years so far to play out, but after getting louder every decade, it is
now getting louder every year. When the "Stratfordians," who still issue content-free "biographies" of Shakespeare, finally give up, this one
insight will have wiped away perhaps a thousand times the print volume
that Copernicus' insight did. Encyclopedias will have to be re-written
because of Looney.

Another book that may qualify is Iman Wilkens' *Where Troy Once Stood*.[2] While I know enough about Shakespeare to be sure that Looney is correct, I cannot say the same about the *Iliad* and *Odyssey* of Homer. Yet Wilkens' book so thoroughly wipes away discrepancies between the descriptions in Homer's books and the standard scholars' attempts to locate their battles and voyages in and around the Mediterranean that the reconciliation is stunning. In a nutshell, Wilkens says that the stories are accurate accounts of a Celtic-era war between British and European continental forces and of sea voyages in the Atlantic, with astrological imagery employed to facilitate navigation. As to how the tales got to Homer, you will have to read the book. Unfortunately, that's not so easy to do. Published in 1990, the book is already out of print; you can get it only from used book dealers. This fact seems to bear out Schopenhauer's dictum, "Without exception, every original thinker is surrounded by a conspiracy of silence." Established scholars should take a stand on the book, whether in agreement or disagreement, stating *why*. Some books, to be sure, are rightfully to be ignored, such as New Age tomes. Even in such cases, however, a crafted response can devastate any claim to validity, and it stands for all time. To be silent in the face of a substantial effort, on the other hand, implies stubbornness and fear. Is Wilkens' thesis too challenging to scholars who have published volumes on the traditional interpretation? If so, we have an explanation for the silence. One reviewer anticipates the defense, "Homer wasn't being literal." That's what the Stratfordians say about Shakespeare's intimate descriptions of court life. When the truth, if that's what Wilkens has given us, becomes accepted, then the time-honored attempts at mapping the *Iliad* and the *Odyssey* from a Greek perspective will appear as a fool's errand. They all will have been due to a stubborn premise, born of a reasonable—yet ultimately untenable in the face of contradictory evidence—assumption of a connection between the Greek language of the author and the "Greek" names in the book and the location of its subject matter. This is the same simple-minded deduction that rules Stratfordianism: The name "Shakespeare" is on the cover, so the author must be a guy with that name. (Tell that to Sam Clemens.)

I also include *Stonehenge Decoded*,[3] by Hawkins and White, on my list. In a brief, scholarly volume, Hawkins vaporizes the condescending view of the designers of Stonehenge as a gaggle of mystic Druids and showed us why it was actually a team of intelligent, stone-age astronomers and engineers.

Probably also in this category is *Dr. Atkins' Diet Revolution*,[4] by Robert C. Atkins, MD. His thesis has been updated and expanded in such books as *The Zone*[5] and *Protein Power*.[6] These writers present anthropological and biological evidence that a healthy diet is high in protein, fat and vegetables, and low in starch and sugar. This thesis virtually *inverts* the standard "food pyramid" so widely promoted by nutritionists and the government in the twentieth century. Until recently, one could hardly cite Atkins without being called a crank, but research from Harvard on up is lately validating the diet.

Last is a recent book called *Drunks, Drugs and Debits*,[7] by Doug Thorburn, which might better be titled, *Turmoil—How to Spot the Secret Alcoholic/Addict in Your Life*. Doug draws from myriad sources to contend that people do not become addicts because they suffer from psychological problems, but rather they suffer from psychological problems because they are addicts, by genetic disposition. The symptom and the cause are the reverse of what most people believe. An army of psychologists and psychiatrists has wasted years treating people— sometimes with more drugs—for severe psychological problems that in fact are the symptoms of undetected addiction. Rehabilitation is erroneously focused on symptoms when it should be focused on the cause. A psychoanalyst friend tells me that Doug is not the first to propose this argument, and I have no reason to doubt that to be the case, but if so, the idea has been mostly ignored. Thorburn's book is an independent investigation and a comprehensive tour de force. After reading it, you can diagnose probable addiction not only in people close to you but also from afar based on reports of behavior patterns. If he succeeds in popularizing this information, it will save many lives and billions of dollars. I like the thesis of this book because it posits *a reversal of the presumed order of causality*, which is what I have tried to do with respect to social events and social mood in *The Wave Principle of Human Social Behavior*.

The following discussion will introduce you to a new book on my list, which has yet to be published: Lewis E. Little's *Theory of Elementary Waves—A Causal Explanation of Quantum Phenomena*.[8] This thesis, in contrast to most of those in the above list, is in the hard sciences, specifically, physics. It is of additional interest because the revolution that the author will ultimately bring about parallels the revolution that I hope socionomics will effect in the social sciences.

**Foreword**

The path I have taken to get to the point of composing this investigation might be of some interest. In college, I switched majors twice because there are some things upon which I refuse to waste my time. For example, after spending a day with philosophy books by Kant and Hegel, I vowed to avoid philosophy courses at all costs. Hegel's obliqueness seemed purposeful, as if the author deliberately chose to make it nearly impossible to follow his trains of thought. Kant's challenge to reality and its perception was a clever mind game but contradictory and false, so there was no point in studying it. (Much later, I came to appreciate the fundamental value of philosophy, but that's another story.)

I quickly rejected my first two majors, physics and economics, for similar reasons. In physics, the biggest topic was quantum theory, which sounded absurd. It proposed that a subatomic particle had multiple identities simultaneously when it was not being observed but condensed into one upon its being observed. A famous analogy is that of a cat in a box that is not dead *or* alive but both dead *and* alive simultaneously, the final state to be determined by the action of someone opening the box to look.[9] Broadly speaking, we were told, one's consciousness can change the nature of reality simply by deciding to observe it. People who introduced this idea to you would look at you with a mischievous grin, as if they were supremely clever and your skepticism was sad ignorance. I could not imagine pursuing such ideas as my life's work.

I was interested in economics, so I took an economics course in my freshman year, soon thinking that it would be my major. As we ploughed deeper through Samuelson's *Economics*, though, I began to get discouraged. While the book is scholarly and wide in scope, many of the formulae were too "pat," ignoring the changeability of people, and the book is cavalier on the matters of central banking, forced redistribution of income and other government monopolies and intervention. I saw these things as errors in principle (and evils as well) and was aghast at the intertwining of politics—the use of force—and economics, as if the two belonged together. (Of course, I now realize that the idea of a legitimate intertwining is the dominant view of economists.) In the final week of class, our professor took a deep breath and said, "I have now taught you what I am paid to teach you. But you may be surprised to find out that I don't believe most of this stuff." Five of us—you could tell who we were by glancing around—sat up straight and quickly adopted a state of keen attention. Would he finally dismiss all the errors? Would he deliver us from Keynesianism? "Actually," said the professor, "I'm a Marxist." The five bodies deflated back into their seats. We listened for the rest of the period as he described how each neighborhood should have a mass meeting every Saturday to vote on who would do what jobs and how much they would be paid. I did not take another economics course after that.

After two years of uncertainty, I finally settled on psychology. At least the professors were honest about the subject's shortcomings and its conjectural nature. It was years later before I realized that actually I *had* majored in macroeconomics by majoring in psychology. That path has led me, via R.N. Elliott, to formulate what I believe is a revolutionary idea of macroeconomic causality, so it turned out to be the right path after all. Maybe in a sense, I also took a path parallel to the one I could only have hoped to pursue in quantum physics, our next topic.

### What's Wrong with Twentieth Century Quantum Mechanics

Scientists have accurately observed the patterns of sub-atomic particle emission and diffusion, yet they have come to bizarre conclusions about the universe as a result. Here is a highly simplified version of the situation: Sub-atomic particles travel by waves. The intensity of a wave affects the probability that a particle, emitted from a source, will arrive at a detector. The problem is that waves, and thus particles, do not appear to behave as one would initially expect. The famous "double-slit" experiment shows that when particles with multiple trajectories are screened by narrow slits in a barrier, the particles that arrive at various points on the surface of a flat-screen detector on the other side of the barrier create a distribution pattern. Fine. But when the detector is moved forward or back with respect to a fixed source of particles and a fixed slitted barrier, the pattern of particles reaching the detector remains constant not with respect to a straight-line trajectory from the source but *with respect to the surface of the detector*, which means that the trajectory of particles along the waves that carry them changes depending upon the location of the detector.[10] Physicists have had extreme difficulty explaining this phenomenon. Once a particle has left a source, it must go in a straight line, yet the straight line is different depending upon where the detector is placed. So physicists have proposed that reality itself changes to accommodate the observer. Werner Heisenberg, who described quantum mechanics in 1925, formulated in 1927 what has come to be called the "uncertainty principle" or "principle of indeterminacy," in which he postulated, "The 'path' [of a subatomic particle] *comes into existence only when we observe it.*"[11] To accommodate this conclusion, physicists have attempted to describe waves and sub-atomic particles not as things but only as co-existing potentials, "wave-particles," that follow all paths corresponding to all possible detector locations simultaneously *as long as they are unobserved*. These non-entities "collapse" into actuality only upon *being* observed, the very act of which literally creates an actual particle. Bingo. The mere act of looking turns an unexplained (and unexplainable) potential into an entity, which shows up on the detector one is using.[12]

The uncertainty principle, which most physicists have accepted since its formulation, states that accurate measurement of quantum behavior is *impossible in principle* because the very existence of sub-atomic particles depends upon the action or non-action of an observer, so the simple act of attempting to observe such particles alters reality, making it impossible to detect and measure any sub-atomic system without disrupting the system and thus altering the measurements.[13] Our mental/visual powers of reality alteration, which operate *whether we want them to or not*, therefore present an insurmountable impediment to truly knowing reality *because there is no constant reality to know*. The inescapable further conclusion is that there is *no direct causality from one physical event to the next*; it all depends upon consciousness, which in turn affects the paths of particles backwards in time.

How atomic particles would behave were there no conscious beings to observe them is not satisfactorily explained. How consciousness can remain constant when its domicile—a brain—is built only from unobserved non-actual potentialities is not satisfactorily explained. How certain conscious entities—we, the observers—can maintain a single identity while entities that make us up—atomic particles—have multiple potential identities whose ultimate actualization is determined by the consciousness of the observer they constitute as well as other observers simultaneously is too complex a question even to have been addressed.

The German philosopher Immanuel Kant proposed that our means of knowledge, i.e., our senses, cannot be trusted to detect any actual reality and in fact create discrete personal realities apart from "real" reality, which is in principle unknowable. Kant's formulation is surely the philosophical origin of the uncertainty principle. Heisenberg challenged the idea that "if we know the present exactly, we can calculate the future" by saying, "it is *not the conclusion that is wrong but the premise.*"[14] In other words, even the present is unknowable because reality is inconstant.

Whether stated as philosophy or as quantum physics theory, the idea is just as bogus and contradictory. If there is no constant reality, what is a detector? What is a particle? What are you? What is your mind? None of these things has definition or reality if there is no definition or reality possible. You cannot even discuss your philosophy when you have this belief, because none of your words can be trusted to mean anything. You can imagine the intellectual gymnastics required to hold such a contradictory idea. As George Orwell, an astute observer of the human mind, once observed, "There are some ideas so wrong that only a very intelligent person could believe in them."[15]

It takes no more than common sense to dismiss the resulting concoction, but it takes an objectivist intellectual to recognize the fundamental error in such ideas and to challenge them on principle. Einstein knew that the conclusion of quantum mechanics was wrong because, as he put it, "You believe in a dice-playing God and I in perfect laws in the world of things existing as real objects." In other words, consistent physical causality is a universal principle. He diplomatically stated his opinion that quantum mechanics was therefore "incomplete."[16] As we will soon see, Einstein's view has now been vindicated.

### A Parallel Error in Finance

As argued in *The Wave Principle of Human Social Behavior*, accepted "explanations" of social causality likewise begin with a false premise, a pure *assumption*, which the evidence, properly applied, refutes. This false premise, that social events shape social mood, has supported a long-standing error pyramid comprising much of the literature on social causality, which includes macroeconomics, finance and history. This fundamental error has suffused the practice of social forecasting, which is why it has a nearly unblemished record of failure (unlike quantum physics, whose predictions are accurate). This error, one would presume, has been around since the dawn of humanity, which makes it one of the longest-standing errors of human thought. We have explored the magical thinking in conventional quantum mechanics, so let us turn to why some financiers and economists, probably without realizing it, are also using magic to "explain" how things work.

First, we are forced to take a detour because of the miserable state of what passes for knowledge in macroeconomics today. Good economists know that the stock market is the single best leading indicator of the economy, but they are few and far between and rarely quoted in the press. Most economists are so lacking in knowledge about their field that they do not even *realize* that social mood trends precede compatible social actions. All day, newspapers and television present interviews with economists and financial professionals who offer "forecasts" for the stock market by reference to current events or by guessing what future events will cause it to move. They are oblivious to the fact that trends in the stock market, which is an immediate register of shared mood, *precede* events that are compatible with those trends. An analogous situation in physics would be one in which the majority of physicists did not realize that wave trajectory precedes particle detection. They all know that fact because they are scientists who pay attention to details.

As it happens, some financial professionals are indeed observant enough to see that stock market trends precede economic trends. To explain this chronology, they offer the idea that "the stock market discounts the future." In other words, while most economists believe that *current* events are causal to present stock price movements, these financiers believe that *future* events are causal to present stock price movements. The essence of their premise—that social events dictate the trend of the market—is the same; only the chronology is different.

The discounting idea has been around for at least a century, as evidenced in the writings of Charles Dow, founder of *The Wall Street Journal*, who died in 1902. The succeeding *Journal* editor, William Peter Hamilton, packaged and expanded upon Dow's ideas. In 1911, he wrote,

> The superficial observer is constantly startled to find that the stock market fails to respond to sudden and important developments; while it seems to be guided by impulses too obscure to be traceable. Consciously or unconsciously, the movement of prices reflects not the past but the future. When coming events cast their shadows before, the shadow falls on the New York Stock Exchange.[17]

In Hamilton's 1922 book, *The Stock Market Barometer*, a title that accurately reflects his view, he added, "The price movement represents the aggregate knowledge of Wall Street and, above all, its aggregate knowledge of coming events."[18] Dow Theorist Robert Rhea used similar words in his 1932 book, *The Dow Theory*:

*The Averages Discount Everything.* Whenever a group of market students get together, some one of them nearly always starts a debate as to whether stock prices, by their action, discount events not foreseen by the individual speculator. Surely all students who have an understanding of the Dow theory *know* this to be a fact.[19]

As market forecaster E. George Schaefer put it,

Since investors by their very nature constantly scan the news and react either bullishly or bearishly to it, the movements of the averages reflect the sum total of collective investment thought through the willingness of investors to purchase or sell stocks. As a result, trends in business are usually discounted six months to a year ahead.[20]

This idea is so common that I ran across it again just this week in a magazine, in which an advisor and money manager agrees, "The market is a mechanism for discounting the future, most notably earnings per share for the coming two or three years."[21] If all economists understood the proper chronology between the market and events, this theory of social causality would undoubtedly be as widely accepted as quantum theory is among physicists and even used successfully to forecast macroeconomic trends. The question is whether the theory behind that success would be correct.

I do not wish to deduct anything from the brilliance of the seminal thinkers Dow, Hamilton and Rhea, who remain ahead of their time a century later in many ways. Not the least of these is simply in having observed that movement in the stock averages precedes compatible economic events. Pundits today are routinely "startled to find that the stock market fails to respond to sudden and important developments" because of their entrenched yet erroneous belief that the market reacts to news. Hamilton, moreover, made wise accommodations in saying that the process is "guided by *impulses*" and takes place "consciously *or unconsciously*," phrases that anticipate elements of socionomics. Nevertheless, can we really embrace beliefs that "the movement of prices *reflects* the future," as if the future is a fixed edifice impacting the present, that "stock prices, by their action, discount events not foreseen by the individual speculator," as if a mass of individuals can know what separate individuals cannot, and that "coming events cast their shadows before," i.e., *backwards in time*? Did investors six months ago really divine today's newspaper?

These beliefs are as flatly espoused among certain financiers as conventional quantum theory is among physicists, and they are, to be blunt, just as ridiculous. How can a non-existing social future months or years ahead impress itself upon a mass of presently existing people? The social future must be unknown to the mass of investors because *it hasn't happened yet*. The very idea that investors en masse divine the future is a lazy explanation for the properly observed chronology between stock market trends and parallel economic trends. I seriously doubt that anyone has stopped to think about what he is saying with such a theory. Indeed, I have never seen a convincing attempt to account for it. As a typical example, MIT professor Paul Samuelson's discussion of this idea contains (1) the fundamental error of event causality, (2) the idea that the majority of people can guess the future trend of the economy and (3) the fact that it is impossible for anyone to do so, all in one statement. Here is what he says in his classic textbook:

> To the age-old question, Does the market follow business activity or business activity the market? no simple answer can be given. It is reasonably clear that business activity, national income, and corporate earnings determine stock prices and not vice versa; and also that the psychological effects of market movements no longer have primary importance. But still the market can occasionally *anticipate* changes in national income and total purchasing power. It then appears to be leading them when really it is following what it thinks they will be later.
>
> *How to Invest*: There are no simply stated fool-proof rules for making money out of the stock market. Anyone who can accurately predict the future course of business activity will prosper; but there is no such person.[22]

Notice the irony: No individual can predict anything at all about the social future, but the mass of investors supposedly can and does, all the time.

Rhea's and Schaeffer's explanations attempt to accommodate this contradiction by asserting that individuals can divine their own personal business futures, and the resulting *aggregation* of small divinations creates the stock market's trends, while no one individual can divine the whole process.[23] Clearly, though, if the majority of investors could divine even their own future business success, they would then be correct on the macroeconomic trend, so this proposed dichotomy between micro and macro divination is untenable. Further distressing to the theory of individual divination is that the data contradict it. Indicators of market psychology typically reveal aggressive bullishness during and well after market peaks and aggressive bearishness during and after market lows. For a good example, see Chapters 6 and 7 in *Conquer the Crash*. This, of course, is as it must be because investors (aside from socionomists) are necessarily aware only of the events and conditions of the present and the past, not the future. The passage below from *The Wave Principle of Human Social Behavior* addresses this aspect of the "discounting" theory:

### Reasoning from Conditions to Markets – in Advance
The belief that news affects the market is the lowest level of misunderstanding, and it is the most common. There is a higher level of misunderstanding, which at least pays tribute to the fact that the market moves ahead of events. Technicians say that the reason earnings lag stock prices is that smart investors anticipate, or "discount," the future, in other words, guess the future correctly.

While this position is a time-honored and valiant attempt to explain why events lag stock prices, I believe it is false. The idea of the mass of investors possessing near-omniscience about the economic future is difficult to defend. Nor does it explain why in 1928 the market foresaw nothing but blue sky, in 1929 very suddenly foresaw depression, and in early 1930 saw a recovery that never happened.

One might try to make a case that smart investors sell stocks when they get a whiff of trouble in their own businesses. If the economy typically turned before or even coincidentally with stocks, this argument might be plausible. But stocks lead the economy, normally by months. Then there is the problem that when you ask investors what they think, they express no inkling of coming economic changes. In fact, in the aggregate, they always erroneously anticipate the opposite of what then happens. At the start of a bull trend, the vast majority is bearish and wrong, and at the start of a bear trend, it is bullish and wrong.[24]

Technical analysts incorporate the idea of discounting but make a contradictory claim, namely that patterns exist in the market. You can have one or the other but not both. If investors discounted the future, the market would still turn ahead of future developments, but it would not display reliable patterns, because the future is chaotic. Which claim should be jettisoned? For me, the answer is easy. Discounting is absurd. No one knows the future. The only potentially valid claim is that patterns exist.

Up to this point, I have taken the time to challenge the two conventional views on non-Elliott-wave grounds, but there is a shortcut to understanding why they are wrong. The fact that the market is patterned according to the Wave Principle establishes the primacy of social mood in financial market valuation and contraindicates the primacy of events. As *The Wave Principle of Human Social Behavior* observes,

> Because markets are patterned, the idea of near-perfect collective forecasting must be false. Otherwise, future events would have to be patterned according to the Wave Principle, and the collective would have to anticipate each nuance perfectly. This is an untenable position.[25]

The idea that investors price stocks today according to events in the future parallels one of the great errors in the conventional theory of quantum mechanics. Little states, "[The current theory of] quantum mechanics forces one to conclude that...*events can affect one another backwards in time....*" This is exactly what the current theory of "discounting" espouses with respect to social causality, and it is just as erroneous. "What must one say of a belief in the existence of inexplicable phenomena?" asks Little about his field. "This amounts to a reversion to the ideas of the middle ages—the very ideas supposedly overridden by modern methods."[26] Discounting theory amounts to the same thing. These parallel errors have parallel solutions.

### Socionomics Clears Up the Mystery of Apparent Discounting

R.N. Elliott took finance out of the Middle Ages when he said properly, "At best, news is the tardy recognition of forces that have already been at work for some time."[27] Better stated, news is the tardy *manifestation* of those forces. The following passage, from *The Wave Principle of Human Social Behavior*, gives the proper explanation for why trends in the stock market precede trends in the economy:

> The truth is that the stock market does not see into the future, as the discounting idea suggests; it reflects instantaneously the causes of the future. Optimistic people buy stocks and decide to expand their businesses; depressed people sell stocks and

decide to contract their businesses. The economic results show up later as an apparently "discounted" economic future. The actions of human beings spurred on by an increasingly ebullient or pessimistic social mood cause earnings to rise or fall. Rising earnings are the fruits of a bull market, and falling earnings are the result of a bear.[28]

The socionomic explanation dispenses with reverse-temporal causality. It relies entirely upon chronological cause and effect. In so doing, it dispenses with magic. This is exactly what Little has done in revolutionizing quantum physics.

### Lewis E. Little Clears Up the Mystery of Quantum Mechanics

From the beginning, physicist Lewis E. Little thought properly about the problem of explaining quantum mechanics because, like Einstein, he knew that the conventional explanation is contradictory, which means that it is wrong. He did not *wonder* if it was wrong; he *knew* it was wrong, for the same reasons that one cannot properly "wonder" about ghosts, which are impossibly defined as both an entity and a non-entity, both corporeal and non-corporeal, at the same time, just as so-called "wave-particles" are defined today. Conventional attempts to explain quantum mechanics, Little observes, are fundamentally flawed: "Proofs claiming that one couldn't avoid contradictions didn't prove that those contradictions were real. They rather proved that the premises of those proofs already contained a contradiction."[†] The proper orientation to conventional quantum mechanics theory is dismissal on philosophical grounds because metaphysically, reality precedes and is independent of consciousness. To be conscious means to be conscious *of* something and *within* something, each of which must exist and have identity for consciousness to occur.

Understanding the basic error of thought led Little to look for a proper explanation for quantum behavior that did not rely on ghosts and psychokinesis. He began by recognizing that the whole idea that *observation*—mere consciousness—should be credited for the results of measurements of quantum activity is an unwarranted conclusion, because the only thing that physicists have shown to affect the path of sub-atomic particles is *the placement of a physical detector*, which is an entirely different thing from consciousness. By thus isolating the physical cause from the metaphysical conclusion, Little's mind paved the way for a solution.

Little describes 20th century quantum mechanics as the second-biggest error pyramid ever constructed in the hard sciences, and he has taken a deep breath and blown it over with one mighty puff. In 1996, *Physics Essays* published his ground-breaking paper, "The Theory of Elementary Waves." Little's thesis challenges the conventional view of quantum mechanics and presents a new theory that places activity at the sub-atomic level on the same grounds of cause and effect as all other physics. "Bell's theorem," says Little, "coupled with the experiments confirming the associated quantum mechanical predictions, does not 'refute reality,' as is so frequently claimed." Rather, quantum mechanics "can be understood in an objective manner, in which facts are facts, causality is valid, and reality is real."[†] To do this, he has challenged one of quantum physicists' unexamined premises, a pure assumption, which the evidence, properly applied, refutes.

## Little's Insight from Elementary Waves:
## The Direction of Waves Is Opposite the Conventional Assumption

Here is a summary of what Little says:

Conventional theorists are making a false presumption. Because it seems natural and reasonable, they assume, without evidence (indeed, in contradiction to the evidence), that the waves that carry sub-atomic particles travel in the same direction as the particles. It seems to be a logical assumption, but it leads to a nonsensical theory. In fact, he proposes, *waves actually travel in the opposite direction*. Waves travel *from the particle detector to the particle source*. If the intensity of a wave is strong enough to stimulate the emission of a particle, that particle travels along the path of the stimulating wave back to the detector from which the wave originates. The number of particles emitted depends upon the intensity of the stimulating wave. The qualities of an emitter also affect the number of particles that it will emit in response to a wave. Throughout the universe, waves travel from all points on the surface of all objects (including detectors) in all directions, stimulating countless emissions of particles. Each such particle then travels back to the source of the wave that stimulated its emission. Waves travel endlessly, continually stimulating emissions. Particles exert no influence on the waves that they follow. The direction of initial causation is not from particle source to destination but from destination to source. Everyone else is looking at it backwards.

**The Socionomic Insight from Elliott Waves:**
**The Direction of Causality Is Opposite the Conventional**
**Assumption**

You can imagine that when I read of Lewis' insight two years ago, I was excited. After all, I had come to the same conclusion about *social* causality, which parallels Little's thesis as follows:

Conventional theorists are making a false presumption. Because it seems natural and reasonable, they assume, without evidence (indeed, in contradiction to the evidence), that any influence that relates social events to social mood carries in the direction from events to mood. It seems to be a logical assumption, but it leads to a nonsensical theory. In fact, I propose, *the influence actually travels in the opposite direction.* Waves *originate in social mood.* If the intensity of a wave is strong enough to stimulate a social action (an "event emission"), that action will be of the same character as the mood that generated it. In collective terms, it "travels back" to impact the society that was the source of the wave. The number of participants in, and the intensity of, social actions depend upon the degree of the stimulating wave. The qualities of an individual affect the extent to which he will undertake social actions in response to a wave. Throughout the world, waves animate various groups in many ways, stimulating countless social actions, which then impact the societies whose waves stimulated their occurrence. Waves develop endlessly, continuously stimulating actions. Actions exert no influence on the waves that generate them. The direction of causation is not from social actions to social mood but from mood to actions. Everyone else is looking at it backwards.

**The Two New Theories Correct the Same Type of Errors**

Quantum physicists have gotten their mathematics down properly, so they can make probability forecasts of particle appearance at a detector. From that standpoint, their theory appears to "work." Discounting theory is almost never applied to macroeconomic forecasting, but when it is, it also appears to "work." The rare financier who gives the idea more than lip service can watch the stock market and successfully forecast changes in the economy. He assumes that the stock market has a mystical knowledge of the economy's future path, an idea similar to conventional explanations of quantum physics. In contrast, both new theories offer explanations that rely upon direct cause and effect. *Elementary waves precede and stimulate particle emissions; Elliott waves precede and stimulate social actions.*

Physicists cannot predict every particle emission, and a socionomist cannot predict every social event, but we can both make probability statements about the physical and social future, respectively. The socionomic insight brings sociology to the same point as Little's quantum physics in providing a proper theory to account for the fact that certain aspects of the future are predictable, at least to a degree of probability and generalization.

### Differences from a Perfect Analogy

Before exploring the striking parallels between the theories of elementary waves and Elliott waves, we should note that they are not precisely analogous. Here are some of the imperfections in that regard, at least in my mind, along with some possible resolutions for them.

(1) According to Little's theory, elementary waves are fundamental, i.e., irreducible to components or causes. Elliott waves are probably fundamental to growth patterns in a universal sense, because evolution for example appears to travel in Elliott waves,[29] and human thought is irrelevant to that process. Elliott waves may further be viewed as the fundamental waves of sociology in that they stimulate actions, much as Little's waves stimulate particle emissions. Without Elliott waves, there might be no social growth or progress, perhaps no social action at all. In human society, though, Elliott waves may be viewed as reducible in having a more fundamental cause, such as the cooperative herding impulse common to all human minds[30] or perhaps some outside physical cause of which we are unaware.[31]

(2) In Little's physics, waves and particles are discrete physical objects. The Wave Principle operates *within* physical entities and effects actions *through* physical entities, but I am not sure whether Elliott waves themselves are physical objects. They are objects in the sense of comprising electrical impulses within brains and nervous systems, but I am inclined to call Elliott waves processes, not objects. At the same time, there is an analogous aspect respecting the manifestations of the two types of waves. We cannot see Elliott waves, but we can plot their various effects—such as decisions about securities prices—on a graph to make them manifest and thus *see them* as if they were physical objects. Likewise, we cannot see elementary waves with our eyes or even with instruments, but we can plot their effects—such as the patterns of particles reaching a detector—on a graph. That is why Little postulates a *theory* of elementary waves; if we could see them, it would not be a

matter of theory. The same is true of Elliott waves and the socionomic hypothesis.

(3) The results of the two types of waves are not identical, but they do seem to be similar: Elementary waves stimulate physical emissions, and Elliott waves stimulate physical actions.

(4) The particles within entities organize environmental elementary waves into mutually coherent elementary waves, which then stimulate particle emissions from *other entities*. Discrete limbic systems in a social setting may similarly organize various individuals' mental waves into mutually coherent Elliott waves, but they then stimulate actions, for the most part, from some of the *same* entities that participated in those waves. One possible exception that would mimic the results of elementary waves would be an Elliott wave among a population stirring action from an individual who had no emotional stake, merely a dispassionate one, in that action (for example, someone who sells beverages at a pep rally or trades markets based on Elliott waves).

(5) In Little's theory, particles on the surface of all objects reflect and organize elementary waves, although only some objects emit particles in response. Elliott waves may be similar: All people participate in the organization of Elliott waves, but only some of them take actions in response to particular Elliott waves. Even then, though, the emitter of a particle in physics is never the same as the source of the wave that stimulates it. Those taking social actions are always among the participants in the Elliott waves that stimulate them.

(6) Little asserts, "One derives the behavior of larger systems from the behavior of the parts. (Even 'emergent' properties can—must—be so derived.) In the elementary waves theory the waves simply exist, with their various properties. They are primary constituents of reality. Thus there is no need to deduce their behavior from anything." We can look at this statement several ways with respect to Elliott waves. (1) Elliott waves are primary, like elementary waves, and need no explanation from the action of constituent parts. (2) Unlike elementary waves, Elliott waves are emergent properties that derive from their primary constituents, i.e., the unconscious mentation of individual participants in social trends. (3) The premise is wrong. In formological[32] systems, the behavior of the whole is a function of its organizational form, to which smaller parts conform. Human beings, for example, have overall behavioral properties over and above the behavioral properties of the atoms that make them up, as evidenced by the fact that one's atoms change all the time without affecting the organization of the larger

system. The behavior of the parts is a function of the behavior of the whole, not the other way around.[33] Elliott waves are a formological system, not a summation of component properties. Economists lament the "butterfly effect" destroying all ability to predict social events when in fact, the system is not only chaotic but also formological, which is why substantial prediction—prediction specifically of the character of social action—is possible. Individuals' rational thinking does not register in an Elliott wave; only impulsive herding behavior does, so the individual property of rationality coexists apart from the Elliott wave dynamic. The herding impulse in an individual limbic system cannot express itself within an Elliott wave without other human beings to mimic, the larger context giving form to the component.

(7) The physical world is fully deterministic. The social world is much less so, and the individual far less than that. As far as limbic system stimuli and responses go, there is substantial collective determinism, because these unconscious mental processes produce Elliott waves. Yet differences in individual knowledge, rationality and free will preclude determinism in individual thinking, and those same differences preclude determinism in both individual actions and specific social actions, the latter of which are akin to chaotic processes subject to the "butterfly effect" in which previous actions and situations affect later ones. Nevertheless, quantum physics still suffers from unpredictability, if not as much as with Elliott waves. Compare these formulations to see the difference:

*From Little's paper*: "There is some unpredictability, as opposed to indeterminism, in this theory, in that we do not know in advance which wave the source will respond to in emitting a particular particle photon. However, unlike the situation in the usual theory, here the unpredictability can be described as resulting from a random process following an ordinary probability distribution. All the wave states exist as real waves. The source then simply has a constant probability of responding to the intensity of each incident wave. The randomness thus reflects lack of knowledge of the value of some parameters in the source, rather than representing a fundamental indeterminism."

*Regarding socionomics*: There is likewise unpredictability in this theory, in that we do not know in advance exactly which people will respond, and precisely how they will respond, to a wave in terms of taking specific actions. All waves have the potential to stimulate actions. People simply have a certain probability of responding to the intensity of each wave. The imperfect predictability of specific individual and social actions reflects a lack of knowledge of individual limbic system parameters and the variations in understanding that individuals possess. The capacity for free will—holding, as I do, that it is a valid aspect of human nature—makes individual actions indeterminate. These attributes preclude both specific social event determinism and individual response determinism, which produces unpredictability in those areas.

*From Little's paper*: "The exact value of the particle momentum is unpredictable. We don't know which wave will lead to the emission of a particle at which time and hence do not know in advance the value of the parameters describing a particular particle. But this is now due solely to ignorance of the value of parameters in the emitting system and not to any fundamental uncertainty."

*Regarding socionomics*: While waves provide for predictability with respect to the character and intensity of future social action, the exact details of any specific future action in response to a wave is unpredictable. We do not necessarily know which person or social group will respond to a wave at which time. This is due to indeterminism attending human free will and unpredictability due to variations in humans' understanding of situations as well as our lack of knowledge of the mood-thresholds that impel individual humans to take actions.

I may not have expressed all the differences and possible reconciliations between elementary waves and Elliott waves for the purposes of pursuing an analogy. Suffice it to say that the analogy is not perfect or at least that I have not grasped its perfection if it is.

The remainder of this paper will present the details of Little's thesis while exploring parallels between it and socionomics. Because the analogy is not perfect, the pairs of quotations below sometimes fit each other perfectly and other times fit only when one of them is taken out of strict context or implies an otherwise unsupported conjecture about socionomics. I am aware of the expressions with these differences but include them because of their possible compatibility.

### Primary Parallels between the Two New "EW" Theories in Physics and Sociology

The parallels between the Theory of Elementary Waves and Elliott waves/socionomic theory are legion and exciting. Here are some key correlations:

(1) Elementary waves and Elliott waves are both fundamentally causal to subsequent actions.

(2) Elementary waves' stimulation of the emission of subatomic particles relates to Elliott waves' stimulation of individual and/or social actions.

(3) Elementary waves do not travel from the emitter to the detector but from the detector to the emitter. Similarly, Elliott waves of shared mood do not "travel" from actions to minds but from minds to actions.

(4) These new theories properly account for why particle direction correlates with the position of a detector (in the first case) and why the character of social action correlates with the trend of social mood (in the second case).

(5) The volume of particle emission varies with the intensity of the elementary waves that stimulate the source of particles. Similarly, the number of participants in, and people affected by, social actions—and the intensity with which they act and are acted upon—vary with the degree of the Elliott waves that stimulate the source of those actions.

(6) Conventional quantum mechanics divorces cause and effect from the proper chronology, asserting that an observer in the present affects the past path of a particle, which means that an observer in the future can affect the present path of a particle. A conventional view of social behavior, that the stock market discounts the economic future, similarly places the cause in the future and the effect in the present, asserting that an event in the future affects the present mood of investors, which means that an event in the present has already affected the past mood of investors. Elementary waves theory obeys proper chronology, as the demonstrable effect of waves, the emission of particles, occurs in the future. The socionomic hypothesis obeys proper chronology, as the demonstrable effect of Elliott waves, social actions, occur in the future (whether immediately or later, depending upon the nature of the action).

(7) Elliott waves determine the trends of social mood, and those trends stimulate actions, which are reported as events. The actions and events, like particle emissions in physics, are final results *with no consequences of their own in terms of changing or reinforcing the waves that stimulated them.* Events "bombard" minds and thus often shape the *specific* actions that owners of those minds take, but they do not alter or affect the waves of shared mood trend. Likewise, particles bombard detectors and thus effect a specific action at the atomic level, but they do not alter or affect the elementary waves.

(8) In quantum physics, when an observer moves the detector around, he seems to be affecting the future action of particles, *and he is*. Likewise, as observer-participants move the stock market up and down, they seem to be affecting future social actions, *and they are*.

### Some Parallel Statements in the Two EW Theories, the Theory of Elementary Waves (TEW) and the Elliott Wave Theory (EWT)

In this section, I take quotations directly from Little's paper and book chapter and cast parallel expressions relating to socionomics. Some of these renditions may be little more than mental exercises, but they convey the similarly fundamental changes in thinking that these two theories require.

**TEW:** "Nonlocality [in conventional quantum physics] implies that distant events can affect one another instantaneously by no physical means. But no effect can be produced by no means."

**EWT:** Conventional discounting theory implies that events distant in time can affect human thinking in the present by no physical means. But no effect can be produced by no means.

**TEW:** "...it was *simply assumed* that both [the wave and the particle] had to move intromissively, and thus in the same direction as one another. ...Common sense also seems to dictate that the wave is intromissive."

**EWT:** It is *simply assumed* that causality has to move in the direction from event to mood. Common sense also seems to dictate that it moves in this direction.

**TEW:** "The essence of the proposed answer is very simple: it is the quantum wave itself that moves in reverse."

**EWT:** The essence of the proposed answer is very simple: the causality moves forward in time.

**TEW:** "We know by direct observation that particles move forward... so the only thing left to move in reverse is the quantum wave itself."

**EWT:** We know by direct observation that actions move forward in time, so the only things left to move in the reverse of the conventional assumption—i.e., in the forward direction—is the causality between thoughts and actions.

**TEW:** "All of the evidence supporting the hidden variables proofs actually is evidence of the reverse motion."[†]

**EWT:** All of the evidence supporting the idea of markets discounting the future actually is evidence of the reverse direction of causality.

**TEW:** "The contradiction involved in the forward wave theory's attempt to explain the double slit—this in any interpretation, conventional, Bohm's, or others—is that of trying to capture the dependence on the screen location without any physical means for that dependence."[†]

**EWT:** The contradiction involved in the discounting theory's attempt to explain the correspondence of the present (stock prices) with the future (the economy) is that of trying to capture the dependence on the future without any physical means for that dependence.

**TEW:** "Many of the properties currently assigned to particles will be shown in this work to in fact be properties only of the waves."[†]

**EWT:** Properties normally assigned to social events, those of affecting shared mood and of causing specific styles of responses, for example, are properties only of the waves.

**TEW:** "All particle emission in this theory is stimulated by a wave."[†]

**EWT:** All social action in this theory is stimulated by waves.

**TEW:** "If one wishes to validate the [conventional] wave-particle theory, it is thus not enough simply to say that the formulas work. One must also be able to demonstrate, based on empirical evidence, that the further physical hypotheses are correct. Specifically, one must be able to demonstrate that the waves move forward and not in reverse. But this cannot be done for wave-particle theory."

**EWT:** If one wishes to validate the [conventional] "discounting" theory, it is not enough simply to say that the formulation seems to work. One must also be able to demonstrate, based on empirical evidence, that the further physical hypothesis is correct. Specifically, one must be able to demonstrate that human reactions move backward in time and not forward. But this cannot be done for the discounting theory.

**TEW:** "The test of any hypothesis is this: does the hypothesis fit all the facts with no contradictions? …If one accepts the forward-wave picture of things, one is forced to accept the existence of non-local behavior: interactions over long distances by no physical means. But an interaction by no means is a contradiction."

**EWT:** The test of any hypothesis is this: does the hypothesis fit all the facts with no contradictions? If one accepts the backward-impact picture of things, one is forced to accept the existence of non-chronological behavior: interactions backward in time by no physical means. But an interaction by no means is a contradiction.

**TEW:** "Clearly, reverse waves imply a radically different theory. No longer are the waves somehow the particles. Rather, the waves are present in the environment already, and the particles then follow those waves."

**EWT:** Clearly, wave causality implies a radically different theory. No longer are the waves somehow the product of future actions. Rather, the waves are present in society already, and actions then follow those waves.

**TEW:** "The waves were always assumed to move forward, with (or as) the particles. The physical effects caused by the 'information' carried by the reverse waves could only be accounted for through one kind or another of nonlocal interaction."

**EWT:** The waves (of mood or knowledge) were always assumed to move backward, from future actions. The mental effects caused by the "information" carried backwards in time could only be accounted for through one kind or another of non-chronological interaction.

**TEW:** "At every point on the screen, the number of particles arriving is proportional to the intensity, at the particle source, of the wave emitted by that point."

**EWT:** The number of people stirred to and affected by social action is proportional to the degree of the wave in force.

**TEW:** "The wave is present at all times and not only when the particle is emitted."

**EWT:** Waves are acting at all times and not only when dramatic social events result.

**TEW:** "Waves are waves and particles are particles, and both have an exact state at all times. [Particles are not simultaneously waves.]"

**EWT:** Waves are waves and actions are actions, and both have their own states. Actions in the future are not simultaneously waves that travel backwards in time to trigger the discounting that anticipates those actions.

**TEW:** "[In the conventional view,] the act of measuring the state of a particle after it passes through an apparatus appears to affect the earlier process...but of course such reverse-temporal causality is impossible. What we have here is direct experimental evidence of the reverse time sequence."[†]

**EWT:** In the conventional view, later events appear to affect the earlier process of mood change...but of course such reverse-temporal causality is impossible. What we have here is direct empirical evidence of the forward time sequence.

**TEW:** "So instead of having the wave emitted as the photon, the photon is simply a particle emitted in response to the already existing 'available state' wave."

**EWT:** So instead of the wave being emitted with an event, the event is emitted in response to the already existing wave.

**TEW:** "These waves exist independently, in addition to the elementary particles. ...They are primary constituents of reality on the same level as the elementary particles."

**EWT:** These waves exist independently, in addition to social actions. They are primary constituents of social reality on the same level as actions. Without waves, there would be no actions. Without actions, there would be no social reality to experience.

**TEW:** "Th[e] wave intensity at the source determines the probability that a particle is emitted by the source in response to the particular wave."[†]

**EWT:** Th[e] degree and therefore the intensity of a wave determines the probability that an individual will take social action in response to the particular wave.

**TEW:** "In current theory the wave-function is not considered to be a real, physical wave, but rather merely part of a 'formalism' which 'works.' ...The reverse waves in the new theory are real, physical waves, not merely a formalism that 'works.'"[†]

**EWT:** In current theory, the reverse-temporal effect of future events is not considered to be a real, physical wave, but rather merely part of a "formalism" that "works." The forward waves in the new theory are real, causal waves, not merely a formalism that "works."

**TEW:** "All the dynamics of particles are determined by the waves. The particle itself needn't carry any of the 'classical' dynamic quantities generally attributed to particles: mass, momentum, energy, etc. All these properties describe only the waves, with the particle then acting accordingly…. One might say that the particle has mass or momentum or what have you. But the actual numerical quantity is carried by the wave."

**EWT:** All the dynamics of actions are determined by the waves. The action itself needn't carry any of the "classical" dynamic quantities generally attributed to action: mass, momentum, energy, etc. All these properties describe only the waves, with people then acting accordingly. One might say that the action has mass or momentum or what have you. But the actual numerical quantity is carried by the wave.

**TEW:** "Particles are emitted in response to waves of particular frequency/momentum. The behavior of the particle then reflects exactly the momentum of the wave."

**EWT:** Actions are taken in response to waves of particular position, degree and momentum. The style of the action then reflects the position, degree and momentum of the wave.

**TEW:** "The source responds 'randomly' to the various wave 'pieces' which arrive there. However, that randomness can now be understood in terms of additional variables—the so-called 'hidden variables'—in the source. One simply has a constant probability, proportional to the wave intensity, that the source will respond to each particular wave 'piece.'"[†]

**EWT:** The limbic system of each unidentified person responds "randomly" to the various wave "pieces" that reach him. However, that randomness can now be understood in terms of additional variables—the so-called "hidden variables"—in each person. One simply has a constant probability, proportional to the wave intensity, that each unidentified person will respond to each particular wave "piece."

Regarding those hidden variables, each individual has his own trigger point with respect to becoming stimulated to act in accordance with a wave. Some people respond early, to mild stimuli; others respond later, to intense stimuli, and some do not respond at all if the wave never reaches beyond their particular threshold of reactivity. This explains why some people buy or sell early or late, or are the first or last to adopt new fads or fashions, or choose not to participate. (It is unlikely that people maintain a constant probability of reacting throughout their lives. Probabilities change as people age and as they experience more of life.)

**TEW:** "The reverse wave theory thus eliminates all of the physical arguments, based on quantum mechanics, which allege to prove that the nature of reality is somehow intimately tied up with human consciousness."[†]

**EWT:** The forward wave theory thus eliminates all of the arguments, based on discounting theory, which allege that future social reality is somehow detected by present human consciousness.

**TEW:** "A particle must always follow an existing wave—the wave by which it was generated; it is that wave that determines the dynamics. If that wave disappears, the photon must jump into 'coherence' with one of the new waves; it cannot remain in its original state because the corresponding wave is gone."

**EWT:** A social action must always follow an existing wave—the wave by which it was generated; it is that wave that determines the dynamics. If that wave disappears, the action must jump into "coherence" with one of the new waves; it cannot remain in its original state because the corresponding wave is gone.

For example, a rising Elliott wave of major degree may stimulate a peace negotiation and determine its dynamics. If the advancing wave ends and a declining wave begins, the peace process will must ultimately resolve into coherence with the new wave, which means that it will disintegrate, because the mental trend that generated it has reversed. Conversely, a declining Elliott wave of major degree may stimulate a war and determine its dynamics. If the declining wave ends and an advancing wave begins, the war must ultimately resolve into coherence with the new wave, which means that it must end, because the mental trend that generated it has reversed.

**TEW:** "When all the unnecessary baggage required by the forward wave theory has been eliminated, it will become apparent to the reader that overwhelming empirical evidence of the reverse motion has been staring physicists in the face for decades."†

**EWT:** When all the unnecessary baggage required by the backward wave theory has been eliminated, it will become apparent to the reader that overwhelming empirical evidence of the forward motion of causality has been staring economists and sociologists in the face for decades.

**TEW:** "What forces one to assign a fundamental uncertainty to particles in current theory is the forward motion of the waves. By assuming that the wave goes from source to detector and that the wave *is* the particle, one is forced to conclude that the particle exists in multiple states simultaneously in order to explain phenomena involving 'widths.'"

**EWT:** What forces one to assign a fundamental uncertainty to the social future in current theory is the presumed backward motion of the waves. By assuming that the wave goes from future actions to present mood and that the action therefore generates the wave, one is forced to conclude that future actions exist in multiple states simultaneously in order to explain phenomena involving surprise news to which the market briefly reacts as if it were unaware of that future event.

**TEW:** "The momentum and energy can now be defined in terms of the 'picture' of the waves, without reference to the resulting behavior."

**EWT:** The momentum and energy in society can now be defined in terms of the "picture" of the waves (showing, for instance, that society is in wave 3 of (3) of 5 of V of (V) of Ⓘ, which tells you all you need to know), without reference to the resulting behavior.

**TEW:** "The response of the original particle will depend on exactly where it is located when the disturbance occurs. But that in turn will depend on the particular path chosen up to that point, which in turn depends on the particle's inner parameters. The overall motion is thus no longer simply a function of the initial motion of all the particles, as in classical physics. The inner parameters also play a role. One cannot predict the future motion of a system simply from a knowledge of its initial state of motion."

**EWT:** The specific response of social action will depend on exactly what the configuration of the actors is when the wave affects them. But that in turn will depend on the particular paths that individuals within society have taken up to that point, which in turn depends on society's and individuals' inner parameters. The specific social actions taken are thus not simply a function of the initial impetus from Elliott waves. The inner parameters of individuals also play a role. One cannot predict specific individual and social actions simply from knowledge of the state of current individual and social actions. (We can nevertheless predict the *character* of social action without any such knowledge.)

**TEW:** "In fact we never directly observe a quantum wave. We only observe the 'quanta' or particles. Any detector, including our eyes, responds to the particles, not the waves. Wave patterns appear only as the result of the observation of numerous individual particles."†

**EWT:** In fact, we never directly observe an Elliott wave. We only observe the actions that it induces. Any detector, including our eyes, responds to the record of those actions, not the waves. Wave patterns appear only as the result of the observation of numerous individual actions.

A stock market graph is a record of human actions (in this case, buying and selling), which take place in response to the waves. It is not a record of the wave itself.

**TEW:** "The wave does not itself carry any energy or momentum from one location to another; only the particles do that. The wave merely serves as a guide, if you will, for the particle motion."

**EWT:** The wave does not itself carry any energy or momentum from one location to another; only actions do that. The wave merely serves as a guide, if you will, for actions.

**TEW:** "Current theory obtains the equations of quantum mechanics by starting with the equations of classical physics and then 'quantizing' them, using the canonical quantization procedure. The premise here is that somehow the classical laws are primary, and quantum mechanics is then derived from them. But this has matters backwards."

**EWT:** Current theory presumes the properties of social mechanics by starting with the equations of classical physics and then "socializing" them, imposing mathematical equations upon mental processes. The premise here is that somehow the laws of physics are primary in social behavior, and mood is a mechanical response to actions. But this has matters both wrong and backwards. The laws governing unconscious mental processes are different from the laws of physics.

**TEW:** "All that needs to be modified from the usual treatment is the direction of the wave, the direction of propagation of the 'principle function.' It must be reversed."

**EWT:** All that needs to be modified from the usual treatment is the direction of the causality, the direction of propagation of the "principle function." It must be reversed.

**TEW:** "So there is complete causality at every step, both for the particles and the waves."

**EWT:** So there is complete causality at every step, both for actions and the waves.

**TEW:** "Most of what has been accomplished [with elementary waves theory] follows simply from the recognition that the waves move in reverse."

**EWT:** Most of what has been accomplished with socionomics follows simply from the recognition that causality moves in reverse of the common assumption.

**TEW:** "Virtually all the principle mysteries of twentieth-century physics disappear as soon as one corrects the one error."

**EWT:** Virtually all the principle mysteries of conventional macroeconomics and the chronic failures of social prediction disappear as soon as one corrects the one error.

**TEW:** "All of this is accomplished with a theory that is far simpler than current quantum mechanics. Occam's razor does not say that the simpler theory is correct. But it does say that one cannot validly add further aspects to a theory without additional evidence, evidence going beyond what is explained by the simpler theory."

**EWT:** All of this is accomplished with a theory that is far simpler than current discounting theory. Occam's razor does not say that the simpler theory is correct. But it does say that one cannot validly add further aspects to a theory without additional evidence, evidence going beyond what is explained by the simpler theory.

**TEW:** "While the simplicity of the reverse wave theory is certainly beneficial, most significant is the fact that the theory is free of any contradictory, unphysical aspects."[†]

**EWT:** While the simplicity of the forward wave theory is certainly beneficial, most significant is the fact that the theory is free of any contradictory, non-chronological aspects.

**TEW:** "Quantum mechanics is indeed an error pyramid—the most gargantuan error pyramid in the history of humankind"[†] (at least in the area of physical science).

**EWT:** The idea of social event causality with respect to social mood is indeed an error pyramid—the most gargantuan error pyramid in the history of humankind (at least in the area of social science).

**TEW:** "Clearly, the fact of reverse elementary waves has been demonstrated. Too many things are explained by the one simple hypothesis to conclude otherwise."

**EWT:** Clearly, the fact of forward socionomic causality has been demonstrated. Too many things are explained by the one simple hypothesis to conclude otherwise.

**TEW:** "Furthermore, the theory accomplishes what has been sought for many years: a single framework within which all known physical phenomena can be comprehended."

**EWT:** Furthermore, the theory accomplishes what has been sought for many years: a single framework within which social phenomena can be comprehended.

## The Two "EW" Theories Explain Special Relativity

The Theory of Elementary Waves explains special relativity neatly and simply and without resorting to contradiction and magic, whereby, for example, objects change shape when an observer moves while simultaneously not changing shape for other observers who do not move.[34] In Little's words:

> "The elementary waves theory provides a simple, physical explanation for the fact that light travels at the same velocity $c$ relative to all observers and thus serves to explain the Lorenz transformation.... What we see is the particle photon, not the wave. It is the particle that imparts any energy or momentum to the retina, thus producing a visual effect.... But if the dynamics of the particle photon is determined by a wave that comes from the observer, then it is the observer's frame that determines the velocity. The constancy of $c$ relative to the observer is thereby explained.

> "Light, then, does not simply move from object to observer or from observer to object; it does both. Nor is it simply a wave or simply a particle. It consists of a wave from observer to object and a particle from object to observer. ...In the standard derivation it is assumed that the light seen by both observers is physically the same light—the same photons. Space and time are then distorted [by theory] in order to account for the fact that both observers see a spherical pulse. But this is because the light is different, not because of a deformation of space-time. The two observers in two different frames do not see the same photons.

> "Objects do indeed appear to change when one moves. But facts are facts; facts do not change because one looks at them differently. So one knows for certain that it is the means of observation that changes when one moves, not the objects observed. But motion of the observer can affect the means of observation only if the means involves something traveling from the observer.

> "Given the fact of Lorenz transformations, all the consequences of that transformation occur in the elementary waves theory exactly as in current theory. Moving objects appear shorter, time intervals in moving systems appear dilated, etc. However, none of these apparent changes require any change to the objects themselves. Only their appearance changes, due to the change

to light. ...The nature of light as a particle following a wave from the observer dictates that simultaneity is relative. ...It is thus clear that there is no contradiction involved in the fact that two observers in relative motion each see objects as being shorter in the other observer's frame. ...Reality is the same for all observers. It is not the case that 'everything is relative.'

"The fact that the theory which accounts for quantum phenomena also at the same time accounts for special relativity serves as the best evidence I will cite that this theory is correct. Had special relativity not yet been discovered, the reverse wave theory would have predicted it!"†[this paragraph only]

If economists were as creative as physicists, they would have formulated their own theories of uncertainty and special relativity. They would have observed that when their "detector" of future events, the stock market, moved from one trend and level to the next, the future would change right along with it! They would conclude that even with perfect knowledge, the future would be unknowable. Surely, they would argue, there must be an infinite number of pre-existing future social realities, or "wave-futures," in which the economy is both strong and weak, and cats are both alive and dead, simultaneously. The "observer," i.e., society, can bring any one of these futures into actuality simply by changing its financial position from favoring stocks over cash or vice versa. It would not occur to such "quantum economists" that the observer[35] behind the presumed detector actually *originates* the waves of social mood that *direct* events in the future—the *only* future. A socionomist can also see that social causality has its own naturally produced special relativity. As society undergoes changes of mood, the social future changes right along with them because trends in mood produce trends in actions. In other words, the social future remains constant with respect to the present mood of the observers, who produce it. Now we know why, and the answer requires no magical reversal of temporal causality. Instead, the causality is direct and sensible.

### Some Potential Questions and Implications for Socionomics Implied by the Analogy

(1) TEW: "The elementary waves are not actually emitted by the observer, as indicated earlier. The observer merely rearranges the organization of the passing wave." Like elementary waves, are Elliott waves

everywhere present, stimulating organized actions by living entities in the universe, or do they originate inside the living entities?

(2) TEW: "Waves corresponding to all possible free-particle states exist at all times. In the absence of particles the waves are 'disorganized.' Particles have the effect of imposing coherent organization on the waves." Like elementary waves, are the waves governing living processes disorganized until living units impose organization upon them, in which case they become Elliott waves? Are life forms essentially organizational? Are people's unconscious minds the organizers of disorganized social waves that exist independently?

(3) TEW: "In the elementary waves theory the waves simply exist, with their various properties. They are primary constituents of reality. Thus there is no need to deduce their behavior from anything." Like elementary waves, are Elliott waves primary constituents of social reality, or are they products of underlying processes?

(4) In quantum physics, "The intensity of the wave—the absolute value of the amplitude squared—at any point on the screen gives the probability that a particle is observed there."[†] Little corrects this formulation to say, "The square is performed at the source; and it gives the probability of particle emission, not of particle observation."[†] Similarly, the intensity of actions that people take in response to Elliott waves seem to be multiplicative with respect to arithmetic increases in degree. Effects of waves of one degree are often 1.618, 2.618 or 4.236 times those of one lower degree (as examples, aggregate stock valuation extremes and war deaths).

(5) TEW: "These are not waves in a medium, and the signal is not carried by wave fronts. The notion that any periodic 'thing' must propagate as the result of a field equation is a carryover from classical physics. One can deduce wave equations for classical waves from the physics of the medium through which the wave propagates. This notion was then applied to quantum waves, even though no medium is involved. But this is erroneous." It is difficult to say whether Elliott waves propagate through a medium. Certainly the minds of human beings contain electrical impulses that carry herding directives, but can we say that the coherence of those impulses through the cooperation of many minds is accomplished through a medium? The minds are not physically connected. Further, we have Elliott waves in processes outside human society, such as the Elliott waves that describe the flow and ebb in the number of species on Earth. It seems at least possible to conclude that Elliott waves are external entities, not internal waves in

a medium, and that they shape living processes from without, which is why disparate parts conform to the whole. Just as various atoms, molecules and compounds participate in the human body yet a person retains its identity, so various people participate in Elliott waves yet the waves retain their identity. This is what I meant in *The Wave Principle of Human Social Behavior* when I called Elliott waves a formological system, not one of linear or nonlinear causality. Such external waves could serve to "explain" or account for formological systems as being the product of outside forces.

(6) TEW: "If one has indeed reached the most 'elementary' level, one can only describe what exists, not explain it. ...If the waves are primary things, without there being any medium, then one simply describes the waves." I often feel that it is enough simply to describe Elliott waves. They exist; we can see their effects on graphs. Several chapters of *The Wave Principle of Human Social Behavior* attempt to explain where they come from, but ultimately, these explanations describe primarily their media and their ubiquity, not their cause. Elliott waves may be just as elementary as elementary waves. Perhaps, as postulated in Chapter 21 of that book, they are a manifestation of phimation, a force opposing entropy.

(7) TEW: "Each point on the screen [and on all objects] is actually emitting [more accurately, organizing and re-directing] waves of all frequencies corresponding to all possible energies, masses, and other characteristics of particles."† "Particles are emitted in response to waves of particular frequency/momentum. The behavior of the particle then reflects exactly the momentum of the wave. ...An object 'emits' only those waves that correspond to particles that it would absorb." People are capable of experiencing all manner of emotions induced by waves, but their minds participate only in those that pertain to them at a time. Whatever waves people participate in then stimulate actions that are in accordance with those waves and only from people whose internal "hidden variables" are constituted so as to respond with action to those waves.

(8) TEW: "The reverse wave theory thus predicts not merely the relative distribution but rather exactly the correct number of particles arriving at any point on the screen." Knowledge of the effects of Elliott waves within populations can allow socionomists roughly to predict the "mass" and "energy" of their social effects, for example, the number of people that will be unemployed in an economic contraction of each different degree, or the percentage of Earth's population that will be at

peace or war. Already there is evidence that the effects of waves vary according to degree, as illustrated in *The Wave Principle of Human Social Behavior*, Chapters 7 and 16.

## Conclusion

Little says succinctly, "A physical theory is acceptable only if it is able to account for all experimental evidence *without any contradictions*."[†] This fact not only damns conventional quantum theory but also conventional assumptions and theory regarding social causality. Conventional macroeconomics is replete with contradiction. For example, economists assert that logically, "Falling interest rates are bullish for stock prices," except that they are not always so; in fact, during deflations, interest rates on sound debt fall to very low levels right along with stock prices. So, the macroeconomic assertion contradicts evidence. Conventional sociologists tell us, "Terrorist attacks and corporate scandals make people less optimistic and more fearful of investing," except that the evidence utterly contradicts this assertion, as our studies of *actual* optimism and investing trends during and after such attacks and scandals demonstrate. The discounting theory of markets, in which effects purportedly move backwards in time, is an even more fundamental contradiction of reality.

"Before one can base an explanation on some aspect of reality," says Little, "one must have evidence—observational evidence—that the aspect in question actually exists. Otherwise one would simply have a fantasy, not a scientific explanation."[†] This is precisely the problem with conventional ideas of social and macroeconomic causality. They are not scientific explanations but *fantasies* based upon a false premise, which is unsupported by the evidence and indeed contradicted by it.

The Theory of Elementary Waves corrects the fundamental error in conventional theories of quantum mechanics. Socionomics corrects the fundamental error in conventional ideas of social causality. They are, in many ways, parallel scientific revolutions.

## APPENDIX

### Elliott Wave Influence on the Mental States of Physicists and the Nobel Committee

Figure A provides some anecdotal evidence that Elliott waves stimulate similar actions in people at similar points in wave structure. As you can see, the two Elliott waves shown there are nearly identical in *form* despite a 3-times difference in their absolute quantities of duration and percentage rise.

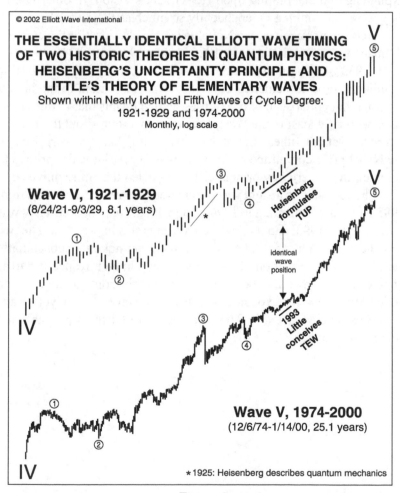

*Figure A*

Heisenberg formulated his uncertainty principle in 1927, and Little conceived of his theory of elementary waves in 1993. These years are almost precisely analogous in terms of their Elliott wave position. In other words, we may speculate that these Elliott waves coordinated a mental energy that induced historic "aha" experiences in individual quantum physicists at almost the same moment in the progression of Elliott wave form, which is early in Primary wave ⑤ of Cycle wave V in the 1921-1929 and 1974-2000 periods, respectively. From these insights, they formulated grand theories that changed the direction of science.

In all the time in between, physicists dedicated themselves to explaining and elaborating upon Heisenberg's vision. In other words, they were not thinking independently so much as they were herding.

Heisenberg received the Nobel Prize for physics "for the creation of quantum mechanics" not in 1925, 1926, 1927, 1928, 1929, 1930, 1931, 1933 or any year thereafter. He received it in 1932. This timing is unlikely to be coincidence. July 1932 was the bottom of the largest stock market collapse in two centuries, which means that in the aggregate, people (at least in the West) felt more uncertain about their social future than at any other time in that period. It is hardly a surprise that the Nobel prize committee at this time was psychologically primed to embrace an "uncertainty principle" that infected the entire universe.

The socionomic insight was formulated over a period of years from 1985 forward, culminating in 1999 along with the bull market. TEW was formulated in 1993, and its final exposition is still in progress. The two new theories of physics and sociology, then, are not only substantially parallel in their correction of previous thought in their respective areas of science but have also been developed nearly coincidentally. Both gelled into summary expositions in Primary wave ⑤ of Cycle wave V of Supercycle wave (V). This temporal parallelism is probably not coincidence, either.

## NOTES

[1] Looney, J. Thomas. (Reprinted 1996). *Shakespeare Identified.* Northampton, MA: The Oxenford Press.

[2] Wilkens, Iman. *Where Troy Once Stood.* 1990, London: Rider Press; 1991, New York: St. Martin's Press.

[3] Hawkins, Gerald S. and White, John B. (1965). *Stonehenge Decoded.* New York: Dell Publishing.

[4] Atkins, Robert C. (1972). *Dr. Atkins' Diet Revolution.* (Republished 2002, M. Evans & Co.)

[5] Sears, Barry, Ph.D and Lawren, Bill. (1995). *Enter the Zone.* New York: Harper Collins.

[6] Eades, Michael R. and Eades, Mary Dan. (1996). *Protein Power.* New York: Bantam Books.

[7] Thorburn, Doug. (2000). *Drunks, Drugs and Debits.* Northridge, CA: Galt Publishing.

[8] Little, Lewis E., (2009). *The Theory of Elementary Waves—A New Explanation of Fundamental Physics.* Gainesville, GA: New Classics Library.

[9] Proposed by E. Schrodinger, *Naturwissenshaften* 23, 807 (1935). I wish I had had Lewis Little's words back then. He says, "The notion that the act of looking at the cat can either kill it or determine that it lives is perhaps the single most absurd prediction of current quantum mechanics. This amounts to a sort of vitalistic psychokinesis."[†]

[10] For a detailed explanation of the "Double-Slit Experiment," please see Chapter 2.1 in *The Theory of Elementary Waves*, as referenced in note #8 above.

[11] Heisenberg, uncertainty principle paper, 1927, as quoted on pages 1 and 2 of http://www.aip.org/history/heisenberg/p08c.htm

[12] This is very like the stance of analysts and reporters when "explaining" the stock market movement of the day. On any typical trading day, all sorts of news is reported, and reporters stand at the ready as if they were applying conventional quantum theory by accepting the fact that all the news has infinite potential causality *until the day is finished*, at which time all those potentials collapse into the *actual* causality. The analysts create reality by looking, and only after looking do they discover which among the myriad potential causes actually pertained to the result! If one were to provide such reporters and analysts with every bit of news for the day *in advance* except the action of the stock market, they would have no hope of determining what the stock market would do because in fact there is no causality of news to mood. (Few people actually investigate history

to uncover this fact.) Indeed, most news events have two contradictory causal arguments attached to them prior to knowledge of what the market actually did that day. As examples, (1) war is bad for consumers' mood, which is *bad* for stocks, and war is good for the economy, which is *good* for stocks, and (2) a decline in interest rates repels investors away from bonds, which is *good* for stocks, or a decline in interest rates indicates a weakening economy, which is *bad* for stocks. And so on.

[13]   There is a parallel between Heisenberg's uncertainty principle and an occasionally expressed assumption on the part of financial analysts. They argue emphatically that any attempt publicly to analyze or forecast the market is doomed because as soon as it becomes popular, it affects the behavior of the market, which destroys not only the forecast but also the basis upon which it was made. You can read this argument in any one of a hundred books on the stock market. Once again, the true causality is in the opposite direction. A forecast's popularity does not cause people to change their mood with respect to the stock market, thereby invalidating it; people's moods with respect to the stock market dictate which forecasts are popular, which by definition are ones that will not succeed at that time. The result is the same, but the explanation is wrong, just as with Heisenberg's uncertainty principle.

[14]   Heisenberg, in his uncertainty principle paper, 1927, as quoted on page 2 of http://www.aip.org/history/heisenberg/p08c.htm.

[15]   I would say the same thing about the conventional idea of social causality, except that common people believe it just as readily as intellectuals, which is not the case for the implications of quantum theory.

[16]   As quoted on page 3 of http://www.aip.org/history/heisenberg/p08c.htm

[17]   Article in *The Wall Street Journal*, March 27, 1911, as quoted in *The Dow Theory* (1932) by Robert Rhea, p.20.

[18]   Hamilton, William Peter. (1922). *The Stock Market Barometer*. Reprinted 1960 by Richard Russell Associates, New York, pp.7-8.

[19]   Rhea, Robert. (1932). *The Dow Theory*. Barron's, New York, p.19.

[20]   Schaefer, E. George (1960). *How I Helped More Than 10,000 Investors To Profit in Stocks!* Englewood Cliffs, NJ: Prentice-Hall, p.22.

[21]   Quickel, Stephen W. (2002, September). "Excessive Stock Prices?" *On Wall Street*.

[22]   Samuelson, Paul. (1967). *Economics: An Introductory Analysis*, 7th edition, McGraw-Hill, Inc.

[23]   The true dichotomy is the opposite of that espoused by discounting theory: The mass of investors knows nothing accurate about the future, but occasionally an informed individual can apply socionomics to forecast

successfully the next trend.

²⁴ Prechter, Robert. (1999). *The Wave Principle of Human Social Behavior*. Gainesville, GA: New Classics Library, pp.331-332.

²⁵ *Ibid.*

²⁶ Little, Lewis E. (1996). "The Theory of Elementary Waves." *Physics Essays*, volume 9, number 1, pp.100-132.

All unmarked quotations attributed to Little in this essay are from this paper. All quotations marked with an endnote style "†" are from Chapter 1 of the book cited in endnote 8.

† See endnote 26.

²⁷ Elliott, R.N. (1946). *Nature's law: the secret of the universe.* Republished: (1994). *R.N. Elliott's Masterworks—The Definitive Collection*. Prechter, Jr., Robert Rougelot. (Ed.). Gainesville, GA: New Classics Library, p. 277.

²⁸ See endnote 24.

²⁹ See Figures 13-1 through 13-3 in *The Wave Principle of Human Social Behavior*.

³⁰ See Chapter 8 of *The Wave Principle of Human Social Behavior*.

³¹ "Astroeconomists" postulate that electromagnetic waves bombarding Earth are regulated by the position of the moon and the planets, and those waves in turn affect humans' aggregate mental states. So correctly or not, some people do propose an outside cause for extremes of shared mood, which would then be an outside cause regulating Elliott waves.

³² For a discussion of this term, see *The Wave Principle of Human Social Behavior*.

³³ This idea goes back to the ancient Greeks, who viewed form as a primary force of nature.

³⁴ Little also dispenses with the nonsensical idea that "space" is "curved" or has any properties at all. He explains, "Space, after all, is nothing. Space is merely the place where real objects can be located. What is real are the objects, not the space.... Nothingness cannot have properties.... The elementary waves are curved, not space." His solution is, "The electromagnetic field...is actually itself simply an elementary wave, with particle photons then following the wave."

³⁵ There is a nuance of difference in this analogy, because in sociology, human thought is causal; in physics, physical action is causal and humans are merely observers.

*Part VIII:*

# *MISCELLANEOUS ARTICLES, LETTERS, SPEECHES AND OBSERVATIONS*

### Chapter 44

# *Elliott and Hamlet*

A few years ago, subscriber Mike Flagg alerted me to a paper in the field of modeling that was published in *System Dynamics Review* in 1992. The data for the study derived from a collective process among students. Author Pamela Hopkins explained, "The students discussed the effect that each event would have on Hamlet's desire to kill Claudius as he became aware of the information, and they assigned accordingly each event a value on a scale of impact from one to ten.... I entered the data into the STELLA model as the students debated the issues related to each event."[1]

| Input | Output |
|---|---|
| 0.000 | 0.000 |
| 1.000 | 0.000 |
| 2.000 | 4.800 |
| 3.000 | 2.000 |
| 4.000 | 4.500 |
| 5.000 | 8.000 |
| 6.000 | 5.500 |
| 7.000 | 6.000 |
| 8.000 | 7.500 |
| 9.000 | 8.000 |
| 10.00 | 9.000 |

Data Points: 11

Edit Output:

To Equation    Delete Graph    Cancel    OK

**Figure 2**: STELLA window for the "revelation of evidence" flow variable, showing a portion of a typical scene-by-scene-development, suggested by the students, of evidence that would motivate Hamlet to kill Claudius.     © 1992, *System Dynamics Review*

*Figure 1*

It took an *Elliott Wave Theorist* subscriber to notice the Elliott wave form of the progression of evidence revealed to Hamlet in the first half of the play. Perhaps one of the reasons this portion of the play is so compelling is the five-wave impulse of discovery, as shown in Figure 1 (Hopkins' Figure 2), which is reproduced from that paper.

Shakespeare's greatness is due to many things, but one of them is his pacing. All his plays follow a five-act format, and, if this graph is representative, he may have regulated shorter plot developments in a five-wave fashion as well.

## NOTES

[1] Hopkins, Pamela Lee, "Simulating Hamlet in the Classroom," *System Dynamics Review*, Vol. 8; No. 1 (Winter 1992), John Wiley & Sons. Ltd. 91-98.

Prechter
*The Elliott Wave Theorist*
July 2002

## Chapter 45

# Another Example of a Link Between Nature's Trees, Waves and Spirals

Chapter 3 of *The Wave Principle of Human Social Behavior* (1999) proposed the following hypothesis:

> Are nature's developing waves, branching arbora [i.e., trees] and expanding spirals all the same thing? Figures 3-15, 3-16 and 3-2 express the Fibonacci sequence in three different ways: as a *tree*, a *spiral* and a *wave*.... Natural processes express this cross-representational property as well. For example, evolution is a process that makes *waves, spirals and arbora*.... This transformation property may cover other types of fractals as well. For example...a topographic fractal (mountains, hills, hillocks, etc.) [is] also an arborum...when water, snow or flowers fill the cracks. See Figure 3-20.... It is also true that price trends can be graphed in such a way as to reveal not a line but a spiral.... All these pictures resemble many natural expressions of growth and expansion [or recession and decay], from life forms to galaxies. In terms of their essence, then, there may be little difference among nature's progressing forms. The only difference may be the template upon which nature projects them.[1]

The work of a scientist in the field of fractal geometry has allowed us to view another example of this idea. Benoit Mandelbrot's latest book, *Gaussian Self-Affinity and Fractals* (2002) presents an illustration of a highly stylized tree, "a Peano motion in the plane." The illustration may be conceived of as "rivers that flow into the black 'sea'" or as trees with "new layer[s] of shorter branches," which you can see in Figure 1. This is a simple stylized arborum (branching fractal).

The more interesting depiction is Figure 2, which displays "the graph $\mathcal{S}$ of the limit curve," i.e., "the $X(t)$ coordinate function of the Peano motion in Figure 1."[2] The fact that the *tree* in Figure 1 can be

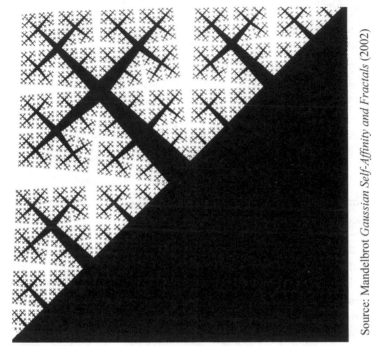

Source: Mandelbrot Gaussian Self-Affinity and Fractals (2002)

*Figure 1*

The Arborum in Figure 1, Plotted as a Wave

Source: Mandelbrot GaussianSelf-Affinity and Fractals (2002)

*Figure 2*

shown as a *wave* in Figure 2 supports the observation quoted above from *The Wave Principle of Human Social Behavior*.

## Nearly an Elliott Wave

The details of the result are even more fascinating to a trained eye because as detailed in Figure 3, the self-affine fractal in Figure 2 reflects the 5-3 form of net progress described by R.N. Elliott's Wave Principle. It follows Elliott's observations of market behavior even to the point of including alternation (see *Elliott Wave Principle*, pp. 61-63) between waves two and four. *This stylized tree, then, does not reflect an indiscriminate line fractal but something extremely close to an ideal Elliott wave.*

The pattern's detail is interesting. Corrections bottom at the level of the preceding wave four, as under the Wave Principle. With respect to alternation, it sports a short-long declining pattern in the "wave 2" position and a long-short pattern in the "wave 4" position.

*The Arborum in Figure 1, Labeled in Elliott Fashion*

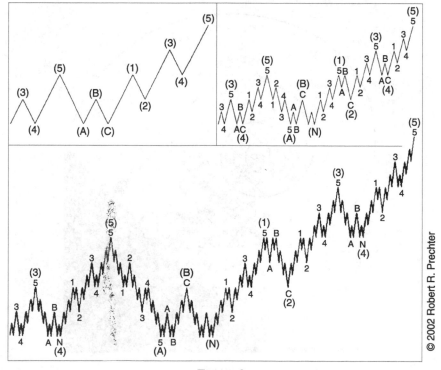

*Figure 3*

There are two main variations from the rules of Elliott wave construction. The first is that wave four in this pattern continually falls to the level of the peak of wave one, which never happens in financial markets. Secondly, what should be wave C under the Wave Principle alternately subdivides into three waves instead of five. (I have labeled this construction "N" in Figure 3.) There are other variations in terms of guidelines. For example, in Figure 3, all advancing subwaves are the same length, which does not typically occur in financial markets or in Elliott's model, which reflects reality.

### The Expanded Hypothesis

Since plotting an aspect of a stylized tree produces a stylized Elliott wave, we may reiterate the suspicion that plotting aspects of robust fractals in the form of arbora in nature is likely to produce robust fractals called Elliott waves, with all the natural order and variation that we have come to know from their expressions in financial markets.

*The Spiral Implied by the Arborum in Figure 1*

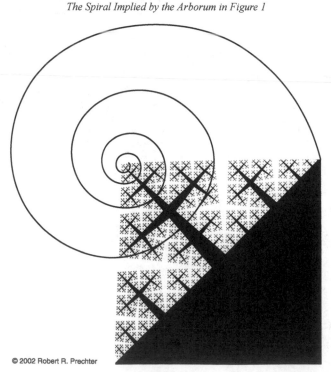

*Figure 4*

*The Spiral Implied by the Wave in Figure 2*

© 2002 Robert R. Prechter

*Figure 5*

They should have this property because arbora and Elliott waves both depict aspects of natural growth patterns. Indeed, as shown in *The Wave Principle of Human Social Behavior*, they can depict the *same* natural growth patterns, such as the number of families of fauna produced through evolution.

Both the stylized tree in Figure 1 and the stylized advancing wave in Figure 2 may be circumscribed with spirals, as shown in Figures 4 and 5. (See also Figures 2-29 and 3-14 in *The Wave Principle of Human Social Behavior*.) Thus, once again, we have expressions of all three of nature's primary growth forms in a single process.[3]

## NOTES

[1] Prechter, Robert R. (1999). *The wave principle of human social behavior and the new science of socionomics*. Gainesville, GA: New Classics Library, pp. 75-82.

[2] Mandelbrot, Benoit B. (2002). *Gaussian self-affinity and fractals*. New York: Springer. Note: As the author explains, the illustration in Figure 1 exaggerates one-dimensional branches into two-dimensional ones for effective visual illustration.

[3] Scientists are getting so close to the Wave Principle that they are within smelling distance of it. An educated nose would prove a useful resource. Ironically, Mandelbrot's aloofness with respect to Elliott's model has provided an opportunity for a wave practitioner to make an observation that otherwise he could have made.

*Chapter 46*

# Another Indication of Possible Elliott Wave Tendencies in Physical Phenomena

Chapter 21 of *The Wave Principle of Human Social Behavior* showed a possible Elliott wave in a graph of the infrared light absorbance of cement. Recently, Charles V. Berney forwarded a copy of his 1973 study[1] on the spectroscopy of trifluoroacetic acid ($CF_3COOH$) and wondered if a similar form was manifest. Included were graphs of the neutron inelastic-scattering spectra of both solid and liquid $CF_3COOH$.

In the accompanying illustration, I have labeled these graphs with the Wave Principle in mind. These forms are not Elliott waves because, in one instance apiece, they exhibit "overlap" between the values of waves one and four. In social trends, wave four in an impulse does not enter the value territory of wave one. Yet there seems to be a strong hint of an Elliott wave *tendency* in these graphs, as you can see by the labeling.

No one has conducted a comprehensive investigation into the existence of Elliott wave tendencies in non-life phenomena. It would be interesting to know whether nature has such tendencies within certain non-living compounds apart from their participation in life forms.

---

**NOTES**

[1] Berney, C.V. (1973.) "Spectroscopy of $CF_3COZ$ Compounds. V. Vibrational Spectra and Structure of Solid Trifluoroacetic Acid," *Journal of the American Chemical Society*, **95**, 708.

## Possible Elliott Wave Tendencies
## in the Spectroscopy of Trifluoroacetic Acid

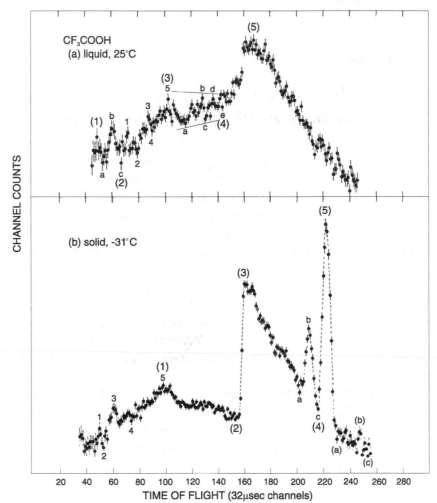

Figure 2. Neutron inelastic-scattering spectra of CF$_3$COOH.
Wave number equivalents of some of the channels are indicated
(458. . .27 cm$^{-1}$). Intense Bragg peaks are observed in the solid
for neutron wavelengths of 5.23 and 5.55 Å; they can be interpreted as the 100 and 002 reflections of a monoclinic unit cell with
parameters $a$ = 5.25, $b$ = 9.165, $c$ = 11.142 A, and $\beta$ = 85 .

© 1973 Journal of the American Chemical Society
wave labels © 2002 Robert Prechter

Alan Hall
*The Socionomist*
April 2015

*Chapter 47*

# Elliott Waves Manifest in Stars, Minerals and Fossils

In 1999, Robert Prechter gave me his new book, *The Wave Principle of Human Social Behavior*, and suddenly, history and sociology—never my favorite subjects—became as fascinating as biology and physics. Socionomic theory elegantly connected these fields. In brief, the book argued that the Wave Principle could be the underlying signature of many structures and processes in the universe, mostly pertaining to living systems but in some cases to non-living systems. As a concrete example, Chapter 21 of Prechter's book charts what may be an Elliott wave in "the absorbance by cement slurry of each wavelength of infrared light, a property that is important for timing the hardening of cement for oil-well drilling operations." Let's look at four additional charts that depict Elliott wave patterns in non-human systems, which span from 12 billion to 550 million years in length. The first process is non-living, the second is also non-living but was created by life, and the third and fourth are measures of life on Earth.

### The "Life" of Stars

Stars, including our Sun, evolve and devolve in patterns that resemble an Elliott wave. Figure 1 plots Northwestern University's rendering of the Sun's luminosity to date[1] and its projection into the future, which required twice magnifying the timescale. We simply added Elliott wave labels to the graph of the 12-billion-year pattern.

Over the 4.5 billion years of the Sun's existence to date, its brightness slowly increased by about 30%. The nuclear furnace at the center of every star begins to overheat as it ages. Before wave 1 is over, the Earth will be roasted to bare rock. During wave 3, Earth will have lakes of molten aluminum and copper. In wave 5, Earth will be burnt to an iron core, if not completely vaporized. At the peak of wave 5,

*Figure 1*

the Sun's helium core will explode, ignite and burn within a matter of minutes, leading to a crash in luminosity. Much like the latter stages of a bear market, the final 140 million years of the Sun's life—waves B and C—will be complicated and volatile. In four or five huge bursts roughly 100,000 years apart, the outer layers of the Sun will separate from the core and be completely blown away, leaving a white dwarf, an immensely dense stellar remnant whose faint luminosity comes from the emission of stored thermal energy. White dwarfs will eventually fade completely, but none have so far, because the process takes billions of years longer than the universe is estimated to have existed.[2]

### Earth's Minerals

The number of Earth's minerals has increased in a pattern that resembles an Elliott wave. Figure 2 plots the number of Earth's minerals, which has risen from about a dozen 4.6 billion years ago to about 4400 today. In contrast, Mars and Mercury are estimated to have only about 350 minerals apiece, because those planets are missing two things crucial to the creation of new of minerals: oxygen and life. Robert Hazen, a research scientist in geophysics at George Mason University, said, "If you think of

*Figure 2*

all the nonliving world as a stage on which life plays out its evolutionary drama, think again. The actors renovated their theater along the way."[3] More than half the mineral species on earth "owe their existence to life."

Viewing minerals in an evolutionary context fits the general theme of evolving systems throughout the cosmos. Simple states evolve into increasingly complicated states in many contexts, such as the evolution of chemical elements in stars, mineral evolution on planets, the molecular evolution that led to the origin of life, biological evolution through natural selection, and human social and cultural evolution. There seems to be a common pattern underlying increases in complexity.

### Earth's Species

Chapter 13 of *The Wave Principle of Human Social Behavior* showed Figure 3, which plots the total number of families of marine species.[4] Michael J. Benton of the University of Bristol compiled these fossil data in 1995. Prechter wrote,

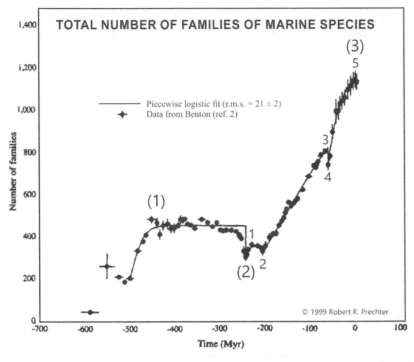

*Figure 3*

As you can see by the wave labels that I have applied to the graph, particularly the advance from 250 million years ago [wave (3)] shows the classic five-wave form, complete with an extension in wave three. From collective life's extreme micro-scales to its extreme macro-scales, there is the Wave Principle, time and again.

It is not that surprising to me that evolution develops according to the same principle that governs social systems. Societies and evolution share the essential traits of self-regulating complex dynamical systems. I contend that evolution is a social phenomenon, as it involves the constant intermingling of life forms. On this basis alone, I am inclined to postulate that the Wave Principle applies to all interactive systems of life, not just the human.

About the wave labels on the chart, Prechter wrote,

For a wave analyst, the implication of this pattern is obvious, though not comforting, as five waves up portends in the relatively near future the largest extinction since the one that occurred 300 to 250 million years ago. If this were a graph of the stock market,

I would add that the slowing of upside rate of change in the past forty million years is a classic precursor of a reversal, which is strong support for the case that five waves are indeed ending.

Figure 4 plots more recent and detailed data, which suggest a slightly different labeling of waves yet with a similar Elliott-wave outlook. The previous chart, Figure 3, plots *families* of marine species. Within families there are many genera, and within genera, innumerable species. The top line in Figure 4 plots the estimated number of marine *genera*

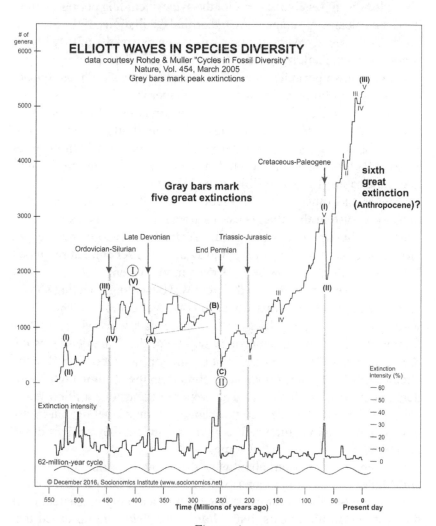

*Figure 4*

over the past 550 million years. The data are from Robert A. Rohde and Richard A. Muller's 2005 paper, "Cycles in Fossil Diversity."

Scientists have named the most important retracements in this chart the Five Great Extinctions, which we have marked with vertical bars. Rohde and Muller identified a 62-million-year, best-fit cycle in species extinctions, shown in the oscillating line at the bottom of the chart. Each of the five great extinctions occurred during a downtrend in that cycle. Extinction intensity, shown in the jagged line near the bottom of the chart, spiked during each cyclic decline. The authors tested and discarded seven possible reasons for the cycle, including periodic comet impacts, volcanism, solar cycles and orbital oscillations of the Sun and Earth. They wrote, "Although no explanation exists, the 62-Myr cycle is not a subtle signal. It is evident even in the raw data, [and it] implies that an unknown periodic process has been having a significant impact on Earth's environment throughout the Phanerozoic."[5]

This graph also forms an Elliott wave, making it look somewhat like a stock chart. Waves ①, (I) and (III) all subdivide into five waves. Wave ② forms a corrective pattern (called a zigzag), which includes a wave (B) triangle. Even the smaller-degree waves show fractal fluctuation. Chapter 13 of *The Wave Principle of Human Social Behavior* explained, "In other words, evolution is a self-regulating, complex dynamical system that fluctuates in a fractal pattern, just as the stock market and human society in general." As the fossil record provides yet more data over time, the pattern of growth and retrenchment regulated by the Wave Principle has become even more evident.

The newer data require a different wave labeling than that shown in Figure 3. It indicates that wave ③ is not yet complete. The Elliott wave pattern in Figure 4 nevertheless suggests wave (IV) of ③ is imminent. The coming retracement will be of the same degree as the preceding wave (II), the Fifth Great Extinction, which occurred in the Cretaceous-Paleogene period. No decline from the all-time high is evident in Figure 4, in which each data point represents one million years. Newer and better fossil data could change the wave labeling, but in any case, it may be a long time before humans—unless they are part of the next extinction—learn the outcome.

Scientists are curious about what drives major extinctions. Rhode and Muller ruled out a number of factors but did not propose an answer. The 62-million-year cycle has been remarkably consistent over the past 600 million years, but *Elliott Wave Principle* observed that stock market cycles may manifest for long periods but also "fade in and out of existence at times, usually with little or no warning." If the 62-million-year cycle ever disappears, the Wave Principle will probably continue to manifest.

Fluctuations in unconscious social mood naturally produce the fractal pattern of progress and regress in the stock market and in human prosperity. We have proposed that all of life undergoes waves of progress and regress that are regulated just as naturally. Paleontologist Peter Ward offered an opinion on this subject. He thinks the Gaia Hypothesis, the idea that life makes the world better for itself, is rubbish. He instead offered the opposite, the Medea Hypothesis, the idea that multicellular life, understood as a superorganism, is periodically unintentionally suicidal. Ward thinks mass extinctions were short periods of return to microbe-dominated worlds with hydrogen sulphide atmospheres deadly to complex life. He says he suspects that "life does actually try to do itself in—not consciously, but just because it does."[6] In this natural process, stocks, species and even stars seem to follow an underlying pattern of least resistance and maximum efficiency that is well described by the Elliott wave model.

## NOTES

[1] Solar luminosity image (Figure 1) retrieved from David Taylor, The life and death of stars, The end of the sun, Weinberg College of Arts and Sciences, Northwestern University.

[2] Holberg, J. B. (2005). "How dDegenerate sStars cCame to be kKnown as wWhite dDwarfs". American Astronomical Society Meeting 207. 37207: 1503. Bibcode:2005AAS...20720501H.

[3] Hazen, R.obert M. (March 2010). Evolution of minerals. Scientific American., 302:, 58-65.

[4] Stewart, I. (1999). Life's other secret. New York: John Wiley & Sons, Inc.

[5] Rohde, R.A., & Muller, R.A. (2005). Cycles in fossil diversity. Nature. 434:208-210.

[6] Ward, P. (200813, February 1). Earth's mass extinction. So if not impact? YouTube.A theory of earth's mass extinctions. TED Talks.

*Chapter 13 of* The Wave Principle of Human Social Behavior *(p.217)*
*discusses evidence of the Wave Principle in individual life forms. We*
*may have additional evidence along these lines in David Goodman's*
*study of human emotional biorhythms.*

## Chapter 48

# Evidence of the Wave Principle in
# Human Emotional Biorhythms—
# A Starting Point for Further Study

The Foundation for the Study of Cycles publishes a magazine called
*Cycles*. Volume 46 included a submission by member David Goodman,
who recorded his mood swings with great precision for twenty years,
from January 1977 through September 1996. Rather than finding a
regular cycle, he found that since 1977, the cycle of his mood swings
got progressively shorter, from 30 days to 30 *hours*. Now, this might
mean nothing; one sample has little value for generalizing, and this is
barely a glance at a neglected area of scientific research. However, if
this study does prove to reflect an aspect of human psychology, what
would be the implications? It might suggest that people's emotional
cycles shorten with age, perhaps explaining why people perceive time
accelerating as they get older. (My preferred theory is that people experience time as a percentage of their age.) Some clues in the data point
to another explanation.

Figure 1 is Goodman's chart, but it is inverted and annotated to
reveal a familiar pattern: an Elliott wave, labeled 1 through 5. This
picture suggests a link between patterns of individual mood and social
mood in the production of Elliott waves.

More intriguing is that the one-way longer term trend and the timing
of its interruptions are highly reflective of the stock market's concurrent
advance, with pauses in the areas of the corrective periods of 1979-1982
and 1987-1991. Notice in Figure 2 that the five-wave sequence reflects

*Figure 1*

*Figure 2*

the same development in the stock market. This parallelism suggests the possibility that *social mood trends are related to the frequency of human mood swing*. Now observe that concurrently with the upward accelerations in stock prices, the length of Mr. Goodman's emotional cycle fell particularly swiftly after 1982 and again after 1991. These are precisely the times that recessions ended. We already know that the stock market bottoms as or before recessions end, indicating that social mood trends are the engine of aggregate rates of production. Now we might postulate that accelerating biorhythms support an increasingly active sociology that results (among other things) in production and a desire to buy stocks, while decelerating biorhythms bring on a sluggishness that results in retrenchment, conservatism and selling. An increase in the frequency of mood swings might explain why exercise becomes popular in bull markets and unpopular in bear markets. It might also be the reason behind a demonstrable increase in the personal performance of sports stars during bull markets, and vice versa, as revealed in "Basketball and the Bull Market" (1996). Perhaps the frequency of mood swings correlates with preferences for fast-tempo music in bull markets and slow-tempo music in bear markets. In sum, maybe frequency of mood change correlates with direction, which in turn drives the social events that we socionomists observe.

To say that this is conjecture is an understatement, but the potential value of proving such a possibility is so great that this avenue of inquiry should be explored. If a large sample of members of society were found to produce a similar graph, it would add weight to the possibility; if the changes continued along the same lines over several bull and bear cycles, it would become a probability. A proven correlation would add to the predictability of social mood trends and therefore of the timbre of historical events.

It is important to note that Hersey, the originator of the idea of emotional cycles, concluded that for the most part, biorhythms were regular at about a month. However, his studies mostly took place in the 1930s and 1940s, years of a Supercycle degree bear market. Goodman's study shows that cycle lengths can vary from one month to one day. In his experience, the one-month variety occurred near major bear market lows. That is the environment in which Hersey's studies were conducted.

Goodman also lists descriptive terms, based on work by Jung, Pao and Grof, that reflect what he perceives to be four stages of his emotional cycle, as follows:

(1) Calm, contented, friendly, at ease, inventive, imaginative, humorous.
(2) Energetic, happy, affectionate, enthusiastic, successful, influential, loving.
(3) Fatigued, sad, inhibited, fearful, imperiled, distressed, insecure.
(4) Tense, anxious, suspicious, angry, aggressive, hostile, antagonistic.

Read these terms carefully, and you will recognize the moods that *society* progressively projects in the four stages of a stock market cycle: uptrend, top, downtrend and bottom. Roughly speaking, at Cycle degree, the 1920s were (2); the early 1930s were (3); the late 1930s to mid-1940s were (4); the 1950s were (1); the early 1960s were (2); the late 1960s through 1970s were (3) and (4); the 1980s were (1); the 1990s have been (2). You can see that if the majority of investors felt progressively as above, they would buy and sell in such a way as to produce a bull and bear market.

To conclude, the frequency of *bio*rhythmic mood swings may determine the character of *socio*rhythmic moods. Since in most cases, each sociorhythmic cycle would begin from a higher base of retained production value, all that would be necessary for overall progress would be a repeating Elliott wave of biorhythmic frequency. The fractal nature of social mood change may in turn suggest that in the aggregate, biorhythms follow Elliott-wave patterns of frequency and duration, thus generating Elliott waves of human progress and regress.

*Chapter 49*

# A Socionomist Looks at Bankruptcies

A correspondent wants to know, "If things are so great in the U.S., why is the bankruptcy rate so high?" Indeed, for the year ended September 1997, there were 1.37 million personal bankruptcies, another new all-time high. It seems logical that bankruptcies would contract in booms and expand in recessions/depressions, doesn't it? Finance is often not so simple. This chart of annual bankruptcy filings from 1930 to 1997 reveals that a rising trend in petitions for relief from creditors is not reliable evidence of economic decline. To the contrary, despite a flurry of debtor-friendly alterations to the bankruptcy code in the 1930s, filings remained flat. Since 1942, bankruptcies have risen along roughly the same path as the stock market, producing an Elliott

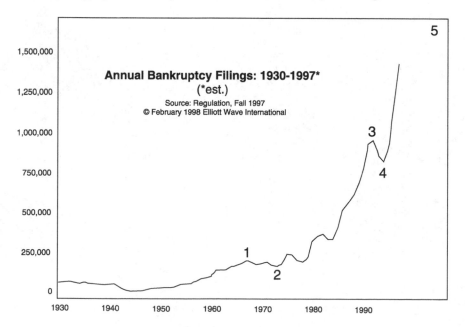

five-wave advance. Not shown is a similar quadrupling in the number of bankruptcies during the booming 1920s. The numbers continued to edge higher to a peak in 1932, when the stock market bottomed, and finally receded in the late 1930s and early 1940s, when conservatism returned to finance.

In the late 1920s, a presidential commission searched for ways to toughen the bankruptcy code. Similarly, today Congress is debating ways to reverse the 1978 law that further loosened creditors' grip.

Why does the trend of bankruptcies go mostly counter to what seems logical? The answer is that bankruptcy rates are a function of lending quality, and lenders are more active when they are more confident, which is in uptrends. Today's record-high bankruptcies reflect lenders' record-high willingness to lend more money to less qualified borrowers, which is a symptom of good times, not bad times. So to answer our subscriber's question, the bankruptcy rate is high *because* things are great. They will stay high through the coming bear market and depression and then recede.

*Technically Speaking*
(the newsletter of the Market Technicians Association)
June 2000

## Chapter 50

# Seminar Speaker Summary

### by Mike Carr

### Keynote Address, May 18, 2000

Robert Prechter, CMT, of Elliott Wave International, in a rare public speaking appearance, delivered the keynote address after the Friday evening meal. The topic was "The Wave Principle and the Socionomic Perspective." In it, Prechter promised to provide an answer to what effect the Department of Justice antitrust action against Microsoft will have on the overall market.

First, he shared an insight into the Elliott Wave Principle that idealized wave progressions are contained within a channel. Prechter noticed that if the lower channel line is broken, then the fifth wave should be expected to break the upper channel line. This leads him to believe that we are in the final stages of an extended Wave V, completing the formation that began at the 1932 bottom.

Other technical indicators support his interpretation of the wave structure. He has found that sentiment extremes correlate to waves' peaks and troughs. Using the DJIA dividend yield, sentiment is at a record peak, implying that we are near a Supercycle peak in the market. Wave V is not expected to show the same technical strength as Wave III, and the weakening advance/decline line, which peaked in Wave III, supports this idea.

Economic and financial fundamentals are also expected to be weaker in Wave V. Key economic measures, such as real GDP, industrial production, capacity utilization and unemployment are all, on average, weaker in the current wave than they were in Wave III (1942 to 1966). Financial fundamentals include measures of household liquidity, debt in various sectors of the economy, the prime rate and the current account surplus or deficit. All of these measures are also weaker, on average, in the current wave.

Prechter believes that technicals produce fundamentals, and it is well known that the stock market is a leading indicator of the economy. In fact, eleven of the last twelve recessions occurred after stock market tops. It is the social mood, in Prechter's theory, that is reflected in Elliott waves. It is the social mood of the society that governs the economy.

If this is true, then wars should be expected to result when the social mood is angry. In fact, the major wars our country has fought, from the Revolutionary War through World War II, occurred during or immediately after the completion of C waves, when conditions and the social mood were at their worst.

His work, and the work of academics, finds no correlation between the demographics of 40-year-old "spenders" and the stock market, the commonly touted explanation for the strength of this bull market. However, Prechter does find another correlation between demographics and the market. He sees the decision to conceive as a reflection of positive mood. Shifting the birth rate back one year to reflect the timing of conceptions, he is able to correlate demographics to the stock market. This approach reflects the bottoms in 1932 and 1974. The more popular approach of shifting the birth rate forward by 40 years or more to account for the retirement savings of the Baby Boomers fails to explain these bottoms.

Returning to his original question, Prechter explained that the actual question should be, "What is the social mood of the nation when the government takes antitrust action against the most successful companies?" He has found that this type of action is taken at major peaks, while bailouts occur at bottoms. These peaks correspond to both the social mood and the stock market.

In summary, Prechter concluded that the mood of the market is the real fundamental and that mood is reflected in the charts we study. The Elliott Wave Principle provides an insight into the pattern and progression of the social mood.

Prechter
Private communication in response to an academic paper
1999

*Chapter 51*

# Challenging Another Myth of Market Rationality

I enjoyed your 1999 paper and hope that it triumphs in influence over the [competing] piece. I have one dissenting point. Theory and empirics must agree. If they do not, then one of them is wrong.

The Efficient Market Hypothesis and its reliance on "market rationality" is in the process of destruction. Your work is helping that process along, but in my view your model nevertheless maintains a relic, a key pillar of the argument for randomness, which is market rationality. You propose that when a bubble accelerates, buyers are rationally requesting an increasingly larger return—in terms of capital gain—for the increasing risk of a crash. This idea applies the laws of economics to those of finance. It initially sounds reasonable, being akin to the practice of paying higher fees to stuntmen for riskier movie stunts, which is rational economic behavior. I see several problems with this theory.

First, both the actual and potential return to investors accelerate downward during an accelerating market advance. The actual return via dividends falls as fast as stock prices rise, so the risk of stock ownership is decreasingly compensated in those terms, which are the most reliable terms available. As for potential capital gain, with every tick upward in stock prices, the chances for a higher return diminish in terms of the probability that the price rise will continue. The faster the market's rise, the sooner the inevitable reversal. A truly rational investor would take such factors into account. Buyers in a fast-rising overvalued market either must know that they will be ruined sooner or later, in which case their buying is irrational, or they ignore or are unaware of the fact. Either way, it is like agreeing to play Russian Roulette for more and more money until you shoot yourself dead. This is not economic *or* rational behavior. It is *financial* behavior, which differs by being impulsive.

The empirical problem with the rational-risk-taking explanation is the fact that investors do not report the mindset required by the theory but in fact precisely the *inverse* of it. Statistics on market psychology show a consistent correlation between price rise and complacency. Investors' concern about a market crash *decrease* as prices rise. Poll after poll proves this point. At major market tops, fears of decline are virtually non-existent. Your theory and empirics, then, are at complete odds. Stuntmen will tell you that they charged a higher fee due to higher risk. Investors say the opposite. They perceive less risk and therefore buy with impunity, which is the very reason that prices rise so rapidly. So the theory that an upwardly accelerating market is a rational economic response to buyers' perception of increased risk does not describe new buyers' actual motivation. If what investors actually think does not support what they are expected to think according to the rationality theory, then there must be problems with the theory.

Parabolic-rise-and-crash structures in financial market behavior challenge the idea of rationality. Reason does not lead to these types of patterns. What you are observing is a pattern of paleomentational impulsivity. While such thinking has a rational purpose (survival), it is not based upon reason. The proof is that it leads to failure, and the reason is that the impulse is misapplied by the unconscious mind to finance. The market punishes people for their impulsivity and rewards people for true rationality, which applies only when they understand the market's psychological dynamics.

Then why do markets rise exponentially and then crash? I think bubbles accelerate not because people fear a crash *more* but because they fear one increasingly *less* as the market rises. Markets crash not because people think it will do so but because they become *certain that it will not*. When that conviction reaches a critical point (at the end of an Elliott wave) and cannot expand further, the market stops going up. People are out of money and out of room to expand their bullish conviction. As social mood changes and disappointment in the lack of further price rise spreads, a bear market develops.

Your scientific observations are important, but you may wish to reconsider the proposed explanation for them. Dumping the rationality argument and adopting the unconscious impulsivity argument will strengthen the theoretical foundation of the very real phenomena that you are observing.

*Chapter 52*

# Why Teenagers Lead Fads of Social Expression

Why do teenagers participate so widely and passionately in fads of self-expression? Do they herd less discriminately than adults? Apparently, they do rely more than adults on the primitive portions of the brain, which house the herding impulse. Here is a discussion from the transcript of an ABC News report on the subject of teen vs. adult brain activity:[1]

> Are teens really that different from adults? Well, yes, say researchers here at Harvard Medical School's Brain Imaging Center. Here, they put teenagers, and then people my age, into the MRI so they can watch how our brains work. The doctor in charge, Deborah Yurgelun-Todd, says when I and other adults answer questions, we use the rational, thinking part of our brain, the "dorsal lateral prefrontal cortex," and the teenagers use a different part. [DYT]: "Kids use the region behind here called the amygdala." That's the instinctual part of their brain. This may explain their creativity. Some of our better creative work occurs during this time of life because there's not that sense of "I shouldn't do this or I can't do this."

> Harvard researchers say that not only are teens more likely to use a part of the brain that may allow for more creativity, they're also less likely to use the part that does critical thinking, that helps people make mature judgments. Teens use the "gut reaction" part of the brain. They're using the more emotional, automatic parts; we smarter adults use our critical thinking. [DYT]: "That's exactly right. You activated more up in this region, and the boys that we saw today activated more down in this region."

---

**NOTES**

[1] Stossel, John. (1999, March.) "Teenagers." *20/20*, ABC Network.

## Chapter 53

# *Response to a Question from a Renowned Scientist*

**Question:** *What is the essence of your argument that outside causes do not affect the stock market?*

**Answer:** There are two main arguments for why mood dictates the character of events, not vice versa.

First, if the Wave Principle is true, then the market is hierarchically patterned. The only way to maintain the presumption that outside events move market prices would be to assert that those outside events are perfectly patterned to produce the Wave Principle. This appears to be an untenable position.

Second, whether the Wave Principle is true or not, if you pay attention, you can see that events lag stock market trends. I can always point to the social results of a rise or decline, but economic historians often cannot locate or agree upon the presumed causes of a market move even decades after it occurs. Distinguished attendees at a recent international economic summit admitted that armed retrospectively with the data and the news of 1928-1930, they cannot determine reasons justifying the market's historic crash. (Economist Hernan Cortes wrote a paper on this topic.) On the other hand, you can see its result in the Great Depression without difficulty. Once you understand that a crashing social mood has consequences, understanding the result is easy.

Finally, there is a more subtle and perhaps less compelling point but also valid whether the Wave Principle is true or not: The market is a fractal with a specific dimension, which means that its roughness is about the same at all scales. Even if one were to accept only this fact, it really weakens the "outside causes" argument because one would have to take the position that those outside causes of the market's changes are also a fractal with the same specific fractal dimension! This stance would render useless virtually all economic commentary. The entire cadre of economists who think that the Fed (an "outside cause" in their view) has the market under control would have to close up shop. If the Fed were smoothly controlling the economy, then the market would not be a fractal. The same would be true of every presumed outside force that they would cite. If all forces together are an indefinite fractal, then what's the point in discussing them or forecasting anything? Outside-causality advocates who have integrity would be resigned to mumble, "The market will fluctuate" and leave it at that.

## Chapter 54

# *Letter to a Curious Objectivist*

Objectivists should definitely be open to the Wave Principle and socionomics, which are observations about the workings of mass psychology, as follows:

(1) The desire among many, if not most, individuals to belong to and be accepted by the group, as well as their penchant for second-handedness in epistemology, make their unconscious minds dominate their conscious minds in emotionally charged social settings.

(2) When the unconscious mind dominates, it does not do so randomly (as that would mean no thought at all) but in patterns peculiar to it.

(3) The behavior that results is so repetitive that it is observable as displaying patterns.

(4) Once you perceive patterns of social behavior and understand how they typically develop, you have an objective basis for occasional speculation about probabilities for future courses of social behavior.

(5) The mechanics of the patterns appear to reflect mathematical characteristics of a family of patterns found throughout nature. This fact that gives rise to some speculation about why they might exist and how, biologically and evolutionarily speaking, they arose.

Think of a mob in the square listening to a Hitler speech. If the points above make sense to you in that context, then you can see that it makes sense with respect to other highly emotional socially shared experiences such as auctions, which are hotbeds of crowd psychological forces. The stock market is an auction for substantially intangible goods whose attractiveness to general participants increases as prices *rise*. This is a crucial point that makes economic supply/demand/price formulas inapplicable to market analysis, thereby segregating the disciplines of economics and finance.

If you can live with the above five points, then you should have no problem philosophically with the Wave Principle. The only potential problem would be scientific, i.e., whether you could investigate the evidence enough to verify, reject, or dub insufficient the data that suggests that there are patterns in investment behavior.

Chronologically, #3 above came first, as it was empirics that got the train of thought going. The Wave Principle *began* with percepts and can be *reduced* to percepts. At bottom, I can point and say, "*Look.*"

Now, this fact is diametrically opposed to most of what passes for economics. For instance, how many times have you read that "the wide and widening U.S. trade deficit is bad for the economy and bearish for the market"? Hundreds of times. And it sounds logical, doesn't it? Well, here is a chart [produced later as Figure 19-3 in *The Wave Principle of Human Social Behavior*] that juxtaposes the trade deficit and the stock market, which has quite closely paralleled the trend for the economy. What do you *see*? You see that the trend of the trade deficit has waxed and waned in precisely the opposite way from what the conventional wisdom presumes. So, what are you going to believe, the initially seemingly (omitting percepts and deep thought) logical answer, or your eyes? It is on that question that your decision on my work will depend.

Obviously, the "logical" answer is indeed logical. It is just that the premise behind the logic is false, and the fact that the premise has no clothes can be seen simply by looking. These parallel trends in the chart *can* be explained quite sensibly and logically. But what do you think happens when you show this chart to someone who believes otherwise? He evades it. He does not comment. He will not believe that trees are green if he thought they should be blue. Paradox stymies him instead of igniting his mind to inquire.

The result is that economists encourage Congress to "reduce the trade deficit at all costs," i.e., by force, including trade war. Forced or not, the trade deficit *will* come down in an economic contraction, just as it has before.

Economics is diseased with thought like this, and many of its errors are far more fundamental. My biggest objection to macroeconomic formulas, for instance, is that they assume people are machines following physical laws, which they are not, because people can change their minds.

I believe that socionomics will become the first true social *science*, as opposed to armchair deliberating and theorizing about sociological forces, usually based on whimsy. My arguments are a challenge to the majority of professionals' false premises in this field, so many of them do not wish to investigate them, probably because they don't feel any need to spend mental energy on a challenge to ideas that appear to them as obvious. No negative response is likely to be formidable to me, though, so if you are convinced that a good point in opposition has been scored, I would respond to it. I get far more communication from people who are ecstatic and say they have suspected much of what I contend about markets because their experiences have contradicted what people told them should happen. Objectivists should embrace this new science, as some already have, quite fervently.

One problem that people might rightfully encounter is that, as I mentioned, my books to date are mostly a practical application of what I know, not an exposition of it. Unfortunately, there is no *Atlas* on the Wave Principle, so I cannot point you to a source with that scope or level of integrity. There will not be one until I write it, which will be in my 50s, ten years from now.

If my commentary on socionomic causality does not appear perfectly logical to you despite the sometimes-resulting seeming paradox, then I would certainly want to hear about it. Objectivism contains or implies many seeming paradoxes, as deep truths do. For instance: The worst way to help the poor is to give them something.... If you are truly selfish, you should be kind and benevolent.... The virtue of honesty is contextual.... "Thou shalt not kill" is not a call to virtue.... A society of independent people would be the most harmonious one.... To achieve happiness, you must be disciplined enough to postpone fun and pleasure.... Faith and hope are destructive. People who come across these ideas piecemeal assume you are crazy, and dismiss them. They must "get it" in the broad sense before they can get it in the particulars. They must care enough about the particular *realm* of ideas to bother to do so, which is true of my field as well.

P.S. I am disturbed to see that some Objectivists (two that I know of) are arguing for a state-sponsored "gold standard," which is like arguing in favor of no standard backed temporarily by a misleading title. Recall what the English "pound" originally meant and how the dollar was originally defined. The better position would be to favor free-market money. The market would quickly choose the best form of money and ensure its integrity.

Prechter
Speech introduction for James Grant
Market Technicians Association Conference
May 1989

*Chapter 55*

# Contrasting Three Styles of Financial Analysis

In 1983, Jim Grant left *Barron's* to start his own publication, *Grant's Interest Rate Observer*. It also happens that 1983 was the year that subscriptions to *Barron's* peaked, immediately beginning a substantial decline. Now I submit that this fact is highly relevant. But in exactly what way is a question about which there is some debate. Let's look at it as a fundamental analyst, a technical analyst and an Elliott-wave analyst would.

A fundamental analyst would conclude quite logically that the exit of Mr. Grant from the staff of *Barron's* caused such disappointment among *Barron's* readers that thousands of them jumped ship. The numbers in fact show that *Barron's* subscriptions peaked at 299,000 the last year Jim was there and subsequently dropped to 245,000. Armed with these statistics, it would then be obvious to the fundamentalist that *Grant's Interest Rate Observer* has... 54,000 subscribers. Finally, the fundamentalist would point out, with annual subscriptions costing $495, Jim Grant is hauling in $26,730,000 per year.

Now let's look at it from the standpoint of technical analysis. The technical analyst of course also notices that *Barron's* subscriptions peaked when Jim left the magazine, but the technician understands the fact that markets move ahead of fundamental events. His reasoning is that markets discount the future. So, the technician might wonder, were all those subscriptions to *Barron's* pouring in during 1983 on the *anticipation* that Jim would soon be leaving? If so, the conclusion with regard to the current number of subscribers to *Grant's Interest Rate Observer*, and Jim's gross receipts, would be quite different. That does leave a question as to where *Barron's'* 54,000 subscribers went, but undoubtedly they would conclude, it has something to do with hedge funds, derivatives or program trading.

The Elliott wave analyst sees it much more simply: It was time for a change. Jim ended one pattern in his life and started another, right when he should have.

Still, if Jim didn't inherit those missing 54,000 subscribers, why does he toil late into the night week after week to bring us the wit and wisdom for which he is so widely and justly famous? Is it because he has a great message to deliver? Certainly he does. Is it because he's fascinated with markets and history and people? No question about it. However, the central reason I believe, is expressed by a quote from the author Kingsley Amis, who said, "If you can't annoy somebody, there is little point in writing."

Which brings me to the question of why people read *Grant's Interest Rate Observer*. I think the answer lies in another insightful quote, this time from Claude Cockburn, who said, "Never believe anything until it has been officially denied." Jim Grant has that healthy sense of skepticism, that gimlet eye of cold observation, that penchant for questioning the comfortably obvious that makes his articles "must reading." And now, as I am sure we will discover, he is "must listening," too. Will you please welcome our next guest speaker, James Grant.

## Chapter 56

# Miscellaneous Observations

### Thoughts on Forecasting

(April 30, 1984) What would you think if you had heard this forecast tomorrow: "I believe prices are likely to trade in a narrow range between 1120 and 1190 on the Dow for the next several months." Would you recognize this forecast for what it is? Most published forecasts are merely descriptions or extrapolations of what has already happened. As a rule of thumb, I never give any forecast a second thought unless it addresses the point at which a change in trend may occur.

As an example outside the markets, a sportswriter for *The Atlanta Journal* published on April 1 his ratings (scale 1-5) for each of the players on the 1984 Braves baseball team. He rated last year's "Most Valuable Player" a "5," Atlanta's slugger a "4," and the right fielder a lowly "2" due to bad performance in 1983 (following two excellent years). At this point in the season, the MVP is batting only .215 and the slugger is batting a dismal .179 while the lowest-rated player, the right fielder, has hit 8 home runs and leads the team in batting average and RBI's. The point is not that the sportswriter was wrong in his predictions. The point is that he *didn't make any predictions*, even though he thought he did. He was merely rating the *1983* Braves, in retrospect. Things like motivation, cyclic changes in talent, [pre-season training efforts, stresses in personal life,] etc., weren't even considered.

Read forecasts carefully. Descriptions of recent price behavior or mild-mannered extrapolations of a recent trend are usually not based on useful forecasting methods.

(February 1, 1988) One of the oldest adages on Wall Street is "use stops." That's great as far as it goes, but the obvious question is, "which ones?" As pointed out numerous times, the Wave Principle is one of the few approaches to market analysis that provides a method for establishing stops objectively. Fundamental approaches use no stops.

If you turned bearish in 1982 because the trade deficit was rising, you had no mechanism to force you to change your mind, and presumably stayed short until you were wiped out.

(August 28, 1992) At the peaks of expansions, most people feel a stronger kinship with animals and trees. The environmental, or ecology, movement, when expressed in terms such as, "let's work together to clean up the environment," is a manifestation of the last stage of the trend toward inclusion. At bottoms of major economic contractions, people care less about the environment and more about survival.

(1998) I would argue against the widespread notion among economists that "wars create jobs." War jobs cost tax money, and the money has to come from the destruction of other jobs. (See *Economics In One Lesson* by Henry Hazlitt.) The latter jobs produced goods and services that the market wanted; war jobs don't. Moreover, war jobs ultimately result in the mass destruction of capital and therefore of the means to create jobs. So on two fronts, the net result is that wars destroy jobs.

(2000) I think there is an important difference between the gambling impulse and the impulse to speculate. The former is a drive to get lucky, to be showered with unearned gain. The latter is a drive to prove you are smarter than everyone else. It's very powerful. Some games—such as poker—involve a combination of both.

(2002) John Stuart Mill asserted, "Panics do not destroy capital; they merely reveal the extent to which it has been previously destroyed." This is close to the truth. Panics do destroy capital, but the *setup* for the destruction occurs beforehand. Dynamite likewise destroys a building, but earlier, someone has to collect the gunpowder, build the stick and light the fuse. Actions accompanying the positive social mood trend *preceding* a panic carry out the equivalent of those activities.

*SPI Report* (Australia), Issue #667
July 31, 2002

*Chapter 57*

# A Craftsman's View

by Adrian Pitt

Even after 20 years of following this market, it never ceases to amaze me just how incredible the Elliott Wave Principle is. These days I get to the point of just casual application as if it's just taken for granted. Not because I apply counts slapdash, but because I've been doing it for so long that much of it just stares right back at me without a lot of thought. There are many occasions, mind you, when deep thought and analysis is required to make sure the most accurate count possible is used, but when you sit back and just look at the wiggles that have occurred since the September 2001 low and how every wave has been perfectly accounted for by the correct wave structure, and market action following the completion of each little pattern has moved exactly as it should have, I don't think anyone can be anything but amazed. I know I am! I can guarantee, there isn't another method that comes close to forecasting moves into the future in time and price, on all levels, whether it be economic or technical.

*Technically Speaking*
(the newsletter of the Market Technicians Association)
February 2000

*Chapter 58*

# Book Review: *The Wave Principle of Human Social Behavior and the New Science of Socionomics*

### by Roman Franko

Robert Prechter's new book is unquestionably a ground-breaking work in the development of technical analysis. Its purpose stated at the outset is "to establish the idea that in humans, an unconscious herding impulse impels social mood trends and changes that are specifically patterned according to a natural growth principle and which in turn is the engine of cultural expression and social action." In other words, the book aims to establish that the Wave Principle that flows naturally out of human behavior is the primary cause of social, historical, cultural and economic changes, including market fluctuations.

These audacious arguments can only be described as stunning and revolutionary in intent and scope. They speak broadly for the study of all human efforts and specifically for the place of technical analysis in the study of financial markets. Today, technical analysis is often viewed as a secondary or supplementary form of market analysis. It is supposedly dependent on the study and interpretation of underlying factors that can be accessed only by so-called "fundamental analysis." Prechter explicitly aims to reverse this causal relationship by arguing that the so-called fundamental factors and events are ultimately dependent on the working of the Wave Principle as manifested in social mood and then the financial markets. In short, the form of technical analysis founded on the Wave Principle studies the causal or independent variables while the misleadingly named fundamental analysis studies the dependent financial factors.

The first of the five sections of the book introduces the idea of the Wave Principle. Even here, Prechter goes beyond merely summarizing ground previously covered in his (and Jack Frost's) 1978 *Elliott Wave Principle*—the five-wave impulse or "motive" and three-wave corrective patterns uncovered by Elliott, as well as the Fibonacci or phi-based (.618... etc.) mathematical relationships underlying these patterns. Rather, the emphasis is on showing how these patterns and relationships are evidence of recurring forms called robust fractals. This form of fractal lies between self-identical and indefinite ones that are similarly irregular at all scales. Robust fractals, which replicate forms within a certain latitude in a branching-like manner, are found not only in the stock market as 5-3 wave patterns but are also being found throughout nature by researchers such as Benoit Mandelbrot. Further, researchers are uncovering that Fibonacci mathematics regulate all fractal branching systems, including the branching characteristics of DLA (not DNA) clusters. "In its broadest sense, then, the Wave Principle communicates the seemingly outrageous idea that the same law that shapes living creatures and galaxies is inherent in the mentation (thinking emanating from both the rational and pre-rational or limbic systems) and activities of men en masse."

Before going on to elaborate upon this claim, Prechter devotes the second part of the book to validating the Wave Principle. First, he demonstrates through the use of rules and modeling that consistency of interpretation under that Principle is possible. He then goes on to review a series of major and astonishingly accurate historical forecasts made by Elliott, Bolton, Collins, and himself between 1941 and 1983 to demonstrate that the Principle is a valid approach to forecasting market behavior. While admitting that these leading Elliotticians have made errors from time to time, he is quite correct in stating that there simply is no other approach to market forecasting which provides a methodological basis or more precisely a rule-based model for such predictions, particularly more than one swing ahead.

The third section is a ground-breaking argument that the Wave Principle is based on biological, psychological and sociological factors. Other technical analysts have previously attempted to explain why, for example, overhanging supply can turn into resistance as money-losing investors begin to sell when a stock rallies back to their buy levels. Prechter, however, attempts to take the analysis of investor behavior to much deeper and causal levels. He provides an explanation of why market participants would collectively act so as to create such overhanging resistance.

His basic thesis is that "the prime mover of aggregate stock market prices is mass emotional change, which itself must be, and demonstrably is, independent of outside influence." While most readers would probably be comfortable with the first half of that thesis, the notion that mass emotional change must be independent of outside influence will undoubtedly elicit more controversy.

To support this thesis, Prechter has assembled and linked together an amazing array of arguments and evidence that will be boiled down to three principal ones. The first step is a discussion of how the limbic part of the human brain that gives rise to emotional responses kicks in quicker than the cerebral cortex that generates rational thought. He then reviews psychological studies that argue that people, including investors, are driven by the interaction of their goal of self-preservation with the emotion-driven limbic system to participate in unconscious herding behavior. "When a herd 'thinks,' the result is not reason but an emotional interpersonal superorganic dynamic that must be the source of waves." Prechter buttresses this idea of unconscious herding behavior with several other processes, all of which help explain investor behavior. The idea of mental contagion, which explains how fads like the slinky, jacks and Pokemon propagate from brain to brain, suggests that individuals in herding mode depend upon the thoughts and actions of others. Feedback mechanisms operate so that investors' decisions make the Dow move in a certain direction and this direction then influences other investors' decisions and so on.

The second step in the argument is that this unconscious herding impulse produces a robust fractal pattern of social interaction. After reviewing robust fractals found in the human body, he concludes "the brain may be disposed to participating in a fractal of collective sentiment because circumstantially it, along with the rest of the human body's structures and function, is of and for fractals in so many ways."

A third step is to provide evidence that unconscious herding is expressed in a Fibonacci form because numerous studies show that individuals' decision making is predisposed to a 62/38 inclination and in the absence of clear parameters tends to default to phi. These far-reaching hypotheses are a testament to Prechter's unequaled ability to weave together emerging evidence into a stunning new model.

The fourth part of the book provides an introduction to 'socionomics.' As Prechter estimates, it will take another ten years to construct a full theory of the components, processes and structure of social mood. He categorizes this initial exposition as observational summaries but not yet a fully-fledged hypothesis. Some might take issue with some of the components of social mood and the cultural trends that he identifies as manifestations of social mood trends. His argument that historical events and economic trends result from social mood trends is certainly thought provoking. As a political scientist by training, I was more than partially persuaded by his argument that "the social psychology that accompanies a bull or bear market is the main determinant not only of how voters select a president but also of how they perceive his performance."

Nonetheless, many readers including myself, will have problems, at least at this early pre-hypothesis, with his flat-out assertion that "Elliott waves, like them or not, are the first cause of history." To his credit, Prechter takes his argument to the logical limit: "As opposed to the traditional mechanistic models of aggregate behavior that are based upon presumptions of multiple exogenous [external] causes and ultimate effects, socionomics recognizes that patterns of aggregate human behavior are endogenous [internally-generated], self-causing, self-regulating, self-reinforcing and, to a far greater degree than has heretofore been imagined, predictable."

Given this perspective, it is not surprising that Prechter spends a good deal of the fifth and final part of his book refuting conventional approaches to financial markets. Even if many technical analysts are not prepared to agree that the Wave Principle is the primary cause of all events, they ought to be able to enjoy his dissection and disproving of the efficient market hypothesis, the presumption that the Federal Reserve Board is able to propel or rein in economic growth through the manipulation of interest rates, and other common chestnuts.

Readers of this review must understand that this is but a cursory exposition of some of Prechter's main hypothesis and observations. This review deliberately avoids most of the new terminology and concepts that Prechter is developing to describe these ideas for it is well nigh impossible to explain even some of them adequately in a relatively short review. It also must be said that some of the evidence, while suggestive, is insufficient to be persuasive and that as Prechter readily admits, much more work will have to be done to flesh out the arguments.

Are Prechter's claims for a new science of socionomics implausible or at least premature? It is certainly not implausible for this reviewer, who has personally witnessed two leading Canadian politics departments both change their names, from political economy in one case and political studies in the other, to political science. These changes were effected to reflect a growing use of quantitative methods but with methods still far short of scientific methods employed in the physical sciences. They were also a reminder of the goal of many of its practitioners to ultimately create a fully-fledged science of politics. As Prechter accurately observes in his introductory comments, "The social sciences today are where the physical sciences were three hundred years ago." However, this has not stopped the social sciences from appropriating the term scientific and it can be very plausibly argued that they are no more so than technical analysis.

For technical analysis to advance at an accelerated rate toward the status of a science, all serious technical analysts ought to first read this book with open minds. Many may object to Prechter's assertion that "the Wave Principle is to sociology and related sciences what Newton's laws were to physics," but there simply are no other approaches to technical analysis that have a basis for even making such a claim. For that matter, this reviewer, after reviewing his not inconsiderable library of key political science books, is unable to find any that are as sweepingly important and have the same potential to bring about a paradigm shift in the study of social events as the book under review.

It must be said that an objective discussion of the merits of these arguments would certainly be enhanced if Prechter, who is so intimately associated with the Elliott Wave approach, would in turn keep an open mind on the markets and reconsider his multi-year belief that the markets are at 'the crest of the tidal wave.' In this book, he applies traditional tools in a questionable manner (see for example the unconventional placement of channel lines on the chart of the DJIA on page 329) [Note: They are conventional for Elliott waves.—Ed.] to continue to advance this argument. Despite good calls in his career, Prechter's bearish outlook on U.S. stocks in the 1990s has generated so much criticism so as to undermine not only his very real and seminal contributions to technical analysis but also allow detractors to dismiss the validity and utility of the Wave Principle altogether.

Having read this book, technical analysts ought to give thoughtful consideration to his hypotheses and realize that it is in our collective self-interest to contribute to their further development. One way to do this is to channel any relevant evidence to Prechter's organization (care of comments @socionomics.org) that contributes to the further elaboration of these arguments. Another way is to critically analyze these hypotheses and supporting evidence at each and every annual conference of IFTA, MTA, CSTA and other national association meetings. The preferred method would be that used by social and natural scientists at their annual nationwide conferences, with a main presentation followed by responses by two discussants. The more these hypotheses are developed and the more persuasive they become, the more technical analysis will be able to assume a rightful position of equality with mainline fundamental analysis.

Let the debate begin, and let it be a constructive one for the advancement of technical analysis!

*Roman Franko obtained a Ph.D. in Canadian and Comparative Politics from Queen's University in Kingston, Canada where he taught for several years. He then worked for the Canadian federal government as a policy analyst before moving on to pursue his passion for technical analysis.*

*Futures Magazine*, www.futures.com
November 2004
[excerpt]

*Chapter 59*

# How Social Mood Drives Markets and Events

*The madness of crowds often is examined in relation to cultural movements and stock market crashes. Robert R. Prechter, author and renowned interpreter of Elliott waves, describes here how social moods are the cause, rather than the effect, of not only market moves but key events.*

by Ginger Szala and James T. Holter

*Robert Prechter is a well-known author, market analyst, publisher and as he says, the first socionomist, who is best known, at least in the markets arena, for his writings on Elliott waves. As president of Elliott Wave International, Bob has interpreted and parsed the writings of R.N. Elliott to make Elliott waves a popular tool and area of study for serious traders. Today, although he still stays involved in the markets, Bob has grown more involved in the study of socionomics, which he discusses here. As an author of [numerous] books, he has a larger view of the markets than most do. In an interview,* Futures *editors asked him to discuss this study of socionomics and how traders can use it in today's markets.*

**FM: What's this we hear about someone filming a documentary on your social mood work?**

Bob Prechter: A filmmaker in Atlanta got intrigued by socionomics, so he proposed doing a documentary, the kind you see on PBS. It has taken him two years of work, and it shows. It's an hour-long program called "History's Hidden Engine" that lays out the case for the idea that human herding produces patterns of mood, which in turn motivate social actions. He's got film clips, news footage, and a killer sequence showing how the mood of popular songs tracks the Dow. He also interviewed about a dozen PhDs in various fields and even gets into the pros and cons of the Wave Principle. It's more fun—to me, anyway—than reality TV. This is real reality TV. The Socionomics Foundation, which is non-profit, is funding the project. Of course, he's got to get someone to air it, which is the next hurdle. [It never happened. A DVD is available.—Ed.]

**FM: Please discuss socionomics. In about two sentences, I mean.**

RP: Socionomics is the study of social action that expresses social mood. Social mood arises endogenously from unconscious herding impulses inherited through evolution and is patterned according to the Wave Principle.

**FM: Endogenously, meaning that nothing impacts social mood?**

RP: Right. No outside forces change the trends and patterns of social mood. This idea is counter intuitive, but studies demonstrate time and again that even the most dramatic news events do not change the dynamics of stock pricing, which is our measure of social mood.

**FM: Can you describe these studies?**

RP: The best introduction to the evidence is a paper I wrote this year called "The Stock Market Is Not Physics." [Reprinted as "The Myth of Shocks" in 2016 in *The Socionomic Theory of Finance.* —Ed.] It demonstrates that even advance knowledge of the most shocking news events in history would not have helped anyone make money in the market.

**FM: Then can you explain the palpable depressed mood of the crowd after 9/11? It seemed the event put a gloom over everyone, which is contrary to what you are saying. Was that an aberration?**

RP: On the contrary, it is exactly in accordance with socionomics. What you say didn't happen. People had been getting gloomier for a full year and a half *before* the attack, not after. Five trading days after the attack, social mood trended positively non-stop for half a year to a far more optimistic level than it was at the time of the attack. The positive trend showed up in stock prices, consumer sentiment and measures of advisor and investor optimism. When the event occurred, people unconsciously latched onto it as an explanation for their waxing gloom. "Ah, there's a reason!" And they wrote articles about it in financial magazines. But if the attack really were the reason, then it should have occurred when optimism was strong and preceded a change toward pessimism. That's not what happened. The opposite happened. You can read our study on this in Chapter 29 of this book. Chapter 31 shows unequivocally that the Enron scandal did not upset investors. In fact, mood improved throughout the erupting Enron scandal and the anthrax scares, which were concurrent. And that was in the middle of a bear market! It should go without saying that scary news in a bull market has no negative effect. If you really want to get down to what I'm talking about, the eruption of scandals did not cause a negative social mood; a negative social mood caused the eruption of scandals. In fact, we predicted that it would.

**FM: Then why do people believe that it does?**

RP: Because people's brains naturally default to mechanics when they think about social events. A knowledge of mechanics has helped keep the species alive. We know that an object in motion will continue in motion unless acted upon by a force. So we duck when a rock is thrown at us and we swerve out of the way of a drunk driver who is drifting across the median. People also assume, with deep conviction, that any change in the stock market's direction must have been caused by some outside force. If they can't find one, they make one up. That's what the newspaper writers do every day after the market closes. But the stock market is not an object in motion, and outside forces are not required to change its trajectory. Unlike rocks, people have minds and they can change them. In fact, they do change them, all the time, in accord with the impulse to herd. That is what moves markets. It's also what makes markets patterned. Herding is not rational, but neither is it random. It trends and reverses by its own dynamics.

**FM: As the Chinese might say, these certainly are interesting times, with Iraq, rise in terrorism, economic issues, the coming of age of China and India, etc. Are the effects of crowd psychology more pointed when we find ourselves in a more turbulent and critical era?**

RP: Crowd psychology creates peaceful eras and turbulent eras. After the mood has trended positively for a long time, peace reigns, as it did in the 1920s, from the mid-'40s to the mid'60s, and during the 1990s. After the mood has trended negatively for a long time, turbulence reigns, as it did in the 1930s, the 1970s and since the peak in 2000. Social mood induces social actions, which express that mood.

**FM: Discuss cause and effect a bit. You say that notable social events follow, rather than precede, corresponding stock market waves (hence socionomics). Does the market cause changes in mass psychology or does mass psychology drive market prices?**

RP: Mass psychology drives markets. But it also drives other things. Changes in social mood cause people to take certain types of actions. A positive mood induces people to expand businesses, dress with flair, buy happy music, make peace with others and buy stocks. A negative mood induces people to contract businesses, dress conservatively, buy morose music, fight with others and sell stocks. So social mood moves not only the stock market but other measures of social action as well.

**FM: Isn't crowd or mass psychology just another way of refer-ring to supply and demand? If not, how is this approach different than traditional economic analysis?**

RP: It is definitely not the same as supply and demand, at least not in the sense that economists talk about it. I've written a paper called "The Financial/ Economic Dichotomy" [reprinted in *The Socionomic Theory of Finance,* 2016.—Ed.] on the stark difference between the Law of Supply and Demand, which causes equilib-rium in prices for utilitarian goods and services, and the Law of Patterned Herding which causes dynamism in prices for financial instruments. In economics, higher prices deter buyers; in finance, higher prices seem to attract buyers. Think about how dichotomous that is. The first law operates in situations of substantial certainty in an economic context, and the second in situations of substantial uncertainty in a financial context or arbitrariness in a broader social context, such as with fads and fashions. Supply has almost nothing to do with these things. They are regulated by demand, which is regulated by patterns of herding.

---

## CONTRASTING MODELS OF FINANCE

### Economic Model

1. Objective, conscious, rational decisions to maximize utility determine financial values.
2. Financial markets are random.
3. Financial markets are unpredictable.
4. Financial markets "tend toward equilibrium" and "revert to the mean."
5. Investors' decisions are based on knowledge and certainty.
6. Changing events presage changes in the values of associated financial instruments.
7. Economic principles govern finance.

### Socionomic Model

1. Subjective, unconscious, pre-rational impulses to herd determine financial values.
2. Financial markets are patterned.
3. Financial markets are probabilistically predictable.
4. Financial markets are dynamic and do not revert to anything.
5. Investors in financial markets typically use information to rationalize emotional imperatives.
6. Investors' decisions are fraught with ignorance and uncertainty.
7. Changing values of financial instruments presage changes in associated events.
8. Socionomic principles govern finance.

Source: Robert Prechter

**FM: Are sentiment indicators what you call sociometers (bounded and unbounded)? Could you describe these and how traders can use them in measuring social moods?**

RP: Wow, you're getting technical here. In a nutshell, any record of social actions that express social mood is a sociometer (see Chapter 7 of *The Socionomic Theory of Finance*—Ed.). The measures that have endless trending potential such as the stock market, are the "unbounded" type, and the ones that oscillate between extremes are the "bounded" type. Most standard sentiment indicators are bounded, such as the put/call ratio, the percentage of bullish advisors, and so on.

The key to the utility of a sociometer is how quickly it responds to mood changes. The stock market moves almost instantaneously with the social mood, while the economy and politics take longer to respond. That's because it takes time to implement the long range plans that people make when their moods change. That's why the stock market is a great tool for predicting the trend of the economy and the climate for peace or war. So sociometers are for people who want to predict the tenor and character of important news. But traders have to be able to predict where the leading sociometer is going, and that's a whole other ball game. The best way to do that is with Elliott wave analysis.

**FM: Elliott wave analysis generally is placed in the context of technical trading. However, exploiting mass psychology in your trading seems almost fundamental. Does this mean that Elliot wave analysis acts as a bridge between the fundamentals and technical worlds?**

RP: Yes! And the connection is very subtle. First, the Wave Principle is not just another technical tool. It is the foundation for all technical analysis. The market's fractal pattern is the reason that technical analysis works, and mass psychology is the driver of the pattern. The Wave Principle is not just fundamental; it is *the* fundamental. Now let's look at what other people call "fundamentals," the economy, politics and so forth. When we started this discussion, I said that social events such as economic and political trends are the result of social mood trends. If that is so, then these so-called

---

**PERCEPTION VS. REALITY**

To get a feel for how a socionomist understands social causality in a variety of areas, consider the following list of examples:

| Standard View (exogenous cause) | Socionomic Hypothesis (endogenous cause) |
|---|---|
| **Social events determine the tenor of social mood. Examples:** | **Social mood determines the tenor of social events. Examples:** |
| • Recession causes businessmen to be cautious. | • Cautious businessmen cause recession. |
| • Talented leaders make the population happy. | • A happy population makes leaders appear talented. |
| • Epidemics cause people to be fearful and depressed. | • Depressed and fearful people are susceptible to epidemics. |
| • A rising stock market makes people increasingly optimistic. | • Increasingly optimistic people make the stock market rise. |
| • Scandals make people outraged. | • Outraged people seek out scandals. |
| • The availability of derivatives fosters a desire to speculate. | • A desire to speculate fosters the availability of derivatives |
| • War makes people fearful and angry. | • Fearful and angry people make war. |
| • Happy music makes people smile. | • People who want to smile choose happy music. |
| • Nuclear bomb testing makes people nervous. | • Nervous people test nuclear bombs. |

Source: *The Elliott Wave Theorist*, September 17, 2004

---

fundamental causes are nothing but results. Being results, social events lag markets, which is why they are of no value in forecasting. But there's your bridge: The technical world of mass psychology creates the so-called fundamental world of economics, politics, fashion and culture.

**FM: Are people listening to these ideas?**

RP: They're starting to. I gave a two-hour presentation to graduate students at MIT and another at the London School of Economics. In

December, I'm going to speak at an academic/professional conference, the First International Workshop on Intelligent Finance, in
Melbourne, Australia. One academic is working on a new institute
to conduct studies on these ideas. Another has done a socionomic
study and written a paper about it. Some have been speaking about
it at conferences. So it's starting to get some traction. [For an update
on socionomists' activities, see the Appendix to *The Socionomic
Theory of Finance*.—Ed.]

*New Scientist*
August 31, 2002

*Chapter 60*

# I Know What You'll Do Next Summer

John Casti

*What do galaxies, stockbrokers and style gurus have in common?
A set of numbers describing everything they do. Does nature's
hidden program mean we're deeply predictable? asks John Casti.*

When was the last time you bucked a trend? Really swam against the tide? Chances are, you never really have—at least, not for long. But it's not your fault. You may not have as much free will as you think.

Most of us are aware of our tendency to go with the herd. We tag along with fashions: our hemlines rise and fall, our trouser legs widen and narrow, or we buy technology stocks when others are doing the same. We accept that, much of the time, we're not being "individual." What we're not aware of is why.

There are evolutionary arguments, of course: if you haven't enough information on which to base a judgement, the next best thing is to assume that the herd knows where it's going. But a mathematical analysis of our activities indicates that there may be something deeper going on. We seem to be fated to act in a way that mimics patterns found elsewhere in nature.

We already know that some actions of society appear to follow laws that often apply to otherwise completely unrelated phenomena in the universe. The numbers behind the fractal shape of a snowflake can also describe our society's financial activities, for instance. Financial data is one thing, but why should the maths that describes a seashell's spiral also underlie our technological progress? Why can our shopping habits be described by the same rules that dictate how galaxies are spread through the cosmos? It's as though we are somehow programmed by mathematics. Seashell, galaxy, snowflake or human: we're all bound by the same order.

Mathematical laws are already used to describe human activity, of course. There are various tools such as Bayesian theorems, power laws, hidden Markov processes and cellular automata, just for starters. All of these have been used in modelling financial markets, with varying degrees of success and popularity. But now an old mathematical idea, first dreamed up in the 1930s, has come to the fore again and is proving itself more powerful than anyone ever thought possible. It has enabled people to make specific predictions about the financial markets, forecasts that are now unfolding with uncanny accuracy. The fact that this technique also has something to say about what it is to be human makes it all the more remarkable.

To begin at the beginning, you have to go back to California during the Great Depression. Ralph N. Elliott, a Los Angeles accountant, is in frail health and unable to find work. While recuperating, he has plenty of free time to investigate the stock market and try to work out why it has just lost 90 per cent of its value over a three-year period. He becomes convinced that there are repetitive patterns within market indices such as the Dow Jones Index. Of course, Elliott knows it's not really saying much to point out that the Dow Jones moves in cycles. What he needs to understand is how to characterise the kinds of cycles, and then to look for patterns within them. He realises that such an understanding would enable alert investors to predict the rising prices of a bull market, foresee the decline of a bear market and even anticipate great crashes such as those of October 1929.

Elliott, a hands-on specialist in corporate financial rescue, was no stranger to market analysis or the ebbs and flows of business and eventually managed to fit together the pieces of a fascinating puzzle. Elliott's great leap forward was the realisation that the cycles don't originate within the financial markets but are a product of the humans that drive them. "Human emotions are rhythmical; they move in waves of a definite number and direction," Elliott observed. "The phenomenon occurs in all human activities, be it business, politics, or the pursuit of pleasure." And so, by analysing stock market data, he picked out certain fundamental rhythms. Today they are known as Elliott waves.

The connection between Elliott waves and the Fibonacci sequence is intriguing, because it links the Wave Principle that underlies the stock market with other natural patterns and processes found in living forms. The Fibonacci sequence appears all over the scientific landscape: it describes the spiral patterns found in seashells and the DNA helix, as well as the number of spirals on pinecones and sunflower seed heads, to give just a few natural examples. It also crops up in fractals. Its self-similarity at different scales is the hallmark of fractal patterns, which are seen everywhere in nature in things like fern fronds, coastlines and blood vessels.

According to Prechter, who produces a monthly publication called *The Elliott Wave Theorist*, these patterns reveal a direct connection between nature's numbers and all of human behaviour. Prechter believes the wave patterns are an organising principle for myriad social behaviours, ranging from newspaper sales figures to the fortunes of national leaders.

As you might expect, the area in which Elliott waves have been most extensively applied is in finance. For instance, the value of the Dow Jones between 1932 and the present can be broken down in terms of Elliott waves. If you can identify the waves and sub-waves and if know where you are on a wave, you know exactly where you're going next (see "Riding the wave"). For example, Elliott used his wave theory to announce, in the middle of the worst of the Second World War, that a multi-decade stock market rise was about to begin. And financial guru Robert Prechter did the same in the midst of recession in September 1982, by announcing that a "super bull market" had begun and forecasting a fivefold increase in stock values. In both cases, the Elliott waves enabled them to get it right.

The reason Elliott waves can tell us all this is simply because they are a direct reflection of human psychology—the rhythms of human emotion, as Elliott put it. It doesn't matter what the exact mechanism is; the point is that they're a result of human behaviour. Their success at predicting stock movements stems directly from the fact that price movements in financial markets mirror the collective beliefs of investors about the future. If the majority are optimistic, prices rise; if not, they fall.

But the stock market is just one way to take society's emotional temperature. If you look at the average length of hemline as fashions change and plot it against the Dow Jones, there is a striking correlation: the stock market faithfully rises and falls with hemline length. The obvious explanation is that when people are feeling bold and adventurous, they buy stocks and wear more revealing clothes. When they feel threatened and conservative, they do the reverse. The mood is pervasive, and almost everyone gets swept along with it.

Prechter's theory, which he calls socionomics, is that the units in a social system, whether they are investors, voters, music fans or shoppers, tend to base their decisions on what they see others doing. In other words, they herd. These decisions are then translated into a social mood, which shows up in indicators such as the Dow Jones, hemlines, lyrics in songs and so on. Armed with Elliott waves, you can start forecasting all sorts of things. Indeed, Prechter has had astonishing successes with the method in areas where no one else is even trying.

Take Major League Baseball, for example. In 1991, the sport enjoyed what some commentators felt was its most exciting season ever. Fans got so enthusiastic that a record 760,000 of them turned out to welcome the two teams returning to Atlanta and Minneapolis from the World Series, despite the fact that it was sleeting in Minneapolis. Players, owners and leagues predicted ever-increasing popularity for the sport, and cities began building new stadiums.

But socionomics predicted exactly the opposite. Prechter plotted the 90-year annual ticket sales for Major League Baseball and identified an unmistakable Elliott wave. Immediately following the 1992 season he wrote, "If you're an investor, take profits on baseball cards. If you're a player, sign a long-term contract. If you're an owner, sell your club." In the ensuing months, the speculative bubble in baseball-card prices burst, the stock price of card maker Topps collapsed, and a player's strike cancelled the 1994 World Series and the TV ratings for the World Series began a steady fall to an all-time low. And he says the retrenchment is not over yet.

Prechter has also used these principles to anticipate the peak and subsequent fall in the popularity of a financial guru—himself. Using the number of subscribers to *The Elliott Wave Theorist* as a measure of popularity, he saw that the subscription levels obeyed an Elliott wave pattern of their own. As wave 5 of his overall upward surge began to slow in late 1987, he knew that the end of his ride as a guru was near. And sure enough, despite the fact the 1988 was one of his best forecasting years ever, various members of the media had had enough of Prechter and began to attack the persona that they and their colleagues had overpromoted. He's now written about far less, and far less lionised.

Socionomics completely turns on its head the idea that events shape social mood. Since trends in social mood produce Elliott-wave patterns, the mood itself must follow a definite pattern. And if that's true, it certainly cannot be the result of external events, which are random and don't follow set trends. The only possible conclusion, Prechter argues, is that the direction of causation goes the other way: social mood actually shapes events. Work out the social mood by looking at stock market data, Prechter says, and you can then predict future social events.

## Ruling herds

The Enron scandal in the US illustrates that socionomic viewpoint very well. For weeks, newspapers and magazines trumpeted the conventional direction of cause and effect: the scandal deeply unsettled investors, they said, triggering the collapse. But socionomic thinkers argue just the opposite: worried investors precipitated the scandalous behaviour. [See Chapter 31 of this book.—Ed.]

The conclusion of Elliott wave theory is that the herding instinct in society governs events in economics, politics, and even war and peace—and all these events follow exactly the same kinds of cycle. This idea has deep implications. If Elliott waves can describe all of human activity—economic trends, wars, shopping habits and political ideas—and a sequence of numbers that is ubiquitous in nature can describe Elliott waves, is our behaviours somehow dictated by those numbers? Is what we do just a natural process, like the way a snowflake or a seashell forms?

Conspiracy theorists and fans of science fiction would love to take it as indication that we're helping to carry out some cosmic computation. But, whatever the real answer, we may well not like it. Somehow, for all our cleverness and cherished free will, it seems we might simply be living by numbers.

*Chapter 61*

# A New Paradigm

by Hernán Cortés Douglas

One might ask, 60 years after Elliott and with much data and experience, "Why are there no signs of economists' recognition of the Wave Principle?" The answer is that it is a totally different paradigm. Economics is still in love with the Newtonian physics paradigm, primarily the ideas that the same cause always generates the same effect, and if you know the parts, then you understand the whole.

Elliott is like modern physics. You do not need to understand the parts to understand the whole. Content is not important; form is important. If an alien being 3000 years from now asks what cathedrals were for, he will not get the right answer if he examines the composition of bricks or the coffins of bishops in the cellar. He will need to look at form; therein lies the path to the answer. This approach is alien to economists. They have become enamored with the mathematics and the mechanical causality of Newtonian physics, which are irrelevant to markets and business cycles.

Private correspondence
2002

*Chapter 62*

# Why Socionomics Will Be a Tough Sell to the Entrenched Majority of Professionals

by Valeri S. Safonov, PhD

While reading *The Wave Principle of Human Social Behavior*, I realized many times that it was a kind of "this-is-it" stuff. After studying the whole field in terms of what else was available, which distracted my efforts for years to other fields of market analysis, I see quite clearly that, though the Wave Principle is not perfect, it is nothing but the best available alternative to any other theory of market behavior.

Thank God that the Wave Principle is not a religion. Of course, the Wave Principle should be convincing not only to those who blindly accept it but also to sincere skeptics (as opposed to the hostile opposition, which will never be converted for any reason). Friendly seekers should have every opportunity to see that the Wave Principle is based on scientific, consistent and independently verifiable ground. Of course, there is still some work to do to reach this objective. One wonders, though, whether socionomics will even have a chance to succeed. I think it may present too powerful a challenge to the academic and professional status quo.

I would like to answer your question, "Why does the conventional approach remain so entrenched?" (p.385). One of the related questions worth attention is why the Wave Principle so quickly breaks people into "love-it" followers and "hate-it" opposition. I think that both the limbic system and the neocortex are responsible for this result, which clearly shows in the "conventional entrenchment" phenomenon. In general, I see a rather gloomy prospective for the Wave Principle to be appreciated *comme il faut* in the near future, while socionomics does not seem to stand any chance at all.

To explain why, I will not stop at the fact that people do not accept easily any unpleasant truths about themselves. Quite evidently, it is humiliating for a Homo Sapiens—the King of Nature—who has reached the top place in the spiral of evolution, to see himself as a part of a stone-age herd acting impulsively rather than intelligently.

But here is the real problem: You showed with sometimes scary clarity not only that nothing else can be compared to the Wave Principle in its predictive power but also that the whole army of conventional economists, politicians and many others, who pretend that they control the waves, do not deserve their salaries. The Wave Principle makes users of the conventional approach feel that they are not only stupid but also insecure, which is something much, much worse.

In the Statement of Value (p.6), you urge "economists and sociologists" to consider the material of your book seriously. How could they? That would mean one thing for sure: After accepting the thesis of your book, conventional social science would be ashamed of itself. What are they all paid for, and why were they getting Nobel prizes in economics? Mr. Greenspan, what the hell you are doing with taxpayers' money? When are the World Bank and the IMF, with their thousands of employees, going to stop wasting international funds? Sociologists measuring public opinion, trash your assumptions and use this new one!

Those potentially under siege by socionomics must perceive by their limbic systems that it is a clear and present danger to their very existence. Socionomics stands tall against the bulk of the educated world, which keeps on learning conventional ways of seeing things. (Those academics who die of natural causes are immediately replaced by their students.) The same thing goes for political planners and national leaders, who are so erroneously sure of their effectiveness. Socionomics would ruin their professional careers, destroy otherwise impeccable images, establish them as worthless. After what you have done to herds of economists, politicians, central bankers, etc., one should not expect them to worship socionomics. They would prefer stubbornly to express their good-for-nothing "expert views" on television and in newspapers in order to keep playing leading roles in new "tragicomedies of never ending wrongness."

Right now, the *status quo* is closely guarded by all sorts of unconsciously working Freudian defensive mechanisms. No one could ever show that economics or related sciences can take over brilliantly where the Wave Principle or socionomics fails to yield satisfactory results, but no ones cares to admit that inability. The illusionary conventional world is convenient and almost risk-free because "market experts" and "social scientists," unlike traders, are never in immediate financial danger if they are wrong. Thus, it is very smart of the neocortexes of those people to work to prevent their illusionary world from the destruction that you hopelessly call for. Although I like how well you formulated two fundamental principles of success (both "living in harmony" with trends and yet "acting independently" at crucial turning points), for most people, independent thought—much less an actual reversal of opinion—is anathema.

It will probably take generations to replace, in an evolutionary way, the old-guard mentality of conventional minds. Eventually, perhaps Nobel Prize winners will be Elliotticians. The primary hope for a faster evolution is to establish proper university courses on socionomics, with students becoming bachelors, masters and Ph.Ds in this science. In this regard, I have a dream: to establish something like an Institute of Socionomic Research (ISR) in Russia or Latvia. I have just begun to discuss the idea with my friends and colleagues. I, for one, love this theory, and I am eager to learn more of what I am really in love with.

Prechter
2002

*Chapter 63*

# On the Outlook for Socionomics

In discussing the socionomic hypothesis with intellectuals and professionals, I find that some people are receptive—if not passionate—about it once they examine the idea and study a few examples. The main reason why people in general are not initially attracted to the idea is that they presume that outside event causality—a staple of physics—applies to social mood, which it does not. Some economists reject the idea because they do not care to abandon the illusion that their policies can manage macroeconomic trends (an illusion that is easy to hold in uptrends yet which leads to disorientation and panic in downtrends). Hurdles such as these notwithstanding, truth triumphs in the end.

On the way to that triumph, socionomics will not so much ruin old careers as it will make new careers, ones that are valuable, useful and fascinating to pursue. Until 20 years ago, science either ignored the stock market or developed and defended erroneous hypotheses to model it. In the past two decades, it has mostly made progress in re-hashing some of the simpler market observations that practitioners of technical analysis have been making for decades. The exceptions are the fields of fractal geometry, in which the roughness of markets has been measured, and behavioral finance, in which psychology is finally being taken into account. What has been missing until now is a unifying force. I believe that the Wave Principle and the resulting science of socionomics constitute that unifying force.

As for how long it will take for academia to embrace socionomics, Arthur Schopenhauer made this observation:

> *"All truth passes through three stages. First, it is ridiculed. Second, it is violently opposed. Third, it is accepted as being self-evident."*

I agree with most of that statement, although as Schopenhauer said at another time, radically new ideas are first primarily *ignored*. Ridicule is only one mechanism—employed when a response is unavoidable—that keeps discussion at bay.

The Wave Principle has suffered through the first stage for seven decades. Its recent introduction to the academic world and the inauguration of the Socionomics Institute (www.socionomics.org) should create enough visibility to assure that the second stage—violent opposition—is nigh. Yet I trust that any thinking person who reads this book and its predecessor cover to cover will become thoroughly ensconced in the third stage. We will win eventually, one open mind at a time.

*Appendix:*

# TOWARD QUANTIFYING SOCIOMETERS OTHER THAN THE STOCK MARKET

*This section is relegated to an appendix because the studies presented here were developed without benefit of the socionomic insight. They have some value to socionomics nevertheless, which is why they are included.*

Prechter

*Appendix A*

## *Quantifying Social Mood in Popular Song Lyrics*

My 1985 study, "Popular Culture and the Stock Market," made this observation:

> Although the stock market would probably remain the single best indicator because of its reliably precise measurement of mood and mood change, other social phenomena *could* be detailed, numericized and studied, and used to forecast social events and even changes in mood trends themselves when extremes are achieved. If reliable data on social activities other than stock valuation were available, we could undoubtedly graph and interpret them with a similar degree of reliability. The main difficulty in assessing indicators of mood other than stock prices is the woeful lack of precise numerical data produced by social "scientists." A precise, measurable detailing of sporting event attendance figures, the number of notes and note changes in popular melodies, the lyrical content of popular songs, story content in popular books, hemline lengths, tie widths, heel heights, the prominence of various fashion and pop art colors, the angularity vs. roundness of automobile styling, the construction of various architectural styles and a host of other reflections of the popular mood, all weighted according to volume of sales, would allow us to read graphs of the public mood in the same way we read graphs of aggregate stock prices now. By comparing the evidence to stock price movement, their implications could be assessed and the general hypothesis presented here could be tested. It is highly likely that plots of the net existence and dominance of these various popular cultural elements on a daily basis would parallel those of aggregate stock prices and reflect the Wave Principle.

In fact, I had taken these words to heart many years earlier, quite without understanding where it would all lead. As a 19-year-old sophomore in college, I took a tentative first step in quantifying popular song lyrics and hypothesizing the meaning of the results. Herewith is presented what we might perhaps term a Paleolithic study in socionomics.

# An Investigation of Achievement Motive Level as Expressed in the Musical Art Forms Appreciated by Today's Youth, and Implications

by Robert R. Prechter, Jr.
Psychology of Communication/Psychology of the Arts
January 1969

### Background

Mass media today provide their listeners with a barrage of different communications for a variety of different purposes. McLuhan (1964) encourages us to look beyond the content of these many different communications to the effects of the communications themselves. In this paper I ask that the reader look beyond the immediate purpose of the content of individual communications to investigate the results, not of each communication separately, but of the collective body over a period of time. With this outlook it is possible to discover a hidden purpose, one which is probably not intended, except in rare cases, but nevertheless has its effect.

Today's popular music communicates to the youth of our society messages which are highly powerful and quite diverse. This medium is one of the most effective means of communication we can experience, for at the same time it both delivers its message and provides entertainment for its audience, thus making its reception an enjoyable and sought-after experience. Moreover, these communications are spoken most often through a youth medium to a youth audience, thus eliminating one of the most difficult psychological barriers that other communicators must continually deal with: that of overcoming boredom, fear, dislike or mistrust of the communicator. In view of these factors, it seems to me appropriate to investigate this medium in order to attain a more adequate conception of the nature of the communications produced by and affecting today's youth, and the consequent expectations we may formulate regarding the future of our society. The aspect of this medium which I have chosen to investigate is the expression of achievement motive level and its implications.

The research conducted for the preparation of this paper is, in essence, an extension of the work of D.C. McClelland (1953, 1961) concerning the correlation of Achievement Motive with the national rate of economic growth. McClelland found that the level of achievement motivation expressed in stories found in children's readers provides a basis for accurate predictions concerning the overall economic growth rate of a nation. Approximately thirty to fifty years after the achievement themes of these stories become widespread, McClelland discovered, the economy of the nation usually reflects their themes. In effect, early childhood training concerning the value of hard work and competition produces high achievement motivation, which in turn is conducive to an entrepreneurial character; when this entrepreneurial character becomes widespread and entrepreneurial roles are filled competently, the result, as may be expected, is positive economic growth. (See Table One.)

One of the most indicative elements of culture reflecting a nation's collective potential for achievement decades before this potential is evidenced in the national economic growth rate is art. These reflections are not proposed as causes for the development of

*Table 1*

high or low achievement motivation in the population but merely as indices for measuring national attitude toward it. In other words, the social environment in which children are raised to regard diligence as a positive or negative good produces at the same time works of art which express this feeling.

Several different art modes can be used to investigate this relationship. Literary art is used both in modern societies, where scholarly attention has been focused upon the stories in standardized children's readers, and in older societies, such as Britain from the 1400s and even as far back as ancient Greece from 900 to 100 B.C. In these older societies, the index used is representative literature from each era, which in turn is correlated with economic development of the country, as measured in a variety of different ways. In ancient Greece, for instance, the size of the area in which large Greek earthenware jars have been found indicates the size of the trade area during different periods of its history. When these jars are carbon-dated, they provide an index for comparison of the relative economic well-being of Greece for these different periods. The visual arts are also used to score level of achievement motivation. Since no written records have survived the civilization of Pre-Incan Peru, investigations were concerned with scoring the achievement level indicated in the choice of characteristics of art work found on Peruvian pottery. Urns dated by carbon-14 calculations were scored for appearances of S-waves and diagonals, characteristic of doodles of high achievers, and multiple waves, characteristic of low achievers. It was discovered that where designs characteristic of high achievement were most abundant, Peru, with an approximate thirty-year lag, entered upon a period of economic growth, as registered by the number and size of public buildings erected during that period. Similarly, drawings characteristic of low achievers preceded periods of low growth rate and even Peruvian conquest by outside forces. This ingenious measure was even used by McClelland to compare thirty modern nations from 1925 to 1950, correlating the achievement motivation level as indicated by their literature with the consequent change in level of kilowatt-hours of electricity produced per capita and the national income in international units per capita.

One important aspect of McClelland's discoveries is that the level of economic growth of a country is characteristically cyclical. The reasons for this phenomenon will be discussed later. However, consider the implications of these cycles upon the future economic outlook for

| Cycles Listed by Sorokin Which May be Related to Present Trend Indicated in This Paper |
| --- |
| © 1969 Prechter |

| | |
| --- | --- |
| 3 1/2 - 4 years — | Business cycles |
| 7 - 11 years — | Business cycles |
| 15-16 years — | Political life (opinions in government) |
| 30-33 years — | Dominating literary movements and schools, dominating political parties and governmental policy |
| 48-60 years — | Business cycles (accompanied by social phenomena such as revolutions, wars, social and political changes) |
| 300 years — | Great changes: beginning and end of many dynasties and social, religious and political institutions; appearance, development and decline of literary and idealogical systems |
| 500 years — | Approximate period for the growth and decline of some cultures and states |

*Table 2*

the United States. (See Table Two.) This country has been enjoying healthy economic prosperity for approximately twenty-five years. Is this prosperity to continue, or is there reason to expect a decline in relative economic activity in the near future? A strong indication of the answer lies within the art forms appreciated by the younger generation of our culture and the attitudes toward achievement inherent in it. I undertook this research for the reasons that an investigation concerning the economic future of the United States is highly relevant to our times and secondly that the field of music is an art form which to my knowledge has not been utilized in a study of this sort.

My first major assumption, based upon the preceding evidence, is that the music appreciated, listened to, and bought by the younger generation of the past decade will contain evidence of the popular attitude toward the value of achievement and thus, I hope, provide an accurate basis for scoring the achievement motivation level expressed in this material. My second assumption is that music is one of the most, if not the most, important and relevant art forms in the lives of young people today and that therefore this art form would provide the most assurance of a reliable source for investigation. For evidence supporting this assumption, we can refer to the Sunday, November 24, 1968 issue of *The New York Times*, in which an entire section is devoted to "Rock 1968." "In the scant decade and a half of its life," reports recordings editor Theodore Strongin, "rock has become a prime cultural force, one that has captured the attentions and emotions of youth en masse." Never before in history has a society produced in such a short time such a tremendous volume of artistic material which is so expressive of the youth element in a society. With this confidence, I began an investigation of this topic.

## Method

My task was to choose in the most random way possible a relatively large number of songs represented by many artists in different fields of recent popular music, score each song for achievement motivation level, and tally the results. I selected a total of seven hundred songs performed by a group of sixty different artists,[1] representing the categories of rock, rhythm and blues, pop, folk and independent singer-songwriters. Most of the songs chosen were single "hits" or from albums highly popular within the last five years. The elements of each song could fall into one or several of nine different categories and in some categories more than once. The two major categories were "Pro-Achievement" and "Non-Achievement," the latter of which was subdivided into "Anti-Achievement" and "Escape." Each of these three categories was further subdivided into three smaller categories, labeled "total theme," "major reference" and "minor reference," depending upon the extent to which the attitude toward achievement was expressed in each song.

Those songs falling into the category of "Pro-Achievement" were those expressive of acceptance of, praise of, or participation successfully in matters concerning economic, social or personal advancement. One example of a work that fell into the "Pro-Achievement—total theme" category is "It's My Life," performed by Eric Burdon and the Animals, with lyrics thus:

It's a hard world to get a break in
All the good things have been taken
But girl there are ways to make certain things pay
Though I'm dressed in these rags I'll wear sable some day

...Hear my command, I'm breakin' loose
It ain't no use holdin' me down
You're gonna cry, I'm squeezin' you dry
Takin' all I can get; no regrets when I openly lie
And live only money...

(These lyrics may not endorse *honorable* achievement, but they endorse achievement nevertheless.) A typical line meriting entry in the "major reference" category, is "For my baby I work part time/ Down at the neighborhood five and dime," from Stevie Wonder's "Nothing's Too Good For My Baby." An example for "minor reference," from Percy Sledge's "When a Man Loves a Woman," indicates acceptance of the responsibility of achievement; "I couldn't wait to see that little girl of mine/*When I got home from work*."

On the other side of the scale are the categories, "Anti-Achievement" and "Escape." These are in turn the antitheses of praise of or participation successfully in competitive action, and of acceptance of achievement behavior, respectively. These last two categories were divided in this manner in order to reveal more about the direction that the non-support of achievement was taking. I made this division after pre-testing several songs and noticing this definite division of sentiment. An example of material falling into the category of "Anti-Achievement—total theme," is Donovan's "Writer in the Sun," which concerns the meditations of a man who has wasted his life striving for the "good things": "Too many years I spent in the city/ Playing with Mister Loss and Gain." A line meriting inclusion in the "major reference" category is "Daytime turns me off and I don't mean maybe/ Nine to five ain't takin' me where I'm bound," from Neil Diamond's hit, "Thank the Lord for the Night Time." Deserving inclusion in "minor references" is "Who makes me feel like smiling when the *weary day* is through/ You, baby, you..." from the Mamas and Papas' "You Baby." Finally, we have the "Escape" category, which is characterized by songs which reject responsibility and embrace non-realities or dream worlds. A song scored under "total theme" is "A World of Our Own," by the Seekers, which claims, "We'll build a world of our own that no one else can share/ All our sorrows we'll leave far behind us there/ And I know we will find/ There'll be peace of mind/ When we live in a world of our own." Then, in the category of "major reference," I included from "A Day in the Life," by the Beatles, the reference at the end of the line spoken by a man who has just rushed to work, "Ran upstairs and had a smoke/ Somebody spoke, and I went into a dream…Ahhhhhhh…" Under "minor references" I included such lines as "I've got sunshine on a cloudy day/ When it's cold outside I've got the month of May," from "My Girl," performed by several artists, including the Temptations, the Outsiders and the Mamas and Papas.

Each song could be scored once only in a "total theme" column, and if "total theme" were scored, no other column (either "major" or "minor reference") could be scored under the same major heading (i.e., "Pro-" or "Anti-Achievement" or "Escape"), although the song could score under "major reference" or "minor reference" under a different main heading. If "total theme" were not scored for the song under any of the three main headings, the song could be scored any number of times under any of the "major reference" and "minor reference" categories. This procedure was adopted in order to avoid overweighting a single song by scoring it both under "total theme" and then several times under "major" and/or "minor reference." In this study, no song received more than three checks under a single subheading.

## Problems and Potential Objections

Before reporting the results of my research, I would like to mention some of the problems I encountered and answer some of the possible objections to my method. My most egregious problem was that of thematic ambiguity. Some of the songs were often open to two opposing interpretations. For example, "Five Hundred Miles," sung by Sonny and Cher, concerns someone who finds himself penniless after years away from home and feels ashamed to return: "Not a shirt on my back or a penny to my name/ Lord I can't go home this-a-way..." Now, is this to be scored "Pro-Achievement" since the singer regards financial success as a positive value, or "Anti-Achievement" since he has participated in the achievement process and failed, leaving the listener to conclude, "It's no use trying for anything; you never win"? I felt that a score of "Pro-Achievement—total theme" was most consistent with the scale I had constructed. One song I encountered, "Strange Young Girls," by the Mamas and Papas, discouraged the use of LSD. I felt that this was somewhat relevant since it seemed to fit under a heading of "Anti-Escape," which I had not provided for. However, this was the only song which presented this problem, so I decided that since it fit none of my categories concerning achievement motivation I would count it among the "unrelated" songs. Problems of this magnitude, however, were few, and I feel that they have not affected my results significantly. Other problems included the occasional fine line between "major reference" and "minor reference," and between a score of say, three "major references" as opposed to one "total theme." This problem was one of subjective judgment and one which would have a tendency to compensate for itself on both sides of the spectrum.

As far as major objections to my investigation, I see three. The first concerns the validity of my categorical headings. Why did I not use the scoring method used by McClelland in his evaluations of stories produced by subjects for psychological study (under the pretense that their creativity was being tested)? This point requires rather involved discussion. McClelland's scoring was based upon whether or not his stories "showed concern with competing successfully with some standard of excellence." First, a desire to achieve something does not necessarily mean competition. For example, "Hitch Hike," by Marvin Gaye (and the Rolling Stones), promises, "I'm gonna find that girl if I have to hitch hike 'round the world." There is certainly concern with achieving a goal here, although no competition with a standard or another person is required. Secondly, McClelland's breakdown of points for each interrelated element that may enter into an achievement situation seems somewhat arbitrary, and his concern more for whether or not the story displays achievement imagery and the extent to which it does rather than the opinion expressed by the story concerning the value of such activity leads to the complication that a story scoring 5 could be just as favorable toward achievement as a story scoring 11. Finally, McClelland is dealing with stories, whereas I am testing song material, which is more conducive to direct statements of sentiment rather than a symbolic or representative expression of situation and outcome. Thus, in song lyrics, interpretation by the scorer is at a minimum. The second objection I see is that possibly my category of "Escape" is unrelated to achievement imagery or that a fourth, polar category should have been included, labeled something such as "Acceptance of Involvement." As I have previously mentioned, escape from reality is a rejection of responsibility and thus a rejection of the major prerequisite for achievement. Besides, all songs which do not advocate escape from reality do accept reality and therefore involvement. However, as can be seen in so many examples, one may be involved in reality and still express negative feelings toward achievement. Therefore, the category of "Escape" is merely the antonym of acceptance of achievement as a value, statements of which were scored under the heading of "Pro-Achievement." The third major objection to my research could be that my selection of song material was not random enough and therefore may produce biased results. About ten percent of the songs were chosen randomly from a card file of all the single records owned by radio station WYBC at Yale University. The bulk of the songs were from albums that I chose from libraries of Yale students, including myself, in an attempt to get a wide range of artists included in the scoring process. Although I feel that my choices provide a good representative sample of the more popular recordings of the past five years, the choice was not made by random selection and therefore constitutes a valid criticism.

## Results

The results of my research are as follows: from 700 records tested, 134 (approximately 19 percent) contained relevant material. Of these 134 records, there were 36 total "Pro-Achievement" references and themes and 128 total "Non-Achievement" references, with 60 in the "Anti-Achievement" category and 68 under the "Escape" heading. For a breakdown of the scores, refer to Table Three.

It is evident from these results that the general attitude expressed in songs representing today's youth is not favorable toward the values of achievement, competition or diligence. In every subheading, "Anti-Achievement" references top those which are "Pro-Achievement," even up to more than double in the case of "major references." Of the records tested, far more were found to have their total themes concerned with escape from reality and its responsibilities than for the other two categories combined. Strongin (1968) saw an indication of this escape trend in his description of rock music, in which songs "...lend a touch of sadness and a sense of 'being free from the crush of society.'" In fact, of the four instrumentals I encountered on albums used for this research, two of them had escapist titles: "Flying" and "Embryonic Journey." The next highest in total thematic statement is for the "Anti-Achievement" category, suggesting a rebellious, rejecting attitude toward the values of the industrious capitalist. However, the split between pro- and anti-achievement values in entire themes is not very great. The deciding

*Table 3*

factor is the encouragement for those who wish to escape reality and responsibility and lose themselves in carefree, non-competitive world, thus greatly enlarging the gap between the "Pro- Achievement" and "Non-Achievement" categories. Moreover, upon closer examination of the data, I find that a greater percentage (23 percent as opposed to 6 percent) of those included in the "Pro-Achievement" category are themes dealing with concern about achieving a better love relationship with a member of the opposite sex. These songs usually proposed a plan to better a relationship through means of achieving better economic or social status. "Do You Love Me?" by the Contours, for instance, concerns a man who returns to ask his girl if she loves him now that he can dance well, giving a positive value to social achievement. "For Your Love," by the Yardbirds and "Hey Gip" by the Animals are both promises of riches to women in return for their love, therefore giving a positive value to economic achievement. On the other hand, most of the entries under the heading of "Anti-Achievement—total theme" are social commentaries. Whether one should consider these entries more relevant or less, however, is questionable.

**Forecast**

What do these results indicate concerning the future of economic development in the United States? If this measure and these results are to be trusted, one is led to predict a decline in economic growth activity for the United States as a whole in a period of time approximately thirty to fifty years after this tendency began to manifest itself. Since my investigation is not chronological, I cannot speculate upon when this negative attitude toward achievement became so prevalent, although it would seem appropriate to suggest that it was nurtured soon after the emergence of rock music some fifteen years ago.

**Possible Psychological Causes of Social Attitudes Toward Achievement**

What, we may ask, is the reason for the negative attitude toward achievement? Max Weber's Key Hypothesis, as modified by Roger Brown (1965), tells half of the story. (See Table One.) An ideological movement, he says, often impels parents to train their children to be independent. An entrepreneurial character is then assumed, the recruitment of which provides for economic growth of a country. But, as Sorokin (1928) and Spengler (1926, 1928, 1932), as well as McClelland, indicate, societies are cyclical. The state of economic growth produces, in its turn, economic prosperity. Thus, an environment of affluence is created which is conducive to child dependency and thus a non-achieving-oriented adult. On a personal psychological level, Erikson (1963) indicates support of McClelland's argument in his discussion of the eight ages of man, in which the development of a dependent child results from lack of independence training by his parents (as Weber implies), which makes difficult or impossible the child's expected act of dissociating himself from his family and embracing roles of productive diligence within society. The crucial stage of development here is under the heading "Industry vs. Inferiority," which, if not resolved successfully, is highly conducive to the development of a non-achievement-oriented adult:

> For before the child, psychologically already a rudimentary parent, can become a biological parent, he must begin to be a worker. With the oncoming latency period, the normally advanced child...learns to win recognition by producing things. He has experienced "a sense of finality regarding the fact that there is no workable future within the womb of his family. He develops a sense of industry...the work principle teaches him the pleasure of work completion by steady attention and persevering diligence.

> The child's danger, at this stage, lies in a sense of inadequacy and inferiority. If he despairs of his tools and skills or of his status among his tool partners, he may be discouraged from identification with them and with a section of the tool world. To lose the hope of such "industrial" association may pull him back to the more isolated, less tool-conscious familial rivalry of the oedipal time ...this is socially a most decisive stage, since industry

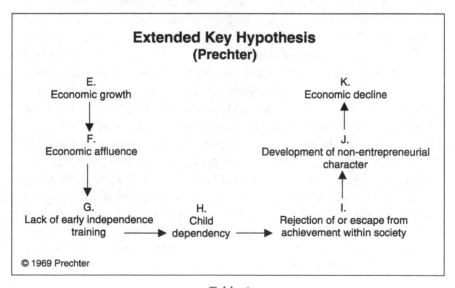

*Table 4*

involves doing things beside and with others, a first sense of division of labor and of differential opportunity, that is, a sense of the technological ethos of a culture, develops at this time.[2]

The result of non-resolution of this stage of child development, then, is a lack of willing and diligent entrepreneurs and thus a tendency toward economic decline if the conflict is on a national scale. (See Table Four.) This state of affairs may well be the one in which the United States is situated today. Moreover, the communication of such anti-achievement sentiments is not merely the result of such a feeling or tendency but a cause of it as well, reaffirming and strengthening such sentiments:

> "The people of our own age, we are trying to express something,"
> one teenager said recently. "We do it through the music we call
> rock. It tells our feelings about the way society is today, about
> war, the system, about relationships today." (Strongin, 1968)

### Impressions of These Results in Other Social Trends

The conclusions of this research are manifest in other art forms and in other areas of society as well. In the visual arts, "impressionism" has to a great degree replaced the style of true representation, in which the achievement of producing the work of art was of greater importance. Today one doesn't marvel so much at the painstaking task of producing the work of art as he marvels at the effect or impression that it has upon him. The "mind-expanding" drug movement, supported by Barron and Leary, slogans of "turn on, tune in, and drop out," LSD as a religion, and a liking for psychedelia all put emphasis on the experience of the surreal. They are oftentimes merely means of escape from the responsibilities imposed by a world of reality. Even social changes and political movements reflect this anti-achievement tendency. The peace movements and the move to abolish ROTC are rejections of the value of military achievement as a positive good. Student movements at Yale University have changed in the last year and a half no less than five major requirements of students to engage in competition, effecting the abolition of the letter grading system, the abolition of required physical education until judged "fit," the abolition of freshmen course requirements, the reduction of the course credit requirements for graduation and, finally, the abolition of the dean's list.

**Looking Forward**

The topic I have chosen is open for many more extensive investigations concerning the nature of this anti-achievement sentiment. Is there a difference between the feelings communicated in white rock and black "soul" or rhythm & blues? Research here could lead to discovery of problems confronting these two groups as well as to predictions concerning their relationships with each other. Has the anti-achievement element declined, increased or remained the same in musical expression during the last ten years? A systematic scoring of the "Top 100" songs of each year from 1958 to 1968 would probably answer this question. How about aspects related to achievement motive in the visual arts, such as discreteness vs. fuzziness? Are such terms applicable to musical quality? I would be interested in seeing the results of such investigation, as indeed I am going to be interested to see how these trends continue and whether or not my prediction is realized in the future.[3]

## A List of the 134 Songs (Out of 700) Scored For Relevant Content

| | Pro-Achievement | | | Anti-Achiev. | | | Escape | | |
|---|---|---|---|---|---|---|---|---|---|
| | Tot. | Maj. | Min. | Tot. | Maj. | Min. | Tot. | Maj. | Min. |
| Soul Train | | | | | | ✓ | | | |
| Crystal Ship | | | | | | | ✓ | | |
| Time to Dream | | | | | ✓ | | ✓ | | |
| Do You Love Me | ✓ | | | | | | | | |
| Gimme Some Lovin' | | | | | ✓ | ✓ | | | |
| New Orleans | | | | | | | ✓ | | |
| California Nights | | | | | | ✓ | | | |
| Museum | | | | | | | ✓ | | |
| Sidewalk Surfin' | | | | | | | | ✓ | |
| Dancing Bear | | | | ✓ | | | | | |
| England Swings | | | | | | | ✓ | | |
| People Got to Be Free | | ✓ | | | | | | | |
| A World of Our Own | | | | | | ✓ | ✓ | | |
| Don't Look Back | | | | ✓ | | | | ✓ | |
| Call Me Lightning | | ✓ | | | | | | | |
| For Your Love | ✓ | | | | | | | | |
| Don't Bother Me | | | | | | | ✓ | | |
| I'll Get You | ✓ | | | | | | | | |
| Hitch Hike | ✓ | | | | | | | | |
| Good Times | | | | | | | ✓ | | |
| One More Try | ✓ | | | | | | | | |
| Play With Fire | | | | | ✓✓✓ | | | | |
| 19th Nervous Breakdown | | | | | ✓ | | | | |
| As Tears Go By | | | | | ✓ | | | | |
| Mother In Law | | | | | | ✓ | | | |
| Groovin' | | | | | | ✓ | | ✓ | |
| You Baby | | | | | | ✓ | | ✓ | |
| Is It Any Wonder | | | | | | ✓ | | | ✓ |
| Let Me Be | | | | | | | | ✓ | |
| It Ain't Me Babe | | | | | ✓ | | | | |
| Outside Chance | | | | ✓ | | | | | |
| You Know What I Mean | | | | | | | | | ✓ |
| With A Little Help/Friends | | | | | ✓ | | | | |
| A Day In The Life | | | | | ✓✓ | ✓ | | ✓ | |
| My Girl | | | | | | | | | ✓✓ |
| King of the Road | | | | ✓ | | | | | |
| Do You Believe in Magic | | | | | | | | ✓ | |
| Daydream | | | | | | | ✓ | | |
| Up Up and Away | | | | | | | ✓ | | |
| Summer in the City | | | | | | | | ✓ | |
| Ruby Tuesday | | | | | | | | ✓ | |
| On a Quiet Night | | | | | ✓ | | | ✓ | |

*Table 5*

| | Pro-Achievement | | | Anti-Achiev. | | | Escape | | |
|---|---|---|---|---|---|---|---|---|---|
| | Tot. | Maj. | Min. | Tot. | Maj. | Min. | Tot. | Maj. | Min. |
| Pretty Ballerina | | | | | | | | ✓ | |
| Barterers and Their Wives | | | | ✓ | | | | | |
| Lazy Day | | | | | ✓ | | | | |
| The Sailing Ship | | | | | | | ✓ | | |
| In the Café | | | | | ✓ | | | ✓✓ | |
| The Town/Back To | | | | | ✓ | | ✓ | | |
| Up On the Roof | | | | | ✓ | | ✓ | | |
| Mr. Unreliable | | | | | ✓ | | | | |
| Cobblestone Road | | | | ✓ | | | | | |
| You've Got to Hide Your Love/ | | | | | ✓ | | | | |
| There's a Place | | | | | | | ✓ | | |
| Groovy Kind of Love | | | | | | | | ✓ | |
| Summer Place | | | | | | | ✓ | | |
| Poor Side of Town | | ✓ | | | | | | | |
| Michael | | ✓✓ | | | | | | | |
| The Gypsy Rover | | | | | ✓ | | | | |
| Tuesday Afternoon | | | | | | | | ✓ | |
| Early Morning Fantasy | | | | | | | | ✓ | |
| Turn Down Day | | | | | ✓✓ | | | | |
| Itchycoo Park | | | | | ✓ | | ✓ | | |
| When a Man Loves a Woman | | | ✓ | | | | | | |
| We Ain't Gonna Make It | | | | | ✓ | | | | |
| I Got You Babe | | | | | ✓ | | | | |
| Flying | | | | | | | ✓ | | |
| Embryonic Journey | | | | | | | ✓ | | |
| 500 Miles | ✓ | | | | | | | | |
| Straight Shooter | | | ✓ | | | | | | |
| California Dreamin' | | | | | | | ✓ | | |
| No Salt on Her Tail | | | | | | | | | ✓ |
| Sing For Your Supper | ✓ | | | | | | | | |
| Did You Ever Want to Cry | | | | | | | ✓ | | |
| Turn Turn Turn | | | ✓✓✓ | | | | | | |
| Satisfied Mind | | | | ✓ | | | | | |
| The Times/Changin' | | | ✓✓ | | | | | | |
| Wait and See | ✓ | | | | | | | | |
| Mr. Tambourine Man | | | | | | | ✓ | | |
| All I Really Want to Do | | | | | | ✓ | | | |
| Don't Doubt Yourself | ✓ | | | | | | | | |
| It's My Life | ✓ | | | | | | | | |
| Gonna Send You/Walker | | | ✓ | | | | | | |
| House of the Rising Sun | | ✓✓ | | | | | | | |
| We Gotta Get Out/Place | | | | | ✓✓ | ✓ | | | |
| Little Bit O' Soul | | ✓ | | | | | | | |
| Sugar Town | | | | | | | ✓ | | |
| Nobody But Me | ✓ | | | | | | | | |
| Hey Gip | ✓ | | | | | | | | |

*Table 5 (cont'd)*

| | Pro-Achievement | | | Anti-Achiev. | | | Escape | | |
|---|---|---|---|---|---|---|---|---|---|
| | Tot. | Maj. | Min. | Tot. | Maj. | Min. | Tot. | Maj. | Min. |
| I'm Gonna Make You Love Me | ✓ | | | | | | | | |
| Let's Live for Today | | | | ✓ | | | | | |
| Thank the Lord for the Nighttime | | | | | ✓ | | | | |
| Dock of the Bay | | | | | ✓ | | | | |
| Papa Was Too | | | | | ✓✓ | | | | |
| Nothing's Too Good | ✓ | | | | | | | | |
| Uptight | | | | | ✓✓ | | | | |
| People Get Ready | | | | | | | ✓ | | |
| Pushin' Too Hard | | | | ✓ | | | | | |
| Enchanted Gypsy | | | | | | | ✓ | | |
| Voyage Into/Screen | | | | | | | ✓ | | |
| Mandolin Man and His Secret | | | | ✓ | | | | | |
| Epistle to Derroll | | | | | ✓ | | | | |
| Skip-a-Long Sam | | | | ✓ | | | | | |
| There Was a Time | | ✓ | | | | | | | |
| Land of Doesn't Have To Be | | | | | | | ✓ | | |
| Writer in the Sun | | | | ✓ | | | | | |
| Guinivere | | | | ✓ | | | | | |
| The Fat Angel | | | | | | | ✓ | | |
| Poor Cow | | | | | | | | ✓ | |
| White Rabbit | | | | | | | ✓ | | |
| Makin' My Mind Up | | | | | | | | ✓ | |
| Think I'll Run Away | | | | | | | ✓ | | |
| Somebody Tell/Name | | | | | ✓ | | | ✓ | |
| Downtown | | | | | | | ✓ | | |
| Then You Can Tell Me Goodbye | | | ✓ | | | | | | |
| Alabama Song | | | | | | | ✓ | | |
| A Girl Like You | | | ✓ | | | | | | |
| Beautiful Morning | | | ✓ | | | | | | |
| Flowers Never Bend/Rainfall | | | | | | | | ✓ | |
| Paint It Black | | | | | | | | ✓✓ | |
| Flight 505 | | | | | | | | ✓ | |
| Ben Franklin's Almanack | | | | | | | ✓ | | |
| July | | | | | | | ✓ | | |
| A Well Respected Man | | | | ✓ | | | | | |
| Hard Day's Night | | ✓ | | | | | | | |
| Can't Buy Me Love | | | | ✓ | | | | | |
| Think for Yourself | | | | | | | | ✓ | |
| 5D | | | | | | | ✓ | | |
| Mr. Spaceman | | | | | | | | ✓ | |
| Lear Jet Song | | | | | | | ✓ | | |
| I Am a Rock | | | | | | | ✓ | | |
| I Gotta Dream On | | | | | | | ✓ | | |
| Moody River | | | | | | | | ✓ | |
| School is Out | | | | ✓ | | | | | |
| Johnny B. Goode | | ✓ | | | | | | | |

*Table 5 (cont'd)*

## NOTES

[1] Here is a sample of some of the artists included: Animals, Association, Beatles, Byrds, Cryan' Shames, Neil Diamond, Donovan, Doors, Fifth Dimension, Herman's Hermits, Jefferson Airplane, Kinks, Left Banke, Lovin' Spoonful, Mamas and Papas, Roger Miller, Outsiders, Rascals, Johnny Rivers, Rolling Stones, Simon and Garfunkel.

[2] The next stage of child development is "Identity vs. Role Confusion," which seems to have been a major problem of the new generation. The question of "finding oneself" is becoming more critically important and more commonly asked and searched out.

[3] Or should I remain unconcerned, a disciple of the Grassroots, who preach, "Live for today/ and don't worry 'bout tomorrow...."

## REFERENCES

Brown, Roger. (1965). "The achievement motive." *Social psychology.* New York: The Free Press, pp. 423-476,

Erikson, Erik H. (1963). *Childhood and society.* New York: W.W. Norton & Co., pp. 255-263.

McClelland, D.C., et al. (1953). *The achievement motive.* New York: Appleton-Century.

McClelland, D.C. (1961). *The achieving society.* Princeton: Van Nostrand, 1961.

McLuhan, Marshall. (1964). *Understanding media: The extensions of man.* New York: New American Library.

Sorokin, Pitrom. (1928). *Contemporary sociological theories.* New York: Harper & Brothers, pp. 730-735.

Spengler, Oswald. (1926, 1928, 1932). *Decline of the west.* New York: Alfred A. Knopf.

Strongin, Theodore. (1968, November 24). "Rock 1968." *The New York Times,* section 14.

### A Discussion of Outcomes (2002)

Socionomics regards the expression of sentiment in the popular songs of the late 1960s as a *concurrent* expression of social mood. Since the mood of the time was escapist and anti-achievement, it probably accurately reflected the mood of a fledgling bear market, which began in February 1966. That bear market ultimately had economic (and other) consequences.

Whether we should credit the fortunate timing of the author's interest in the subject or the forecasting value of the information, the fact

*Figure 1*

is that the study was just about perfectly timed for the rather dramatic change in trend for stocks and the economy that ensued immediately thereafter. The paper was completed in December 1968 and submitted in January 1969, after a period of eight recession-free years, an all-time U.S. record. As you can see in Figure 1, the Value Line geometric average of stock prices reached a speculative top in December 1968 and lost 74 percent of its value over the next six years, ushering in the recessions of December 1969-November 1970 and December 1973-February 1975. In constant-dollar terms, the Dow Jones Industrial Average, which had topped in 1966, continued lower until August 1982, ushering in two more recessions, those of January-August 1980 and August 1981-November 1982. Overall, those fourteen years were the worst comparable period for stock prices and the economy since 1928-1942. In other words, the social mood observed in the study had immediate effects.

**The Forecasted Outcome Is Due Now**

There is another way to look at the results, which is the way they were construed in the paper: as a harbinger of economic change decades in the future. In the paper, I cited D.C. McClelland's conclusion about timing: "Approximately thirty to fifty years after the achievement themes of these stories become widespread, McClelland discovered, the economy of the nation usually reflects their indications." With nothing else to go on, I gave the conclusion that he would have given: "If this measure is to be trusted, one is led to predict a decline in economic growth activity for the United States as a whole in a period of time approximately thirty to fifty years after this tendency began to manifest itself." Further review leads me to conclude that the trend in popular song lyrics to an anti-achievement theme started in 1965, which would mean, according to McClelland, an economic decline beginning sometime between 1995 and 2015.[1] Whether this delayed effect of the anti-achievement sentiment of the late 1960s will occur in line with McClelland's' theories remains to be seen, but it is certainly compatible with the outlook from an Elliott wave standpoint as expressed in *Conquer the Crash*. If the stock market continues to fall and depression ensues, then the onset of economic malaise may turn out to have begun right at the time that the original study said it should.

## NOTES

[1] Since the medium of expression was not children's stories but late teenagers' stories, we might today propose an adjustment to the forecasted time reflecting that ten years' difference, producing not a 30- to 50-year range but a 20- to 40-year range for the time before the downturn. Either way, the 30 years that have since elapsed as of the late 1990s represent either the beginning or the center of the range targeted for the start of a period of economic malaise.

*Appendix C*

# Quantifying Pessimistic Rumination in Popular Songs

My 1969 paper cited its own main shortcoming:

> My investigation is not chronological.... Has the anti-achievement element declined, increased or remained the same in musical expression during the last ten years? A systematic scoring of the "Top 100" songs of each year from 1958 to 1968 would probably answer this question.[1]

As if taking a cue from that call to action, in 1990,[2] Harold Zullow of Rutgers University independently undertook to quantify meticulously the degree of "pessimistic rumination in popular songs" over a 34-year period, which was published the following year in the *Journal of Economic Psychology*. For the study, he selected the Top Forty songs of each year from 1955 to 1989 as compiled by *Billboard* magazine and scored them for extent of "rumination," a negative description or evaluation of an event, by the degree of focus and emotion as well as the expressed stability, globality and internality of its cause(s). A chronological table of results is shown on the next page. Here are his primary conclusions:

> Pessimistic rumination in popular music lyrics correlated highly with subsequent values of rumination in *Time* [magazine], the Index of Consumer Sentiment, personal consumption expenditures, and GNP growth. The two-year moving average of pessimistic rumination correlated -.063 (p<0.0002) with the moving average of the year-to-year change in GNP (GNPCHG) in the subsequent two years. In a 2SLS analysis, changes in personal consumption expenditures (PERSCONS) predicted GNPCHG, and the Index of Consumer Sentiment (ICS) in turn predicted PERSCONS. One more step removed, pessimistic rumination and rumination in *Time* predicted consumer sentiment.

Pessimism and rumination in popular music and *Time* magazine, 1955–1989.

| Year | RUMSONG | PESS SONG | PESSRUM | RUMTIME |
|------|---------|-----------|---------|---------|
| 1955 | 24.7% | 8.53 | −2.30 | 1.9% |
| 1956 | 31.7 | 9.77 | 0.30 | 1.9 |
| 1957 | 28.7 | 8.95 | −1.06 | 1.9 |
| 1958 | 31.7 | 10.07 | 0.56 | 9.7 |
| 1959 | 27.2 | 8.57 | −1.72 | 9.7 |
| 1960 | 32.0 | 10.29 | 0.81 | 13.2 |
| 1961 | 33.4 | 10.08 | 0.93 | 17.0 |
| 1962 | 25.4 | 8.83 | −1.89 | 13.5 |
| 1963 | 27.9 | 8.11 | −1.97 | 7.7 |
| 1964 | 27.4 | 9.87 | −0.55 | 5.8 |
| 1965 | 23.2 | 9.14 | −2.10 | 15.1 |
| 1966 | 30.3 | 10.02 | 0.21 | 19.2 |
| 1967 | 32.5 | 10.81 | 1.37 | 19.2 |
| 1968 | 35.3 | 9.83 | 1.13 | 30.8 |
| 1969 | 28.6 | 11.44 | 1.07 | 25.0 |
| 1970 | 27.2 | 9.26 | −1.12 | 36.5 |
| 1971 | 36.8 | 10.56 | 2.09 | 25.0 |
| 1972 | 34.2 | 9.58 | 0.67 | 19.2 |
| 1973 | 36.9 | 11.24 | 2.70 | 41.5 |
| 1974 | 25.4 | 8.96 | −1.78 | 48.1 |
| 1975 | 29.0 | 9.41 | −0.60 | 30.8 |
| 1976 | 17.5 | 8.79 | −3.64 | 23.1 |
| 1977 | 18.0 | 10.98 | −1.63 | 25.0 |
| 1978 | 35.1 | 11.37 | 2.43 | 32.7 |
| 1979 | 36.6 | 10.22 | 1.75 | 47.2 |
| 1980 | 28.9 | 12.59 | 2.14 | 42.3 |
| 1981 | 30.6 | 10.43 | 0.63 | 44.2 |
| 1982 | 27.5 | 11.26 | 0.68 | 50.0 |
| 1983 | 25.9 | 8.17 | −2.36 | 44.2 |
| 1984 | 26.5 | 10.26 | −0.41 | 28.3 |
| 1985 | 26.9 | 9.78 | −0.74 | 40.4 |
| 1986 | 29.2 | 12.40 | 2.04 | 34.6 |
| 1987 | 30.3 | 10.97 | 1.03 | 48.1 |
| 1988 | 25.8 | 10.22 | −0.60 | 30.8 |
| 1989 | 30.7 | 12.08 | 2.09 | 63.5 |

*Note:* Higher rumination percentages, pessimism scores, and PessRum scores indicate greater rumination, pessimism, and pessimistic rumination.

from Harold Zullow, *Journal of Economic Psychology* (1991)

Rumination in *Time*, PESSRUM in songs, and its components of pessimism and rumination correlated strongly with: subsequent economic growth, the occurrence of a recession year, and the hypothesized mediating variables of consumer optimism and personal consumption expenditures.

Pessimistic rumination in popular songs predicts decreased economic growth with a one- to two-year lead. The hypothesis that this relationship is causal was strengthened by the confirmation by simultaneous equations of a plausible path of influence. The path is that pessimistic rumination in the fantasy-based material of song lyrics predicts changes in the degree to which Americans worry about real-world events. PESSRUM in songs predicts rumination about events on the cover of *Time* magazine and consumer pessimism in nationwide surveys. Consumer pessimism in turn predicts decreased personal consumption expenditures, which strongly predicts decreased GNP growth.

Controlling for psychological variables, current GNP growth did not predict the ICS, rumination in *Time* magazine, or pessimistic rumination in songs.

Pessimistic rumination may aid in forecasting economic recessions and growth with a longer lead time than traditional econometric models because it is an early signal for changes in personal consumption expenditures and GNP one and two years later, a longer lead than many economic variables.

Whatever the cause of the fluctuations, high pessimistic rumination in the lyrics of popular songs and rumination on the cover of *Time* magazine have predicted changes in consumer optimism for the last 35 years.[3,4]

For evidence of these correlations, please see three of Zullow's graphs, reproduced below.

Zullow observes that the overall "pessimism score" reached an optimistic high in 1963 (which not coincidentally in my opinion saw the outbreak of Beatlemania) and a pessimistic low in 1980, which marked the low for stocks priced in gold. He also found substantial pessimism in the final year of his study, 1989. Zullow used his sociometer to make a successful forecast:

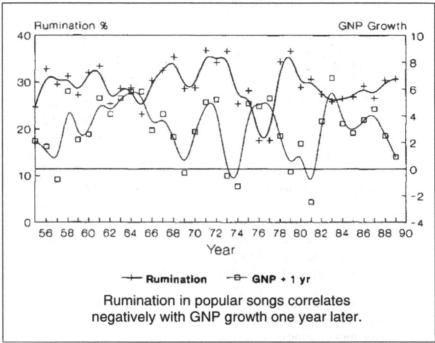

Rumination in popular songs correlates
negatively with GNP growth one year later.

Pessimism in popular songs correlates
negatively with GNP growth one year later.

from Harold Zullow, *Journal of Economic Psychology* (1991)

The two-year moving average of pessimistic rumination in popular songs correlates negatively with GNP growth one year later.

from Harold Zullow, *Journal of Economic Psychology* (1991)

Pessimistic rumination in songs in 1989 (especially the second half of 1989) reached one of its highest levels in the last 35 years. Rumination in *Time* magazine in 1989 reached a historic high, in nearly two-thirds of the cover stories, in spite of an auspicious year of economic growth and the demise of Communism in Eastern Europe. This suggests a downturn in consumer optimism in 1990, followed by a recession year in 1991, with the recession beginning as early as later in 1990—a prediction I first made in May 1990 (Zullow 1990).[5]

Why would pessimistic rumination in popular songs be high in 1989, when the stock market was near an all-time high? The answer is that it was in the middle of an Elliott wave bear market of Primary degree (wave ④), which began in August 1987 and ended in October 1990 at the end of a flat pattern or in January 1991 at the end of a triangle pattern, its social results including recession and war. (For a picture of this corrective wave, see Figure 2 in Chapter 35.) I would surmise that song-lyric pessimism stayed high at least through October 1990. Whatever the trend in rock music lyrics was for the decade of the 1990s, the trend of country music lyrics certainly took a dramatic turn toward optimism as the market resumed its upward path in wave ⑤.

Zullow asks, "Then why do consumer optimism and pessimistic rumination fluctuate?" His tentatively suggested answer naturally assumes an external cause, in this case that bad times might cause people to pursue escapist fantasies and good times might cause them to "expose themselves to negative fantasies in the popular culture." This is similar to one of the assumptions of my paper, as illustrated in Table 4 therein. *His data and mine, however, do not make a strong case that changes in the economy cause changes in mood, opposing or otherwise.* In a footnote, he observes, "Ordinarily, an economist might model PERSCONS [personal consumption expenditures] as a function of income. However, when GNP [change] is introduced as an independent variable in predicting changes in [personal consumption expenditures], its beta weight is non-significant. Only consumer sentiment was significant...." In other words, social mood, not macroeconomic vibrancy, correlates with personal spending. The tendency for pessimistic rumination to follow boom times and its lack to follow bad times is not causation at work but merely the natural ebb and flow of social mood change. His data do show quite effectively, as he reports, that changes in mood precede changes in the economy. This is exactly what the socionomic insight indicates should be the case. Social mood is endogenous; it *precedes* economic change because it *causes* economic change.

## New Directions

To date, the only attempts at creating a sociometer from popular music have involved numericizing lyric content. We each took this path partly because it is easy. I believe, however, that other aspects of popular recordings, such as tempo, melody, harmony, dissonance, noise level and tone of vocal delivery are probably better measures of the mood behind a song than its lyrics. We can *read* the lyrics of "Purple Haze" or "Sunshine of Your Love" and regard them as love songs in a pleasant mood. We can *listen* to their opening notes and their melodies, though, and realize that they are something quite different. Likewise, we can read the lyrics of "Bad Moon Rising" and regard them as a picture of doom, while we can listen to the song's bouncy jump beat and singsong melody and hear something quite benign. Many songs have no ambiguity in any of their aspects and could undoubtedly be rated as utterly positive or negative mood recordings. Until more comprehensive studies are undertaken, we are only scratching the surface.

## NOTES

[1] Prechter, Robert. (1969, January). "An investigation of achievement motive level as expressed in the musical art forms appreciated by today's youth, and implications." Paper submitted for Psychology of Communication/Psychology of the Arts, Yale University.

[2] His paper appeared 21 years later and this book 34 years later, which are Fibonacci durations.

[3] Zullow, Harold M. (1991). "Pessimistic rumination in popular songs and news magazines predict economic recession via decreased consumer optimism and spending." *Journal of Economic Psychology* 12, 501-526.

[4] Each paragraph is an excerpt from the larger paper (ellipses omitted).

[5] Zullow, Harold M. (1990, May). "Pessimistic rumination in popular music and news magazines predicts economic recession, 1890-1990." Paper presented at a joint meeting of the American Association for Public Opinion Research and the World Association for Public Opinion Research, Lancaster, PA.

## Appendix D

# Quantifying Social Mood by Polling

George Katona of the Economic Behavior Program at the University of Michigan apparently made the first successful attempt to quantify a meter of social mood other than the stock market for the conscious purpose of forecasting the economy. To that end, he developed the now widely used Index of Consumer Sentiment. The following account is from Zullow's 1991 paper:

> Since Katona and others in the Economic Behavior Program at the University of Michigan began studying consumer optimism in the 1950s, it has become increasingly evident that national mood changes before a recession begins—typically nine months in advance (Katona 1960, 1980). Surveys conducted two to four times a year until 1977, and monthly since 1978, have asked a nationwide sample of Americans about their current and expected financial situation, and that of the economy. Responses are combined into an Index of Consumer Sentiment (ICS), which the U.S. Commerce Department has used since 1978 as a leading indicator of economic activity. The ICS forewarned us of the last seven recessions and sounded one false alarm before the minirecession of 1966-67. The ICS predicts changes in durable goods purchases, such as automobiles, by American consumers. These expenditures reflect the use of discretionary income and provide an advance indicator of turning points in the economy.
>
> These findings have been replicated by continuing surveys in other countries (Katona and Strumpel 1978; Praet 1985; Williams and Defris 1981). A nation's generalized (non-economic) hopes and fears also predict changes in GNP (Noelle-Neumann 1984, 1989).

Does consumer sentiment predict the economy above and beyond traditional macroeconomic variables? Some have found that the ICS can be explained largely by traditional macroeconomic variables: that consumer sentiment reacts to the economy but does not contribute over and above to predicting economic change (Shapiro 1972; Vanden Abeele 1983). In contrast, Katona and others (Adams and Klein 1972; Pickering 1977; Praet 1985; Van Raaij and Gianotten 1990; Williams and Defris 1981) have shown that changes in consumer sentiment are at least in part independent of economic change and contribute to predicting macroeconomic trends.[1]

The Index of Consumer Sentiment has had an excellent record of anticipating recessions, as have corrective Elliott waves in the stock market. In fact, this index moves up and down pretty much with the stock market. That's not the only index that it tracks. Zullow comments,

PESSRUM, RUMSONG, PESSSONG, and RUMTIME correlated significantly with the annual average of consumer confidence as measured by the Conference Board's nationwide surveys since 1969, providing an independent validation of the predictive relationship between PESSRUM and consumer confidence.[2]

So the stock market, consumer sentiment and the degree of pessimism in popular songs all move up and down roughly together. A socionomist would suggest that the reason for the coincident trends is that changes in mood prompt immediate changes in stock values and the popularity of songs because people can buy or sell stocks and choose to enjoy particular sound recordings almost instantly upon changing moods, while economic actions taken *at the same time* require time to play out and thus have a lagging influence on the economy.

It is pertinent that while some researchers have attempted to bolster the conventional view of social mood causality in purporting to show that consumers are just reacting to present conditions, the bulk of studies to date supports Katona's original observation that changes in consumer sentiment are independent of economic causes and in fact precede trends in the economy. Therefore, the weight of the evidence in this area supports the socionomic insight.

A most important addition to evidence supporting the socionomic insight is that the forecasting ability of public mood is not confined to "consumers" anticipating the economic future. As cited above, Noelle-Neumann (1984, 1989) demonstrates that even the public's general non-economic hopes and fears predict changes in GDP. This is crucial data supporting the case that the limbic system generates changes in general human mood (see Chapter 8 of *The Wave Principle of Human Social Behavior*), which in turn has consequences in *all* areas of social behavior, not just economic behavior.

As useful as the Index of Consumer Sentiment is, it is still not as immediate or detailed an indication of social mood change as the stock market. It takes time to poll the public and publish the results, and the mechanism is not yet there to do weekly, daily, hourly or minute-by-minute polls of public feeling. The stock market, in contrast, stands ever at the ready to register the minutest changes in social mood, instantly, which makes it the ideal sociometer.

## NOTES

[1] Zullow, Harold M. (1991). "Pessimistic rumination in popular songs and news magazines predict economic recession via decreased consumer optimism and spending." *Journal of Economic Psychology* 12, 501-526.
[2] *Ibid.*

## REFERENCES

Adams, F.G. and Klein, L.R. (1972). "Anticipations variables in macro-econometric models." In: B. Strumpel, J.N. Morgan, and E. Zahn (eds.), *Human behavior in economic affairs: Essays in honor of George Katona*. San Francisco, CA: Jossey-Bass.

Katona, G. (1960). *The powerful consumer: Psychological studies of the American economy*. New York: McGraw-Hill.

Katona, G. (1980). *Essays on behavioral economics*. Ann Arbor, MI: Institute for Social Research.

Katona, G. and B. Strumpel. (1978). *A new economic era*. New York: Elsevier.

Pickering, J.F. (1977). *The acquisition of consumer durables*. London: Associated Business Programmes.

Praet, P. (1985). "Endogenizing consumers' expectations in four major EC countries." *Journal of Economic Psychology* 5, 255-269.

Shapiro, H.T. (1972). "The Index of Consumer Sentiment and economic forecasting—A reappraisal." In. B. Strumpel, J.N. Morgan and E. Zahn (eds.) *Human behavior in economic affairs: Essays in honor of George Katona*. San Francisco, CA: Jossey-Bass.

Vanden Abeele, P. (1983). "The Index of Consumer Sentiment: Predictability and predictive power in the EEC." *Journal of Economic Psychology* 3, 1-17.

Van Raaij, W.F. and Gianotten, H.J. (1990). "Consumer confidence, expenditure, saving, and credit." *Journal of Economic Psychology* 11, 269-290.

Williams, R.A. and Defris, L.V. (1981). "The roles of inflation and consumer sentiment in explaining Australian consumption and savings patterns." *Journal of Economic Psychology* 1, 105-120.

Zullow, Harold M. (1990, May). "Pessimistic rumination in popular music and news magazines predicts economic recession, 1890-1990." Paper presented at a joint meeting of the American Association for Public Opinion Research and the World Association for Public Opinion Research, Lancaster, PA.

Zullow, Harold M. (1991). "Pessimistic rumination in popular songs and news magazines predict economic recession via decreased consumer optimism and spending." *Journal of Economic Psychology* 12, 501-526.